*The*
# CHRISTIAN
# DOCTRINE
*of* GOD
## DOGMATICS: Vol. I

*Books by*
EMIL BRUNNER
*Published by The Westminster Press*

The Christian Doctrine of God
(*Die christliche Lehre von Gott*)

Man in Revolt
(*Der Mensch im Widerspruch*)

The Mediator
(*Der Mittler*)

The Divine Imperative
(*Das Gebot und die Ordnungen*)

Revelation and Reason
(*Offenbarung und Vernunft*)

The Divine-Human Encounter
(*Wahrheit als Begegnung*)

EMIL BRUNNER

# The
# CHRISTIAN
# DOCTRINE
# *of* GOD

## DOGMATICS: Vol. I

*Translated by*
OLIVE WYON

*Philadelphia*
THE WESTMINSTER PRESS

PRINTED IN THE UNITED STATES OF AMERICA

# PREFACE

In the realm of doctrine the Christian Church has always recognized a twofold task: one concerning the Church itself; the other concerning the outside world, the world of doubt and unbelief. Although, at a time like the present, the conflict with unbelief and false ideologies may seem the more urgent one, yet the first task is always fundamental. For how can the Church do justice to her missionary calling in an un-Christian world if she is not herself clear about the content of her message? All down her history the Christian Church has given much thought to the basis, meaning and content of the message she has received—and is bound to proclaim; this process of reflection is what we mean by "dogmatics".

Dogmatics is not the Word of God. God can make His Word prevail in the world without theology. But at a time when human thought is so often confused and perverted by fantastic ideas and theories, spun out of men's own minds, it is evident that it is almost impossible to preserve the Divine Word without the most passionate intellectual effort to re-think its meaning and its content. The simple Christian may, it is true, understand and preserve God's Word without theology; but for those Christians who are involved in the thinking of their own day, and who, as children of their own day, are deeply influenced by these currents of thought, an all-inclusive and thorough effort to re-think what has been "given" to faith is absolutely indispensable. This is particularly true for those whose calling it is to proclaim this faith to others.

Hence dogmatics serves first of all those who themselves exercise a teaching-office in the Church, as clergy and missionaries, evangelists, pastors and catechists. In addition, it is useful to all those members of the Christian Church who desire to grapple with the religious problems which their faith creates in their own minds. Upon the ladder of reflection on that which is given with the Word of God, dogmatics, as the science of Christian doctrine, holds pride of place. Hence it is not "everybody's business", but only that of those who are capable of, and in need of, a thoroughgoing effort of thought.

There is no lack of dogmatic works in the Church. But the theological renaissance of the past twenty years has not produced any comprehensive work which expresses the spirit of this renewal. The monumental work of Karl Barth, which in spite of the five weighty volumes which have already appeared, has not yet covered one-third of the doctrinal material, makes us wonder—even when we take into account the great industry and creative powers of the great theologian of Basle—whether this massive work, in spite of (or on account of) its unusual length, will be able to do justice to all the claims of a comprehensive presentation of Christian doctrine. In any case, there is room for other attempts.

One who for more than twenty years has been lecturing on dogmatics in the usual four terms a year, and so has tried nearly a dozen times to re-cast the doctrinal material as a whole, does not need to fear the charge of "superficiality", when he produces the result of this work of so many years as a whole, having dealt with it hitherto in single monographs—as Christology, anthropology, the doctrine of the Holy Spirit, and of Revelation. Perhaps it is not too much to expect that the comprehensive presentation may succeed in overcoming and dispelling prejudices and misunderstandings which have arisen in the course of the last twenty years, and have led to controversy on points of detail; possibly this general method may achieve results which could not be reached by the method of "frontal attack".

Owing to my long co-operation with the Œcumenical Movement, I am fully aware both of the needs and the hopes of the World Church. Hence I have been very careful to keep as closely as possible to the external form of dogmatics—to the theological tradition common to the Church as a whole. In the main, therefore, I have tried to follow the order of the *Loci theologici* which, from the days of Peter Lombard onwards, has formed the framework of Christian Dogmatics, and was also in all essentials adopted by that master of Reformed theology, Calvin. Over and over again I have proved that this procedure is fundamentally sound.

In order not to overburden the non-theological reader who is willing to make the effort to think through theological questions, all the more technical historical material has been relegated to special appendices; this has also had the advantage of enabling me to introduce surveys from the History of Dogma which will meet the needs of students, and may perhaps sometimes even be useful to scholars. My thanks are due to Herr Pfarrer R. Rockenbach for the Index. It is my earnest desire that this work of dogmatics (of which the present volume is the first of three or four which have already been planned) may help to preserve the knowledge of the Divine Word, and to contribute to its expansion in a world which is fainting for lack of it, and is in such sore spiritual need.

EMIL BRUNNER

ZÜRICH,
 *Lent* 1946

# CONTENTS

ix

## Section Two

## THE WILL OF GOD

# TRANSLATOR'S NOTE

THE present work is an unabridged translation of Professor Brunner's first volume of his *Dogmatics: Die christliche Lehre von Gott*. It was published by the Zwingli-Verlag, Zürich, in 1946.

I have re-arranged the *Table of Contents*, and have added a *Subject-Index*, for the convenience of English-speaking readers. While I was preparing this translation Dr. Brunner kindly sent me a list of printer's errors discovered in the first German edition; at some points, therefore, I have been able to correct the German text.

For help on particular points I am indebted to the kindness of my friends: The Rev. C. H. Dodd, M.A., D.D.; the Rev. H. H. Farmer, M.A., D.D.; and the Rev. F. Hildebrandt, Ph.D.

OLIVE WYON.

*Cambridge*, 1949.

*The*
# CHRISTIAN
# DOCTRINE
## *of* GOD
## DOGMATICS: Vol. I

# PROLEGOMENA
## THE BASIS AND THE TASK OF DOGMATICS

## CHAPTER I

# THE POSITION OF DOGMATICS

THE intellectual enterprise which bears the traditional title of "dogmatics"[1] takes place within the Christian Church. It is this that distinguishes it from similar intellectual undertakings, especially within the sphere of philosophy, as that is usually understood. Our immediate concern is not to ask whether this particular undertaking is legitimate, useful, or necessary. The first thing we have to say about it is that it is closely connected with the existence of the Christian Church, and that it arises only within this sphere. We study dogmatics as members of the Church, with the consciousness that we have a commission from the Church, and a service to render to the Church, due to a compulsion which can only arise within the Church. Historically and actually, the Church exists before dogmatics. The fact that the Christian Faith and the Christian Church exist, precedes the existence, the possibility, and the necessity for dogmatics. Thus if dogmatics is anything at all, it is *a function of the Church*.

It cannot, however, be taken for granted that there is, or should be, a science of dogmatics within the Christian Church; but if we reverse the question, from the standpoint of dogmatics it is obvious that we would never dream of asking whether there ought to be a Church, or a Christian Faith, or whether the Christian Faith and the Christian Church have any right to exist at all, or whether they are either true or necessary? Where this question does arise—and in days like ours it must be raised—it is not the duty of dogmatics to give the answer. This is a question for apologetics or "eristics". But dogmatics presupposes the Christian Faith and the Christian Church not only as a fact but as the possibility of its own existence. From the standpoint of the Church, however, it is right to put the question of the possibility of, and the necessity for, dogmatics.

But when all this has been said, the "place" of dogmatics has still only been defined in a very provisional sense. Further, this definition of its "place" is obliged to start from the fact that the Christian Church is a Teaching Church. But even as a Teaching Body the Church precedes dogmatics, both histori-

[1] See below, pp. 89 ff.

3

cally and actually. From its earliest days the Church, the Christian Community, has been pre-eminently a teaching body; one of her outstanding characteristics has been "teaching" or "doctrine".[1] As the Lord of the Church, Jesus Christ was Himself a Teacher, so also His disciples carry on a teaching ministry. We cannot think of the Christian Church without teaching, any more than we can think of a circle without a centre; teaching and "doctrine" belong to its very nature.

But this does not mean that teaching is the beginning and the end of the Church; rather, teaching is *one* of its functions, and *one* of the basic elements of its life. Like the Lord of the Church Himself, His Apostles did not only teach: they did other things as well. "And they continued steadfastly in the Apostles' teaching and fellowship, in the breaking of bread and the prayers."[2] This is the earliest description of the Primitive Church. Whether the "teaching" is put first intentionally, or by accident, we will not as yet enquire; we may, however, guess that the order is not accidental. For there can be no doubt that from the very earliest days, and all down the centuries, teaching has been an outstanding function and expression of the life of the Church.

Dogmatics is related to this teaching function of the Church; its living basis, its possibility, and—as will be shown later on—its content, all depend upon it; but this teaching of the Church is not "dogmatics". The Apostles are not systematic theologians, and what they teach is not dogmatics. It was two hundred years before the Christian Church produced the first "dogmatics" Thus it is not because there is a science of Christian dogmatics that we have Christian teaching, but, conversely, Christian teaching is the cause of dogmatics. Dogmatics —to put it so for the moment—is the Science of Christian teaching or doctrine. But the subject always exists before the "science" of the subject can be studied. The teaching Church, and the teaching of the Church, is the "place" at which dogmatics arises. Dogmatics is a function of the teaching Church; speaking generally, it is a service which is rendered for the sake of the doctrine of the Church.

But the doctrine of the Church, and the teaching Church, do not merely constitute the presupposition of dogmatics in the sense that a subject presupposes the science of that subject. There may be, it is true, a science of Christian faith and of

---

[1] The German word *Lehre* = both "teaching" and "doctrine". (TR.)
[2] Acts 2: 42.

4

Christian doctrine, for which that general relation between the subject and its science exists, which we might describe as a branch of general religious knowledge, namely, as the science of the Christian religion. It was thus conceived by Schleiermacher in his Short Exposition[1] of the relation between the doctrine of the Church and dogmatics, although he did not adhere to this definition in his own work on the Christian Faith. When we said that the Church is the "place" of dogmatics, we meant that this kind of academic or intellectual knowledge or research was only possible within the community of believers. Dogmatics are only possible or thinkable, not only *because* the Church and Christian teaching exist, but also only *where* they exist. Dogmatics is itself a function of the Church. Only one who is a genuine "believer" and, as such, believes in the Church and its teaching, can render to the Church the service which is implied in the idea of dogmatics. The presupposition of dogmatics is not only the existence of the Church and its doctrine, but life *within* the Church, and *in* its doctrine. Dogmatic thinking is not only thinking *about* the Faith, it is *believing* thinking. There may be various ways of solving the problem of the Theory of Knowledge which this raises:[2] this, in any case, is the claim which dogmatics makes, without which its effort ceases to be dogmatics, and it becomes the neutral science of religion. It is the believing Church itself which, in dogmatics, makes its own teaching the object of reflection; essentially, dogmatics claims to be an academic study controlled by the Church.

[1] Schleiermacher's *Werke*, I, 1, para. 97: "The connected presentation of doctrine, as it is accepted . . . at a given time, is what we mean by the expression 'dogmatics' or 'dogmatic theology'."

[2] Cf. E. Burnier: "*La restauration de la théologie biblique et sa signification épistémologique*", in *Bible et théologie*, Lausanne, 1943.

## CHAPTER 2

## THE NECESSITY FOR DOGMATICS

THE urgent question for a humanity which despairs of all truth: "Is there any Truth which one can believe at all? And, if so, does Christian doctrine, as such, claim to be truth of this kind?" lies, as we have already seen, outside the sphere of dogmatics. The Christian Church deals with this question by means of an intellectual discipline which is closely related to dogmatics, yet which must always be strictly distinguished from it; this study is called "Apologetics", a name which is as traditional as the term "Dogmatics". Apologetics is the discussion of questions raised by people outside of, and addressed to, the Christian Church; therefore at all times it has proved to be as urgent, and as inevitable, as the Christian study of doctrine proper, or dogmatics.

The question of the justification for, and the necessity of, dogmatics, differs from the former question because it arises within the Church. And yet it is a genuine and not a rhetorical question; nor is it even merely academic. The fact is, this question is justified from the standpoint of the "scientific" theologian. Serious objections have been raised to the whole undertaking, objections which must be recognized; to ignore them would simply mean that we had already fallen a prey to that dogmatic "rigidity", and that over-emphasis on the intellectual aspect of doctrine which is so deplorable.

The first objection concerns the loss of directness, and even of simplicity of faith, which is necessarily connected with the process of dogmatic reflection. A person who has hitherto only encountered the Biblical Gospel in its simplest form, and has been gripped by it in a direct, personal way, must necessarily feel appalled, chilled, or repelled by the sight of massive volumes of dogmatics, and his first acquaintance with the whole apparatus of ideas and of reflection connected with this study of theology as a science. Instinctively the simple Christian murmurs: "But why this immense apparatus of learning? What is the use of these subtle distinctions and these arid intellectual definitions? What is the use of this process of 'vivisection' of our living faith?" When, further, this "simple believer" becomes aware of the theological controversies and passionate dogmatic conflicts which seem inevitable, it is easy to under-

6

stand that the simple Christian man or woman turns away from all this with horror, exclaiming: "I thank Thee, O Father, Lord of heaven and earth, that Thou didst hide these things from the wise and understanding, and didst reveal them unto babes!"[1] He sees the contradiction between the simple Gospel of the New Testament and this world of extremely abstract conceptions, between the living concreteness of the speech of Jesus and His Apostles, which speaks straight to the hearts of all who listen aright, and this ruthless analysis, this massive labour of systematic theology, in which only people of high intellectual gifts can share, which seems to be possible only at the cost of losing the freshness and directness of a living experience. Like a certain French theologian, he says, rightly: "A Gospel which cannot be put on a postcard cannot be the Gospel which was preached to the fishermen of the Lake of Galilee!" From this point of view dogmatics seems to be a perversion of the Gospel.

The second objection is closely connected with the first. It is raised by people who feel that the Biblical Gospel calls them to *action*. Their faith has awakened them to see and feel the sufferings of humanity, the terrible need and the burning questions of their own day, and they feel that "love constrains them" to give the world all the help they possibly can, both inwardly and outwardly. This being so, they feel: "Who would waste time trying to answer such difficult intellectual problems? Dogmatics is theory, but faith is obedience and fellowship. How can we waste time in speculations about the mysteries of the Trinity while there are human beings in trouble—both of body and soul!"

This direct and non-reflective rejection of dogmatics by the practical Christian layman is austerely expressed[2] by the philosopher in intellectual terms. Dogmatics, he says, like all theory, belongs to the "sphere of recollection", of reflection, of thought which is concerned with ideas; faith arises in the "reality" of encounter. Between these two there is an impassable gulf. The truth which is given to faith is only understood by one who meets the "Other" in action and in suffering, but it is not understood by the man who seeks truth in the sphere of solitary thought. Therefore the introduction of the truth of faith into that intellectual process of reflection, which

[1] Matt. 11: 25.
[2] Cf. E. Grisebach: *Gegenwart; Freiheit und Zucht; Die Schicksalsfrage des Abendlandes.*

is so remote from reality, can do faith no good, indeed, it can only do harm, because it diverts the Christian believer from his real duty of active love to God and his neighbour.

There is another equally important objection. It runs rather like this: "Dogmatics comes from 'dogma'. However you may define it, still by your precious 'dogma' you want to force us to accept an objective authority, an impersonal doctrinal authority, inserted between us and the Source of faith, Jesus Christ Himself; you want to set up a system of doctrinal coercion, which is in opposition to the freedom of faith. You want to establish an ecclesiastical heteronomy which restricts the liberty of the children of God! You want to repeat the ancient error, and to perpetuate it, that doctrine is the object of faith —a doctrine preserved by the Church, on which she bases her clerical authority. Inevitably, dogmatics leads to ecclesiastical tyranny, which, more than anything else, obstructs our view of the Gospel of the New Testament."

Finally, there is a fourth objection, which represents the views of those who admit the necessity for thinking about the Gospel, but who regard dogmatics as a perverted form of such thinking. Those who take this position claim that what the Church of our day needs is not a continuance of the dogmatic labours of previous centuries, which, as we know by experience, divides the Church by its definitions, but an intellectual effort which, recognizing the peculiar need of our own times, and the widespread lack of faith at the present day, tries to seek to win the outsider by answering his questions, and by entering into a real discussion with him. A dogmatic analysis of ideas does not make the Gospel more intelligible to the unbeliever, but less; it does not help him to understand why he ought to accept the Christian Faith. The true task of the Christian thinker, however, should be the very opposite—a task which hitherto has only been undertaken by great men who are exceptions in the realm of theology, men like Hamann, Pascal, or Kierkegaard. So long as the Church still uses her intellectual powers on the old traditional lines, she is neglecting the one and only important and fruitful intellectual task, which is her real duty.

Faced by these objections, are we to regard the enterprise of dogmatics, in spite of the weighty tradition behind it, as unnecessary? Or even if not actually dangerous, as at least a bypath for the teaching Church?

In the following pages the effort will be made to allow the

History of the Church itself to give the answer to this question. We must, however, begin at this point: namely, that the Bible itself knows nothing of that process which from time immemorial the Church has known as "dogmatics". For more than a thousand years Israel existed as a religious community without anything like a system of dogma, in the sense, for instance, in which Calvin uses it in his *Institutes*—indeed, the Jewish Church did not even possess a Catechism, and even the Early Christian Church—that is, the Christian Church at the time of its highest vitality and purity, did not produce anything of the kind. This fact does make us think. *One* thing it does prove, beyond a doubt, namely, that dogmatics does not belong to the *"esse"*, but at the most to the *"bene esse"* of the Church. For the *"esse"* of the Church consists only in that without which she could not possibly exist. But the Church existed for two hundred years without dogmatics. Thus if dogmatics is under no circumstances an *absolute* necessity, is it perhaps a *relative* necessity? That is, something which, under certain circumstances, is necessary. The History of the Church[1] gives a clear affirmative answer to this question—a threefold answer. Dogmatics springs from a threefold source: there are three urgent necessities for dogmatics which spring from the life of the Church itself, and cannot be ignored. (*a*) The first root of dogmatics is the *struggle against false doctrine*. The sinful self-will of man takes the Gospel—at first imperceptibly, and indeed perhaps unconsciously—and alters the content and the meaning of the message of Jesus Christ and His Mighty Act of Redemption, of the Kingdom of God and the destiny of Man. This process produces "substitute" Gospels, introduces "foreign bodies" into Christian truth, and distorts the Christian message: the very words of the Bible are twisted, and given an alien meaning, and indeed, one which is directly opposed to its purpose. The Christian Church is in danger of exchanging its divine treasury of truth for mere human inventions. This being so, ought not those who know the original Truth feel called to make a clear distinction between truth and illusion—between "gold" and "cat-gold" (Yellow mica)? This necessity of distinguishing between truth and error, and of warning the members of the Church against false teaching, makes it quite impossible to adopt the naïve attitude which can ignore these things. Comparison and reflection become necessary, and the more subtle and refined are the errors, the more urgent does

[1] Cf. below, pp. 93 ff.

9

this become. Where the very words of the Bible have been twisted to mean something different, it is not sufficient to appeal to the "words" of Scripture; where whole systems of alien thought have been "smuggled" into the message of the Church, it becomes necessary to set the whole on the one side over against the whole on the other, and to show clearly how each is built up into a system. It is the perversion of doctrine which leads to the formation of the ideas and systems of dogma. It was out of the fight against heresy that the dogmatics of the Early Church arose; the dogmatics of the Reformation period arose out of the struggles to purify the message of the Bible from Roman Catholic errors.

(b) The second source from which dogmatics is derived is that of catechetical instruction, or preparation for Baptism. Even the simplest Christian faith contains a doctrinal element. We have already pointed out that the Church never can, and never will be, without doctrine. Even the simple, non-theological teaching of Jesus is full of "theological" content. A person cannot become a Christian without *knowing* something about the Father in Heaven, the forgiveness of sins, Atonement through the Son of God, and the Work of the Holy Spirit; and when he "knows" these Biblical phrases he must go further and grasp their inner meaning. The teaching Church has to become the Church which instructs catechumens. But the thoughtful person cannot receive these doctrines without finding that they raise questions in his mind. The more alert and vigorous is his thinking, the more urgent and penetrating do his questions become. The Christian message must mould and penetrate not only the heart of man, but also his mind, and his processes of thought. But this can only take place if the Christian Message is thought out afresh and re-formulated in intellectual terms. The thoughtful believer is constantly perceiving new depths and heights in the truth of the Gospel. Thus the Christian catechetical instruction which was given through the rich intellectual medium of the Greek world of culture became a method of theological and dogmatic teaching. The instruction of educated catechumens developed into Dogmatics.

The third root of dogmatics is that of Biblical exegesis. Where there is a living Church, a living spiritual life, there men feel the need to penetrate more deeply into the meaning of the Bible, to draw water from the richness of its wells of truth, to enquire into the hidden connections between its main ideas. Such people are not satisfied with an approximate and pro-

visional knowledge—they want something exact and per-
manent. But this means that when the great "words" of the
Bible, such as "Sin" or "Grace", are studied, it is not enough
to study them in the particular passage in question: they must
be investigated from the standpoint of Biblical doctrine as a
whole, and *this*, they feel, they must grasp as a whole. It is not
sufficient, for instance, to know what the Apostle Paul means
by the "righteousness of God" in a particular passage in the
Epistle to the Romans: we want to know what he means by
this expression as a whole, and also how this specifically
Pauline phrase is related to other phrases which, although they
sound different, contain a similar meaning in other Biblical
writers. Then when the Biblical scholar has done his work—
when he has explained the Epistle to the Romans, and has
related it to "Pauline theology" as a whole—then the reader of
the Bible, who wants to learn not only from Paul but from the
whole revelation contained in Scripture, starts a fresh process
of questioning, and it is such questions that the systematic
theologian tries to answer. It is at this point that the "Dic-
tionary of the Bible", or the *"loci theologici"*, comes into being.

This threefold root is still visible in the titles of the three
standard dogmatic works of the Reformation period. The
struggle against heresy is represented by Zwingli's *Commentarius de vera et falsa religione*; the instruction of catechumens
by the *Institutio christianae religionis* of Calvin—which developed out of an expanded Catechism; the need for a "Dic-
tionary of the Bible" for the Bible reader, by the first dogmatic
work of Melanchthon, his *Loci theologici*.

For the sake of the Gospel the Church cannot ignore its duty
to distinguish false doctrine from true; to this end it must
make the effort to express the content of its simple teaching in
more exact and thoughtful terms. The Church must help the
reader of the Bible by giving him a comprehensive explanation
of the chief Biblical terms; Church leaders cannot ignore the
fact that it is their duty to give thoughtful members of the
Christian community a body of instruction which goes further
than the most elementary elements of the Faith, and to answer
their questions. Hence the Church cannot fail to develop her
doctrine in the sense of giving more exact and precise definitions
of ideas; then, she must show the connexion of these ideas with
the whole body of Christian truth. This process is "Dogmatics".
This is the answer from Church History.

But this historical answer alone is not sufficient; primarily,

11

because it starts uncritically from an historical position which is not impregnable; that is, it assumes that the original doctrine of the Church was clear and uniform.

The New Testament is not a book of doctrine, but it is a collection of apostolic confessions of faith and historical records which have been written down in order to awaken and strengthen faith. But in these believing testimonies to God's revelation in Jesus Christ there is already a good deal of intellectual and theological reflection—in some more, and in others less. From this it is possible to construct a "theology of the Apostles" —as we shall see later on—and this New Testament doctrine will become the basis of all dogmatic instruction. Now, however, this process of development—from the relatively non-reflective, immediate character of the doctrine of the New Testament, to the highly developed doctrinal system of the Church, proves to be inevitable, because this "theology of the Apostles" is not an absolute unity, but is presented in a series of different types of doctrine, which differ considerably from one another. In a variety of doctrine the one Christ and the one Gospel bear witness to the Divine Act of Redemption. The fact that this "unity" exists within a partly contradictory multiplicity, evokes critical reflection. It is not the task of the Church to teach what Matthew, Paul, or John teach, but it *is* her duty to proclaim the Word of God; therefore she must teach the one divine truth in these differing Apostolic doctrines. If there were an absolutely uniform, and therefore unmistakably "apostolic doctrine", or "doctrine of the New Testament", then perhaps the work of dogmatics might be superfluous. But since this is not the case, and since the truth of revelation must be sought in and behind the unity of the different testimonies to Christian truth, the work of reflection upon dogma is indispensable.

Hence a simple reproduction of "the" doctrine of the Bible is impossible. Every theology or proclamation of the Church which claims to be able to do this is based upon a fiction; in actual fact it is accomplished by an unconscious, and unacknowledged process of systematization of theology. The teachers or preachers of the Church who claim for themselves and others that *"they* have no dealings with theology, but that they stick quite simply to the teaching of the Bible", deceive themselves and others. Whatever the Church teaches, she teaches on the basis of a normative decision—even though this decision may have taken place unconsciously—concerning the nature of "sound doctrine". Open and honest consideration of "sound doctrine" can never end in appealing to any "standard" doctrine. "Sound doctrine", when more closely examined, always proves to be a task which is never ended, and it is never something which exists "ready-made". Even behind the most primitive forms of Christian teaching, behind the teaching of Jesus and of the Apostles, "sound doctrine" is always something which has to be sought. If the New Testament witness to revelation is the basis and the content of all dogmatics (as will be shown in the following pages to be the case), then its necessity has already been proved by the fact that the task of discovering the unity of sound doctrine behind the different doctrines of the New Testament is unavoidable. Thus the truth of revelation and human doctrine do not only diverge in the sphere of dogmatic reflection, but this contradiction exists already, even in the simplest Biblical witness to revelation and faith. Here already it is evident that the divine Truth is a light which cannot be received by the human mind without being refracted. The one truth of Christ is refracted in the manifold doctrines of the Apostles; but it is the task of the Church—which has to proclaim the truth of Christ, and thus also has to teach—to seek continually for the one Light of Truth within these refractions. Dogmatics is the science which enables the Church to accomplish this task.

## CHAPTER 3

# THE BASIS OF CHRISTIAN DOCTRINE: REVELATION[1]

THE doctrine of the Christian Church, which dogmatics exists
to serve, like all doctrine, points beyond itself to a concrete
reality; it is doctrine about "Something"; that is, it is the
doctrine which concerns God and His Kingdom, His Nature
and His Will, and His relation to man and to the world. Christian doctrine, however, is fundamentally different from all
other kinds of doctrine. For the Reality with which Christian
doctrine deals—God—by its very nature, is far above all
human doctrinal conceptions. This "Something" with which
Christian doctrine is concerned cannot be "taught" by man,
for "It" transcends all human doctrines; indeed, all human
doctrines are excluded precisely because this Reality is not a
"Something", not even a "concrete reality", since God is
Absolute Subject. By his own knowledge, all that man can
grasp is the world.

God, however, is *not* the world; therefore He stands outside
the circle in which human knowledge and human doctrine—
acquired by man's own efforts—can move, and with which
they are competent to deal. Knowledge of God exists only in so
far as there is a self-disclosure, a self-manifestation of God,
that is, in so far as there is "revelation". There is a doctrine of
God, in the legitimate sense of the words, only in so far as God
Himself imparts it.[2] The human doctrine of God—which is
undoubtedly the doctrine of the Church—is thus only legitimate, and can only claim to be "truth", in so far as the divine
revelation—that which God teaches about Himself—is validly
expressed by it. Thus Christian doctrine not only points away
from itself to its actual "subject", but it points away from itself
to the divine "doctrine", *i.e.* to that which God Himself manifests and "teaches" about Himself. It is evident that in so
doing not only the origin and content of this divine "teaching"
(or doctrine), but also the manner of "teaching", of the manifestation or self-communication, must be of a special kind. The

---

[1] This chapter is a condensed summary of the content of my book, *Offenbarung und Vernunft*, 1941; its First Part contains a doctrine of Revelation,
which is here presupposed.

[2] There is a play on words in this paragraph, which is impossible to reproduce in English. *Lehre* = "doctrine" or "teaching"; *Lehren* = "To teach".
(TR.)

concept, the "Word of God", does not solve the problem of the nature of this divine teaching; for when God "speaks", if it is really *He* who speaks, something is said which is evidently quite different from that which men usually call "speaking".[1]

Thus all Christian doctrine, even in its primitive form in the New Testament, in this twofold sense, is merely a pointer to something outside itself; it is the pointer to "Him, Himself", and it is a pointer to that which He discloses concerning Himself, which human speech or teaching "reproduces", or repeats, or expresses in human language. The Biblical expression for this twofold character of Christian doctrine as a "pointer" is called: "Witness". The Apostles, the first teachers of the Christian community, know themselves to be witnesses to the divine revelation. The divine revelation is not only the *basis* and content of their teaching, but it is its authorization; their teaching claims to be true and valid because, and in so far as, the divine teaching itself is accomplished in their teaching. But what is this divine revelation which constitutes the basis, the content, and the authority of their teaching? Since the discussion of this question constitutes the content of another of my books we must here confine ourselves to a brief account of the content of that book.

(1) In the New Testament the idea of *revelation* does not denote a single entity, but a complex one; there are many "forms of revelation";[2] it is only as these are welded into a unity that they constitute that which lies at the basis of Christian doctrine, and determine its claim to truth and validity.

In the centre of this New Testament testimony stands the historical event: Jesus Christ.[3]

The fact that "the Word became flesh" is the centre of the divine manifestation, towards which all the teaching and witness of the original witnesses is directed. Obviously, this means that the "Word of God" is not that which we human beings mean by a "word": He Himself, Jesus Christ, is the "Word" of God; it is therefore impossible to equate any human words, any "speech-about-Him" with the divine self-communication. Jesus Christ Himself is more than all words about Him; the "Word" of God, the decisive self-communication of God, is a Person, a human being, the man in whom God Himself meets us. The fact that He is "here", that He has "come",

---

[1] Cf. *Offenbarung und Vernunft*, pp. 24–33.
[2] Karl Barth also speaks of the "Three Forms of the Word of God", *Kirchl. Dogm.* I, 1, p. 125.　　　　[3] *Offenbarung und Vernunft*, pp. 95–117.

that we may see and know Him in His action and His suffering, in His speech and in His Being, as Him in whom God's Holiness and Mercy stand before us in person, inviting us to Himself, and giving Himself to us—this is the revelation, the self-manifestation of God. In Him, through Him, God makes Himself known to us. But this unique historical event cannot be understood as an isolated Fact; it can only be grasped in the light of a twofold "before", and a fourfold "afterwards".

(2) The witness borne to Jesus Christ attests Him as the One in whom the promises of the Old Covenant are fulfilled, as the Messiah whom the Prophets foretold.[1] Jesus Christ wills to be understood, and indeed must be understood, in connexion with the preceding and provisional revelation of the Old Covenant just as, on the other hand, this Old Testament revelation itself can only be rightly understood as the precursor of the revelation in Jesus Christ. It is precisely this duality, the fact that the revelation of the Old Testament in its wholeness "intends" Jesus Christ, and yet that it witnesses to this only in a preparatory and provisional manner, which is the decisive fact. If anyone identifies the revelation of the Old Covenant with that of the New, he misses the meaning of the New Testament witness, as that which distinguishes the two forms of revelation from one another.

The revelation of the Old Testament, for its part, contains a variety of forms of revelation; but the decisive and standard one is that of the prophetic Word. God reveals Himself here through the Word, through speech. This constitutes both the greatness and the limitation of this revelation—its *greatness*, in the fact that because the Word, the speech, stands in a distinctive relation to the mystery of personality and its self-manifestation; its *limitation*, because no speech, no word, is adequate to the mystery of God as Person. The provisional nature of this revelation comes out precisely in the fact that God only "speaks" in it, but does not yet reveal Himself in Personal Presence.

It is precisely this twofold nature of the relation to the Fact of Christ that is meant by the expression in the Gospel of John —a phrase which is both an antithesis and a synthesis—"The Word became flesh . . . and we beheld His Glory".[2] That of which the Prophets could only "speak", is now actually here in person; in itself "speech" is only a provisional and preparatory revelation.

(3) The revelation in Jesus Christ and the revelation in the

---

[1] *Offenbarung und Vernunft*, pp. 82–97.　　　　[2] John 1: 14.

prophetic Word are both historical; that which took place and was proclaimed within Israel was a "New Thing"; so again was that which took place in Jesus Christ; it was something completely new. But now, according to the witness of the New, as well as of the Old Testament, this historical revelation presupposes a pre-historical revelation.[1] The revelation in history is retrospective in character. It is not addressed to an emptiness in man but to a false "fullness". It does not point to an ignorant and therefore innocent being, but to a guilty creature, who is therefore aware that all is not right with him: in a word, it is addressed to sinful man.

But sin, as the broken relationship between man and God, presupposes a relation with God which preceded the breach, and a knowledge of God which was given with this relation to God, that is, an original revelation. Whenever we use the word "sinner" we imply the Original Revelation; to deny the original revelation means to deny the fact of sin. Thus the Old Testament begins its account of the Prophetic revelation of the Covenant in Israel with an "*Ur*-geschichte" or primal history, which precedes that of Israel, and the revelation of the Covenant. God has revealed Himself not only to the Hebrew, but to Man as a whole, to "Adam". The witness of the Primal Revelation is inseparable from the witness of revelation of the Old Testament; for the Primal revelation precedes history as a whole, and the history of Israel in particular.

In the New Testament, moreover, it becomes plain why it is impossible to keep silence about this revelation which precedes all history, and why it must be taught. It alone makes man a responsible being—or, to put it more exactly: through it alone is man responsible for his sin. Without some knowledge of the will of God there is no sin; for sin means turning away from God. But how could we turn away from God unless we had previously been in His presence! How could we despise His will if we knew nothing of His will! To understand man as sinner, therefore, means to understand him from the standpoint of his original relation to God, and of the original revelation which this presupposes. It is the dialectic of sin, and of responsibility *for* sin and *in* sin, which means both a knowledge of God and an ignorance of Him. If we knew nothing how could we sin! And yet sin consists precisely in the fact that this knowledge has been lost, that the knowledge of the True God has degenerated into superstition and idolatry.

[1] *Offenbarung und Vernunft*, pp. 59–81.

Apart from revelation there would be no insane idolatry, and no sin.[1] But the fact that the revelation of God is turned into the insanity of idolatry, constitutes *sin*. This is the teaching of the Bible, and all down the ages this is what the Church has taught. Without this revelation which precedes history, the historical revelation is not intelligible. And yet the real nature of this "pre-historical" revelation can only be *understood* from the standpoint of this historical revelation; for sinful man no longer understands it, although the fact that he is a sinner is certainly based upon this fact.

(4) The revelation in the historical Fact of Jesus Christ does not only contain this twofold *presupposition*; it is also necessarily connected with a manifold form of revelation which comes after it. As an historical revelation to us who are not contemporaries of Jesus, but who are separated from Him by the history of more than nineteen hundred years, it is only accessible to us through the testimony of the first teachers and witnesses. The revelation of Christ comes to us in the words of the Apostles,[2] in the New Testament. Their witness—in accordance with the fact that in Jesus the Word became flesh—contains two elements: the record which bears witness, and the teaching which confirms it.

To us, who have not seen Him in the flesh, and as the Risen Lord, He does not come in the same form as He came to those who saw Him when He met them as their Risen, Living Lord. And yet He comes to us as the Same, and He is truly present to us. To us also He reveals Himself; but He reveals Himself to us through the revelation of the apostolic testimony in their narrative and their teaching concerning Him, the Christ. When the eye-witnesses were no longer in this earthly life, the Church was so conscious of the revelatory power of the Apostles' Word that she called it *the* "Word of God", pure and simple.

This phrase, however, may give rise to a serious misunderstanding—a misunderstanding which throws the Christian Church back to the level of the revelation of the Old Testament, namely, that God's revelation is identical with a human "word" about God, whereas the revelation of Christ fulfils the Old Testament revelation, and leaves it behind, in the very fact that "the Word became Flesh". This designation of the New Testament as the "Word of God" is correct, however, in so far as it recognizes and emphasizes in it a standard form of

---

[1] Cf. Luther, *W. A.*, p. 14, p. 588. *Nisi divinitatis notitiam habuissent, non potuissent eam tribuere idolis.*　　[2] *Offenbarung und Vernunft*, pp. 117–34.

revelation which cannot be severed from the Christian revelation.

(5) The New Testament testimony to Jesus the Christ does not, however, reach us apart from the mediation of the teaching Church.[1] Only those who take an unthinking Fundamentalist view can fall into the error of imagining that we are here directly confronted by the witness of the Apostles—is it not indeed only through the medium of the Church that we possess the New Testament, the writings of the Apostles, who collected them, preserved them, copied them again and again, had them printed, translated, and proclaimed to us? The community of believers itself, however, does not live first of all on the Bible— the Christian religion is not the religion of a Book—but on the living word of our contemporaries who can testify to us themselves that Christ is the Living and Present Lord. *Praedicatio verbi divini est verbum divinum*—this daring phrase of Bullinger's is not exaggerated if it is applied to the meaning of the Church's message, to that which ought to happen, which, by the grace of God, continually does happen. Thus the message of the Church—which is in living union with Christ—is also a form of revelation. The teaching of the Church about revelation is itself the bearer of the revelation.

(6) In all these forms revelation is understood as something objective, as something which confronts us, something outside ourselves. But this is a very improper and inexact way of speaking; for revelation is certainly not a "Something", a "thing"; but it is a process, an event, and indeed an event which happens to us and in us. Neither the prophetic Word of the Old Testament, nor Jesus Christ, nor the witness of the Apostles, nor of the preachers of the Church who proclaim Him, "is" the revelation; the reality of the revelation culminates in the "subject" who receives it. Indeed, it is quite possible that none of these forms of revelation may become revelation to *us*. If there is no faith, then the revelation has not been consummated: it has not actually happened, so to speak, but it is only at the first stage. All objective forms of revelation need the "subject" in whom they become revelation. The Bible itself calls this inward process "revelation".[2] It was a new particular intervention of God which opened the eyes of Peter to the Mystery of the Messiah, so that he could then confess Him as the Son of the Living God.[3] Again, it was the same

[1] *Offenbarung und Vernunft*, pp. 134–61.
[2] *Ibid.*, pp. 161–80.        [3] Matt. 16: 16.

intervention of God which happened to Paul when "it pleased God to reveal His Son" in him.[1] And the same process of revelation takes place wherever Christ manifests Himself to a human being as the living Lord and is received in faith. Our spiritual forefathers used to call this the *"testimonium spiritus sancti"*; but we ourselves, in accordance with the Scriptures, will not deny the title of "revelation" to this *"testimonium spiritus internum"*.

(7) We have not yet said, however, all that must be said if the word "revelation" is to have its full weight. As the Prophet of the Old Testament knew that the "Word" which he proclaimed was not yet the final revelation, and therefore looked forward into the future, where the fulfilment still had to take place, so we also look beyond the "Word made flesh" to a future form of revelation, when we shall no longer merely "believe", but we shall "see", face to face;[2] indeed, this future revelation, which is taken for granted in the New Testament, is frequently described with great emphasis by the word "revelation" ἀποκάλυψις.

This word ἀποκάλυψις is a synonym for the *Parousia*, for the perfected revelation at the end of the ages.[3] How, indeed, could it be otherwise! The very fact of the Incarnation of the Word in Jesus Christ proclaims that revelation means the fullness of the Presence of God with us, and therefore, that we are with Him. Revelation is, it is true, never the mere communication of knowledge, but it is a life-giving and a life-renewing communion. But so long as we are "in the body of this death", this revelation is always incomplete; thus the meaning of revelation is only fully achieved where all that separates has been removed, and where the fullness of the Presence has been realized. From this final form of revelation alone do we fully understand the meaning of each form of revelation.

Above all, from this standpoint we also understand that in all the various forms of revelation[4] there is *one* meaning: Emmanuel, God with us. It is the same Son of God who in Jesus Christ became man, whom the Prophets discerned dimly from afar; He is the same in whose image man has been created, and in whom lies both the meaning and the foundation of the Creation of the world. It is He who constitutes the secret or

---

[1] Gal. 1: 15.  [2] 1 Cor. 13: 12.
[3] Cf. Romans 2: 5; 1 Cor. 1: 7; 2 Thess. 1: 7.
[4] *Offenbarung und Vernunft*, pp. 181–89.

manifest centre of all the testimony of Scripture; He it is whom the Word of the Church has to proclaim and to teach, whom the Holy Spirit attests in the heart of the believer, and through whom the "new man" is created. It is also for that complete revelation at the end of the age that the Church waits, in whom the "faithful" will see God "face to face".

We need to see both this unity and this multiplicity of the forms of revelation in their variety and their distinctive character. In their unity they are "the revelation"; none of these links in the chain can be dispensed with, none may be neglected or ignored at the expense of another. It is important to know two things: first, that from the very beginning God has revealed Himself in His Creation, but that we can only know what this means through His revelation in Jesus Christ; and to know that we men, from the very beginning, have been created in and for this Image of God, and that no sin of ours can destroy this original destiny of human nature. Secondly, it is equally important to realize that it is only in Jesus Christ that we know our original destiny, and that it is only through Him that this "Image" is realized in us: in our present state, imperfectly, but in the age to come, in its full perfection.

CHAPTER 4

# REVELATION AS THE WORD OF GOD

THE presupposition of all valid speech or teaching of the Church about God is the self-revelation of God. The previous chapter —which gathers up in brief compass the results of a former detailed study—has dealt with this subject. But there is still a final step to be taken: the question still remains: How can human *doctrine* spring from divine revelation? We have seen, it is true, how rich and varied is the drama of historical events to which the Christian Church points when she speaks of "revelation". But this does not establish a relation between it and valid speech about God. The decisive middle term is still absent, that is, the fact that God Himself speaks—the Word of God.[1]

The task would be much easier if we could confine our investigations to the Old Testament. For there the standard form of revelation is the fact that "God speaks". It is true that even then the relation could not be established as simply as in orthodox theology, whether Catholic or Protestant, where the human doctrine of God is based upon the assumption that *revelation is a divine doctrine,* a doctrine revealed, that is, by God Himself; thus where the revelation itself already bears the stamp of a formulated doctrine, and even of the fixed word of Scripture. In the Old Testament, it is true, there can be no question of such a point of view. Revelation is not only that Word of God which is communicated through the "word" of the prophets, but it is at the same time an *action* of God in History, an *Act* of God, which cannot be ranged under the heading of the "Word" or the "Speech" of God.[2] Yet it is possible to say this: In the prophetic revelation the revelation of the Old Covenant attains its highest point; the prophetic teaching is the standard and characteristic form of this revelation. From this standpoint it would be easy to find a point of transition to the teaching task of the Church; does not the form of the revelation itself already contain the decisive pre-condition for valid human teaching, namely: that God Himself actually speaks, using human words, in formulated sentences, which, like other sentences, are formed of intelligible words? Thus here the Word

[1] Cf. the excellent article on the word λόγος in the *Theol. Wörterbuch z. N.T.*
[2] Cf. Grether, *Name und Wort Gottes im A.T.*, pp. 127 ff.

of God is present in the form of revealed human words, not behind them—which human words merely seek to express, just as a poet tries to express in words what an impression of Nature or of a musical work of art "says" to him—but in direct identity, in the complete equation of the human word with the "Word of God". There is no reason to doubt that the Prophet, who was conscious that God had "put His words into his mouth", combined this idea with the conception of the "Word of God", and regarded himself as a wholly passive instrument of the Divine revelation.[1]

Between us and the Old Testament, however, there stands a new form of revelation, the fulfilment of all that was only promised in the Old Testament, and the actual content of the divine revelation proclaimed by the Apostles and the Church: Jesus Christ Himself. Thus this "revelation" is not a "Word" but a Person—a human life fully visible within history, a human destiny so like, and so unlike, every other: Jesus of Nazareth the Rabbi, the wonder-worker, the Friend of publicans and sinners, and the Crucified and Risen Lord, now exalted to the Right Hand of God. Whatever He may be—so much is plain: He is not a "Word"; He is not "speech", or a summary of sentences like the prophetic utterances; and it is this very fact which is joyfully proclaimed: that for this very reason, just because He is quite different from a speech, namely, God Himself present, acting in His own Person, that He is the consummation of the revelation of God. For what the prophets could "only" say, towards which their word could "only" point, as something which was yet to come, a Perfection yet to be realized in the future, has now happened: Emmanuel, God with us. *God* Himself, not only a Word about Him, is now here. It is this that characterizes the New Age as contrasted with the past as a whole, even as contrasted with the revelation in the Old Covenant: the fact that He Himself is now *here*; He Himself is speaking, but for that very reason He is not merely the One who *speaks*, He is also the One who *acts*. That is why the Kingdom of God has now dawned; hence now the old is over and past, even the Old Covenant with all the forms of revelation proper to it. These are all severed from the new revelation, towards which they all pointed as heralds, as a light which shone out into the future, pointing towards the Coming One, Jesus Christ, in whom God Himself is present, speaking and acting.

[1] Cf. Eichrodt, *Theol. des A.T.*, II, pp. 21 ff.

23

This profound change is the content of the Prologue to the Fourth Gospel. This new revelation, which is the subject of the whole New Testament message, is presented in the Johannine Prologue as a theme expressed as the transition from the Word to the Person: "The Word became flesh." This means: He who could only be foretold previously in human language through the speech of the Prophets, is now present "in His own Person". What here takes place is not an hypostatization of the Word; on the contrary, the hypostatization of the Word, like that which took place in the work of Philo, the Jewish-Hellenistic thinker and writer, or the hypostatization of the Torah, of the Word of the Law or of the Scriptures, as became the custom in Rabbinic Judaism,[1] has now become impossible; it has been eliminated. That which was previously "Word" has now revealed itself in such a way that henceforth it has become evident that the "Word-about-Him" is different from Him, Himself, and that the real revelation is the fact that He Himself is here present. The message of the Johannine Prologue, therefore, is this: that He Himself, Jesus, the Son of God, is the principle of the Creation, or which the Old Testament could only say: "God spoke". It is Jesus whom the Scripture, and indeed all the Prophets, mean. He, Jesus, is the content of all previous speech, which took place under God's orders. Previously—so we may paraphrase the meaning of the Prologue —the Revelation of God assumed the form of the Word, of speech; now, however, its form is no longer this merely provisional, indirect form—a "pointer" to something beyond, but *now* the form of revelation is Himself, the One who speaks and acts in His own Person. Therefore the predicate "Logos", "Word", has become an inaccurate expression. For a Person is not a spoken word, but One who speaks, who, however, for that very reason is not merely One who *speaks*, but One who *acts*, a living, active "Subject". A Word is not a Subject, but it is the function of a subject. Jesus, however, is not a "function" but a "subject". And He Himself, not His speech, is the revelation proper, even though His speaking is part of Himself, as well as His action and His suffering. Hence the Johannine Prologue—in order to make this situation quite plain—has set alongside of the idea of the "Logos" the ideas of "Light" and "Life". The one concept of "Word" cannot now express *everything* that revelation means in the Old Testament. Behold! more than the "Word" is here—God Himself is here! The

[1] Cf. *Theol. Wörterbuch*. IV, p. 138.

prophetic "Word" is full of force and power—"Is not my Word like as a fire?" saith the Lord, "and like a hammer that breaketh the rock in pieces?"[1] But here the atmosphere ·is different. "Light" and "Life" are not characteristics of the "Word", but they are equally valid terms to describe Jesus Christ Himself in Person, as the self-manifestation of God.

The opening verses of the First Epistle of John show that this is the meaning; obviously, here the Logos is deliberately paraphrased in order that it may become clear that this is more than "Word": not only: "That which we have heard", but— "that which we have seen . . . and . . . beheld, . . . and . . . handled."[2] The correlation of "Word" and "hearing" which the spoken word clearly implies, is no longer the only meaning; it is expanded and enriched by equally valid terms: to see, to behold, to touch, and to handle. Hence the Logos is no longer only the Word *about* life, as it was with the Prophets, but it is "the Word *of* Life",[3] which may also be described as the "Bread of life"[4] or the "Light of life".[5]

This event which John has summed up in such a pregnant phrase is in harmony with the whole outlook of the New Testament. Henceforth revelation is no longer a "Word", but Himself; it is true, He *may* also be called the "Word";[6] it is not necessary, however, to apply this term to Him, who cannot be fully expressed in any of these conceptions, because He, as Person, is beyond and above all intellectual concepts. Certainly this does not mean that the idea of the "Word of God" has disappeared from the witness of revelation. There is still an excellent relation between the revelation and the spoken word; but with the Incarnation of the Word the meaning of the formula, the "Word of God", has been drastically altered. The spoken word is now no longer the revelation itself, or, to put it more exactly, it is no longer directly "revelation", but only indirectly. The spoken word is an indirect revelation when it bears witness to the real revelation: Jesus Christ, the personal self-manifestation of God, Emmanuel. The spoken word, the "word" in the actual sense of speech, "saying something in words", has thus been relegated to a secondary position, because the first place is now occupied by Him to whom the Old Testament prophetic Word pointed as the Coming One. Hence the meaning of the Old Testament revelation has now —and only now—been fulfilled, and its fulfilment is the Man

[1] Jer. 23: 29.   [2] I John I: I.   [3] I John I: I.
[4] John 6: 48.   [5] John 8: 12.   [6] Rev. 19: 13.

25

in whom God Himself is present: speaking, acting, suffering, reigning.

Further, this also implies that man's "reaction" to this revelation can no longer be simply described by the word "hearing". The relation has now become as personal as the revelation is personal. We are here no longer concerned with a relationship in "word", but with a personal relation: no longer are we content to "believe *it*", but our one concern is to come to *Him*, to trust Him, to be united to Him, to surrender to Him. Revelation and faith now mean a personal encounter, personal communion. He has come, in order that He may be with us, and that we may be with Him;[1] He has given Himself for us, that we may have a share in Him.[2] Whatever the significance of the "word", of "speech", may be in this happening, and its significance is great and indispensable—one thing is clear: it has still been relegated to the second place, it is a servant of the revelation; it is not the revelation itself. The "Word" —in the sense of speech or doctrine or preaching—is witness to Him, pointing to Him, the story of Him, of what He has done, and teaching about what He is. Our service to Him, to whom both act and speech are subject, is gathered up into this twofold activity of the historical recording of events and the doctrine which interprets their meaning.

It is therefore no accident that the Johannine Gospel in particular, which begins with the concept of the Logos, and thus describes Jesus directly as the Word of God, *only* uses this term in the Prologue, and nowhere else in the Gospel. The use of the idea of the Logos, therefore, does not mean that *Jesus is the Word*, but that *the "Word" is Jesus*. All that was called the "Word" in the Old Testament, all that was indicated in the Old Testament narrative of the Creation by the words "and God said", all that had to be said in words in the Old Testament, is now here Himself in Person, no longer merely in speech about Him. It is for this reason that the One whom men describe as the Logos, may also be described in other terms: Light, Life, and above all: Son of God.

In order to make it clear that this change has taken place, henceforth the expression "Logos, Word of God" will no longer be used. The way in which the Early Church spoke of the Logos, and in which the orthodox theological tradition still does so, betrays an alien influence, not in accordance with the testimony of the Bible, a train of thought which has been

---

[1] Matt. 18: 20; 28: 20.　　　　　　　　[2] Cf. John 15: 4; 17: 23.

introduced into Christian thought by Greek philosophy from
the thought-world of speculation concerning the Logos.

Certainly we can say—and indeed we shall have to say, as
we shall see—that in Jesus Christ God "speaks" with us. But
this expression is no longer, as in the case of the prophetic
Word, an adequate expression; it has become inaccurate. For
a Person is certainly not a speech, in spite of the fact that
without speaking he can "say" a good deal to us through his
life and his work. In the fact that the "Word became flesh",
God's way of "speaking" has changed from the literal
"speaking" (through the Prophets); it has become a more
figurative way of "speaking". The vessel "speech" could no
longer contain the content of this new form of divine revelation.
The prophetic "Word"—however fully it may be understood
as God speaking—is still "only speaking" about Him who is
Himself not a "speech" but a Being, a personal Being, and
indeed a Person whose whole aim it is to come to us as the One
of whom the Prophets spoke. As in the Old Covenant the Word
of Jahweh "came" to the Prophets, so now Jesus has "come".
As the Prophets used to say: "Thus saith the Lord", so Jesus
says: "But I say unto you." The fact that He Himself takes
the place of the spoken word is precisely the category which
distinguishes the Old Testament revelation—the revelation
through speech—from the New Testament revelation, the
revelation in Christ.

Should someone object, and say, on the contrary, that Jesus
Christ alone is the "Word of God" in the full sense of the word,
he is really saying what I am saying here, only he is saying it
on the basis of a misunderstanding. For he has not realized that
when we say that Jesus is the real Word of God we alter the
simple meaning of the notion "word", since a person is different
from a spoken word. If I describe Jesus as the "real Word"
I render the formula, the "Word of God", inaccurate; it then
becomes symbolic language, just as it would be were I to say
that the music of Bach "says" more to me than any poem.

Thus we really mean the same thing: but to avoid confusion
it is important to be quite clear on this point: that the more we
emphasize the fact that God's speaking alone is *real* speech,
that Jesus Christ alone is the *real* Word of God, the more we
are moving away from the direct use of the idea, the "Word of
God", to the indirect. The Word which has been formulated
in human speech is now only revelation in an indirect sense;
it is revelation as witness to Him.

This truth is of decisive importance for theology; only by its means will it be possible to repair the damage inflicted on Western theology by the Logos theologians, who infected Christian thought with their sterile intellectualism. This over-emphasis upon the intellectual aspect of the Faith came out in two facts—both of them well known—but, as it seems to me—never fully understood. The first of these facts was the equation of the "Word" of the Bible with the "Word of God"; this produced the doctrine of Verbal Inspiration, with all its disastrous results; the second fact was the view of revelation as "revealed doctrine". Behind both these facts there lies a misunderstanding of the idea of the Logos as expressed in the Prologue to the Fourth Gospel. But these two facts simply mean that the view of revelation given in the New Testament was abandoned in favour of an Old Testament idea of revela-tion—with a strongly rational element—thus, that the Divine revelation is a spoken Word of God, and even a doctrine. It is obvious that once this had been accepted, the idea of faith, and the understanding of the Christian life as a whole, of what it means to be a Christian, was coloured by the same misunder-standing. Here, however, we cannot deal with this problem any further. Our immediate question is: What is the basis upon which the Church can carry on its teaching work?

Orthodoxy, which understands revelation as revealed doc-trine, finds it very easy to establish correct doctrine. All one has to do is to formulate the revealed doctrine—in a formal sense—for purposes of instruction, in a systematic or cate-chetical form. The doctrine is already there, in the revelation. We find it impossible to take this enviable short-cut; but we are also aware at what a price this short-cut was purchased, what terrible consequences sprang from it, and indeed, that these consequences are still bearing their own fruit. Hence we know that we shall not have to regret choosing the longer way. Another "short-cut", which is not warranted, exists, where the question is put: "How can revelation, which is not doctrine, become doctrine?" and is answered by pointing to the fact of the testimony to the revelation, without which indeed Jesus would not be present for us at all. Up to a point, of course, this observation is correct, and in the next chapter we shall be dealing with the question of this testimony. *But:* although the connexion between the testimony of Christ and Jesus Christ Himself is very close, they are not identical. Jesus *is* not the testimony, but He *is* the revelation. The question should, therefore, be thus expressed: How does legitimate human speech about Jesus, about God, arise out of the revelation, which is Jesus Christ Himself, and therefore is not a spoken word? Is there a point of identity between the revelation of the Person and the word in human speech?

Actually this point of identity does exist; it is *the witness of the Holy Spirit*. We are now speaking not of the human witness to Jesus Christ, but of the Divine testimony. Before there can be a legitimate human witness, speech about God, genuine, valid testimony to Jesus Christ, there *must* be a Divine testimony to Him, which makes use of human forms of thought and speech—and it is precisely this that is meant by the witness of the Holy Spirit "in" the human spirit. By this we do not mean, first of all, what our fathers used to call the *"testimonium spiritus sancti internum"*; for this refers to a situation which we cannot yet presuppose, but which is indeed the result of that of which we are now speaking. For the *"testimonium spiritus sancti"* means the understanding of the Word of Scripture, of the Apostolic testimony which has already become a human message under the guidance and illumination of the Holy Spirit. Here, however, our question is: How did this "understanding" arise? The Apostles themselves give us the answer: the Spirit of God testified *in their hearts* that Jesus is the Christ.

This was what took place at Caesarea Philippi—perhaps for the first time—when Jesus for the first time was confessed as the Messiah and the Son of God: "Flesh and blood hath not revealed it unto thee, but my Father which is in heaven."[1] This took place because "it was the good pleasure of God . . . to reveal His Son in me"[2]—as Paul explains to the Galatians.

The revelation in Christ is not completed with the Life, Death, and Resurrection of Jesus: it only attains its goal when it becomes actually manifest; that is, when a man or woman *knows* Jesus to be the Christ. Revelation is not a starkly objective process, but a transitive one: God makes Himself known to someone. This revealing action of God is a twofold stooping to man: historically objective, in the Incarnation of the Son, and inwardly subjective, in the witness borne to the Son through the Spirit in the heart of man—first of all, in that of the Apostles. God stoops down to us, in that He who was in "divine form"[3] took on Himself human form; and God stoops down to us when He Himself speaks to us in human

---

[1] **Matt. 16: 17.**   [2] **Gal. 1: 15–16.**   [3] **Phil. 2: 6.**

speech, in the witness of His Spirit, who bears witness to the Son.[1]

We do not usually pay enough attention to tne fact that the expression "in us", "in the heart" is a parabolic expression. This localizing "in" means, when its parabolic dress is removed: "in the form of human inwardness" or "in the form of the human spirit". Here there are two points to note: The Spirit bears witness to our Spirit—that means: He has not become human spirit; and it means: in that He bears witness, He has taken on Himself the manner of existence and the form of action of human spirit-activity. This is the meaning—from the point of view of the Theory of Knowledge—of the New Testament witness of the Holy Spirit: identification of the divine spirit with the human spirit, and at the same time the fact that the Spirit of God and the human spirit confront one another.[2] Nowhere does this situation become clearer than where Paul repeats the most inward, the most central experience of faith of the Christian community—in the cry of "Abba", which is sometimes regarded as the cry of the spirit, and sometimes as the witness of the heart illuminated by the Spirit.[3] Thus "The Spirit Himself beareth witness with our spirit, that we are children of God";[4] so the witness is both the witness of the Holy Spirit and the witness of the believing heart. The same may be said of the confession of Jesus as Lord, which is mentioned in connexion with the gifts of the Spirit.[5] In such central acts of "knowing", in faith, man experiences the working of the Holy Spirit as a real utterance of God in language and thought familiar to mankind. Only in this Word of the Holy Spirit does the Divine revelation in Jesus Christ become the real, actual word of God to man, in which the parabolic term of the historical revelation, *Deus dixit*, becomes *Deus dicit*, which is to be taken literally.

Now there are three points to note: First, even as the Word of the Spirit "in" a human being, the witness of the Spirit to Jesus Christ does not cease to be "over against" him. "The Spirit beareth witness *to our* spirit." That identification *may* take place; but man does not possess the power to achieve this identification. The witness of the Spirit thus *can* be rightly received by the human spirit, so that the "echo" corresponds to the Word, whose echo it is; but it is also possible that this identity will *not* take place: the human spirit may, more or less,

---

[1] John 16: 14.   [2] 1 Cor. 2: 16 ff.   [3] Gal. 4: 6; Rom. 8: 15.
[4] Rom. 8: 16.   [5] 1 Cor. 12: 3.

fail to receive the witness of the divine Spirit. We cannot find an unambiguous criterion for the one or for the other. Thus the apostolic testimony to Christ has, it is true, its basis in inspiration; but it nowhere claims, *eo ipso*, to be inspired, either because it *is* apostolic testimony, or in the whole range and detail of its formulated doctrine.

This first point is very closely connected with the other two points. The second is the fact from which we started: that the real revelation is Jesus Christ, and that the witness of the Spirit points to Him, and to Him only. Functionally, therefore, the witness of the Spirit is subordinated to the revelation in Christ. As the Son is subject to the Father, so the Spirit in His testimony is subject to the Son. As the Son has been sent in order that the Father may be glorified, so the Spirit is sent in order that the Son may be known and glorified as the Son of God.[1] The witness to the Son constitutes the genuineness, and thus the validity of the witness of the Spirit. And the testimony to the Son constitutes its inexhaustible content. It has been said, it is true, that "The Spirit . . . shall guide you into all the truth";[2] but this future is a Future Imperfect, it never becomes a Future Perfect; this process of witnessing, this teaching (of the Spirit) is never ended, never finished. From the human standpoint the Spirit retains the right to teach mankind more and more clearly, never, however, establishing once for all a definitive doctrine, "dogma" pure and simple.

Then comes the third point: that the *witness* of the Spirit is not the whole work of the Spirit. The Holy Spirit is not only the One who witnesses and speaks, He is also the God who pours out vitality and creates new life. It is true that from this point of view His activity is just as impenetrable and mysterious as the process of procreation in the natural sense is impenetrable and mysterious: *"arcana spiritus efficicia"* (Calvin).[3] This is in accordance with the fact (which has already been mentioned) that Christ Himself is not only the Logos, but is also "Life" and "Light"; thus that even His work in the believing human being consists not only in the understanding of the Word, in the believing act of perception, but beyond that in happenings which lie beyond the range of clear knowledge, and indeed even beyond the range of human consciousness. At all these three points the new element in the New Testament revelation, contrasted with the revelation of the Old Testament, becomes evident. The idea which lies behind the theory of

[1] John 16: 14.  [2] John 16: 13.  [3] *Institutio*, III, 1, 1.

Verbal Inspiration corresponds to some extent with the Old Testament, prophetic, level of revelation; but it is not in any way in harmony with the New Testament stage of revelation, and precisely for this reason: that, unlike the revelation of the Old Testament, the New Testament revelation is not to be understood simply and solely as the revelation in the "Word". As the Person of Jesus is more than a Word, so the working of the Holy Spirit is more than merely a witness, in spite of the fact that the witness through which, and in which, Christ becomes to us the Word of God, is the Centre of everything. But for this very reason, because neither Jesus Christ nor the working of the Spirit of God who bears witness to Him is adequately defined as "letting the Word of God speak"—so also the testimony to Jesus Christ borne by human speech is never simply the same as the "Word" of God: hence the idea of a Verbal Inspiration of divinely revealed doctrine is entirely inadequate as a definition of the New Testament revelation.

In contrast to the Prophets, therefore, the Apostles do not assert that their teaching activity—all that they say and write —is dictated by the Holy Spirit, but they let us see, quite naturally and without self-consciousness, into the human and psychological process of their apostolic testimony. They know that all that they teach can never exhaust the revelation which God has given in Jesus Christ: that their words, therefore, are only continually renewed attempts to say "it". Hence the freedom with which, without trying to construct a doctrinal "standard", they place one formulation alongside another, and struggle unceasingly to find better forms of expression, and to formulate them as well as they possibly can.

Now for my last point: where the knowledge of Jesus Christ given through the Holy Spirit is concerned, in the very nature of the case there is no difference between the Apostles and the members of the Christian Church, thus also there is none between the Apostles and the Christians of later generations. If it is really true that every Christian is to have the Holy Spirit, indeed that he who "hath not the Spirit of Christ, he is none of His",[1] there *can* be no difference. To be united with Christ through the Holy *Spirit* means: to be *directly* united with Him.[2] Here there is no difference between an ordinary Christian of our

---

[1] Rom. 8: 9.
[2] Think of that bold word of Luther: that we, as Christians, "can make new Decalogues, as Paul does in all his Epistles".

own day and an Apostle. And yet this difference does exist, and it has great significance. Only it is not significant for the content of the revelation, but only for the way in which it is given: namely, for the *way* in which we, in contrast to the Apostles, receive the Holy Spirit and therefore the knowledge of Christ.

The second generation, and all the succeeding generations, receive faith, illumination through the Spirit, *by means of* the witness of the first generation, of the Apostles, the eye-witnesses.[1] Jesus Christ is not directly *"here"* for us, as He was for the disciples. We possess Him only in their narrative which tells us about Him. Their narrative and their doctrine are the *means*, which God uses, in order to unite us with Him. This is inherent in the very nature of the historical revelation. As an historical revelation, it can only reach us along the historical path, through the testimony of eye-witnesses. But this testimony, in accordance with that to which it points, is not simply an "historic fact"; the Apostles are not for us simply the biographers or chroniclers of Jesus. The historical revelation is something more than an "historic fact". What they have to tell and to teach is indeed the fact that the Word became flesh, that the Son of God has come to us in human form. The Christian message tells us not only of the Crucified Lord who "suffered under Pontius Pilate", but of the Risen Lord, who rose again on the third day; but the Resurrection is not a "fact of world history", it is a fact of the history of the Kingdom of God, which can only be reported by "eye-witnesses" who have "beheld His glory" as the glory "of the only begotten Son, full of grace and truth".[2] The fact of our redemption— the history of salvation—is transmitted by the proclamation of facts, that is, by the testimony of the Apostles, under the guidance and inspiration of the Holy Spirit.

It is this testimony, then, that stands between us and Christ; not, however, that it may be a barrier, but a bridge. Through this message we may receive the same Holy Spirit, and may therefore receive from the Spirit Himself the witness that He is the Christ, just as they received it. That means, however, that their witness can never be the *basis and the object* of faith, but only the *means* of faith. We do not believe in Jesus Christ *because* we first of all believe in the story and the teaching of the Apostles, but *by means of* the testimony of their narrative and their teaching we believe, as they do, and in a similar

[1] Cf. Kierkegaard, *Philos. Fragmts.*   [2] John 1: 14.

33

spirit of freedom.[1] Faith in Jesus Christ is not based upon a previous faith in the Bible, but it is based solely upon the witness of the Holy Spirit; this witness, however, does not come to us save through the witness of the Apostles—that apostolic testimony to which our relation is one of freedom, and, although it is true, it is fundamental for us, it is in no way dogmatically binding, in the sense of the theory of Verbal Inspiration. The Scripture—first of all the testimony of the Apostles to Christ—is the "Crib wherein Christ lieth" (Luther).[2] It is a "word" inspired by the Spirit of God; yet at the same time it is a human message; its "human character" means that it is coloured by the frailty and imperfection of all that is human.

[1] German: *Autopistie* . . . "self-evidence of faith." (Tr.)
[2] "*Vorrede auf das Alte Testament*", *Bindseil-Niemeyer*, VII, 303.

## CHAPTER 5

## DOCTRINE AND THE WITNESS OF FAITH

THE witness of the Apostles, by means of which they were able to perform their "service of the Word", is twofold in character: it is the *story* of Jesus, and it is the *teaching* about Jesus. This dual character of their witness is in harmony with the actual fact of revelation: that the "Word became flesh". The revelation of God in Jesus Christ is not itself a doctrine, but a Person, with His story.

The fact that the first disciples *told* the story of Jesus was not a mistake, nor was it a deviation from the right path. It is not due to a misunderstanding that the stories of Jesus are called the "Four Gospels". They are unique, for they contain the very heart of the Gospel. It was therefore an exaggeration—which had an unfortunate influence at the beginning of the theological renewal derived from Kierkegaard—when the great Danish thinker maintained that in order to become a Christian, in order to establish the Christian Faith, there was no longer any need of "narrative" or record; all that was required was to state that God became Man.[1] God's Providence was more merciful: He gave us the Four Gospels. The stories of Jesus must have played a very great part in the primitive Christian *kerygma*, just as they do to-day in all healthy and fruitful missionary work. In contrast to the doctrinal activity of the non-Christian religions or philosophies, the Christian message is, first of all, narrative, not doctrine.

Through the story of Jesus in the Gospels we are ourselves confronted by Him. The fact that the Apostle, the missionary, must above all "tell a story", and can only teach on the basis of this narrative, brings out very clearly the distinctive element in the revelation of God in Jesus Christ. In other religions there are *doctrines* which claim to deal with a supposed "revelation", but there is no *story* of revelation. To proclaim the Word of God means, in the New Testament, first of all to *tell the story* of Jesus, of His life and His teaching, of His sufferings, His death and His resurrection. So long as the Church is vitally aware of this, the idea of the "Word of God" is not in danger of being misunderstood in ultra-intellectual "orthodox" terms. Conversely, where doctrine is emphasized at the expense of the Biblical

[1] Kierkegaard, *Philos. Brocken*, pp. 94 ff.

35

narrative, there the intellectualistic misunderstanding of orthodoxy has already begun.

Reformation theology, if measured by this standard, cannot
be wholly acquitted from the reproach of having confused the
Word of God with doctrine; just as we cannot fail to be amazed
at its one-sided doctrinal instruction, based on the Catechism,
not only on didactic grounds, but also on those of theology.

The Reformers constantly maintained that the mere "story"
of Jesus was of no use to faith; up to a point, of course, they
were right, for in actual fact the *mere* story is as powerless to
awaken faith as *mere* doctrine. It is essential to the witness to
the Incarnate Son of God that the story of Jesus and the teaching about Jesus should be indissolubly united. Even the narrative as such cannot give us "Himself". A "sound film" of the
life of Jesus taken by a neutral reporter, or an account of the life
of Jesus written by an unbelieving compiler—such as Josephus,
for instance—would not have the power to awaken faith in
Jesus. But the Gospel narratives of the New Testament are not
neutral, for they do not give an "objective" account. They are
not photographs but portraits; they are not merely narratives
of something that happened, they are testimonies in the form of
narrative. This result, which the New Testament research of our
generation, in the sphere of criticism, has undoubtedly brought
out very clearly, has not yet been fully integrated into theological thought: even the telling of a story may be a testimony
to Christ, indeed this is the primary form of the primitive
Christian witness. This fact is so significant because it shows
very clearly that the essential Gospel, the "Word of God", the
revelation, is contained, not in the words spoken by the witness,
but in that to which he bears witness.

Here the oft-repeated formula, that "witness" is the act of
"pointing", gains its clearest meaning. We cannot "point"
away from ourselves to "the other" more clearly than by em-
phasizing the fact that the story we tell is itself the whole point
of our message, that it is itself "the Gospel". The story of Jesus
makes it very plain that it is not what *we* say that matters, but
Himself—so we must look away to Him, Himself. The story of
Jesus with this absolute emphasis: He of Whom I tell you is
the revelation of God—that is the meaning of all the Gospel
narratives, and the form of the earliest witness to Jesus
Christ.

It is certainly no accident, but is actually in the highest
degree significant, that the Risen Lord Himself said: "Ye shall

be My witnesses."[1] Only when the "life of Jesus" is seen and narrated from that standpoint is it truly a witness, is it a "Gospel", and not merely a series of "anecdotes about Jesus".[2] It is the Jesus who proved Himself to be the Christ in the Resurrection, whose earthly life and words are to be narrated. The orientation towards this point, which alone makes the picture correct in the sense of testimony, is, however, only possible, and can therefore only then shape the narrative, of one whose eyes have been opened by the Holy Spirit, so that in the picture of the Crucified he is able to "behold" the "Glory of God, full of grace and truth". *Thus* the Holy Spirit at the first "spoke" in the Apostles, so that they were able to see the picture of the earthly Jesus, of the Rabbi Jesus of Nazareth, as that of the Messiah and the Son of God. The picture of His earthly life came first; the fact that it gradually dawned on them that this was the picture of the Messiah was the first sign that the Holy Spirit was witnessing in their hearts. Accordingly, this is why the narrative of the acts and words of Jesus the Messiah was the first form in which they gave their own testimony. We ask: How did the Primitive Church carry on its missionary work? How did the Apostles carry out their calling as witnesses of Jesus? The standard answer to this question is not the *Corpus* of the Apostolic Epistles—they were written to communities which were already Christian—but the Gospel narratives. The "Gospels" represent the finest missionary preaching of the Apostolic period, of which otherwise we know so little.

Because the Word became *flesh*, the story of Jesus had to be told, and this story about Him is the primary witness;[3] but because the *Word* became flesh, alongside of the witness in story form, there had to be the witness in doctrinal form. In the narrative-witness the revelation is emphasized as the *Act* of God; in the witness in doctrinal form, the revelation is emphasized as the *Word* of God. Neither can be separated from the other; nor can they ultimately be distinguished from one another. For just as the story of Jesus, as the story of the Messiah Jesus, the Son of God, already contains "doctrine", so the doctrine of Christ as the doctrine of the Incarnate, Crucified, and Risen Son of God, already contains the "story". And yet the difference between the teaching of the Apostles and their

[1] Acts 1: 8.
[2] Cf. K. L. Schmidt, *Die Stellung der Evangelien in der allg. Literaturgeschichte*, Festschrift für H. Gunkel, 1923; and other works on *Formgeschichte*.
[3] Cf. *Theol. Wörterbuch*, IV, p. 121.

Gospel narrative is obvious. It is the task of the doctrinal testimony to make the subject of these deeds and words, of this suffering and victory, visible, which is invisible in the narrative as such. While this is only suggested in the narrative of the Gospels, it comes out clearly in the doctrinal testimony. Just as the narrative moves deliberately, in order to show who He is, and what is His secret, within the sphere of time and space, so the doctrine develops gradually, within the sphere of thought, in order to make the meaning of the mystery clear.

If, however, we go back to the origin of both, to the point at which "it pleased God to reveal His Son in me"; that is, where the revelation becomes the *Word* of God, then we perceive that an important change has taken place between this point and the witness. Peter, who was the first to confess Jesus as the Christ, because this "was not revealed unto him by flesh and blood, but by the Father in heaven", does not tell the story of Jesus, nor does he teach about Christ. His confession, the primitive form of his witness, is still accomplished in the dimension of personal encounter: "Truly Thou art the Christ, the Son of the Living God!" The original form of all genuine witness is the confession of faith in the form of the answering "Thou", evoked by the "Thou"-word of God addressed to the soul. This is true not only of the confession of the Apostle, but also of the confession of every true believer, of that "Abba, Father", which the Holy Spirit utters, evoking the response of faith in the same inspired words. The act of faith is a confession in the form of prayer, in the dimension "Thou-I";[1] it is not a doctrinal statement in the third person: "He-you".

Thus the first step in the development of the doctrinal testimony is to move away from the "Thou-relation" to God; this signifies a change of front: from God towards the world. In doctrine man speaks no longer in the "Thou"-form to God—as in the original confession of faith—but he now speaks *about* God as "He". Doctrine is no longer a spontaneous, personal response, in the form of prayer, to the Word of God, but already, even in its simplest form, it is reflective speech *about* God. The process of leaving the sphere of personal encounter in order to enter into the impersonal sphere of reflection is the presupposition of all doctrine. God is now no longer the One who speaks, but the One who is spoken about. It is no longer God who is addressed, but a person, or a number of people. This change of dimension, this transition from the personal sphere into the

[1] Cf. *Offenbarung und Vernunft*, pp. 119 ff.

38

impersonal, is the same as that of reflection. Hence all doctrine is reflective; but all doctrine does not represent a process of reflection to the same extent. The extent to which the personal relation is broken by the impersonal depends on the extent of reflection and also of the didactic element. The more that God becomes an *object* of instruction, instead of being One who is addressed with believing fervour, the *further* the doctrine moves away from the direct confession of faith, the more it becomes theoretical and doctrinal. It is an essential characteristic of the Biblical "doctrine", and especially of that of the New Testament, that it contains a minimum of doctrinal reflection.[1] Doctrine (or teaching) continually passes into worship, thanksgiving and praise, into the immediacy of personal communion. This comes out very clearly in a second process of refraction in that which we describe as "doctrine".

The witness of the Apostles, as a personal confession of faith, is always at the same time a call to obedience. The "Thou" has not disappeared: it has only changed its *vis-à-vis*. The Apostle who is both witness and teacher no longer addresses God, but he speaks in the Name of God to Man. "We beseech you in Christ's stead, be ye reconciled to God."[2] All apostolic teaching is speech which calls for faith and obedience, speech which tries to win others, which tries to bring others within the circle of those who believe. Even where the Apostle is giving direct "teaching", what he says is more than a "lecture". Even in this teaching, in spite of the fact that God is being "spoken about" the "Thou"-relation still determines the attitude of the speaker and the tendency of his message, because, and in so far as, the speaker addresses man in the Name of God: with the authority of a Divine commission, in absolute harmony with the God who reveals Himself to him. Thus such teaching, even where it takes place in the third person, for the sake of *this* "Thou", is not really reflective. It is not what we usually mean by "doctrine"; it is *witness* which demands an answer.

This witness, which is also a summons to faith and obedience, already differs in a significant way from instruction, as, for instance, the instruction of catechumens for Baptism in the Early Church. It is true that here also the *faith* of the learners is the aim, but it is not the immediate aim. The change to the third person, to teaching-about-God, goes deeper than in the

---

[1] The very word "teaching" or "doctrine" has a far less theoretical and academic meaning in the New Testament than it has to-day. Cf. article on διδάσκειν in the *Wörterbuch z. N.T.*, II, pp. 147 ff.      [2] 2 Cor. 5: 20.

witness of faith; the extension into the dimension of the third person covers and includes a wider sphere, more time is given to a reflective, and rather more scholastic, form of teaching.

The teaching of the Catechism, with its questions and answers, is directed primarily to the intellect; the subject must be understood, and to this end it is explained. Here we no longer hear— or if we do, only from very far off—that urgent cry: "Be ye reconciled to God! Repent!" But the deflection of the pupil's mind from the sphere of faith, of existence in the "Thou"-dimension by doctrinal teaching, is strictly limited to the explanation of that which is elementary and necessary. It is only the intellectual questions which clamour for consideration which lead to that theoretical extension which we call "theology" or "dogmatics".

In this sphere reflection predominates: thought and prayer are separated, not, it is true, in principle, but in practice. The teacher may, of course, remain aware that the subject he is teaching is his confession of faith, and that the instruction of the pupil ultimately demands the obedience of faith; but this faith is a distant source and a distant goal. Between both there extends the broad space of mental reflection—and the further it extends the more does the unlikeness increase between the subject that is discussed, and Him whom we address in the response of prayer. The further dogmatics extends, the more remote is its relation to its Primal Source; the further it drifts away from the confession of faith as "being laid hold of" by God, the more is the personal relation with God replaced by an impersonal one.

The change which this makes in the confession of faith is so great, and the danger of drifting away completely from the Origin and from the Goal is so acute, that we must ask ourselves why, then, does this take place? *Now* we understand all those objections—already mentioned—to the study of dogmatic theology; we must, therefore, repeat the question: Why does this change have to take place? Why should it take place? But we have not forgotten the answer which was given earlier: The transformation of the adoring confession of faith into a "doctrine-about-God" *must* take place—not for its own sake, not because faith itself requires it, but—for the sake of the believer, in face of doctrinal errors or heresies, in face of the questions which necessarily arise in our own minds, and in face of the difficulties which the original Biblical doctrine provides for the understanding.

In the light of the foregoing observations we can now give an answer to three questions, which, apart from these considerations, could either not be answered at all or could not be answered clearly. The first is that of the relation between faith and doctrine; the second is that of the difference between the knowledge of faith and theological knowledge; the third concerns the limits of theological effort. Obviously the relation between faith and doctrine is twofold in character: Faith springs from doctrine in so far as doctrine springs from faith; the doctrine of the Apostle is ἐκ πίστεως εἰς πίστιν.[1] The Divine revelation makes use of the believing testimony of the man on whom Christ has laid hold, in order that he may comprehend more. Faith urges us to preach and to teach; the preaching and the teaching create faith.

The difference between the knowledge of faith and theological knowledge, which is so difficult to define, and yet so necessary, is not one of subject or of content, but one of the form or dimension of existence. Theological or dogmatic knowledge is, it is true, the knowledge of faith in accordance with its origin, but not with its form. One who thinks in terms of theology must, so long as he does this, pass from the attitude of the worshipper to that of the thinker who is concerned with his subject. Greater clearness and precision of theological concepts can only be gained at the cost of directness of faith, and that readiness for action which it contains. While a person is studying theology he is not in the state of the praying and listening disciple, but he is a pupil, a teacher, a scholar, a thinker. This does not mean that theology *must* inevitably damage faith and obedience, but it does mean that it *may* harm it—that is, when the temper of the theologian replaces the spirit of the man of prayer, who listens for the Voice of God. This is what we mean by the term *"Theologismus"*.[2] When we see this, however, we also see why it is impossible to draw a sharp line of demarcation between the truth of faith and theological truth. The distinction is relative in character: the more that reflection and impersonal objectivity predominate, the greater will be the difference.

This brings us to the third question: that of the limitations of the theological enterprise, and answers it. Theology, dogmatics, doctrine in the highest form of reflection, are not "in themselves" necessary. It is not faith itself which urges us

[1] Rom. 1: 17.
[2] I.e. the danger of putting theology in the place of personal faith. (Tr.)

41

towards theology, but certain definite impulses within the community of believers, or in the heart of the believer himself. Theology is not necessary unto salvation, but it is necessary within the Church, and necessary for a person who must and will think. This sense of compulsion is one reason for studying dogmatic theology; it justifies its usefulness. On the other hand, in order to keep dogmatic theology within its bounds we may claim that only so much theology is good as can be combined with no injury to the attitude of faith, and to obedience itself. To ignore these limitations is already a symptom of that unhealthy process which we call "Theologismus"; but this is itself based upon the failure to distinguish plainly between the truth given by faith and theological truth, of the immediate knowledge of faith, and of that refracted by reflection, which must more or less be laid to the charge of the whole of the older theology.

## CHAPTER 6

## THE NORM OF CHRISTIAN DOCTRINE

ALL sound doctrine claims to be based on Truth. This is the hall-mark of all right thinking. When the claim is made: *"This is what you ought to think about this matter"*, it rests upon the conviction that to think in this particular way is the *right* way to think; that is, it is thinking in accordance with Truth. It is this which distinguishes sound doctrine from propaganda; the man who is "out for propaganda" is not concerned with Truth; all he wants to know is whether a particular view will be useful to him for a particular end. Christian doctrine claims to be true doctrine, that is, the true doctrine of God and His relation to Man and the world. The vastness of this claim, as we have seen, is based on the fact that its foundation does not lie in human knowledge, but in divine revelation. But this basis is at the same time a condition; Christian doctrine can only legitimately make this unconditional claim to Truth in so far as it is based upon revelation. Thus its *basis* becomes its *criterion* and its *norm*. We now have to inquire how revelation becomes the norm of Christian doctrine. Historical experience, indeed, shows us that this question is not superfluous; the very fact that there is such a variety of Christian doctrine, much of it contradictory, suggests that a mere appeal to revelation is not sufficient to form the basis for the legitimacy of its claim to be the true doctrine.

*Because* God has revealed Himself there *can* be, and is, sound Christian doctrine. But the question is: How does this basis of sound doctrine, revelation, become the norm, and thus the criterion of true doctrine? Between the decisive, objective, form of revelation, Jesus Christ, and doctrine, there lies that subjective element in revelation which we call "faith", though perhaps it would be better to describe it as that process which is accomplished within the subject. All Christian doctrine regards itself as a confession of faith, as an expression of the fact that the objective form of revelation has become subjective knowledge. Nevertheless, there *is* the possibility of illusion; for a doctrine may claim to be a confession of faith, and therefore a response to the objective form of revelation, when it is actually very different from that which it claims and seems to be. It may be based upon a misunderstanding of the divine revelation, or

43

upon opinions which have nothing whatever to do with revelation.

It is true that with the recognition of revelation—in the sense in which we have defined it—as the basis of Christian doctrine, we have already done something to distinguish legitimate from illegitimate Christian doctrine. A doctrine which does not appeal to this revelation as its origin, but to some other basis of knowledge, is by this very fact disqualified from the outset; all merely speculative theories, and all relativistic doctrines of God based on Comparative Religion, or on the Psychology of Religion—whatever their value may be in other directions—cannot be recognized as the Christian doctrine of God. In an earlier work of mine[1] I have discussed in detail how this exclusive basis of Christian doctrine deals with the various objections of the reason and justifies them; here all this must simply be presupposed. But this appeal to revelation, in the definitely Christian sense, has merely a limiting significance, not a constitutive one, in order to establish the validity of Christian doctrine; it is the *"conditio sine qua non"*, but it is not yet *"ratio sufficiens"* to establish the legitimacy of the claim of any doctrine to be *Christian* doctrine. This second step is only accomplished when it can be shown how the revelation, to which the doctrine appeals, becomes for doctrine itself the norm of all its teaching, and even the norm of faith itself.

This transition from the basis to the norm takes place within the Church founded upon the Reformation through the establishment of the "Scriptural principle". Christian doctrine is legitimate, is truly based upon revelation, and the faith which is based upon it is the true knowledge of faith, in so far as this doctrine and this faith agree with the teaching of the Bible.

This Scriptural principle of the Reformation is established in contrast to the principle of Tradition of the Catholic Church, in accordance with which the doctrine of the Church, and especially the exposition of Scripture, made by the highest ecclesiastical doctrinal authority, the Pope alone, *ex sese*, without any right of appeal on the part of a critic or inquirer to the Holy Scriptures themselves, determines what is Biblical and what is sound doctrine.[2] The Catholic doctrinal authority, that is, the Pope, is alone qualified to say in a binding authoritative manner what Scripture teaches. In setting up this autho-

---

[1] *Offenbarung und Vernunft*, 2nd Part.
[2] See the *Appendix* on the "Authority of Scripture", and its place in *The History of Dogma*, pp. 113 ff.

rity, however, not *in thesi*, it is true, but *in praxi*, the authority of the Church is set above the authority of Scripture, and the Scripture as a critical court of appeal is eliminated; this position is justified by the fiction that the apostolic ecclesiastical oral tradition contains elements which are not emphasized, or are not sufficiently emphasized in Scripture. Even if one were inclined to admit some truth in this fiction, it would only be in the sense that such truth is a complement to the Biblical doctrine; but this would not justify it in claiming that it invalidates the Scripture altogether as a critical court of appeal. The true reason is obvious, even though it is never acknowledged: the Catholic doctrinal authority, and many of its dogmas, would become insecure, if that court of appeal (i.e. the Bible) were actually allowed to function.

Now, however, what is or should be the basis of the Reformation principle of Scripture? To this question Reformation theology has only been able to give an inadequate answer, because in this theology, alongside of the right view of the authority of Scripture, which distinguishes the revelation in Jesus Christ from the Biblical testimony to it, an erroneous, "orthodox" doctrine of the authority of Scripture was at work, which became increasingly effective.

According to this view there is no question of the authority of Scripture, since the Verbal Inspiration of Scripture and the absolute identity of revelation and Biblical doctrine are the axiomatic presuppositions of all doctrine and of true faith. When the Scriptures are absolutely identified with the Word of God, this axiomatic authority of the doctrine of Scripture, and its absolute character as norm, are taken for granted and need no basis. But if Luther's statement is valid, that Christ is *"rex et dominus scripturae"*, then certainly the *question* of the authority of Scripture, and the kind of *norm* Scripture contains, has been set up.

As in the case of the Reformers, we must express our first principle thus: the Scriptures have the authority of a norm, and the basis for this principle is this: the Scriptures possess this authority because they are the *primary witness* to the revelation of God in Jesus Christ.[1] This revelation is central, both in the Old and the New Testament, in Christian doctrine as well as in Christian faith. But Jesus Christ comes to us through the witness of the Apostles; this witness has for us the validity of a norm because it is that which bases and creates faith. This is

[1] Cf. *Offenbarung und Vernunft*, pp. 124 ff.

the new truth which broke through at the Reformation, and was called to overcome the orthodox axiomatic view of the previous view. "Whatever is concerned with Christ is apostolic." All Christian doctrine is based upon the witness of the Apostles; the primitive witness supports the witness of the Church.[1] The doctrine of the Apostles is the primary medium, through which the revelation comes to us.

This *historical* priority, and this actual basis, are, however, still not the same as the establishment of a norm. A further element must be added, namely, the concrete priority, the fact that the Apostolic doctrine comes first, before all later forms of doctrine. This pride of place is based on the fact that particular dignity is accorded to the original witness because it still belongs to the actual happenings which constitute the Christian revelation. This is the dignity which is ascribed to the Apostle over against all the later teachers and doctors of the Church: that he, as the first to receive, and indeed to have a share in the historical revelation in Christ, has a special measure of the knowledge of Christ. He, in contrast to all who come later, is the eye-witness of the Resurrection, as he was the eye-witness of the earthly life of Jesus.

But this privileged position is not an absolute one, which can be clearly defined. This comes out in two facts which can be established, objectively, quite plainly:

First of all, in the fact that the circle of the Apostles cannot be rigidly defined: is Paul, Mark, Luke, or the unknown author of the Epistle to the Hebrews an "eye-witness" in the same sense as one of the Twelve? Secondly, in the fact that the doctrines of the Apostles, the doctrines of the New Testament, to a great extent differ from one another. Recourse to "the" doctrine of the New Testament is, in the strictly literal sense of legal doctrinal authority, impossible. The unity of the witness of the New Testament in the strict, unconditional sense of the word, lies solely and alone in Him, the One who is confessed, but not in the teaching of the witnesses. They all stand in a circle round Him, and they all point to Him, each from a different standpoint; their witness indeed points to Him, the One, but the witness of each is different. The refraction of the divine revelation in the human medium of the knowledge of faith and the witness of faith is already at work in the primitive Christian testimony, and can only be argued away either by a forcible imposition of dogma, or by a deliberate resolve to ignore

[1] Eph. 2: 20.

46

the real facts of the situation. Anyone who really listens to the Apostolic witness to Christ feels compelled to *seek* the unity of the truth of revelation in the very variety of these testimonies.

The priority of this court of appeal, however, also implies its relative character. Like the historical record, so also the theological doctrine of the Apostles must be subjected to critical examination. This criticism cannot result from human rational truths, but only from the revelation in Christ itself, which is attested in the doctrine of the Apostles. Thus it seems to move in a circle: only *through* the doctrine of the Apostles can criticism be exercised *on* the doctrine of the Apostles. This circle is, however, only real for those who hold a legalistic "orthodox" view of doctrinal authority.

Actually, this is the point at issue: that the real norm is the revelation, Jesus Christ Himself, who Himself witnesses to us through the Holy Spirit, who, however, in addition to this His self-revelation, makes use of the witness of the Apostles. While we are bound in an absolute sense to the medium, to the means of revelation of the Apostolic witness, we are only bound in a relative sense to the *authority* of this witness. The absolute authority is Jesus Christ Himself, whom we only possess through the record and the teaching of the Apostles; but He, whom we only have *through* them, stands above them. Their witness is valid, absolutely binding, in so far as it really witnesses to Him Himself. It is true that, as Luther says: "Whatever is concerned with Christ is apostolic."

A legalistic, immutable authority, such as the human desire for security would so gladly possess—and indeed is offered in an orthodox doctrine of the Scriptures as an axiomatic authority, or in the Catholic doctrine of the infallible doctrinal authority of the Pope—is thus denied to *us*. The word of Scripture is not the final court of appeal, since Jesus Christ Himself alone is this ultimate authority; but even while we examine the doctrine of Scripture, we remain within the Scriptures not, it is true, as an *authority*, but as the *source* of all that truth which possesses absolute authority.

Up till now we have spoken of the Scriptures as the sum of the *Apostolic* testimony to Jesus Christ. This raises two further questions: what is our attitude to the Old Testament as witness to the provisional or preparatory revelation? And what should be our attitude to the statements of Scripture which do not come under the heading of witness to revelation?

So far as the Scriptures of the Old Testament are concerned,

47

the phrase the "Word of God" has far less final validity than in the New Testament. Here, indeed, the still greater variety and lack of unity of the teaching—and also of the narrative—warns us of the necessity for critical distinctions. The orthodox identification of the Word of Scripture with the Word of God could only be maintained at all—so far as the Old Testament was concerned—by leaving the widest possible latitude for *allegorical* interpretation. The less that the Scriptures are taken literally, the more room is there for freedom of exposition—we might even say, for arbitrary interpretation; then every single expositor becomes a kind of Pope who alone possesses the right key to the meaning of the Scriptures. The Scriptures, then, become not a *norm* of doctrine, but a proof of a doctrine which stands firm independently of it; it is no longer a critical court of appeal, but it is used merely to cover, or in any case to illustrate an interpretation of doctrine which is regarded as absolutely convincing.

In principle, however, there is the same relation between the Old Testament witness to revelation and revelation itself as there is between the Apostolic witness and Jesus Christ, with this difference only: that over the revelation in the Old Testament itself there stands the word "provisional". It is an essential part of the Christian Faith: it is part of the Apostolic doctrine of the Old Testament, that the revelation which it contains has the character of "prophecy", of pointing forward, and of preparation. My work on the doctrine of revelation has already shown how this should be treated in detail.[1] The second question, that concerning the statements of Scripture which do not refer to revelation itself, is simple to answer. In so far as the Bible speaks about subjects of secular knowledge, it has no teaching authority. Neither its astronomical, cosmological picture of the world, nor its geographical view, nor its zoological, ethnographical or historical statements are binding upon us, whether they are in the Old Testament or in the New. Here, rather, free course should be given to rational scientific criticism.[2] Even in these sections the Scripture remains the sole *source* of our knowledge of revelation, to which we are absolutely obliged to turn, but it is in no way the *norm* of our knowledge and our doctrine. We possess revelation through the Bible as a *whole*, to which statements of all kinds, ideas of the universe

[1] *Offenbarung und Vernunft*, pp. 131 ff.
[2] On the relation between a "Bible-faith" and historical criticism, see *Offenbarung und Vernunft*, Chap. 18.

of the ancient world, Jewish and Early Christian systems of chronology, etc., belong. We cannot disentangle the one from the other, for these cosmological ideas are, moreover, the alphabet in which the witness of revelation is spoken to us. But that is no reason why we should confuse the witness itself with this alphabet; on the contrary, we should try to distinguish the one from the other, although we cannot separate them.

In all this, all we are trying to do is to free the newly discovered Scriptural Principle of the Reformers from the traditional orthodox, formally axiomatic faith in the Bible, and to show clearly what the teachers of the Reformation period never succeeded in doing—although in principle we owe this truth to them. The result of our considerations is this: the Scriptures are the absolute authority, in so far as in them the revelation, Jesus Christ Himself, is supreme. But the doctrine of Scripture as such, although it is the absolute basis of our Christian doctrine, is only in a conditional sense the *norm* of the same. Critical reflection on the adequateness, or inadequateness, of the Biblical doctrinal testimony for the revelation to which it bears witness, is not eliminated; we still have to face it; a final resort to a single Scriptural passage is impossible for us. Hence in each instance all Christian doctrine is, and remains, a venture of faith.

## CHAPTER 7

# DOGMA AND DOGMATICS

SINCE Christian doctrine is itself a form of revelation, one of its essential characteristics is a claim to absolute truth and validity, a claim to obedience. If we posit the alternative: either an attitude of "tolerance" with its "relativistic" spirit, or one of dogmatic intolerance, then undoubtedly Christian doctrine is on the side of the latter. But this alternative is false. The fact that various forms of widely divergent "Christian doctrine" have always existed within the Christian Church shows us clearly that the "revelatory" authority of such doctrine is limited. This, as we have seen, is a recognized reason for the necessity of dogmatic theology or dogmatics. The Church is forced to distinguish "sound" doctrine from "unsound", that which conforms to the "orthodox" standard from that which does not.

But while doctrine as such is primarily the individual concern of individual teachers, the Church must endeavour to distinguish "standard" doctrine from that which is not, "sound" doctrine from "unsound" in such a way that it is evident to all that this verdict expresses the view of the Church as a whole. The Church knows that her unity, and the validity of her preaching and her teaching, are seriously endangered by the fact of contradictory doctrines; for that which is contradictory cannot be equally true, and the preaching and teaching activity of the Church cannot make a strong claim for the obedience of faith if contradictory doctrines are put forth in the name of the Church. Not only the outward unity, but also the inner unity of the Church, and not only the unity, but also the commission and work of the Church—that is, the task of finding a way into the hearts and minds of men for the divine revelation, are seriously injured if the Church is not in a position to distinguish between that which is the standard and correct doctrine and that which is not.

It is the perception of this fact which lies at the root of the formation of dogma.[1] In order to make this necessary distinction the Church uses the form of a public Confession of Faith. A Confession of Faith is primarily a spontaneous and individual expression of faith; the individual Christian "confesses"—for

[1] On the history of the conception of dogma, see below, pp. 103 ff.

instance when summoned before a tribunal—his Christian faith. Secondly, there is the "Confession of Faith" in the form of Christian preaching and teaching. Every Christian preacher and teacher—even the simplest father of a family who instructs his children in the Christian Faith—teaches others by the very fact of "confessing" his faith, and he confesses his faith before others in order to teach them. This, however, does not mean that the Church as a whole may feel the necessity to confess its faith publicly and in common. This may take place first of all in the body of the local Church as a whole, in the gathering for public worship, as part of the response of the local Church in thanksgiving and praise to the Word of God which is proclaimed, as a liturgical act; it may also take place in a universal form, including all the Churches as a whole, if the occasion arises.

This occasion, however, does arise when the Church sees that her commission and her unity are menaced by the variety of contradictory doctrines. It is then that there arises what is called, in the narrower sense of the word, the "ecclesiastical Confession of Faith", the Credo, or the dogma. The aim of this common confession is to express the true faith, and to fix a standard of doctrine. Thus the Church sets up a norm of faith and doctrine which is intended to act as a means of separation, as a criterion of "sound" *versus* "unsound" doctrine. The need for such an instrument to scrutinize and criticize doctrine is all the more urgent since doctrinal aberrations affect not only details of secondary importance, but also the heart of Christian doctrine, the truth of revelation itself.

Since the reasons which force the Church to work out such a "Confession" are almost always operative everywhere, it is not surprising that the Church—in its various branches—has continually felt obliged to set up such norms of faith and doctrine as should provide a "standard", and give the right direction to Christian belief, especially at times where the essence of faith and doctrine was gravely menaced. But the history of the formation of Creeds shows equally clearly both its inevitability and its problems and dangers.

The first and most important question is of the *authority* of the Confession which is thus formulated. The Roman Catholic Church claims for her "confession" absolute, final validity, a claim which includes the whole sphere of faith. While the ancient Catholic Church, the Church of the earlier centuries, claimed this authority for the Œcumenical Church Council, constituted according to ecclesiastical law, and thus established and based this claim, up to the time of the Council of Trent, upon the theory of the infallibility of Œcumenical Councils rightly gathered together, in the Vatican the already very ancient predominance of the Curia won the victory, which thus established the Papal teaching-office as the sole final court of appeal, and thus gave to it absolute doctrinal authority, established by the law of the Church.[1]

The Confessional writings of the period of the Reformation, on the whole, share the ancient Catholic view of the absolute teaching authority of the Church—certainly on the pre-supposition, silently assumed by the Lutheran Church, and explicitly stated by the Reformed Churches—that the Confession of the Church must agree with the norm of Holy Scripture. In both cases belief in the unassailable doctrinal authority of the rightly constituted Church Council representing the whole Church is the controlling factor. Two ideas lie behind this view: firstly, a very strong belief in the effective spiritual power of the Christian community, as compared with the isolated individual believer, or the individual teacher or preacher; secondly, there is a dangerous over-emphasis on the authority of the Christian community and its ecclesiastical organization as the guarantee of Truth.

The acceptance of this principle of the authority of the Confession of Faith is all the more surprising, since the Reformation arose when Luther threw down his challenge, which shook the very bases of this ecclesiastical authority. Who, then, can guarantee that the few hundred Churchmen, who constitute the Synods which create Confessions of Faith, grasp the meaning of the divine authority and express it in their teaching, while the individual thinker who contradicts them has no such authority? Who, then, gives to the Church Council the authority to give an interpretation of Holy Scripture, which is binding for faith? In any case, it is a fact that all previous Confessions, without exception, contain cosmological elements which are in opposition to our scientific knowledge.[2] Thus doctrinal statements were formulated, with *absolute* authority, believed to be based upon the divine revelation itself, which have since proved to be mistaken, even though only in part, and on points of secondary importance.

[1] *Romani Pontificis definitiones* ex sese, non autem ex consensu Ecclesiae, *irreformabiles esse*" ("*Vaticanum*", in Denzinger, 1839).
[2] Think, for instance, of the idea of an historical "Fall" of "Adam"—cf. my anthropology *Man in Revolt*, Chapters 5 and 6.

Thus, both the fundamental perception of the possibility of error of even the most Biblical of ecclesiastical Councils, as well as the testimony of fact, agree that the "Confession", or *Credo*, or dogma, of the Church can only possess limited authority; this implies the possibility of further light being given to the Church on any particular problem. In principle dogma comes under the same provisional authority as the doctrine of the individual teacher. On the other hand, as an act of the whole Church, by which we may assume that particular care in critical examination will be exercised, an act in which, above all, we have the promise of genuine fellowship in faith, there may be ascribed to it a *particular* relative authority or dignity.

This estimate of dogma alone corresponds to the fundamental view of the Reformation; it constitutes the essential characteristic which distinguishes the Protestant from the Roman Catholic understanding of Faith and revelation. For the Catholic believer, as for the individual Catholic teacher, the dogma of the Church is fixed, it is the final court of appeal in matters of religious truth; for the Protestant teacher, on the other hand, the dogma, whether that of his own Church in particular, or that which is common to all the Churches, is, it is true, a court of appeal of the highest importance, which he will find it difficult to ignore, but it is never the *final* authority, forcing him to suppress his own view entirely. That is why the Protestant Churches do not set up a fixed system of "dogma", but instead, they have "Confessions of Faith".

The danger of turning dogma into an absolute is one danger, but there is a second one—certainly closely connected with the first, which is, if possible, still greater. The doctrine of the Church is always the *Confession*, the expression, but not the *object* of faith. The Object of faith is the revelation, Jesus Christ Himself, not the *Credo* of the Church. But if this Creed of the Church is wrongly equated with absolute Truth, then it is almost impossible to avoid setting it up as the actual *object* of faith. Faith becomes faith in dogma, belief in an authoritative human doctrine; it then ceases to be what it is according to the teaching of the Bible: faith in the truth of revelation, which can never be equated with any human doctrine at all.[1] The revelation is Jesus Christ Himself, not a doctrine *about* Jesus Christ. In true faith we have to do with Jesus Christ Himself, not with a doctrine *about* Him. The doctrine points to *Him*;

[1] We owe an abiding debt of gratitude to W. Herrmann for the way in which he continually pointed out this fundamental contradiction.

its aim is to show Him, and to make Him plain and visible before the eyes of men.

Doctrine, rightly understood, is the finger which points to Him, along which the eye of faith is directed towards Him. So long as faith clings to the "finger", to the interpretative doctrine, it has not really arrived at its goal; thus it is not yet actually faith. Faith is the encounter with Him, Himself, but it is not submission to a doctrine about Him, whether it be the doctrine of the Church, or that of the Apostles and Prophets. The transference of faith from the dimension of personal encounter into the dimension of factual instruction is the great tragedy in the history of Christianity. The Reformers were right when they rejected the unconditional authority of ecclesiastical doctrine as such; but when the theologians of the Reformation began to believe in a doctrine *about* Jesus Christ, instead of in Jesus Christ Himself, they lost the best fruit of the Reformation. Reformation theology was right in setting up the *Biblical* doctrinal authority above the *ecclesiastical* authority as their norm; but they were wrong, when they made the Biblical doctrine their *final* unassailable authority, by identifying the Word of God with the word of the Bible. When they did this, in principle, they relapsed into Catholic error; the Protestant faith also became a doctrinal faith, belief in dogma, only now the Biblical dogma took the place of the doctrine of the Church. Protestant orthodoxy arrested the development of the Reformation as a religious awakening.

This distinction between "Jesus Christ Himself" and the doctrine about Him, as final authority, must not, however, be misunderstood in the sense of separation. We do not possess "Jesus Christ Himself" otherwise than in and with the doctrine about Him.[1] But it is precisely this doctrine, without which we cannot have "Him Himself", which is not Himself, and therefore has only a relative authority. This authority increases the more plainly and clearly it is connected with Jesus Christ Himself. Thus it is precisely the duty of a genuinely religious —which means, also, a genuinely critical—system of dogmatics to undertake a careful examination of this necessary, obvious connexion between Jesus Christ and the doctrine concerning Him.

Dogma, that is, the Confession of Faith of the whole Church, does not come into being without much thought and effort on the part of theologians. It is the faith of the Church, it is true,

[1] Cf. K. Barth, *Kirchliche Dogmatik*, I, 1, p. 142.

which it expresses; the faith which in principle is held by each individual living member of the Church. But the spontaneous individual faith knows no definitive, authoritative and exclusive formulation. It is true that out of the common life of the worshipping community the main belief, shared by all, may be continually expressed in the form of the common Confession of Faith, as, for instance, the phrase, κύριος χριστός, was undoubtedly a confessional formula of the Primitive Christian Church, spontaneously arising out of the worship of the Church. Further, the expansion of this very simple, and earliest, Christian Confession into the threefold Baptismal formula which forms the core of the Apostles' Creed, may have arisen spontaneously without special theological reflection. But what a gulf there is between these simple forms of the Creed of the Church and the Confessional writings of the period of the Reformation, as, for instance, the Apology of Melanchthon (for the Augsburg Confession) or the Second Helvetic Confession!

However, not only elaborate doctrinal confessions of this kind, which are absolute masterpieces of the theological craft, but also the "symbols" (creeds) of the Early Church, which arose out of the controversies of the third to the fifth centuries, are the result of theological, "dogmatic" labour—their formulated doctrines, with their intellectual acumen and their antithetical character, could never be regarded as expressions of a naïve, spontaneous, unreflective faith, but only as products of the highest intellectual activity, willingly devoted to the preservation of the purity of the treasure of the faith of the Church. They may be compared with the artificial "settings" with which the jeweller surrounds the pearl as a natural product, in order to protect it from loss and destruction, and in order to enhance its beauty. The dogma is an artificial product of theological reflection, whose "art" must be shown in the fact that it exactly fits the form of the "pearl", that is, that upon a foundation of extreme intellectual activity, it lays stress upon the essential element in faith, brings it out, so to speak, and defends it against all misunderstandings that may threaten it.

Now, however, the simple question: "What, then, is the chief thing in our Faith?" springs from an abstract process of reflection, and indeed evokes another. But this is still more true of the question: "What is the distinctive element in our faith which must be defended against the erroneous belief which menaces our Church?" The history of dogma in the

Early Church, therefore, shows how much patient and penetrating theological labour, in thought and reflection, preceded the formation of these short classical credal formulas. If we compare the language of these dogmas with the language of the New Testament the difference is obvious. The terminology of the doctrine of the Trinity of the Athanasian Creed, and indeed even that of the Nicaeno-Constantinopolitan Creed, is alien to the New Testament. The latter does not contain the terms *homousios*, the *"Persons"*, the *Trinity*; we may say, however, that the New Testament possessed all the elements which were ready for this process of development: the New Testament provides the premises; dogma draws the conclusions. But in order to perceive the truth that these non-reflective, unsystematic, scattered, and (from the theological point of view), naïve ideas of the New Testament are the premises from which this conclusion may be drawn, a vast amount of abstract work was required, in the shape of the analysis and formulation of ideas, and the classification of these ideas in systematic form. Between the formulas of the New Testament and those of the Athanasian Creed there lie four centuries of the most intensive theological, "dogmatic", intellectual toil. In this sense we may, and must, say: dogma is the product of dogmatics.

This, however, is only one side of the question. The second becomes plain when we start from the position of the Catholic theologian. For the Catholic theologian of the present day dogma is that which is "given", behind which he cannot, and may not, go. His intellectual labour, therefore, can only aim at the interpretation and explanation of dogma; it is not his concern, or his duty, to examine the dogma critically, in the endeavour to replace it by a better dogma. Thus his work can only be called "dogmatics" in the sense that it is subordinated to, directed by, dogma; it must start from dogma and return to dogma, and moreover to the given dogma, not to the dogma as an idea or a postulate. The same is true, even if only in a limited way, of the work of every ecclesiastical dogmatic theologian. Even the believing Lutheran theologian starts from his Augsburg Confession and returns to it, just as the believing Reformed theologian does with his Second Helvetic Confession.

He does not want, first of all, to create or prepare a new dogma, but, by using his brain, to penetrate, expound and secure the right understanding of the Confession of Faith of his own Church. His dogmatics, too, is determined by the given dogma, starts from it and returns to it again.

And yet the difference between the Catholic theologian and his Protestant colleague is very great, though this comes out far more clearly in the case of the Reformed, than of the Lutheran, theologian. The very fact that in the Reformed Churches there is nothing which corresponds to these really standard Lutheran Confessional writings is characteristic. There are a large number of Reformed Confessional works, which differ a good deal from one another, none of which possesses the "canonical" validity which is ascribed to both the Lutheran documents. Hence the Reformed theologian, from time immemorial, and down to the present day, has a much freer attitude towards dogma than the Lutheran.

But both are aware—if they have not become completely petrified in that confessional othodoxy which leads back to Catholicism—that the "Confession" of the Church is a product of human labour, and for that reason is, in principle, capable of error, and probably needing reform. For this reason, even if to a greatly varying extent, they are critical of the dogma of their Church, and in so far as this is their attitude, their dogmatic work is fundamentally directed towards a reformed type of dogma. Thus "dogmatics" acquires the meaning of a critical examination of the "given" doctrine, and a forward-looking preparation of a new and better Confession of Faith.

This, however, creates a curious dualism in all dogmatic labour. The ecclesiastical Confession was indeed created with the very aim of establishing the doctrine of the Church as a norm, in order to arrest the development of arbitrary views and tendencies dangerous to faith. The Confession therefore is meant to be binding, and indeed rather more binding in the realm of doctrine and of teaching than in the sphere of faith and in the belief of Christian men and women.

The Church is impelled to formulate dogmas, not because there are different kinds of faith, but because there are varieties of doctrine. Thus it should be the Church's endeavour to instruct, direct, and to some extent control the teachers of the Church by its dogma. Thus in the mind of the Church the work of the theologian is primarily an explication of the *given* dogma. On the other hand, in the interest of the authority of the revelation itself—rightly understood—the Church should not hamper the intellectual freedom of its recognized teachers, but should give them every facility for the critical examination of their present Confession of Faith, in order to extend its scope.

Thus the theologian stands on the threshold which both separates the existing Confession of Faith from the future, improved Confession, and also serves as a point of transition from the one to the other. His point of departure is the existing Confession of faith; but before him there stands the "given" revelation in the Scriptures, "given" to him and to the Church. This revelation, however, is not "given" in a static manner; it is not a system of statements for man to take and use; rather is it something with which the Church has been entrusted, something for which we have to "search the Scriptures".

We now see more clearly a third danger which is connected with the idea of dogma. The dogma of the Church as a Confession of Faith is spiritual, pneumatic, a product of faith, whose authority is spiritual only. Even Church order, and order in the Church, is a spiritual matter. The Christian Church —as the body of believers—cannot tolerate any loophole in its structure by which the enemy of faith could enter. Thus, if the Church, by means of her discipline, expels from her body those who are not true members of the Church, in order that they shall not poison the Body corporate, so also must she deal with the teacher who teaches that which is harmful to the faith of the Church. Doctrinal discipline is a necessary form of Church discipline. This doctrinal discipline—which is exercised in every ordination vow, even of the simplest character—must, however, remain all the time aware of the limits to its exercise, due to the relative character of the authority of all ecclesiastical doctrinal norms. Alongside of the power to "bind" there must be room for freedom.

But in her effort to secure purity of doctrine the Church has not been content to use this spiritual method, but she has claimed the power of the State to achieve her end. The heretical teacher was not only the object of spiritual Church discipline, but was subject to police and judicial measures exercised by the State. The heretic was burnt, or he was hindered and punished in various ways in his natural and civic existence. Although since the time of the Enlightenment and of the French Revolution the State has usually withdrawn from this sphere, yet the memory of mankind in the West has saddled the idea of dogma with recollections of these State sanctions of strict orthodoxy, and these memories are very tenacious; while the practice of certain Churches, which, wherever they have the opportunity, tend to recall this misuse of State authority, cannot fail to keep these memories alight.

The example of the Reformation Churches shows that this incursion from the spiritual into the political sphere is not only a tendency of the Roman Catholic understanding of dogma, but that again and again it slips into the Church, due to man's mistaken desire for security. To the extent in which the prestige of dogma grows does this danger become acute, although almost everywhere the Church now has to be content with very modified political and civil sanctions. This digression, which belongs rather to the sphere of Church history than to that of dogmatics, should not be regarded as wholly irrelevant where we are concerned to exhibit both the authority and the limits of dogma as the point of reference for dogmatics.

## CHAPTER 8

## DOGMATICS AS A SCIENCE[1]

As soon as it has been recognized that dogmatics is quite different from a neutral religious study of the doctrine of any particular religion, as, for instance, of the Christian religion, as soon as we have understood that dogmatics has its own "place" within the life of the Church—that it is itself a mode of knowledge of faith, and that its aim is to formulate the doctrine of the Church, of the Divine revelation, in accordance with divine truth, then the question is bound to arise: Can dogmatics be regarded as a science?

As a mode of Christian doctrine, as a function of the Church itself, dogmatics has primarily no interest in being called a "science". Its primary tendency is certainly not in the direction of intellectual research, but in the direction of the fellowship of faith and the preaching of the Church. The earliest theology of the Church betrays no "academic" aspirations of any kind. It is, therefore, really an open question whether dogmatics can have an interest in being called a "science" and in having to satisfy any kind of intellectual criteria.

When we turn to this subject we are not thinking of re-opening the discussion of the problem of "Religion and Science", at least, not in the sense in which this is usually understood: can faith be combined with the truths of science, or are not the statements of faith rendered questionable, or even mistaken by the discoveries of science? These questions have been thoroughly discussed in another connexion.[2] The result of that critical examination was that it became clear that a conflict between religion and science could only arise, and has only arisen, out of a misunderstanding either on the part of religion or of science.

Our present question is a different one: namely, whether the service which dogmatics has to render to the Church obliges it to apply scientific criteria and methods, or, to put it in other terms, whether the very element which distinguishes dogmatics from faith does not make it necessary for dogmatics to enter into the realm of science (*i.e.* scientific criticism), and thus to use

[1] *Wissenschaft* has a much wider sense in German than in English. The author's meaning comes out plainly in this chapter. (TR.).
[2] *Offenbarung und Vernunft*, Chapters 18–22.

its criteria and its methods? It would reveal a complete mis-understanding of faith were we to give an unhesitating affirmative answer to this question, by appealing to the argument that even theology is concerned with truth; but where truth is envisaged, there science must come into the picture. This brings out a very widespread, and very deeply rooted mis-understanding, which has done serious harm not only to theology but still more to faith and to the Church.

The Christian Faith itself is wholly directed towards Truth; but who would care to maintain that the true knowledge of faith is scientific knowledge! Science leads to truth of a quite definite kind; the truth of faith is of a wholly different order. The Christ who says "I am the Truth" certainly does not mean by this that He, as this Truth, is the Object of scientific know-ledge. The truth of faith, in the sense in which the Bible uses the term, is "truth as encounter", truth in the dimension of the person, "Thou-I", but not in the "thing"-dimension.[1] The truth which faith perceives and grasps is a personal self-disclosure, the truth of revelation, not the truth which can be discovered by research and the use of the intellect.

At first sight, therefore, this contrast seems to suggest a negative answer to the question: Can dogmatics be regarded as a science? And should it be thus regarded? in spite of the title, hallowed by tradition, of Theo-logy, "divine science". Know-ledge of God, in the religious sense, is certainly not scientific knowledge, and the God of revelation is certainly not an object of scientific knowledge. In this respect Schleiermacher's protest against the scholastic conception and practice of a "divine science" was right, even though his conception of faith did not agree with that of the New Testament, nor did his own theory of faith agree with the Biblical doctrine, since his thought lacks the objective content of truth, the fact that the divine Self-revelation confronts us as objective Reality.

But we may grant that he is right in contending that dog-matics is distinguished from faith as the process of reflection is distinguished from all that is non-reflective and immediate. This "immediateness" of faith is certainly not the "pious feeling" of "absolute dependence", but the encounter of the human person—of that personal centre which the Bible calls the "heart"—with the Person of God, in His personal self-revelation in Jesus Christ. This revelation is the "Word of God", towards which faith is directed, which it grasps and by

---

[1] Cf. my book *Wahrheit als Begegnung*, 1938.

which it is created. But theology, dogmatics, is not this faith itself—otherwise the theologian alone would be a true believer —but theology is faith in its reflection in critical thought.[1]

We have already made it clear that any Confession which becomes a "doctrine" is the fruit of a transition from the dimension of the "person" into that of a "thing", and indeed that it consists in this change. God, instead of being addressed, is spoken about; He is the object of doctrine. The further this process of refraction of immediacy goes the more impersonal does the truth become, the more does the knowledge of faith approximate to other forms of "secular" knowledge, the more impersonally objective and remote does it become. A further sign of theological reflection points in the same direction: the more that theological ideas become intellectual concepts, the more abstract do they become, the less do they resemble the vital concreteness of the Biblical way of teaching, especially that of Jesus Himself.

So far as this happens, however, the theological definition of ideas, and its ways of teaching, approaches that of the "scientific" or "academic" teacher. It shares with that kind of teaching the effort to be accurate and precise, and strictly logical in the connexion of thought. The ideas are expounded clearly in definitions, and they lose that fluidity which suggests variety of meaning, akin to poetic speech, which is proper to the directness of the witness of faith. Its "edges" become sharp and hard, and in so doing its connexion can be presented in a rational manner; it is a building composed of stones which are well-hewn and can be fitted faultlessly together. The connexion becomes, or tries to become, a system; the historico-dynamic element becomes entangled in a net of timeless-logical conceptions. Above all, the personal categories are smothered by impersonal objective categories.

All this means that doctrine becomes, so to speak, capable of assuming scientific form. Whether this means that we ought to call dogmatics "scientific" or not is finally a question of terminology; is it not the case that even at the present day controversy still rages round the "scientific" character of philosophy? In any case dogmatics cannot become an independent "positive science", so long as it does not forget its origin and its aim, since it does not operate and represent a

---

[1] It must be because he does not recognize this distinction that Karl Barth, in his observations on "Dogmatics as a Science", ventures to say: "The fear of Scholasticism is the mark of the false prophet" (*Kirchl. Dogm.* I, 1, p. 296).

given finite object, because all its efforts are directed towards the ultimate Truth behind all that exists. Its main concern is for that Truth which is not an "It", not a state of affairs, a situation, but absolute Subject, that Truth which cannot be known in cool detachment, but only in the obedience and confidence of faith.

In its relation to the Ultimate, the Absolute, which lies behind all that is given and actual, dogmatics is like philosophy. Its aim is not to establish facts, but to seek to discover the ultimate and final truth behind the facts, which is both the origin and the aim of all that is. In contrast to all philosophy, however, theology does not need to seek for this truth by its own efforts after knowledge; its task is rather to illuminate by means of thought that revelation which is given to man through faith.

Like philosophy, it is concerned with the Eternal Logos, but in contrast to philosophy it is concerned with the Logos which became flesh; therefore it is not concerned with a timeless and eternal Logos, but with one which has been revealed in history; it is not concerned with an abstract idea, but with the Logos who is the Son of the Father.

For all these reasons the "scientific" character of dogmatics, if we want to use this terminology at all, is *sui generis*; it can be compared with no other "science"; it must be measured by its own criteria, and it operates with its own methods, peculiar to itself, and unknown in any other science.

We should, of course, remind ourselves that, even apart from dogmatics or the "science of faith", science itself is not a unity, but a multiplicity of enterprises which take many forms, and represents a variety of sciences which cannot be reduced to any common denominator; this, indeed, comes out in the contrasts between natural science and "intellectual science",[1] the science of facts and the science of norms, causal science and the science of values, historical science and the science of law.[2] These differences between the sciences which exist outside the sphere of dogmatics provide, it is true, certain analogies for the difference between dogmatics and the other sciences, but they are very remote analogies, or parables, which break down at the decisive point.

From these considerations it has now become clear that the

[1] In English: "The Humanities" (*Geisteswissenschaft*). (TR.)
[2] Cf. Rickert: *Die Grenzen der naturwissenschaftlichen Begriffsbildung* and *Kulturwissenschaft und Naturwissenschaft.*

scientific character of dogmatics varies a good deal; we have also seen that the reason for this is the extent to which theological reflection moves away from, or towards, the immediacy of faith itself. There is no doubt that the Epistle to the Romans is more "dogmatic", more reflective, than the Parables of Jesus. But who would maintain that this makes it a "scientific" work? It is well known that certain important works on dogmatics have grown out of catechisms, and the traces of their origin rather help than hinder their usefulness; who, however, can fix the point at which the non-"scientific" catechism becomes the quasi-scientific masterpiece of dogmatic theology?[1] Here, too, we must be content with a proportional statement: the more that reflection, exact definition, strictly logical argument, reasoned classification, method and system predominate in Christian doctrine, the more "scientific" it becomes, and the further it moves from the original truth of faith from which it proceeds, and to which it must continually refer.

But how can this approximation to a "science" be of any service to faith which has no use for science? Must not the transformation, which, it cannot be disputed, takes place in the knowledge of faith, when, and to the extent, in which it moves into the medium of reflection, be felt as a direct loss for faith? If the explanations of ideas which dogmatics accomplishes, and the broad view which it attains through its systematic work, take place at the cost of the preservation of personal faith and the truth of faith—what, then, is the good of it? We have already answered this question, and indeed in three ways. Theological reflection, as we saw, is intended to serve the purpose of making a distinction between the valid and the genuine, and the non-valid and non-genuine (erroneous doctrine); its aim is also to transcend the remoteness of the Biblical witness to revelation and to make this intelligible (*"loci theologica"* of the Bible); finally its aim is to bridge the gulf between secular and natural knowledge and the knowledge of faith (extended Baptismal instruction).

A parable may make the position clear. As the analytical chemist analyses in his retorts edibles which are offered for sale in the market-place, and thus is able to distinguish that which has real food-value from all mere substitutes, yet in so

[1] The criterion which Barth proposes to enable us to distinguish "regular" from "irregular" dogmatics, that is, the effort to achieve "wholeness" (*op. cit.*, p. 292), does not express the essential element which distinguishes a catechism from a work on Dogmatics.

doing diverts the material intended for human nourishment from its actual purpose, and indeed even destroys it, and yet the result of all his methods of separation and examination serve the nourishment of the people as a whole, so that which the theologian clarifies, separates and re-unites, his dogmatic concepts and his systematic processes, are not the "food" that the believer needs, and not that which has to be preached, and yet it is serviceable to the preacher and the pastor. We do not preach—it is to be hoped—dogmatics, and yet what we learn through dogmatics enriches and deepens our preaching, a result which could hardly have been achieved without the study of dogmatics. Yet in order to understand aright the second and the third of the suggested functions of dogmatics, there is still one final aspect to be considered, which will form the content of the next chapter.

Before we do this, however, we must call attention to a secondary, but not unessential service of dogmatic reflection in respect of science. The Church, in the course of the centuries, has found out by experience that in its origins, and for many centuries in its preaching and its theology, it has not distinguished, or has not made an adequate distinction between the cosmological material used by the primal knowledge of revelation—the "alphabet" of the Biblical witness to revelation —and the revelation itself. So the Church supported the ancient view of the world which the Bible contains with the authority of her witness to revelation, and she included all this within her message, until the contradiction of modern science, which was in the act of destroying this view of the world, made her aware of her error.

But a mighty effort of thought and intellectual labour was required to make the distinction between that view of the world and the witness of faith, and still more, in order to re-formulate the witness of the Bible in a new "alphabet", in terms which do not contradict the results of modern science. This process is still going on, and it seems possible that owing to the continual progress being made by the sciences, it will never cease. For this work of re-formulation, however, there is need of thinking which issues, it is true, from faith, and yet, at the same time, is able and willing to make the effort to know the scientific process, in order to understand it, and in some measure to stand above it and to take a larger view. A theological teacher who speaks about Adam and the Fall in terms which it was right and natural for Augustine to use, leads the

65

Church into the conflict between Religion and Science, which is as disastrous as it is unnecessary.

At the heart of the matter, in the witness to revelation itself, the Church never need be disturbed by the movement of secular rational science. Science always moves upon the surface dimension of secular knowledge, whereas faith is concerned with the dimension of depth, where we are concerned with Origin and Aim. But as the Biblical witness to revelation itself could not escape from the ancient ideas of the nature of the world then current, so the witness of revelation, at every period in human history, must use ideas concerning the world—whether they be cosmological or historical—which, if they are not to lead to that unfortunate conflict, must correspond with the modern scientific view of the world, or at least they must not contradict it. In this sense dogmatics is the mediator between secular science and the supernatural witness of faith. But at this point we have already reached the final aspect which I have just mentioned.

## CHAPTER 9

# THE CONTEMPORARY CHARACTER OF DOGMATICS

THE Christian Church stands and falls with the confession, "Jesus Christ, the same, yesterday, to-day, and for ever", and with the confession that the revelation and reconciliation which have taken place in Him, have taken place ἐφ ἅπαξ, once for all. To this extent doctrine is actually what the Roman Catholic Church loves to call it: *Theologia perennis*. At all periods of history, if faith be true and genuine, it makes itself "contemporary" with Jesus Christ, with His Cross and His Resurrection. Where revelation itself is concerned, there is no room for the ideas of "progress" and "evolution". The Christian Church cannot recognize any "progressive revelation". Neither the fact that we look backwards to the preparatory revelation of the Old Covenant, nor forwards to the Coming Kingdom and the Advent of the Lord, can be used to support that idea. The preparatory revelation, the prophetic one, culminated in the Incarnation of the Word, and therefore cannot be continued. But the Coming of the Kingdom, through the Parousia, is described as a final event, and is thus protected from all confusion with the idea of "progress".

There are no interim stages between the revelation which has taken place in the story of Jesus and that revelation of the End, when faith will pass into sight, "face to face". The situation of the Church, of the community of believers, in respect of their share in the truth of revelation, is, in principle, always the same—at all periods of history—and that means that the truth given to it is at all times, until the end of history, the same. If the idea of the *theologia perennis*, the unchangeableness of Christian doctrine and of the Christian Creed, means only this, then it belongs in point of fact to the fundamental ideas in the Confession of Faith. Whatever else may be altered, whatever else may be exposed to the law of historical relativity, this one element does not change, and is not relative.

And yet the Creed of the Church, theology, dogmatics, ceaselessly alters, and indeed not merely in the Protestant Churches, but—even though only secretly—even within the Catholic Church. Although there is a remarkable continuity of doctrine down the ages, and we still feel the theology of men like Irenaeus and Augustine, and still more of Luther, Zwingli and Calvin, to be so contemporary, so actual, so exemplary, that again and again we feel impelled to sit at the feet of these great masters as their eager disciples, yet we cannot ignore the fact that we think differently and teach differently from them and that we teach differently because we ought to do so, and we cannot avoid it. This brings out the decisive fact—which has already been sufficiently stressed—the fact that the Church is not identical with the revelation itself, although it is a form of revelation.

The fact that the doctrine of the Church is not the revelation itself comes out, as we have seen, in the New Testament witness to Christ Himself in the variety of the New Testament or apostolic doctrines. John speaks a different language from Paul; Paul uses different terms from Matthew. The content is one, but in each case the "setting" is different. And yet even in these writers we can already perceive that these varieties of "setting" are due to their intellectual and historical environment. The statement is apt: "*quidquid recipitur, modo recipientis recipitur*". That is the irrevocable law of appropriation, which, even where revelation is concerned, still has its own validity. Here, then, in the realm of faith, what are the "*modus recipientis*" and the changes which it introduces into the sphere of doctrine by the changes due to historical development?

At first we might think that this fact—namely, that the doctrine is conditioned by the recipient—should refer only to one who does not yet believe; for instance, to the way in which Paul the Missionary says of himself that "to the Jews he is a Jew" and to "them that are without law" (that is, the heathen) "as without law," in order that he "might save some".[1] Undoubtedly this is a very important aspect of the problem, and at the same time it recognizes a very important task of the teaching Church.

As the Bible had to be translated by the missionary Church into the most widely differing languages, and as this translation work has been, and still is, one of the most important achievements of the Mission of the Church, so the Gospel has to be continually re-translated into contemporary terms—a task which the Church ought to take far more seriously than she has done of late. But the problem which is involved in the indication of the "*modus recipientis*" is still more comprehensive, and goes a great deal deeper than merely "missionary translation".

We understand its depth only when we remember that faith is a definite experience of self-knowledge; that is, we learn

[1] I Cor. 9: 21.

to understand ourselves in the light of God and His revelation. Even when confronted by the Word of God, man is not simply "*tabula rasa*", not an empty page upon which God now writes His Word. Here, too, understanding is involved, which—like all understanding—makes use of the "apperceptions" of the human mind. And, moreover, what matters is not to understand "something", but oneself. Only where the Word of God or the revelation leads to a new understanding of oneself, does it become "one's own", in the act of believing understanding it is "appropriated". Thus even in the act of faith man is not just an empty vessel into which something is simply poured from the outside. The very act of faith itself is placed within a "setting" in which the ideas with which man understands anything at all, and with which above all he understands himself, are not eliminated but are utilized and remoulded.

But these ideas vary more or less at different times. Language changes, because ideas change, and the most profound change takes place where we are dealing with man's understanding of himself.[1] The knowledge of faith is always involved in this "setting" which conditions our ideas, and in man's contemporary view of himself. Even as Christian believers we are children of our own time; we cannot say merely that we "used to be", "before we became Christians". Certainly, if Jesus Christ really lays hold on us in faith, we are no longer children of our own day as we were before: Jesus Christ also changes this "being-children-of-our-time" in us; but He does not sweep it all away. Therefore even as Christian believers we use different language from the believers of other days; we say the same thing, but we express it differently. As preachers as well as theologians we use, unavoidably, other conceptions.

To name only *one* example of a theologian who is here a blameless witness, because he himself energetically repudiates the idea of a "point of contact": the idea of "Subject" plays a great part in the theology of Karl Barth—and indeed a very favourable part, and one which helps to clarify the problem! And yet this is an idea which, so far as I know, was never used by any previous theologian. It is a conception which springs from the Idealistic philosophy, from which Barth—like the rest of us—has learned some essential truths. Or again, what a necessary function is played by the idea of history in the dogmatics of the present day—once more, a conception which is practically wholly absent from the theology of older scholars.

[1] Cf. Bultman, *Glauben und Verstehen*, pp. 294, 312.

The same is true of ideas such as person, responsibility, decision, community, act, etc.

Such ideas are necessary aids for the theologian, if he is to make plain to himself and his contemporaries that which in earlier days was intelligible in other terms, apart from these ideas. Conversely, ideas which our forefathers in the Faith used to express the truth we hold in common, must be freshly translated by us, and be replaced by others, in order to make clear what they meant. Thus the ideas of "substance", "person" (in the Trinitarian sense) and "nature" played an absolutely decisive part in ancient theology, but for us they are scarcely intelligible, or, if used without commentary, lead to gross misunderstanding. When we speak of the "Three Persons of the Trinity", it sounds really heterodox and polytheistic to us, yet the theologians of the Early Church did not mean it in this way. The same is true of the idea of the divine and human "Nature" of Jesus Christ. And such ideas have, as is well known, become absolutely essential parts of dogma!

Now we understand why there is such a great need for exposition of the Bible, and why *"loci theologici"* are necessary. Even the Bible makes use of a set of ideas—or rather of a mass of different sets of ideas from different periods—which are not intelligible to us at first sight. The work of Bible translation is not ended with that which usually goes by that name; it is continued in the exposition of the Bible, and is completed in the *"loci theologici"* of dogmatics. This means, therefore— however daring this assertion may sound at first, still it cannot be assailed—Dogmatics *is* Bible translation; or, Dogmatics is the necessary preliminary work for that "Bible transla- tion" in which the true living preaching of the Gospel must consist.

The consideration of the truth of the *"modus recipientis"* also throws light on the third root of dogmatics: the extension of instruction for Baptism to thoughtful Christian believers. Why is it needful to go further than the elementary instruction given to catechumens? What do we mean when we say that among thoughtful Christian people there are questions which dogmatics ought to answer, so that the simple instruction contained in the Catechism leads to the *Institutio religionis christianae*? What is there to ask where revelation is concerned? Questions arise first of all because the "appropriation" has been only partially accomplished. The very scheme of question and answer in a catechism is designed to help the process of "appropriation". Christian doctrine must not be simply "ingrafted",[1] we must make it our own, and this means that it must be the answer to a question. Only that which answers our *own* questions can become our *own*. The more living and rich the mind which the Gospel encounters, the more questions does it arouse which must be answered if the Gospel is to be really made our own. But the questions vary with varying times, because their interests are different, and above all because man's view of himself is different at each period.

This is the cause of the demand for "contemporaneousness" in theology, which also implies the *principle* of "contemporaneousness" as the criterion of sound, good, living theology. What is so often offered to us as "genuinely Biblical theology" is the very opposite: it is a stale lifeless theology, which is unable to make the Gospel intelligible in the language of the day; it is a theology which raises the suspicion that the faith behind it has not been truly appropriated—in any case, it is a theology which is unable to fulfil its task. These theologians would like most of all to use the "language of Canaan", that is, they would really prefer not to translate the Bible at all. They do not want to do so because they are unable to make the message of the Bible fully their own.

Certainly this demand for a "contemporary" presentation of Christian truth contains a danger—the danger of betrayal of the central concern of the Bible. This is the danger of every translation: *"Toute traduction est une trahison"* is a witty remark, but it has been put still more strongly in the phrase *"traduttore—traditore"*. But to give up translation means to abandon the effort to make the message our own; even one who "knows Greek" translates; even one who teaches in the conceptions of Augustine's or Luther's or Calvin's dogmatics, translates—only he does not translate into his own language, but into the language of the fifth or the sixteenth century. We cannot get rid of the danger of translation by trying to evade it. But we must see the danger, and know how to meet it. This is accomplished—as is the case in "faithful" translation in the usual sense of the word—by continual reference to the "text", in order to see what it really says; a good translator does this continually; he continually refers to the text, and then tries to give a "faithful" rendering. The ideas which serve the process of appropriation must remain subordinate to the subject which is the writer's main concern. When these ideas

[1] Rom. 6: 9. (TR.)

become independent, when they are erected into a system, into a form or a mould, into which the content of the Christian message is to be poured, there the Gospel has been violated. In modern times we have two particularly clear and warning examples: the freethinking theology, influenced in a speculative manner by Hegel, and the Ritschlian theology influenced by Kant and Lotze.[1]

Wherever dogmatics becomes a system, or is systematically dominated by a fundamental idea—no matter how Biblical it may be—then already there has been a fatal declension from the attitude of the faithful translator. The very thing that makes such an impression, and attracts people with good brains: rigid unity of thought, in dogmatics is the infallible sign of error. Revelation cannot be summed up in a system, not even in a dialectical one. A system always implies that the reason has forced ideas into a certain mould: it is the "imperialism" of an idea, even when this idea claims to be "Biblical". As faith means the destruction of human self-will, so also is it the destruction of human systems. Dogmatics as a system, even when it intends to be a system of revelation, is the disguised dominion of the rational element over faith.

This brings us to one final question.

[1] The latest developments in Theology provide us with another example: the overshadowing of the Christian message by Heidegger's system of ideas in the theology of R. Bultmann, which yet in many ways has done so much to further this task of "translation".

## CHAPTER 10

# FAITH AND THOUGHT IN DOGMATICS

NOT only the study and interpretation of dogmatics, but even faith itself is a thinking process; that is, it is thought determined by revelation, by the Word of God. This is usually forgotten when faith and thought are contrasted. Certainly, faith is not *only* a process of thinking, but as a central act of the person it is also willing and feeling. Faith, as the Apostle Paul puts it, is ὑπακοή πίστεως—the "obedience of faith".

But when man answers God's Word of revelation, he also accomplishes an act of thinking. Where there is speech, where there is an answer, there also is thought. That confession of Peter: "Verily Thou art the Christ, the Son of the Living God", is a thought which expresses itself as a meaningful, grammatical, logical sentence. Even faith is accomplished in ideas, and in connexion with ideas: God is the Lord, or—in the primary form—"Thou, O God, art my Lord".

To pray, to give God thanks, to praise God—all these are acts of thought, thoughts of the heart. Even faith has clearly connected ideas; it is not merely "pious feeling". Thus we cannot distinguish theology, or dogmatics, from faith, by saying that the one is a process of thought, while the other is not. It would not help matters much to say that faith "is thinking of a particular kind". We have indeed already seen (in the previous chapter) that faith as "appropriation" is accomplished through the use of the usual processes of thought, which again is manifested in language. Faith does not speak with celestial tongues, but with the words of ordinary speech: "Father", "Lord", "Word", "Life", "Light", "doing", "speaking", "hearing", "obeying", etc. Like the language of ordinary life, so also the thought of ordinary life is not superseded by faith, but it is utilized.

And yet without much consideration we know that in theology, in dogmatics, thinking plays a far greater part than in faith itself. A person who has little capacity for thinking can still believe; to make a life-work of theology and dogmatics presupposes a high degree of thinking power. The great theologian does not differ from the rest of the members of the Church by his greater faith, but by his greater powers of thought in the service of faith. The distinctive characteristic of the theologian within the Church is not that he is a believer, but that he is a thinker. Where, then, does the difference lie between the thinking of faith as such, and the believing thinking which theology, dogmatics, produces? This question is not put in the interests of psychology, but in that of the Church and of personal religion. We must be aware of this difference, on the one hand, in order not to make a false distinction between faith and thought, and, on the other hand, in order that we may not bind faith and dogmatics so closely together that it would seem as though the theologian alone were an adult, or mature Christian.

Up to this point we have been considering the difference caused by the transition from one dimension to another, as consisting mainly in the process of reflection which leads from "thought-in-encounter" to "thinking-about-it". But this still does not answer the question: "How is it, then, that through this transition the part played by thought becomes so much greater than it is in faith itself? We may, first of all, establish this difference in a negative manner: this process of turning to the "third person", and the impersonality which this engenders, means that the personal element, the "heart"— so long as the theological process of reflection goes on—is practically ruled out. Now we are engaged with the matter in *thought*, not in feeling and in will; moreover the act of personal decision, which is the act of faith, lies behind us as a completed act. Thus reflection serves as a kind of eye-shade which prevents us from looking at anything we do not need to see. Dogmatic reflection is accomplished by a general process of abstracting all those elements which do not help us to understand the subject with which we are dealing as objectively and clearly as possible.

In positive terms this means: In the process of theological reflection the intellectual element in our faith is developed still further, and in isolation. The characteristic question which determines theological work is: "What does this *mean*?" Faith says: God is the Lord, or rather, "Thou, O God, art my Lord". Now from this prayer, which is a confession of faith, theological reflection abstracts the one element, the concept "Lord", and asks: "Now, what does this mean?"—not: "What art Thou saying to me, O God, here and now, in the very heart of my being?"—but: "What does this mean as a whole? What is the true content of this idea, 'God-Lord'?" The logical content of the statement, or rather the logical content of one element in this statement, is isolated, and made the object of reflection.

74

We ought not to be horrified at this fact, however, as though it were something improper. Certainly, the Word of God is not given to us for this purpose; but in order that the doctrine of the Church about the Word of God should be sound, this abstracting process of thought must be accomplished, which in itself goes far beyond that which faith needs for clarity of thought. Actually, then, it is as we surmised it would be: The greater measure of intellectual labour, which distinguishes theology, dogmatics, from the simple thinking of faith, is conditioned by the process of reflection, by that transition into the objective, impersonal dimension which makes both this process of abstraction and the further analysis of the content of ideas possible.

This is the first step which throws light on our problem—but that is all. Now we know—dogmatics is the further development of the element of thought or of logic which is given with faith itself. This leads us to the further question: What, then, takes place in this further development? We may reply, perhaps, that "the idea is clarified"—or "the word 'Lord' is made more intelligible". In point of fact this is the meaning and purpose of this undertaking; that should be plain by now. This illumination or clarification is indeed the meaning of all thinking. But the unsatisfactory point is this, that a content which does not come from our own thinking but from revelation is "clarified" by this very obviously human process, or at least can be thus illuminated. If this really were the situation, then within the sphere of the knowledge of faith we would have to be very suspicious of this whole proceeding, and of the validity and worth of its results. Now it cannot be denied that this kind of thought does take place in the thought-forms of ordinary, rational thinking, and, if we are to think at all, it cannot be otherwise. It is good to know this, and to remind ourselves of it frequently, in order that it may become evident how great—how immense—is the part played by the purely rational element, the logical power of thought in theological reflection or dogmatics. It is actually the purely human faculty of thought which qualifies the theologian for his work. The theologian ought to remind himself of this when he writes about the "sinful corruption of the human reason". Even if it is divine revelation about which he is thinking, still this process of reflection takes place by means of the natural human reason, with its concepts and thought-forms and its logical processes of proof.

But dogmatics is not *only* a process of thought *about* that which is given in faith, it is at the same time *believing thinking*. The theologian is fully justified in protesting against the idea that his work is a *purely* rational consideration of the truths of faith—just as he certainly has no right to protest against the truth that rational thought plays a great part in his work. What, however, is added in theological thinking, that which differentiates this from all other kinds of thought, is the continual reference to the "subject" itself which is grasped by faith: a reference which, for its part, can only be accomplished in faith. The true theologian does not only think *about* the Faith and about the revelation given in faith, but in the very act of thinking he continually renews the act of faith; as a believing man he turns his attention to the revelation granted to faith.

Thus the act of thought in dogmatics may be compared with a movement which arises through the activity of two differently directed forces, for instance, one tangential and the other centripetal. The purely rational element of thought, logic, has the tendency to go straight forward from each given point; but faith continually prevents this straightforward movement by its pull towards the Centre. So instead of a movement in a straight line there arises a circular movement around the Centre—and that is a picture of real theological thinking. Theological thinking is a rational movement of thought, whose rational tendency at every point is continually being deflected, checked, or disturbed by faith. Where the rational element is not effective there is no movement of thought, no theology; where the rational element alone is at work, there arises a rational, speculative theology, which leads away from the truth of revelation. Only where faith and rationality are rightly interlocked can we have true theology, good dogmatics.

For this very reason systematic unity, and logic pushed to an extreme, in the absolute sense of the word, are a sign of a false tendency in theological work. Certainly there is no other way of thinking than one which is directed towards unity, and strives after logical sequence. But these two most essential marks of rationality would, if taken alone, make an end of theology as the consideration of revelation, just as to ignore them would make an end of thinking, even of theological thinking. Only the constant refraction of the systematic unity and the logical sequence by the direct relation of faith to the revelation itself, produces a way of thinking which may be described as "believing thinking", which produces dogmatics. The more exact analysis of the close interlocking of the act of thought with the act of faith in the thinking of the theologian, must, in so far as it is at all possible and necessary, be left to a special theological Theory of Knowledge.[1]

[1] Important beginnings of a theological epistemology of this kind may be found in Heim, *Glaube und Denken*; in Bultmann, *Glauben und Verstehen*; and in E. Burnier, *Bible et théologie*—especially in the chapters "Le caractère de la valeur épistémologique du témoignage biblique" and "La parole de Dieu et l'analogie de la foi".

## CHAPTER II

# THE CONCEPT AND THE TASK OF DOGMATICS

WE must now try to summarize all that we have been saying in our attempt to answer the question: What, then, is dogmatics? And what is the service we should expect it to render?

Dogmatics is a particular form of Christian doctrine. As doctrine it is, like all doctrine, something prescribed for thought. Its aim is right thinking; its intention is that we should think along certain prescribed lines—and no other—about the subjects with which Christian doctrine deals. Because it is Christian doctrine, the virtual "subject" of dogmatics is the Church: this is what the Church teaches. Dogmatics, however, is not the only form of Christian doctrine. In the main, the primary teaching ministry of the Church is not exercised by the teaching of dogma. The Church teaches in her evangelistic work, in her preaching in the parish, in the teaching of young people, children and adults; she teaches also in the exercise of pastoral work. But in all these other ways of teaching the doctrinal element is not emphasized to the same extent as in dogmatics, hence it does not predominate.

The teaching office of the Church is graded, from the exercise of her pastoral ministry and the act of preaching to the "Instruction of Adult Candidates for Confirmation". Dogmatics is the next stage, and the final one. In it the doctrinal (or "teaching") element is central, and all the other elements, proper to other forms of Christian teaching—which may even be stressed more fully than the doctrinal element—are pushed out of sight. It is not the aim of dogmatics—as such, and directly—to convert, edify, warn, restore, nor even to help people to be better Christians. If dogmatics does effect any of these ends, this does not take place because it has been deliberately sought; rather it is a by-product, even though it is not against the general intention.

The interest of dogmatics is wholly doctrinal, that is, it is concerned with right thinking. In order to be able to do this aright, dogmatics has to look away from much towards which otherwise the teaching of the Church is directed. It is, therefore, so to speak, the *logical function of the Church*, with all the advantages and disadvantages of this specialization.

This logical element—that is, the clear definition of the Church's teaching—is developed to a comparatively high state of completeness within the life of the Church; at least, if we may put it so, the Church *aims* at this perfect clarity and completeness; above all, at a clarity of thought which will present Christian truth with the utmost clearness and comprehensiveness, in the form of a well-knit system.

Like all Christian teaching, dogmatics is based upon revelation. In contrast to the other teaching activity of the Church, however, it is the task of dogmatics to make the basis of Christian doctrine in the revelation itself the object of its teaching. One of its most essential characteristics, and most important criteria of its usefulness, is the fact that the basis of Christian doctrine, or doctrinal statements, is made plain in revelation, and that the specific authority which all Christian doctrine claims for itself is derived from this source alone. This is the meaning of that process of proof which has been exercised throughout the whole history of dogmatics: that of the "Proof from Holy Scripture".[1]

Even if this process has been discredited, on the one hand by its arbitrary character, and on the other by its verbal legalism, yet it does contain the right idea, namely, that there can be no other basis for Christian doctrine than that which comes from revelation, that it should seek no other argument for its basis than this, but that this basis in revelation determines the validity of each of its statements. To show the necessary connexion of Christian doctrine with this basis in revelation constitutes for dogmatics what in the other sciences would be regarded as logical proof, and the relation to the experience of reality.

Since, however, Christian doctrine, like all doctrine, develops by means of thinking, and the truth of revelation is related to the experience of reality, dogmatics, for its part, also uses those criteria and principles of secular science as secondary criteria and principles. Hence its statements must not only not contradict the truth of revelation, but also they must not contradict one another, nor must they be in contradiction to reality; that is, they must not be of such a character that in order to affirm them, actual facts have to be denied or distorted.

Revelation, it is true, stands in opposition to human reality, just as the Divine Goodness is in opposition to the sinfulness of

---

[1] Cf. the observations of J. C. K. von Hofmann in the Introduction to his great work, *Der Schriftbeweis*, Vol. I, pp. 3–32, which are still valuable.

man. But where this sinful reality is mentioned from the standpoint of revelation, nothing is said about it that contradicts the experience of reality, but on the contrary, it is precisely this experienced and experiential reality which is disclosed in its opposition to the truth. The criterion of reality, therefore, like the logical one, applies also to Christian doctrine, and especially to dogmatics.

Dogmatics differs from the rest of Christian teaching in the fact that it presupposes this as something "given", and leans upon this "given" element as a support. Dogmatics presupposes the teaching Church—even apart from itself—it is therefore doctrine, which presupposes the teaching which is always going on, and has been going on in the past. It is, so to say, a secondary form of doctrine: it is teaching which defines the "true" doctrine. It is accomplished as the basis and the criticism of Christian doctrine as a whole. It does this, however, only from a definite standpoint, proper to itself, and one which distinguishes it from all the other teaching functions of the Church: namely, from the point of view of the true content of doctrine. It bases and examines the *doctrinal content* of the doctrine which is always being taught within the Church.

Hence, as its name suggests, it has a very close relation with the dogma of the Church, with the doctrinal confession of the Church, in which the Church gives an account—both to itself and to the world—of the content of its teaching. This close relation is twofold in character. On the one hand dogmatics presupposes dogma—the summary of the content of the doctrine of the Church in the form of a Confession—as that which is given to it, and as that which the Church wills to be understood as the norm of all its teaching, including its dogmatic teaching. In this sense the dogma, or the doctrinal confession of the Church, is not merely the starting-point and the material of dogmatics, but at the same time it is its norm. Since, however, this norm may always only be conceived by the Church as conditioned, and not as unconditioned, there falls to dogmatics a second task, namely, that of critically examining the dogma which the Church lays before it, and, when necessary, of providing a better dogma.

Dogmatics accomplishes this examination on the basis of that form of Christian doctrine, which is also the source and the norm of its teaching of every other form of Christian doctrine, on the basis of the original witness to revelation, namely, the doctrine of Scripture. Above all the teaching of the Church, even above all dogma or doctrinal confession, stands Holy Scripture. This is the source of revelation for the Church; for the Church knows the fact of revelation simply and solely through the Holy Scriptures. Scripture, however, is not only the source of all Christian doctrine, but it is also its norm, in so far as the original witness is the source of all the testimony of the Church. It owes this normative dignity and power to the fact that the original witness itself has a share in the primary historical revelation, in the history of revelation of Jesus Christ. But the norm of Scripture, too, understood as the doctrinal norm, is not unconditioned, but conditioned: namely, it is conditioned by that which also forms its basis: the revelation, Jesus Christ Himself.

As it is part of the task of dogma to clarify and examine the relation of teaching to dogma, to the Confession of Faith of the Church, so also it is part of its work to distinguish within the Scriptures themselves that which is binding and valid from that which is conditioned by human and contemporary circumstances. The norm and the criteria of this distinction, however, are never acquired save from Scripture itself. Only from the Bible itself is it possible to perceive what is truly Biblical, only from revelation that which is truly in accordance with revelation. This is why it is impossible to apply the "Proof from Scripture" in its traditional legalistic form, which presupposes the infallibility of the actual Bible text.

Because dogmatics has a definite place within the Church it is necessarily confessional. By this we do not mean that morbid "Confessionalism", which mistakenly sets up its own Confession as an absolute, without considering that every Church and every theology is only moving towards the goal, and has not yet attained it. Rather the genuinely confessional character of dogmatics signifies that each person who "thinks" in the service of the Church, is first of all under an obligation to the form of the Church, and the doctrine of the Church, through which he has received his own faith. A "confessional" attitude of this kind means thankfulness and loyalty towards those from whom we have received our faith. Hence the dogmatics which is here presented is consciously Reformed Church doctrine. Its concern is to preserve and to emphasize the particular truth of the divine revelation which has been given to the Reformers, and among them, above all to Zwingli, Calvin, and their descendants.

This system of dogmatics, however, is under too profound an

obligation to the absolute divine truth, to make this confessional loyalty into the decisive principle of a final court of appeal. It is not for us to reproduce the doctrine of Zwingli or of Calvin, but to seek the truth, and to give honour to the truth, even if this may lead us, at one point or another, to speak *against* Zwingli and Calvin, and *for* Luther, or even against the doctrine of the Reformers as a whole. In spite of confessional loyalty, we must retain freedom to learn from all the teachers of the Church, and to learn from all Churches. Thought that is in genuine harmony with the spirit of the Reformation cannot be "cabin'd, cribb'd, and confin'd" by "Confessionalism" as a principle.

On the other hand, dogmatics needs to be studied in the spacious setting of a truly "œcumenical" spirit, because knowledge of divine truth is present in all Churches, and because every Church has had some special part of the knowledge of the truth given to it. Truly œcumenical dogmatics, however, has no connexion with that cloudy "œcumenism" which tries to distil an extract from all the Creeds which will not contradict any of them. Just as we must not confuse the truly "Confessional" point of view with "Confessionalism", so that which is truly "œcumenical" must not be confused with a supra-confessional eclecticism. In the last resort we are not concerned with this or that ecclesiastical confession, neither Reformed nor Lutheran, nor with any other, but solely with the truth which has been revealed to us in Jesus Christ.

To find this, the different confessions may do us good service: the one which is our own, that of the Reformed Churches first of all, and after that the others; but we are not bound to any one of them. We seek the Truth alone, and not any agreed ecclesiastical formula, whether it be offered us by our own, or by one of the other Confessions, or by none of them. Above all, the dogmatics which is under an obligation to the Truth alone must guard against all national or continental regionalism, for which the European or the English or the American point of view would be more important than to be in the Truth.

The service which dogmatics, as the "logical function of the teaching Church", has to render is twofold: clarification and translation. Dogmatics cannot "make disciples";[1] it can only serve the Church—whose work it is to make disciples through its teaching—by the clarification of the ideas with which it works, by teaching her to distinguish the false from the true,

[1] Matt. 28: 19.

82

the half-true from the true understanding of the Gospel. And it can help individual believers in their faith by answering the questions which the doctrine of the Church raises in their minds. The fact that in order to do this the Church must give a far more abstract form to her teaching than is and should be the case in the practical teaching activity of the Church, constitutes, it is true, a danger; but it should be no hindrance. The more plainly we see the distinctive character of dogmatic, as compared with the practical teaching activity of the Church, carried on by preaching, catechetical instruction, and in the "cure of souls", the less danger will there be; conversely, where this distinction is ignored, where the teaching activity of the Church is practically equated with dogmatics, there the danger of a sterile intellectualism may become a real danger to the life of the Church.

The second service dogmatics can render is that of "Bible translation". As the exegete continues the work of the translator, by paraphrasing the translated text, and thus bringing it nearer to the understanding, so the dogmatic theologian continues the labours of the exegete by a kind of "collective paraphrase of the Bible". He must venture to listen to that which Isaiah, Matthew and John say, and put it together, in order to discern the Word of God behind the words of the Apostles. Thus he must venture to understand the Word spoken so long ago as a contemporary word; for it is only as a word for our own day that it can be understood, and made intelligible. Through this "collective paraphrase of the Bible" the dogmatic theologian serves the expositor of the Bible, as he first of all has learned from the expositor of the Bible, and has received from him, hence he also renders a service to the preacher and pastor, who in order to speak intelligibly must not speak in the language of Isaiah or of Paul, but in the language of the present day. The transference of the Word of the Bible into the thought-categories of our own day—that is the only possibility of real appropriation. The theologian's understanding of the Bible comes out—paradoxically—in the very fact that he does *not* use the language of the Bible.

This "translation" work of dogmatics can easily lead to error, if the dogmatic theologian does not thoroughly understand the thought of his own day. That is why the task of dogmatics presupposes that of "apologetics", the discussion with the ideologies and substitutes for faith of his own day. Only one who has wrestled with the mind of his own day, and who knows the opposition between Biblical and "modern" thought, is in a position to make Biblical doctrine intelligible to the man of the present day, without compromising with modern thought. The dogmatic theologian must walk along the narrow knife-edge between two precipices: the wrong "offence" of being unintelligible, of teaching a doctrine which does not "fit", on the one hand, and the avoidance of the genuine "Offence" of the Cross on the other.

Dogmatics, therefore, is doctrine based upon the divine revelation, thus upon absolute Truth. Hence it shares the claim of the Word of God to be absolute. This claim is neither foolish nor arrogant, because this Truth has not been created by *man*. All Christian doctrine, including dogmatics, is "speaking the divine Word after Him". But this "speaking", since it is human, also shares in the relativity of all that is human. "We have this treasure in earthen vessels",[1] our knowledge is partial.[2] Only a system of dogmatics which is always aware of both these facts can render its service aright. If it forgets the first, then it becomes an individualistic "religious conception", which is without authority; if it forgets the second, then it becomes guilty of idolizing human forms of thought. Thus as reflexion upon the Word of God, given to faith, it has a twofold relative element.

As reflexion, as the *thinking* of a believer about the content of faith, as the specialized logical function of the Church, dogmatics is, however, also, over against the believing existence as a whole, an abstraction, something which has been "split off". There is no such thing as "theological existence"; there is only theological *thinking* and *believing* existence. While a man thinks as a dogmatic theologian, as in every other act of reflexion, he stands outside the active, "Thou-related" reality, even though it may be true that only a person who belongs to the Christian Church can be a good theologian, and therefore, in reality, stands in that twofold relationship with the "Thou", which is called faith in God, and love to our neighbour. In the act of thought, the theologian does not "live" in this vital reality, but he "reflects upon it". Hence it is possible to be a good theologian but a bad Christian, since it is only the logical side, the "thinking" aspect of faith, which has been fully developed, while the other, that of the personal relation to God and our neighbour remains "under-nourished". This is not

[1] 2 Cor. 4: 7.    [2] I Cor. 13: 9.

inevitable; it ought not to be so; but unfortunately it frequently is so.

The remembrance of this always fatal possibility, and of the fact that again and again this possibility becomes a fact, must make the theologian humble. For one who is intellectually gifted, it is so much easier to be a Christian in the sphere of thought than in that of practical behaviour; and yet the good theologian knows very well that what counts before God is not merely what one thinks, but what one thinks with such faith that it becomes act. For only that faith counts "which worketh through love".[1]

Thus in two directions we see the limitations of dogmatics. It is not the mistress, but the servant of faith and of the community of believers; and its service is no less, but also no more, than the service of *thought* to faith. Its high dignity consists in the fact that it is a service to the highest final truth, to that truth which is the same as true love, and it is this which gives it the highest place in the realm of thought. But the fact that it is no more than this service of *thought*—which, as such, does not maintain that love and loyalty which must be expected from the Christian, is its limitation; a dogmatic which is aware of this, shows it is genuine. The dogmatic theologian who does not find that his work drives him to pray frequently and urgently, from his heart: "God, be merciful to me a sinner", is scarcely fit for his job.

[1] Gal. 5: 6.

85

# APPENDIX TO PROLEGOMENA

# APPENDIX TO PROLEGOMENA

## (1) THEOLOGY AND DOGMATICS

Whereas at the present day we take it for granted that dogmatics, the science of the doctrine of the Church, is one among several other theological "sciences", in earlier times this was not the case. Theology as a comprehensive term covering various intellectual studies connected with the Bible, and in the service of the Church, is a modern idea.[1]

The earliest use of the term occurs in Greek philosophy where θεολογία is used primarily of the speech of poets about divine things. The view that Aristotle already adumbrated a philosophical theology seems scarcely tenable. But we may say that this was true of Stoicism, and especially of Neoplatonism, in which the doctrine of God is the foundation of the whole philosophical structure. Philo is the bridge between the philosophy of religion of late antiquity and Christian theology. For him Moses is "the" theologian *par excellence*, who has penetrated most profoundly into the Divine Wisdom. In the patristic period a θεόλογος was one who participated in the development of the doctrine of the Church, of dogma. But far into the period of the Middle Ages dogmatics was described by the terms *sancta doctrina*, and not by "theology", while *"theologia"*, the doctrine of God in the narrower sense, was regarded as one section of the *sancta doctrina*. In the later Scholastic period *"theologia"* gradually came to be identified with dogmatics, although this latter term was not used. Even the theologians of the period of the Reformation carry on this terminology. They distinguish, it is true, different kinds of theology: the *theologia archetypa*, the knowledge that God has of Himself, and the *"theologia ectypa"*, the knowledge of God which comes into existence in the mind and spirit of man, and in the latter again they make the distinction between *theologia naturalis* and *theologia revelata*. But in their thought, too, there was no idea of a number of theological sciences, as, for instance, of exegesis alongside of dogmatic theology. Neither in the Early Church, which indeed from the days of the School of Antioch, produced outstanding examples of Biblical theology, nor at the period of the Reformation (whose theologians construct their system of truth—at least during the actual time of the

[1] Cf. Nitzsch-Stephan, *Lehrbuch der ev. Dogmatik*—Introduction—and *Prot. Realenzyklopädie*, XXI, pp. 901–13.

Reformation—entirely upon Biblical exegesis) did men ever reflect upon the relation between dogmatics and exegesis. Only with the rise of historical Biblical criticism, and with the more or less independent development of other theological disciplines, such as Church History, the History of Dogma, and Practical Theology, does reflection begin on the relation between these various intellectual undertakings, and the idea of "Theology" comes into being as the all-inclusive term for all the intellectual work which deals with the Bible and the Church. Only now does it become necessary to coin a special term to describe what had previously been regarded simply as "theology", the idea of *"theologia dogmatica"*. Speaking broadly, this took place in the first half of the eighteenth century, from the time of Pfaff and Buddaeus.

Schleiermacher made a great contribution in this sphere, for he was the first theologian to conceive theology as a unity, and to try to present the various theological disciplines as a coherent whole. There is no doubt of the service he has rendered in this field; but whether, in so doing, he really rendered a service to the Church is an open question. From his *Encyclopaedia*, in particular, in which he places Dogmatics as an historical discipline as subordinate to a philosophical theology—it is evident that in this work he was guided by principles which have nothing to do with Biblical Truth. The division of theology into three parts: Historical, Systematic, and Practical which has become usual since Schleiermacher's time, corresponds, it is true, to the practical need for classification and order, but it has little intellectual or ecclesiastical significance. Exegetical theology is not simply an historical discipline, in so far as it takes place "within the sphere of the Church" as the exposition of those who themselves participate in that which they expound. Conversely, dogmatics cannot simply be distinguished from exegetical work as "systematic" theology, since it is not only founded upon exegesis, but is continually being accomplished as exegesis. Likewise the distinction between Practical and Systematic Theology cannot be fully achieved, in so far as— for instance, in the doctrine of the Church—the process of dogmatic reflection passes into the realm of Practical Theology, and Practical Theology also develops out of Dogmatic Theology. Further, there is the fact that the various disciplines are determined by their existence in the Church in very varying degrees, down to the extreme instance of the purely secular secondary studies, such as the grammar of the Biblical languages, archaeology, etc. On the "scientific" character of the theology proper to the Church, see pp. 60 ff.

## (2) ON THE HISTORY OF DOGMATICS[1]

From what has just been said it is evident that it is not possible to make a sharp distinction between dogmatic theology and practical, ecclesiastical doctrine. Already within the New Testament itself the extent of reflection within the various groups of writings varies a great deal. The Epistle to the Romans is obviously much more "dogmatic" than the Synoptic Gospels, or the Epistles of Peter or James. But real dogmatic thinking begins as discussions with Greek philosophy, that is with the Apologists. Yet none of them, and none of the great theologians of the second century, ever undertook to make a systematic statement of the whole of Christian doctrine. The first to do so was Origen, in his work "*De principiis*", a work which we might describe as the first work of Christian dogmatics. But—apart from the Catechetical works of Cyril, which were intended rather to serve the purposes of practical instruction, and the *Little Handbook* of Augustine—this first attempt remained completely isolated, both in the East and in the West, and only found a continuation in the Πηγή γνώσεως of St. John of Damascus.

The Church Fathers of the third, fourth and fifth centuries produced, it is true, formidable works of dogmatics, but they did not produce any single comprehensive "Dogmatics". Even the mediaeval theologians did not at first feel this need, but they occupied themselves with the treatment of individual problems which seemed to them important, most of which were strongly controversial in character. An exception is the great systematic work of John Scotus Erigena, *De divisione naturae*, which, however, represents rather a Neoplatonist philosophy of religion than a work of Christian dogmatics. It was Peter Lombard who created the classical type of Western dogmatics in his work, *Sententiarum libri IV*, which remained a standard work even for the dogmatics of the Reformation period, and still more so for that of the Post-Reformation. Certainly the first work of dogmatics of the Reformation period, Melanchthon's *Loci theologici*, to this extent constitutes an exception, since it does not deal with the whole of Christian (Biblical) doctrine,

[1] No "History of Dogmatics" has yet been written; all that we have at present are, on the one hand, the History of Dogma of the patristic period, and descriptions of mediaeval Scholasticism, and, on the other hand, the History of Protestant Theology, such as those of Gass, Dorner, Pfleiderer, Frank, etc.

like that of the Lombard and the great mediaeval Scholastic theologians who followed him, but merely with special *"loci"*, which were particularly important for the message of the Reformation; Calvin, in his *Institutes*, returned to the earlier classical line of dogmatics. While the early Lutherans followed the example of Melanchthon, later on both Lutherans and Calvinists carried on the tradition of the comprehensive presentation which became the classical type, which begins with the Doctrine of God, and countless summaries of dogmatics appeared during the course of the seventeenth and the first half of the eighteenth centuries, under the most varied titles, in both Protestant Confessions.

The first break in this dogmatic treatment of doctrine was made by Pietism; the second came from the Enlightenment. The Pietist theologian replaced dogmatic doctrine by practical Christian instruction or by Biblical exegesis; the thinkers of the Enlightenment period, having become uncertain of the revealed basis of the Christian Faith, turned in the direction of the teaching of the Philosophy of Religion. With Schleiermacher there begins—(he, indeed, only did so formally, but his successors to some extent at least did so actually)—a return to the Christian presentation of doctrine, to Dogmatics. Even where the actual basis was rather that of philosophical Idealism than of the Christian Faith, as, for instance, with Biedermann, still the *schema* of classical dogmatics is retained, until the gulf between the general philosophy of religion and the basis of revealed Christianity became so evident that even this traditional form broke down. Within a theological school such as the *"religionsgeschichtliche"* there could no longer be any question of real Christian dogmatics.[1] But this does not mean that the line of development of the genuine Christian dogmatics, which in the nineteenth century had gained so much ground, and had produced such important works as those of Thomasius, von Hofmann, Frank, and von Oettingen, had been broken. Even the twentieth century, in the works of Kähler and Schlatter, can show important and characteristic dogmatic achievements; outside the sphere of the German-speaking peoples, too, especially in England and in Holland, the dogmatic spirit was not destroyed by the spirit of the Enlightenment. I need only remind the reader of the dogmatic works of Forsyth, Kuyper

[1] Cf. E. Troeltsch, *Wesen der Religion und der Religionswissenschaft* in P. Hinneberg's collective work, *Die Kultur der Gegenwart* I, IV, 2, pp. 1–36, a work which one may describe as the dissolution of Protestant Dogmatics; it was published in 1909.

and Bavinck. The same can be said, of course, still more decidedly of Catholic dogmatics, which, it is true, since the Reformation, and especially after the Enlightenment, had lost a great deal of weight and power, but which, like Protestant theology, gained a new impulse in the nineteenth century, and since then has been able to maintain a high level of achievement. Protestant Dogmatics has received a very powerful increase of vitality through the Luther revival in Sweden and Germany, and through the "Dialectical" Theology. We would be unjust to the achievements of men like Kähler, Schlatter, Bavinck, Billing and Aulen were we to designate Karl Barth as the one and only thinker who has revived Protestant dogmatics; no one can deny that he has done very much towards the new development, and above all that he has given the Reformed Churches a new consciousness of their task, nor would anyone deny the grandeur of his own massive achievement in dogmatics. Dogmatics is on the way to regain its rightful place within the work of the Christian Church. We shall show below that this does not constitute the only, and perhaps not the most important, doctrinal task of the Church in the modern world.

(3) THE THREEFOLD ROOT OF DOGMATICS IN THE HISTORY OF THEOLOGY

So far as I know, no one has previously noted this threefold root of dogmatics; hence there exists no historical survey of the development of dogmatics from this threefold point of view. The aim of this brief sketch is to try to fill this gap, however inadequately. [We are not here concerned with apologetics, that is, discussion with non-Christian thought; this is an intellectual concern of the Church of a special kind.]

(i) *The Polemical Element*

Controversy has played a great part in the dogmatic labours of the Church. Those arguments with heresy which are nowadays rather contemptuously dismissed as "theological quarrels", at the best periods in the life of the Church had a most stimulating effect upon men of vital spirit and vigorous intellect. This is not surprising—for such theological work is like the effort made by a sound organism to repel infectious germs. We should note, too, that at least in the early days of the Church, the frontier line between polemics within the Church—against heresy—and apologetics—as conflict with the paganism out-side the Church—was not drawn very sharply, because pagan-ism—as, for instance, in the case of Gnosticism—was trying to penetrate into the Church itself. So the enterprise of theological dogmatics begins with a work which, in its very title, suggests its polemic and apologetic aim, the *Elenchus* of Irenaeus. The first great dogmatic work of Christian theology is a contro-versial work against Gnosticism. The work of Irenaeus was carried further in Tertullian's *Adversus Marcionem*, and in the *Refutatio* of Hippolytus, and from this time onwards a steady stream of polemical theological literature pours through the Early Christian Church; it reached a peak in the *Orationes contra Arianos* of Athanasius, and later in Augustine's great controversial works against the Manichaeans, the Donatists, and the Pelagians. In the Middle Ages, regarded as a whole, the polemical element was less evident than the speculative doctrinal element; yet here, too, there was a great dogmatic literature which served the interests of discussion within the Church. We need only recall the controversies between Radbertus and Ratramnus, Lanfranc and Berengar, Bernard and Abelard, and the endless conflicts between Realists and Nominalists, Domini-cans and Franciscans.

In the period of the Reformation, alongside of the interest in exegesis and edification, the polemical element dominated theological thinking; the most important writings of Luther (in which the new understanding of the faith was first expressed in theological terms) are controversial writings, not only against the Roman Catholic Church, but also against the humanistic and fanatical views of the Gospel. The same is true of Zwingli—*de vera et falsa religione*—whereas with Calvin the polemical element is less prominent, although as is well known it is not absent.

The Council of Trent gave a fresh stimulus to Protestant polemics—we need only remind ourselves of the excellent work of Chemnitz, *Examen Concilii Tridentini*. In post-Reformation orthodoxy the doctrinal element—(*definitions!*)—outweighs the polemical; the Scholastics of the Middle Ages secretly be-come the model for theology. Since the Enlightenment the conflict that rages round the foundations of Christian doc-trine, that is, the apologetic interest, outweighs all others; yet even so, the renewal of dogmatics has been due to a great extent to the controversy with theological Liberalism or Idealism.

(ii) *Instruction of Catechumens (preparation for Baptism) and the Speculative Element*

In the theology of the Early Church this is less prominent than the polemical element, but it certainly exists. Among these writings we must reckon not only the "catechetical" writings which have been lost, mentioned by Eusebius, the *twenty-four Catechetical works* of Cyril of Jerusalem, and the *Enchiridion* of Augustine, but also the *Protreptikos* of Clement of Alexandria, and the first—and for a long time the only—dogmatic work of Origen, *De principiis*—all of which, in the main, owe their origin to this element; to these we should also add the *Catechetica magna* of Gregory of Nyssa.

In mediaeval Scholasticism the speculative doctrinal element was magnificently expressed; the method of questioning in the *Summa* of St. Thomas has evident affinities with the catechetical method. Here instruction is being given. We have already mentioned the fact that Calvin's *Institutes* originally arose out of a small handbook on the Luther-Catechism. In the period of Protestant Scholasticism, as we have already seen, the doctrinal element predominated. In a certain sense we may also reckon the "scientific" (or intellectual) element which dominates the newer dogmatics as part of this element. Karl Barth himself would scarcely wish to deny that the method of his *Dogmatics* is based upon the model of the great scholastic systems.

(iii) *Dogmatics as the Summary of Biblical Doctrine*

In early and mediaeval theology the third element—the doctrinal development of the fundamental ideas of the Bible—was weakest. It is, of course, true that Augustine's *De doctrina Christiana*, which is explicitly described as a book to help the reader of the Bible, is a sign that it was not entirely lacking. On the other hand, Melanchthon's *Dogmatics* aims to help the Bible reader; this work—the first Dogmatics of the theology of the Reformation—says explicitly in the Preface: *ut, si quos queam, ad scripturas invitem. Nos certe non aliud agimus, quam ut eorum qui in scripturis versari volent studia utcunque juvemus. Id si non videbitur praestare libellus, pereat sane.* Since then, in the older Protestant theology, the title most often used was *Loci theologici*. It is no accident that with Keckermann (1611) the new title *Systema s. theologia* and with Alsted (1618) the still more revealing title *Theologia scholastica* appears. During the seventeenth century, at least in the titles of their books, the Lutherans remained faithful to the example set by Melanchthon.

In modern times it has been the dogmatic theologians well known for their "Biblical" tendency—Cremer, Kähler and Schlatter—who show clearly, by the very way they construct their dogmatic works, that it is their intention to allow "the Word" to be fully expressed.

*　　*　　　　*　　*

In conclusion, this suggestion of the three different sources of dogmatics should not be confused with a classification of the dogmatic systems themselves. In all works of dogmatics the three elements—the polemical, the catechetical and speculative, and the Biblical, are interwoven, although the amount of emphasis on the various elements varies greatly from one to another. While the creative periods of new ideas and thoughts are characterized by a flood of controversial pamphlets, the leisurely construction of massive tomes of theology (like the *Summa* of St. Thomas and other similar works) is a sign of a purely speculative interest, and of a certain "remoteness" from the general life of the Church.

### (4) DOGMATICS AND THE SCIENCE OF RELIGION

From the time of Schleiermacher it became the usual thing to conceive dogmatics as the doctrine of the Christian religion, and therefore to make the problem of "religion" the starting-point. If indeed the Christian knowledge of faith is subsumed under the comprehensive notion "Christian Religion", then it is only logical to subordinate the Christian Religion itself to a still higher conception, that of "religion in general". While with Schleiermacher this scientific method results logically from his belief in a "religion in general", in an "essence of religion", to which the Christian religion is related as a particular kind within the species[1], this development of dogmatics out of the concept of "Religion" is repellent to all those theologians who, diverging from, and indeed in opposition to, Schleiermacher, conceive the Christian Faith to be the relation of man to the Divine Revelation. Certainly, even for the Christian thinker the phenomenon of "religion" requires thoughtful consideration; he, too, will regard it as one of his tasks to try to understand this phenomenon, from the standpoint of the Christian Faith, and to assign it its rightful place. But for him this is a later development, it is not the starting-point of his theological thinking. For he does not understand the Christian Faith in the

[1] Cf. my book *Die Mystik und das Wort*, 2nd Ed. 1928, Ch. 2.

light of "Religion", but he understands religion in the light of the Christian Faith. The Christian view of religion, with special reference to the various "religions"—(the general concept of "religion" is very problematic)—is part of his doctrine of Man, but it is not the basis of his dogmatics. Dogmatics is not the Science of "the Christian Religion".

The problem of a neutral, objective science of religion (already mentioned in Chapter I) is quite different, and indeed is very complicated. First of all, it is a fact. Research is actually being carried on, in our universities and elsewhere, in the study of the "world of religions", just as other spheres of human reality are examined by those who carry on research. There is an extensive "Science of Religion" in which, with all possible objectivity, on the one hand the various religions, and on the other hand the various religious attitudes and states of consciousness are described. It is obvious that the Christian Religion, too, can be the object of such a descriptive, neutrally objective, science. Here the aim is to describe scientifically the facts of Christianity, which means that "Christian doctrine and Christian dogma" also are *facts*, and, as such, constitute a particular subject of enquiry. It should be quite clear that the purpose and result of such research is something wholly different from that which dogmatics purposes and achieves. For this factual account of what is actually taught within Christianity only aims at giving an account of what *is*, without any claim to establish a norm. Such research does not enquire into the truth of these doctrines, it does not ask, which then of these contradictory doctrines is the right one; it does not even try to erect a criterion of "soundness"; but with equal fidelity it presents an "objective" description of the most primitive and abstruse superstitions, and of the most fundamental Biblical doctrines. It is true that this "science of facts" has certain historical categories at its disposal, which enables it to make a certain hierarchy of facts: those which are original, classical and canonical respectively—in the sense of that which has actually been achieved within history—that which is taught by scholars who are at the height of their profession, or by those scholars who are outstanding in the spheres of social science or culture; but these categories have no normative meaning; they are only a means of classification. The Science of Religion cannot say, and does not intend to say, what the true Christian doctrine is.

Within this objective Science of Religion there is a peculiar position adopted by the Swedish school of "Research into

Fundamental Motives", represented by the theologian A. Nygren and his school, the high value of which is shown in an impressive manner by Nygren's excellent book, *Eros and Agape*. Here the method of objective presentation appears to penetrate not only into the very centre of the Christian Faith, but through the idea of the "fundamental motive" it even seems to gain a *normative* significance, although this may not be its direct aim. Through the working out of the "fundamental motive" of a religion it is claimed that it is possible to work out the "characteristic and typical" elements (Nygren, *Eros and Agape*, I, p. 21, German ed.). The objective freedom of "values" of this process of research is, however, explicitly emphasized. It is not concerned with making a contrast between what is "right" and what is "wrong", but—in the case of the Eros-Agape problem—to contrast the Christian and the non-Christian points of view (p. 23). The "fundamental motive" of a view is defined as "its answer to a question of a fundamental character, which from the point of view of category may be described as a fundamental question" (p. 25). This new method of research seems to have a good deal of affinity with the phenomenological method of Husserl, and it promises to yield rich results; here, however, all we wish to show is that this is not the way of dogmatic theology. For dogmatics does not try to find, or want to find, the "fundamental motive of Primitive Christianity", but the *right* doctrine of God, and in so doing to serve the teaching Church, whose conscience is only easy when she is teaching according to the Truth—not in accordance with a "fundamental motive".

### (5) APOLOGETICS AND "ERISTICS"

Apologetic, or (as I have proposed owing to the unfortunate suggestions attached to this word) "eristic" theology, is the intellectual discussion of the Christian Faith in the light of the ideologies of the present day which are opposed to the Christian Message. The name "apologetic" is hampered by the suggestion of a *defence* of Christianity at the bar of Reason, even if it does not go so far as to claim rational *proof*. Actually, however, what matters is not "defence" but "attack"—the *attack*, namely, of the Church on the opposing positions of unbelief, superstition, or misleading ideologies. It is true that part of this attack consists in proving that the hostile attacks—not on empirical Christianity, for these are as a rule only too fully justified, but—on the Biblical Message, as being contrary to reason, opposed to culture, scientifically untenable, etc., are based upon errors, due either to the confusion of rationalism with reason, of positivism with science, of a critical with a sceptical attitude, or out of ignorance of the real truth which the Bible contains.

Apologetics, as a wrestling with the enemy outside the camp, corresponds to the conflict with heresy within. It is a necessity only where the foundations (and not merely particular doctrines) of the Christian Message are attacked; that is, where in the spiritual conflict the whole is at stake, and not merely certain parts.

Hence this apologetic-eristic theology in the Church has always and everywhere, from time immemorial, been to the fore where the Christian Message as such was menaced. All the great theologians of the Early Church were at the same time "Apologists", and the apologetic or "eristic" works of the first four centuries are at least as numerous and important as those which may be properly described as "dogmatic".[1] Here I will only mention the greatest of them all: Augustine's *De civitate Dei*.

Owing to the fact that at the Reformation theology was very one-sided, certain contemporary theologians have concluded that apologetics (or eristics) is not a necessary, or even a legitimate task of theology. It is true that the period of the Reformation did not achieve much in this direction—for the simple reason that at that time the main conflict was not with unbelief, but with a mistaken faith within the Church itself. The same was true of mediaeval theology, until the actual conflict arose against Islam as a philosophy, and against the polemic of Judaism. In the period after the Reformation, when the philosophy of the Renaissance, and the dawn of the period of the Enlightenment began the attack on the foundations of the Christian Faith, a new eristic movement began, whose most brilliant example was the *Pensées* of Pascal: indeed, to this day this work remains an unsurpassed model of discussion with the educated unbeliever.

Unfortunately, the philosophy of the Enlightenment, and the Idealism which succeeded it, gained such a hold over so many of the finest intellects in the Protestant world that—with the exception of Hamann—the Church was unable to produce any vigorous champions of Christian doctrine. So far as the Church

[1] Cf. Zöckler, *Geschichte der Apologie*, 1907.

itself was concerned, doctrine became increasingly rigid, and it was limited to the defence of positions which only *seemed* to be centrally Christian, because they were connected with the orthodox traditions of the seventeenth and eighteenth centuries; thus the Church usually came off rather badly.

In the first half of the nineteenth century, however, in the person of Søren Kierkegaard, one of the most powerful champions of the Christian Faith arose, a man who was able to stand forth as a witness all the more clearly and plainly because at the same time he ruthlessly summoned the empirical Christianity of his own day to give an account of itself. The largest part of his literary work, however, was not an "attack upon Christianity", but on the contrary it was a single, skilfully constructed attack upon the ideologies of his own day, which were opposed to the Christian Faith, especially the romantic idealism of Hegel, aestheticism, self-complacent bourgeois morality, and the "mass" spirit. We may indeed claim that no other thinker has ever worked out the contrast between the Christian Faith and all the "immanental" possibilities of thought with such clarity and intensity as he has done. Kierkegaard is incomparably the greatest Apologist or "eristic" thinker of the Christian Faith within the sphere of Protestantism. The pioneer task which he began still waits to be carried further; indeed, this work has scarcely been begun.

In our own day the expansion of totalitarian ideologies both of the National Socialist and the Bolshevist variety have made it clear, even to those who formerly had no use for eristic theology, that such discussion is necessary. At last it has once more been recognized that the proclamation of the truth alone is not sufficient, that the immediate command is also to unmask all untruth, and that this summons cannot be avoided; within the Church itself the simple proclamation of the Gospel is not enough, but theological controversy has to be carried on with heresy, and all that is untrue or unreal within her life must be eliminated.

When the objection is raised that we are here trying to "prove" something which can only be "believed", we might say exactly the same about all the intellectual labour expended on dogmatics, and about all polemical discussion with heresy within the Church, and indeed about theology in general. On the other hand, as the present writer has done in his article entitled *"Die andere Aufgabe der Theologie"* (*Zwischen den Zeiten*, 1929, pp. 255–76), we may answer, that every living proclamation of the Biblical message, and indeed this message itself, is full of eristic apologetic elements—is it not indeed an attack upon the self-understanding of the unbelieving "natural" man? In Apologetics this attack takes place in reflective form, which corresponds to the reflective form of the testimony to faith in dogmatics.

Karl Barth's hostility to Apologetics is, however, to this extent justified, because it is true that discussion with non-Christian thought cannot be the basis and the starting-point for dogmatics itself. His opposition to "eristics" was necessary, so long as this was proclaimed as the "foundation" of dogmatics. The task of theological prolegomena, and the task of controversy with the various attacks upon the foundation of revelation, must be clearly and conscientiously distinguished from one another, although from the purely psychological standpoint it is still true that "eristics" helps to create the necessary space for the doctrine of the Church. The confusion of both tasks is evident in the work of such otherwise excellent dogmatic theologians as Kähler and Schlatter; indeed, I myself, in my early writings, also believed that both tasks were the same.

Further, there is a type of theology which it is not easy to distinguish from eristics on the one hand, and from dogmatics on the other; this is called "missionary theology".

## (6) MISSIONARY THEOLOGY

In a single sentence[1] the Apostle Paul has expressed the programme of, and the justification for, both Apologetics or Eristics and of "missionary theology". "For the weapons of our warfare are not of the flesh, but mighty before God to the casting down of strong holds; casting down reasonings"—that is the programme of eristics. He goes on to say that the aim of this process is to bring "every thought into captivity to the obedience of Christ"—that is the programme of what we may call "missionary theology". In the message of the missionary, whether we are willing to admit this or not, to be able to make use of the knowledge which the pagan, unconverted, man already possesses plays a decisive part. No missionary work has ever been carried on in any other way, and it can never be done in any other way.

The mere act of "bearing witness" remains sterile unless it can be integrated with the truth which the listener already

[1] 2 Cor. 10: 4 ff.

possesses. To deny this is to deny an obvious fact; it really means shutting one's eyes to the truth for the sake of a mistaken theory.

Now it is the task of "missionary theology" to accomplish in the sphere of intellectual reflection what every missionary does, as it were, by instinct. In so doing something is achieved which the dogmatic theologian, as such, ought not to do, and cannot do. His task is strictly confined to the subject with which he is dealing; the person who is listening to what he has to say does not directly concern him. He has enough to do to make clear the content of the message in its own proper context. The spiritual situation of the non-Christian hearer does not come directly within his line of vision. This spiritual situation, however, is also a concrete problem. The non-believing hearer—above all the presumptive hearer—is already affected by a definite "spirit of the age"; that is to say, his views of life and its problems, and of his own nature, are all coloured by a definite outlook which claims to rival the Christian view of life. The total sinfulness of the natural man does not consist in the fact that all that he thinks and believes is false, but in the fact that he is wholly unable to distinguish between the true and the false in his understanding of himself or of life. Therefore one to whom the truth of Christ has been granted has the task of making this distinction, and in so doing he has to explain the meaning of the Christian message. And this is the task of "missionary theology", the positive aspect of Eristics. The first part of the Pauline statement described the first, negative, task; the second part describes the positive task. Missionary theology is an intellectual presentation of the Gospel of Jesus Christ, which starts from the spiritual situation of the hearer, and is addressed to it.

As dogmatics is necessarily deductive, missionary theology is equally necessarily inductive. Dogmatics says: this is the revealed truth, and this is the salvation of humanity. Missionary theology says: This is the need and the danger of man—and from this the Gospel of Jesus Christ is the means of rescue. Missionary theology is, first of all, wholly concerned with the hearer, with his need, his helplessness, his scepticism and his longing. Missionary theology unveils the *"cor inquietum"*, and shows why it is *"inquietum"*; it does not, however, do this in such a way that the Gospel appears to be derived from the need of man; rather, its aim is to show that it is only the miracle of revelation in Jesus Christ which can meet man's need, because this distress is caused by man's distance from God, and indeed consists in this alienation.

Missionary theology takes the form of a conversation between a Christian believer and an unbeliever. The Christian believer enters into the questions raised by the unbeliever; he gives full weight to all the truth and insight the unbeliever already possesses. But he shows also how his knowledge, and therefore also his questions, ignore the very thing which brings light and true knowledge. Missionary theology is, so to say, pastoral work in the form of reflection, just as dogmatics is witness in the form of reflection.

Missionary theology removes the hindrances which lie between the Gospel and the hearer—namely, those hindrances which are accessible to intellectual reflection. As in all Christian doctrine—even in dogmatics—the success which attends the instruction does not lie ultimately in the hands of the human teacher, but only in the hands of the Divine Teacher, who is the Holy Spirit. But as in all teaching, so also in this form of teaching, this knowledge of the mystery and the grace of the decisive illumination ought not to prevent us from doing, and from recognizing as a task, that which is set before us as a task, and that which lies within the sphere of human assistance along the line of thought.

When we try to estimate the fruit of human teaching in the Church, then what a thinker like Pascal achieved in his *Pensees*, as an aid to faith, far surpasses all that has been done by dogmatic theologians in the name of the Church. Likewise, I am convinced that the missionary theology of a man like Kierkegaard in the nineteenth century, has done more than any dogmatic theologian, perhaps more than all of them put together. Since his time, however, the task which he then recognized as the proper intellectual task of the Church, has become ten times more urgent. The Catholic Church has recognized this, and has set mighty forces to work to achieve this task; Protestant theology, however, still manages to ignore it, and even dismisses the very idea with contempt. This contempt may even prove its own destruction.

## (7) DOGMA

The word "dogma", although derived from *one* Greek word, actually was used in two senses; this also comes out in the ecclesiastical development of dogma. The verb which lies at the root of it is δοκεῖν, δοκεῖ μοι, δέδοκται. Dogma means, on the one hand, a public "ordinance" or "enactment" for the government of a city, a "decree" enforced with the support of the Law. On the other hand, in the language of the philosophers it meant the common tenets of a "school", which served as a basis for further teaching and research, for which the Latin uses the word "decree" as the equivalent of "dogma": *decreta quae philosophi vocant δόγματα*. (Cicero, *Academ.*, II, 9, 27.) Further, Cicero describes the *"dogma"* or *"decretum"* as the *"lex veri rectique"*, and says of it that it is *"stabile, fixum, ratum, quod movere nulla ratio queat"*.

From philosophy the term was transferred to religion and morality, so that Josephus (*c. Apion. Lib.*, I, c. 8) can describe the content of the Old Testament writings as θεοῦ δόγματα. This usage was then taken over by the early Fathers of the Church and applied to the fundamental Christian truths; at the same time—thus maintaining the ancient twofold meaning —it was used to describe that which the Church had laid down as a religious *law*. But this procedure took place more or less independently of the word "dogma". It came into use when a doctrinal ecclesiastical authority, with power to impose its ordinances, laid down a definite doctrine as valid, as binding for faith, especially when it explicitly judged or condemned the view which diverged from this valid doctrine, and pronounced it "anathema". Hence the great Church Councils and their doctrinal decisions promoted the development of dogma. Yet there was this difference: that in the East it was the doctrinal element, and in the West the juridical element, which predominated. The consciousness of dogma, without the use of the word "dogma", is classically expressed in the introductory sentence of the *"formula quicunque"*, in the so-called Athanasian Creed: *"Quicunque vult salvus esse, ante omnia opus habet, ut teneat catholicum fidem. Quam nisi quisque integram inviolatamque servaverit, absque dubio in aeternum peribit"*.

As such, the Primitive Church only had two dogmas: the doctrine of the Trinity, and its Christology, although in a broader sense we must describe as dogma all that about which the Church pronounced its decrees—as, for instance, the condemnation of a whole series of views held by Origen.

Mediaeval theology accepted the formulation of Duns Scotus: *tenendum . . . pro vero, quidquid tradidit auctoritas* (cf. Loofs, *Dogmengeschichte*, p. 591). This conception of the doctrinal authority of the Church as the right to establish and define valid dogma, was ascribed only to the infallible Council and its formal doctrinal decisions, until the Vaticanum. These decisions alone constitute the "dogma" of the Church. But with the *Vaticanum* this final authority was transferred to the Pope. His doctrinal decisions are *"ex sese, non ex consensu ecclesiae"*, infallible, "irreformable" (Denzinger, *Enchir. symbol.* 1839). "Thus every Catholic dogma bears two essential characteristics: an inward, concrete one, contained within the revelation, and an outer juridical one, the proclamation by the Church" (Bartmann, *Lehrbuch der Dogmatik*, I, p. 4). The meaning of this "proclamation" becomes clear from the formula of the *"Vaticanum"*: *"ea omnia ... (quae) credenda proponuntur"* (Denzinger 1792). Dogma, therefore, is that, and only that, which the infallible teaching Church puts forth as *"credendum"* as that which is commanded to be believed by a law of the Church. It is, of course, *eo ipso*, also a doctrinal law: every doctrine which contradicts it is forbidden, and will be suppressed by the Church authorities. By the *Vaticanum* the idea of dogma was also formally recognized as authoritative: at the outset dogma is all that the Pontifex Maximus of the Roman Church *will* teach in virtue of his authority. This is the strictly logical conception of dogma of the Roman Catholic Church.

The idea of dogma in the Eastern Orthodox Church (especially in the Greek and Russian branches) is far less juridically conceived, and less formally authoritarian in character, because here there is no concentration in an infallible doctrinal authority and still less in its sovereign head. The real dogma of the Eastern Church is the so-called Nicene Creed, the *"unicum symbolum"* which represents "all that is necessary as the sum of those things to be believed" (Loofs, *op. cit.*). "The symbol is a compendium of dogma as a whole" (Loofs, *op. cit.*, p. 135). But this chief symbol is always to be understood as the sum of the whole doctrinal tradition of ancient times, especially of the doctrinal decisions of the seven œcumenical Synods, from the first to the second Council of Nicea, 325–692. Since the Orthodox Church now possesses no infallible doctrinal authority, in so far as no Patriarch and no Synod *ex dogmate* is regarded as infallible, there is here a fair amount of scope for doctrinal freedom, even though this means that the theologians of these Churches are only free to move within the interpretation of faith given in the sacred Creeds, or, at least, this is said to be their scope. In the main, we may say that this view of dogma is approximately that of the Fathers of the Church.

This conception of dogma is also that which was taken over by the Reformers. Both the *Augustana* (Augsburg Confession) and the *Confessio Helvetica posterior* (Second Helvetic Confession) explicitly emphasize their "orthodoxy", with reference to the ancient Creeds of the Church, and the dogma which they incorporate. Indeed, the *Helvetica* goes so far as to preface its own Confession with an Edict of Theodosius of the year 380, which places heretics under heavenly *and earthly* penalties. But if we ask for the authority which is ascribed to the confessional writings of the Reformation themselves, it then becomes plain that the supremacy of the Scriptural principle above the principle of tradition, which governs all Reformation doctrine, has also had an effect on the validity of these newer creeds, and indeed could ultimately be applied to that of the ancient creeds themselves. There are a number of indications which point to this: for one thing the variety of confessions—especially in the sphere of the Reformed Churches—which differ a good deal from one another; secondly, the fact that some of them—for instance, the *Augustana*—even after they had been accepted were altered and "improved"; thirdly, the fact that some of them explicitly emphasized the fact that they only claim validity in so far as they do not require revision in the light of the Scriptures, as for instance, *Conf. Gallicana, Art. V.* By the principle of Scripture, dogma, and also the new ecclesiastical Confession, instead of being an absolute authority, became a conditional authority, a *"norma normata"*, as this was expressed by an orthodox Lutheran, Leonhard Hütter, in the year 1608. The confessional writings of the Lutheran Church only merit conditional belief, *"nempe quatenus cum scripturis sacris ex asse concordant"*.[1]

The genuine Reformation principle of Scripture, especially as it was boldly formulated by Luther, was a severe blow to the authority of dogma. Even the doctrine of Scripture is not, as such, infallible; it, too, must be tested by its own standard, that is, by the revelation which it contains: *Christus dominus et rex scripturae.* Even in the Scriptures the divine dogma is not simply "given", but it is given in such a way that at the same time and continually it must be *sought*. Only then does the truly Biblical conception of truth and faith become valid; no doctrine as such is the object of faith, the *"credendum"*, but only in, and under the doctrine of "Jesus Christ" as God's Own Word, Himself. Faith is not relation to a doctrine, to that

---

[1] Ritschl, *Dogmengeschichte des Protestantismus* ,I, p. 391.

106

which ought to be believed, but it is the obedience of faith, ὑπακοὴ πίστεως, to Jesus Christ Himself, who bears witness to Himself in the Word of the Scriptures through the Holy Spirit in the heart, conscience, and mind of man as the Truth. This truth, made known through the Reformation, destroyed the authoritarian conceptions of dogma, both in the Catholic, and in the Protestant Church—the one with its authority of the Church, and the other with its authority of the Bible; dogma is still only a relative, not an absolute authority, because it is only the human vessel which contains the divine revelation.

## (8) THE AUTHORITY OF SCRIPTURE

From the very beginning the Christian Church possessed a Sacred Scripture which had absolute canonical authority: the Old Testament. Its authority was based upon the fact that it was the work of the Holy Spirit, θεόπνευστος (2 Tim. 3: 16). The doctrine of Verbal Inspiration was already known to pre-Christian Judaism (cf. *Offenbarung und Vernunft*, p. 117) and was probably also taken over by Paul and the rest of the Apostles. Later on, however, in the Early Church and in the Mediaeval Church, the influence of this literalistic theory of the authority of Scripture was actually not only modified in practice, but to a large extent removed by the very free, and often quite arbitrary method of allegorical exposition (cf., for instance, 1 Cor. 9: 9). In point of fact Scripture was regarded as the authority because, and in so far as, it bore witness to Jesus as the Christ. Faith in Christ, and the Holy Spirit operating in the Church, were the actual seat of authority, which was only theoretically equated with "Scripture", but not in practice. From the second century onwards the New Testament was added to the Old Testament as Holy Scripture. Although until the fourth century the range of the New Testament Canon was not always and everywhere the same, yet from the middle of the second century it was established that alongside of the Old Testament there was a second written authority of equal rank, which, even if not in theory, yet in actual fact, was the final court of appeal for the definition of that which was to be considered valid in the Church. From the time of Justin Martyr (*Coh. ad Graecos*, 8) there was also a rudimentary doctrine of Inspiration—God's Spirit makes use of "holy men" as a zither-player plays on his zither—which established the supernatural authority of the Scriptures. "Hence they have taught us . . .

out of one mouth, with one voice, logically, and without contradiction." And Irenaeus already teaches: *"Scripturae quidem perfectae sunt, quippe a verbo Dei et Spiritu ejus dictae"* (*Adv. Haer.*, II, 28), and Tertullian makes the acceptance of the whole *Codex* the criterion of Christian life (*De praescr. Haer.*, 22). It seems to have been he who introduced the idea of "inspiration"—as well as many other ideas—into the theological vocabulary. But in spite of this strict theory, the *actual* view of the authority of Scripture remained to a large extent free, and allowed critical observations on special points of detail. From Origen onwards, the rank growth of the allegorical method of Biblical exposition made it impossible to maintain the Bible text as normative, as compared with the ecclesiastical development of doctrine. By means of allegorical exposition the Scholastics "prove", with the help of Scripture, all that they *wish* to prove.

The struggle of the Reformers for the sole supremacy of Scripture as the doctrinal authority was therefore only significant in the fact that at the same time they followed the line of the literal historical and philological exposition of the Scriptures. So long as a *"regula fidei"* determined the method of exposition, nothing could be done against Roman Catholic doctrine; for naturally the latter also appealed for support in a general way to the Scriptures, and bolstered up its specifically Catholic views by an appeal to the *"analogia fidei"*. With the doctrine of the equal authority of tradition and Scripture—the *"sine scripto traditiones"* are to be accepted *"pari pietatis affectu ac reverentia"*—(Denzinger, 783)—guaranteed not only a second seat of authority, but above all the canonical authority of the Church's interpretation of Scripture. "Neither the Holy Scriptures nor the Divine tradition, but the teaching Church, which infallibly expounds both sources of truth . . . is for us the first rule of faith", so does a responsible theologian of the Vatican formulate the Catholic idea of authority (Loofs, *Symbolik*, p. 209). "The Catholic Christian must believe everything that God has revealed, and that which the Catholic Church presents to be believed, whether the same be found in the Scriptures or not," is said in a Catholic Catechism (*ibid.*, p. 210). Thus, without denying the view of the Early Church on the Scriptures (doctrine of Inspiration), or the Tridentine principle of Tradition, the Catholic Church removes both Tradition and Scripture from the position of critical courts of appeal by the actual and legal establishment of the Papal doctrinal authority as the supreme court of appeal, against which there can be no appeal. The principle of Scripture, already weakened by the theory of the equal value of Tradition, although not contested, was thus, though retained in theory, actually abrogated in practice.

But the Protestant principle of Scripture—deliberately we do not say that of the Reformation—is far from being clear. Certainly, it is true that at first all that mattered was the contrast between Scripture and Tradition. The Reformers saw the immense contrast between the doctrine of the New Testament and the doctrine of the Roman Church, and they decided for the former against the latter. The Word of God alone, not the doctrine of the Church, has final authority: *"Quod sine scripturis asseritur, aut revelatione probata opinari licet, credi non est necesse"* (Luther, *W*. 6, 508). Since, however, the Catholic Church also claims that it is based upon the foundation of Holy Scripture, and claims for herself the right to give the only valid interpretation of Scripture, this first thesis has to be supplemented by a second one: *"scriptura sui ipsius interpres"* (*W*. 7, 97), and this means further: Scripture is to be understood in the *"sensus literalis"*. "The natural language is the Queen" (*W*. 18, 180). The Principle of Scripture requires the renunciation of the allegorical method of exposition: *"Difficillimum autem mihi fuit, ab usitato studio allegoriarum discedere, et tamen videbam allegorias esse inanes speculationes et tanquam spumam sacrae scripturae. Sola enim historica sententia est quae vere et solide docet"* (*W*. 42, 173). Zwingli expresses the same view in his work *"Von Klarheit und Gewissheit oder Untrüglichkeit des Wortes Gottes"*.

What, then, is here meant by "the Scriptures"? If they alone are the authority, *in what sense* is this meant? One of the greatest proofs of the truly spiritual freedom of Luther is the fact that he did not allow himself to be led astray into a literalistic interpretation of Scripture, although this would have been a very easy thing to do, in this situation of conflict and controversy. In spite of the fact that he could fight Rome with the Scriptures only, not only did he not (like the "orthodox" of a later date) set up a doctrine of Verbal Inspiration, and thus of the Infallibility of the Text of the Bible, but, going further than any previous critical views of Scripture, he made a distinction between Scriptures that were "canonical", and those which were not (not in the sense of being included in the Canon or not, but in the sense that some were binding and others were not). His delicate sense of truth did not allow him to ignore the fact that some parts of Scripture contained far more of the quality of "revelation" than others; this prevented him from laying down a principle of the authority of Scripture in formal, general terms—in which all parts of Scripture are regarded as of equal value. His various prefaces to the different books of the Bible are valuable testimonies to his point of view. This is his principle: "This is the touchstone by which all books may be tested, to see whether they proclaim Christ or not, since all Scripture witnesses to Christ and St. Paul will know nothing save Christ. Whatever does not teach Christ is not apostolic, even were it taught by St. Peter or St. Paul" (E. 63, 157). Thus the content and the real authority of Scripture is Christ. "But if I know what I believe, then I know what stands in the Scriptures, and the Scriptures contain nothing save Christ and the Christian Faith" (W. 8, 236). "Si adversarii scripturam urserint contra Christum, urgemus Christum contra scripturam" (Disput. Drews, p. 12). "Scriptura est non contra, sed pro Christo intelligenda, ideo vel ad eum referenda, vel pro vera scriptura non habenda" (ibid.). "Christus dominus scripturae (W. 40, 1, 420). Thus this means: we believe in Christ, not because Scripture, or the Apostles, teach us about Him in such and such a way, but we believe in the Scriptures because, and in so far as they teach Christ. The authority of Scripture is not formal but material: Christ, the revelation. Even subjectively, however, this authority is not based upon the Scriptures as such, but upon the encounter of faith with the Christ of Scripture. "Each one alone therefore must believe that He is the Word of God, and that he knoweth inwardly that He is the Truth" (W. 10, 2, 90). "It is not enough that thou sayest: Luther, Peter or Paul hath said this, but thou must thyself feel in thy conscience Christ Himself, and immovably that it is the Word of God. . . . So long as thou hast not this feeling, so long hast thou certainly not tasted the Word of God" (W. 10, 2, 22).

Here—compared with previous theological views—we find a completely new conception of the authority of Scripture. We are not required to believe the Scriptures because they are the Scriptures; but because Christ, whom I am convinced in my conscience is the Truth, meets me in the Scriptures—therefore I believe. Scripture is not a *formal* authority which demands belief in all it contains from the outset, but it is an *instrumental* authority, in so far as it contains that element before which I must bow in the truth, which also itself awakens in me the certainty of truth. This is what Luther means by the "Word of

God", which therefore is not identical with the Word of Scripture, although it is only given to me through the Scriptures, and as the Word of the Scriptures.

Only from this point of view, then, can we understand how it was that Luther was able to assign various degrees of authority to different parts of the Bible; he went so far as to say that he would like to see certain books excluded from the Canon altogether. Thus he makes very free and critical remarks about the writings which compose the Scriptures of the Old and the New Testaments, their historical origin, and the conditions under which they were composed; many of these views have been confirmed by the Biblical criticism of last century. Thus Luther was the first to represent a Biblical faith which could be combined with Biblical criticism, and was therefore fundamentally different from the traditional, formally authoritarian view of the Bible, which culminates in the doctrine of Verbal Inspiration.

Calvin is already moving away from Luther towards the doctrine of Verbal Inspiration. His *doctrine* of the Bible is entirely the traditional, formally authoritative view. The writings of the Apostles *"pro dei oraculis habenda sunt"* (*Institutio*, IV, 8, 9). Therefore we must accept *"quidquid in sacris scripturis traditum est sine exceptione"* (I, 18, 4). The belief *"auctorem eius (sc: scripturae) esse deum"* *precedes* all doctrine (I, 7, 4). That again is the old view. On the other hand, his *exposition* of Scripture moves along the line of Luther's new understanding. It can indeed hardly be gainsaid that the Reformed Church and its theology departed more swiftly than the Lutheran Church from the original Scriptural principle— that is, from the new and revolutionary principle of Scripture— and returned to the traditional line of the formal authority of the Bible (cf. Ritschl, *Dogmengeschichte des Protestantismus*, I, 62 ff.).

From the end of the sixteenth century onwards there was no other "principle of Scripture" than this formal authoritarian one. Whatever development took place after this culminated in the most strict and most carefully formulated doctrine of Verbal Inspiration which is characteristic of orthodoxy proper —Lutheran as well as Reformed. L. Hütter already says of the Bible that it is *"verbotim dictata ita ut nullum jota a prophetis et apostolis in istis libris sit exaratum, quod non sit theopneuston"* (*Loci theol.*, p. 26a). Johann Gerhard already teaches the inspiration of the Hebrew vowel-points (*Loci theol.*, II, p. 23b).

Still more important than this verbal conception of the authority of the Bible is the view—entirely opposed to the Reformation Principle of Scripture—of the axiomatic, formal authoritarian validity of Scripture: "Believing Christians", says Johann Gerhard, *"de scripturae auctoritate non quaerunt, est enim principium"* (*op. cit.*, I, 9). The doctrine of the authority of Scripture was *not* an *"articulus fidei"*, but rather *"principium articulorum fidei"* (*op. cit.*, I, II). Here explicitly the pre- and super-ordination of belief in the Scriptures is taught as far above all that they contain for faith, and in so doing Luther's view of Christ as the sole content of the Scriptural faith has been completely abandoned. After this it is only the final logical deduction when all the content of Scripture is given the same value—whether this content be historical or geographical or religious in character—as the message of salvation; even the *"res historicae, chronologicae, genealogicae, physicae et politicae . . . sunt divinitus revelatae"*, in spite of the fact that in themselves they have no connexion with the knowledge of salvation at all (Hollaz, *Examen theologicae*, p. 83).

We must, however, admit that even among the Reformers themselves alongside of their new principle they also retained the traditional, formally authoritarian or axiomatic view of the Scriptures, so that the new element of truth did not make a final clean "break-through"; thus, without meaning to do so, it helped the return to the old view. This applies even to Luther himself who was foremost among the Reformers in his efforts to express the new principle of Scripture in the clearest and boldest terms.

So it was only the rise of the science of Biblical Criticism, and the crisis in the belief in the Bible created by the new scientific view of the world, which forced theology to think back to Luther's revolutionary insight into truth, and to disentangle it from its connexion with the traditional doctrine of Inspiration.

This process was carried through mainly by the labours of the "Bible" theologians of last century, Kähler and Schlatter, although we must not forget to mention their predecessors who prepared the way, confessional theologians, like Thomasius and von Öettingen. Thus Thomasius says (*Christi Person und Werk*, II, p. 273): "That these writings have not been directly dictated by the Holy Spirit, but that they have issued from the process of thought and reflection, out of the inmost spirit, out of the heart . . . of the Apostles." Similarly von Öettingen

(*Lutherische Dogmatik*, II, 2, p. 344): "The Bible ought not to be, and must not be regarded as an oracle fallen from heaven or dictated by the Holy Spirit, clothed with legal authority." Kähler, in his important small book called *Der sogenannte historische Jesus und der geschichtliche biblische Christus* . . . has disentangled the new Reformation view of Scripture very clearly from the orthodox tradition and has once more "put it on the map".

Fundamentally, Karl Barth's *Dogmatik* takes the same position: "The Bible is not a book of sacred oracles; it is not an organ of direct communication. It is real witness" (I, 2, p. 562). He says that we could not expect that the Apostles and Prophets, in addition to their encounter with the divine revelation, "should also have had imparted to them a compendium of . . . divine Wisdom concerning everything in the universe. . . ." (*op. cit.*, p. 564). Indeed, Barth even speaks of the possibility of error in the religious, that is, the theological content, of the Bible (*op. cit.*, p. 565). Thus he arrives at a definite and clear rejection of the orthodox view of the Bible (*op. cit.*, 580 ff.) and returns to the original principle of the Reformation. The same view is contained in my book *Religionsphilosophie evangelischer Theologie* (pp. 117–34), which was published in 1925 in the *Handbuch der Philosophie*.

*PART I*

# THE ETERNAL FOUNDATION
## OF THE
# DIVINE SELF-COMMUNICATION

# THE NATURE OF GOD AND HIS ATTRIBUTES

## CHAPTER 12

## THE NAME OF GOD

THE phrase, "The Doctrine of God", must sound strange to any unprejudiced person. How can *man* undertake to formulate a doctrine of God? If there is one point which is clear from the very outset it is this: that God is not an "object" which man can manipulate by means of his own reasoning; He is a Mystery dwelling in the depths of "inaccessible Light". *Favete linguis!* "God is in His Temple. . . . All within keep silence, Prostrate lie with deepest reverence. . . ." "Calmly to adore the Unfathomable" (Goethe)—this, surely, would be more fitting than the effort to construct a "doctrine of God". Do we not read in the Book of Judges: "Wherefore askest thou after My Name, seeing it is wonderful?"[1] And does not the Commandment of the Old Testament against "graven images" bear the same meaning, *i.e.* that we have no right to compare God with anything known to us: that He is incomparable, and therefore cannot be known? A man who thinks he can instruct others about God has forgotten what he is supposed to be doing.

But when we say this we have already begun to know God, and to teach men about Him. For *this* precisely *is* the knowledge of God, and the doctrine of God, namely, that He is incomparable, and that He cannot be defined. We are here confronted by a remarkable dialectic, which will accompany us throughout the whole of our study of dogmatics. The better we know God, the more we know and feel that His Mystery is unfathomable. The doctrine which lays the most stress upon the Mystery of God will be nearest to the truth.

It is precisely this fact which distinguishes the God of the Biblical revelation from the gods and divinities of paganism. The gods of the heathen are not really mysterious, because they can be "known" within the sphere of that which is natural and given, whether in the processes of the world of nature or in the

[1] Judges 13: 18. (R.V.)

mind of man. Their mystery is the mystery of nature, of the Self, of the world, and therefore it is *not* the mystery of that which is genuinely supernatural. Through the Biblical revelation we discover that what we can "learn" to know as "God" by our own unaided efforts is not the True God, precisely because we acquire this "knowledge" by our own efforts. Even the "Unfathomable" which the agnostic sets in the place of God is not a real mystery, but simply denotes the limitations of our knowledge, a fact of which we are fully aware, and one which it is not at all difficult to perceive. One who is only aware of this limitation is not yet aware how mysterious God is. The thought of that limitation to our knowledge, the idea of the Unfathomable which we can acquire by our own unaided efforts, has therefore no power at all to inspire us with genuine reverence, for there is here a confusion of ideas: the conception of that which has not yet been perceived, of the riddle of the universe, and the idea of that which in principle cannot be discovered by man's searching, these two fundamentally different ideas have unconsciously merged into one another. That which we can see to be "unfathomable" is an emptiness, not a fullness. It makes us "resigned", it does not bring us fulfilment. It does not bring us to our knees, and it moves neither heart nor will. It does not draw us to Itself; the only effect it has is that we do not further concern ourselves with something we cannot know. Agnosticism is not an attitude of reverence but of indifference.

Conversely, what the Biblical revelation teaches us is that the very *mystery* can only be understood as a genuine *mystery* by means of revelation. We do not fully realize how unknowable, how mysterious God is until we meet Him in His revelation. Here alone do we understand that all our own processes of knowing, just because they are our own, do not create the true knowledge of God, since through them—whether in a profound or in a superficial way—we remain in our own sphere. The nature divinity is not really mysterious, nor is the god of reason or of Spirit, which we conceive within the sphere of our reason, of our mind, of our Self; He alone is mysterious who comes to us from a region beyond all spheres known to us, who breaks through the barriers of our own experience of the world and the Self, and enters into our world as one who does not belong to it.

From the standpoint of our own knowledge Faust is perfectly right: "Who can name Him, and who can confess 'I know Him'? The name is an echo, resounding amid clouds of fragrant incense, concealing a heavenly glow". But this Nameless One is certainly not the truly Mysterious One; the Mysterious One is He who makes His Name known to us in His own revelation.

"I will proclaim the Name of the Lord before thee; and will be gracious to whom I will be gracious, and will shew mercy on whom I will shew mercy."[1] Because the revelation of the Name is the self-manifestation of the God who is free, and exalted high above this world, it is this alone which confronts us with the real mystery of God. Hence the revelation of the Name of God stands in the centre of the Biblical witness to revelation.

At first, it is true, in the beginning of the history of revelation, the "Name", the "Proper Name" of the God of Israel, means the Name of Yahweh, which distinguishes the God of Israel from the gods of the other nations, and enables those who share in the divine Covenant to call upon Him, *their* God. So long as a plurality of "gods" formed part of the thought-world of the time the "Proper Name" of the True God was a necessity.[2] But at the zenith of the Old Testament revelation both ideas have disappeared. The name of Yahweh remains, it is true, but it is no longer a proper name. Nor in the teaching of the great prophets is there any trace of primitive magic connected with the Name, or of any other magical conceptions.[3] And yet this conception, the conception of the "name of the Lord", remains at the very heart of the Message of the Old Testament revelation. It is still present within the New Testament, where the Name of Yahweh has entirely disappeared. The first clause of the Lord's Prayer is: "Hallowed be Thy Name." In the Gospel of John—where Jesus Christ, at the end of His life on earth, is gathering up everything that God has done through Him, and has given to the world—Jesus says, in the High Priestly Prayer: "I have manifested Thy Name",[4] and His last petition for His "own" is this: "keep through Thine own Name those whom Thou hast given me, that they may be one, as we are."[5]

We ask: Why is it that in the Bible this incomparable significance is attached to the idea of the "Name" of God? Strangely enough this question is rarely discussed by theologians, and still

---

[1] Exodus 33: 19.
[2] Cf. Judges 11: 23 ff.; 2 Kings 3: 27; 1 Sam. 26: 19.
[3] Cf. Grether, *Name u. Wort Gottes im Alten Testament*, 1934, p. 19.
[4] John 17: 6.                                    [5] John 17: 11.

less often is it satisfactorily answered.[1] We here anticipate our answer—which will be fully worked out in the following pages—by this summary statement: this high significance is ascribed to the idea of the "Name of God" within the Biblical revelation because it gathers up, in a simple way which everybody can understand, certain decisive elements in the reality of revelation: God stands "over against us"; we stand "over against" Him; God is not an "It" but a "Thou"; who addresses us; He makes Himself known through His self-revelation; He manifests Himself to us in order that we may call upon Him and have communion with Him. The "Name" of God covers both the revealed Nature of God and His revealing action; the foundation of this revelation in Being and in Act is the Divine will to sovereignty and communion, the purpose of which is the glory of God and communion with God. Thus the Biblical conception of the "Name", and the "manifestation of the Name", contains the meaning of the whole Biblical doctrine of God. We must now proceed to define this in more detail, showing the foundation for our statements.

(1) God is known only where He Himself makes His Name known. Apart from this self-manifestation He is unknowable; from our point of view He is remote, inaccessible. The "Name" is that which is peculiar to Himself, it is that which distinguishes Him from all else, that which cannot be expressed by any general conception; which is not an object of human knowledge of any kind; we cannot discover it by the exercise of our own faculty of reason; it is a knowledge which—in the strict sense of the word—can only be *given*.

The Greek Fathers made a great mistake (and this error bore disastrous fruit) in turning the Name of Yahweh (and especially the Name as described by the Elohist writer in the narrative of the revelation of the Divine Name on Horeb[2] into an ontological definition. The words "I AM THAT I AM" ought not to be translated in the language of speculative thought, as a definition: "I AM HE WHO IS." To do this not only misses the meaning of this statement, but it turns the Biblical idea of revelation into its opposite. The "Name" which cannot be defined is turned into a definition. The meaning of the Sacred Name is precisely this: I am the Mysterious One, and I will to remain so; I AM THAT I AM. I AM the Incomparable, therefore I cannot be defined nor named. This description is similar

---

[1] Compare Appendix on pp. 128 ff.     [2] Exod. 3: 14 ff.

to that in the Book of Judges, which is intended to warn
man off "holy ground": "Why askest thou thus after My
Name?" God is the Unknown God, until He makes Himself
known.[1]

This does not mean that pagans have no knowledge of God
at all; such a foolish statement, and one which is utterly contrary to experience, does not occur anywhere in the Bible.[2] But
it does mean that those who do not possess the historical revelation, those to whom God has not made known His Name, do
not know Him truly, do not know Him in such a way that they
are in communion with Him. The pagan—or what comes to the
same thing in the end—philosophical knowledge of God,[3] does
not create communion with God, because it is not knowledge of
the God who—since He makes Himself known—creates communion with Himself.

Even the man to whom God has not made His Name known
is not without a certain knowledge of God; for a knowledge of
the Creator forms part of the creaturely existence of man.[4] But
this possibility of knowing God is not sufficient to remove the
sinful blindness of man. It extends to the point of making man
"without excuse", but it does not suffice to bring him to glorify
God and to enter into communion with Him. In sinful man this
natural knowledge of God becomes necessarily the delusion of
idolatry, or—what amounts to the same thing in principle—
the abstract, impersonal idea of God. Man who is left alone
with Nature and with himself does not know the true God,
because he does not know the God of revelation, the God whose
Nature it is to be the Revealer, the one who communicates
Himself. God in His Self-communication—that is *the Name of
God*; hence where God does not make His Name known, He
cannot be known aright.

(2) Secondly, the concept, the "Name" of God, suggests
further that God is Person: He is not an "Iт"; He is our primary
"Thou". That which we can think and know by our own efforts
is always an object of thought and knowledge, some *thing*
which has been thought, some *thing* which has been known,
therefore it is never "Person". Even the human person is never
truly "person" to us so long as we merely "think" it; the
human being only becomes "person" to us when he speaks to

[1] Grether, *op. cit.*, pp. 6 ff. and Eichrodt, *Theologie des Alten Testaments*, I,
pp. 89 ff.
[2] Cf. below, pp. 132 ff.        [3] Cf. below, pp. 151 ff.        [4] Rom. 1: 19.

us himself, when he manifests the mystery of his being as a "thou", in the very act of addressing us.

The "Thou" is something other than the "Not-I"; the "Not-I" is the world, the sum-total of objects. But the "Thou" is that "Not-I" which is an "I" (or a Self) as I am myself, of which I only become aware when it is not thought by my own efforts, or perceived as an object, but when it makes itself known to me as self-active, self-speaking, as "I-over-against me".

It is true, of course, that to a certain extent we can know the human "thou" by our own efforts, because, and in so far as it is "also an I", a fellow-human being. The mystery of human personality is not absolute; it is only relative, because it is not only "other than I" but "the same as I". It can be placed under the same general heading "Man" along with me; it is not an unconditioned "Thou" because it is at the same time a "co-I". There is no general heading for God. God in particular has no "I" alongside of Himself. He is the "Thou" which is absolutely over against everything else, the "Thou" who cannot at the same time be on the same level with "me", "over-against" whom He stands.

Therefore I cannot myself unconditionally think God as this unconditioned "Thou", but I can only know Him in so far as He Himself, by His own action, makes Himself known to me. It is, of course, true that man can think out a God for himself—the history of philosophy makes this quite plain.[1] In extreme cases a man can "think" a personal God; theistic philosophy is a genuine, even if an extreme possibility. But this personal God who has been conceived by man remains some-*thing* which has been thought, the object of our thought-world. He does not break through the barriers of my thought-world, acting, speaking, manifesting Himself—He does not meet me as a "Thou", and is therefore not a real "Thou". He is, as something which I have thought, my function, my positing; He is not the One who addresses me, and in this "address" reveals Himself to me as the One who is quite independent of me.

The God who is merely *thought* to be personal is not truly personal; the "Living God" who enters my sphere of thought and experience from beyond my thought, in the act of making Himself known to me, by Himself naming His Name—He alone is truly personal.

It is the prerogative of persons to possess a name. *Things*

[1] Cf. below, pp. 151 ff.

have no names: we describe them in general terms, which we make more specific by using other general terms, as, for instance, "the house, the first in the street . . . on the left". Even animals do not possess names; when we give them names, we "personify" them; we lift them out of their own plane on to the level of personal existence. The "name" means personal being, that kind of being which we do not know and name of ourselves, but which "presents" itself to us, by naming its own name. We human beings have proper names, by which we present ourselves to each other as something that cannot be expressed in general terms. The proper name cannot be repeated: it is unique; therefore it cannot be turned into a definition.

But our human proper name is only a relative proper name since it is at the same time the name of a species. Our individual personal being is articulated out of that which is common to the existence of all men as a whole. We have two names, the human name and the proper name—and it belongs to the nature of man to have these two names, the general one and the "personal" one.

But the Name of God is only a "Proper Name" because it does not stand alongside of a general conception, of an appellation. The plural "gods" is an insult to God; it belongs to the Nature of God that there should be "none other beside Him". Therefore He cannot be known through general conceptions, but only through the naming of His own Name. The truly personal God is He who is not known through thought, but through the manifestation of His Name, the God of revelation.

(3) The communication of a name is the disclosure of one's self to the other, and thus the establishment—or at least the beginning—of a personal relation and communion. When one gives oneself to be known, one gives oneself away. There is an element of truth in that primitive magical idea—which can be discerned even in the Old Testament[1]—that with the disclosure of the name one gives away something of oneself, and that, conversely, to know the name of a person gives one a power over him. In the divine revelation of the Name there lies a twofold truth: God gives Himself to those to whom He reveals Himself, and these, for their part, now have a certain right to Him—even though it is a right which has been given them— those to whom He makes His Name known have become "His

[1] Grether, op. cit., p. 19.

own". They can and may now call upon Him. He gives them free access to His Majesty, which otherwise could not be approached. The disclosure of a name creates communion. Therefore the disclosure of the Name of God is consummated in the self-offering of the Revealer. "I have manifested Thy Name unto the men whom Thou gavest Me . . ." says Jesus on the night before His Crucifixion, and in anticipation of it. There, too, He also tells us the purpose of this manifestation of the "Name": "Keep through Thine own Name those whom Thou hast given Me, *that they may be one*, as we are." When Yahweh manifests His Name He makes the Covenant with Israel; when Jesus in His own Person makes known fully and finally the personal mystery of God, He establishes communion between the Holy God and sinful man.

Even in that apparently primitive and anthropomorphic passage in the Book of Exodus where Yahweh promises to "proclaim the Name of the Lord" to Moses, this proclamation of the Name of God by God Himself is connected with the sovereign, freely electing, grace of God: "I will be gracious to whom I will be gracious, and will shew mercy on whom I will shew mercy." God's self-manifestation is the act by which God steps out of the sphere of His own glory and self-sufficiency, in which the One who exists *for Himself alone* becomes the One who exists *for us*.

Or rather, it is the act in which God shows us that He *is* the One who exists "for us". In that He gives His Name He graciously summons us to make use of His Name, by calling upon Him. He wills to be present to us, when we call upon Him: "Call upon Me in the day of trouble: I will deliver thee, and thou shalt glorify Me".[1] The disclosure of the Name establishes the connexion which man may and should use henceforth. And only through the fact that God becomes for us the One upon whom it is possible to call, does He become to us a real "Thou", the truly personal God.

(4) Thought that has been fed on philosophical abstractions therefore finds the concept of the Name of God, and the revelation of the Name, to be an anthropomorphic degradation, making God finite, which cannot be permitted. This is quite in order, it would indeed be very surprising if such a protest were not made. Only we must be clear how far this goes, how fundamental it is. Then we perceive that behind this reproach of

[1] Ps. 50: 15.

"anthropomorphism" lies nothing less than the rejection of
revelation, and this means the rejection of the truly personal
God. The self-sufficient reason will not admit anything that
comes from a sphere beyond its own possibilities. It wishes to
remain isolated; it has no desire to receive; it will only acknowledge as truth that which, from the very outset, belongs to its
own sphere.

People who think like this want to keep their minds closed to
all that comes to them from outside the sphere of reason, the
sphere, that is, which they can control by their own thought;
they do not wish to see it opened from outside. They recognize
only the truth which they already know, and that which can be
verified by means which are at man's disposal. They have no
intention of admitting that there could be such a thing as
"given" truth. They will accept as truth only that which they
can attain for themselves, but not that which approaches
them from without. They will only receive—and this is the
same thing in the end—monological and not dialogical truth,
only truth which is preceded by the words: "I think", but not
that which is prefaced by the words: "Here it is!" that is, truth
which they can only receive in this way. Thus this habit of
thought is rooted in the self-sufficiency of the isolated "I":
*Cogito, ergo sum.*

But the revelation of the Name of God means the end of this
self-sufficient isolation of the Self, the end of this truth which is
shut up within the Self, the end of this unbroken continuity, of
this truth which can be attained by the efforts of man alone.
Revelation means that this self-centred circle has been broken
down; the truth comes in its own way and in its own power, to
you. You do not possess it, it is not in you, it is given to you.[1]
It is not that *you* are the starting-point, and *God* is the End,
but that *God* is the starting-point, and *you* are the end of the
movement. That which is disclosed does not start with *you*, the
subject, as if that which you know were your own object of
knowledge, but the disclosure starts from the other, from the
non-Self, but which, precisely because it opens and is not
opened, is not an object, not something which has been thought
but it is a subject: the "Thou" who opens His heart unto you,
and in so doing becomes the power which breaks down your
self-centred isolation and makes an end of your self-sufficiency.

This is the decision, which is accomplished in faith in the
revelation of the Name, and in the One who reveals His Name;

[1] Cf. Kierkegaard, *Philosophical Fragments*, pp. 12 ff., German ed.

what is at stake is the autonomy of the human personality. If this is retained, then no faith is possible; the zone of self-sufficiency is unbroken, the message of the God who manifests His Name is rejected as "anthropomorphism". But if, on the other hand, the revelation of the Name is believed, then the autonomy of the *cogito ergo sum* is rejected; the Self is no longer the final court of appeal, but the Divine Thou. Then self-sufficiency is no longer the standard of all truth, but the final highest truth is now truth which has been given, and this truth becomes real and living in God's approach to man, in the gracious movement of God towards man—God comes down to our level—this is the "truth" which is the same as "grace". "Grace and truth came through Jesus Christ."[1]

The self which is imprisoned within its own sphere can only call this "mythology" or "anthropomorphism"; the very fact that it makes these judgments shows that it is imprisoned within its own limits. The correlate of this self-imprisonment, however, is the impersonal God, the God who does not stand "over against" the Self, who does not address it, who does not reveal Himself, who does not alter the situation of the Self by His own initiative, the God who belongs to the thought-world of the Self, who, in the last resort, is the ground of the Self, the deepest content of the word "I", the God therefore who is never addressed as "Thou", and can never be called upon as "Thou". The "God of the philosophers" is the God to whom one does not pray, with whom, it is true, one can be united—but this unity is one of thought only, one in which one thinks the "deepest truth" by one's own efforts—but here there is no communion—no communion established by God Himself. This is the point of the assertion that all this talk about the revelation of the Name of God is "primitive anthropomorphism". This argument is simply the despairing defence of the Self which wants to be left alone in its isolation, which does not want to open up, which does not want to be forced out of its position as the centre of existence, which wants to assert itself against the God who created it. Hence the "anthropomorphism"-argument cannot be countered by argument, because it is not merely an error, but *sin*, namely, the sin of the man who wills to be his own god, who will tolerate no other god than that which is identical with the deepest ground of the Self.

This, then, is what is meant by the idea of the Name of God, an idea which is so repellent to those who defend the philo-

[1] John 1, 17.

sophical Idea of God, and one which is so decisive for the
Biblical testimony: the disclosure of the mystery of the nature
of the true personal God through revelation, which can only be
known in this revelation as the nature of the God who imparts
Himself. The God of revelation is the God who can only be
known through revelation; God, as He is conceived outside this
revelation is quite different; He is something that has been
thought, hence He is not personal; He is not the One whose
nature it is to communicate Himself. Thus the Name of God
means the indissoluble unity of the nature of God with the
revelation, not only in the sense that it is the nature of revelation, but that it is the nature of the God of revelation.

The Nature of God is the will to impart Himself. We do not
speak of the True God if we do not speak of Him who imparts
Himself, who wills to be for us, not for Himself alone. Of this
God, however, whose nature it is to impart Himself, we can
only speak on the basis of His self-manifestation. God's "willingness to impart Himself" can indeed be perceived nowhere save
in the act, in the event of His self-impartation. Only in His
presence in revelation is God to be known as He is, who He is;
only there can He be known as the One who is "for us", where
He really is present for us, where He discloses Himself in His
presence in revelation. Hence the Name of God is only completely revealed where God comes to us personally in Jesus
Christ. There alone does He make known the absolute character
of His will to be "for us", where He gives Himself for us. Thus
truth is identical with grace: "Grace and truth came through
Jesus Christ."

# APPENDIX TO CHAPTER 12

The small part the conception of the "Name of God" plays in the dogmatic work of the Church is in striking contrast to the witness of Scripture, which shows—by the very fact of its frequent use—that it is one of the most important ideas in the Bible. In the Old Testament there are nearly one hundred passages, and in the New Testament more than two hundred, which deal with the "Name of the Lord". Above all, the Biblical statement leaves no room for doubt that here we are concerned with the centre of the whole history of revelation and salvation. To use the language of the Biblical-theological *Wörterbuch*, "The Name of God denotes all that God is for man, and it is intended that this truth will cause men to know God; for men, it is the expression of all that God is, since it gathers up all that they know of God, and have in Him. Thus it is the concentrated expression of their knowledge of God which is derived from God Himself—for they owe it to the self-activity of God; He is the source, and the means, of their relation with God. . . . In His "name" God turns towards man, or in the fact that He utters His Name to them, they know what they possess in Him. . . . The Name of God is the expression of all that God is as the saving revelation . . . and it is not only an expression intended for the communication of knowledge, for man's use, . . . it serves to designate the relation of, and intercourse between, person and person" (Hermann Cremer's *Biblisch-theologisches Wörterbuch*, published by J Kögel, ed. II, p. 800).

The idea of the "Name of God" plays almost no part in the theology of the Early Church, or of the Mediaeval Church, in the Biblical sense of the word. On the other hand, it plays a very dubious part, since the Name which was made known on Sinai, especially the interpretation given in $E$[1] (Exodus 3: 14) of the Name "I AM THAT I AM", was adopted by speculative theology and made the foundation of its identification of speculative ontology with the Biblical Idea of God. There are possibly few passages in the Scriptures which have been quoted and expounded more often in mediaeval theology than this

[1] Where the general term "Elohim" is used for God, instead of the personal Name "Yahweh". (TR.)

phrase. Even the Fathers of the Church used it: for instance, Athanasius (*Epistula de synodis*, 35); Hilary (*De Trin. L, I, nr.* 5); Gregory Nazianzen (*Orationes*, 30, 18), and many others. (See the relevant passages in *Rouët de Journel: "Enchiridion patristicum"* on Exod. 3: 14.) The real trouble, however, only started with the penetration of the Neo-Platonic idea of the identification of the *summum esse* and the *summum bonum,* that is, through Augustine: "*Nefas est autem dicere ut subsistat et subsit Deus bonitati suae atque illa bonitas non substantia vel potius essentia, neque Deus sit bonitas sua, sed in illa sit tanquam ubiecto; unde manifestum est Deum abusive substantiam vocari, ut nomine usitatiore intellegatur essentia*" (*De Trin.* 7, 5, 10). Augustine believes that he has found the point at which the Bible and Plato say the same thing: "*Vehementer hoc Plato tenuit et diligentissime commendavit.*" No one ever said this before Plato save in this passage in the Book of Exodus (*De Civ. Dei, VIII, II*). Maritain, indeed, is right when—speaking of this text, understood in *this* sense, he says: "Such passages contain virtually the whole Thomist doctrine of the Divine Names and of the analogy" (*La sagesse augustinienne*, p. 405).

In reality the Biblical text does not say this at all. Quite apart from the fact that the interpretation of the Name of Yahweh in the sense of E plays no part in the whole of the Old Testament, and "the honour given to the Name of Yahweh is completely independent of its etymology" (*Grether, op. cit.,* p. 15), even the interpretation given in E is quite different from that of "the One who IS", or even "Being". (In addition to Grether, see also Eichrodt, *op. cit.,* I, pp. 91 ff.). Even the Septuagint rendering contains a hint of philosophical suggestion which is entirely absent from the Hebrew text. "The Tetragrammaton lays the stress not upon God's Being as He is in Himself, but upon His Being as it comes forth in revelation, not upon the *Deus absolutus*, but upon the *Deus revelatus*" (Grether, p. 7). The mediaeval use of the general interpretation of the Name of Yahweh (in the sense of E) has led to quite disastrous misunderstanding. The chapters in this book which deal with the Being of God and His Attributes, in their opposition to the mediaeval ontology, will show on what my opinion is based. It would be well worth while to write a critical historical account of the exposition of Exodus 3: 14.

It is not only the Name of Yahweh, however, expounded in a speculative manner, which plays an important—though essentially negative—part in mediaeval scholastic theology, but also the notion of the *Divine Names*. Here, too, the "Areopagite" was a pioneer. His work, *De Divinis nominibus*, founded a school of thought. But what he discusses (in this book) under the title of the "Names of God", has nothing to do with what the Bible says about the Name of God. In this book the author is dealing with the question: To what extent are the ideas with which *we*, by means of thought, can try to conceive the Divine Being, adequate for the task? Naturally the answer is entirely negative: God is the One who cannot be named; all our ideas are inadequate. The Divine Nature is unspeakable. Certainly, just as the Divine Being is "nameless", so also it can be described by all kinds of names, just as the One who transcends all existence is also the All-existing (I, 6). We can therefore say everything about God as well as nothing.

Thomas Aquinas (*Summa theol.*, I, 13) introduced this doctrine of the Name of God into his system. By the "Name of God" he, too, understands the ideas by means of which we can "think" God; he, too, has nothing to say about the Biblical understanding of the Name of God. He has eliminated the pantheistic element in the Neo-Platonic teaching of his master, it is true, because at every vital point, by means of the idea of causality, he introduces the thought of Creation, which plays no part in the thought of the Areopagite. Through the fact that to him (Aquinas) the creaturely, as God's creation, is *analogous*, the creaturely ideas also acquire the validity of *analogical* truths. But all this remains within the sphere of the speculative *theologia naturalis* and is therefore diametrically opposed to all that is meant by the Biblical idea of the "Name of God".

In Reformation theology there are no longer any fanciful etymological speculations in connexion with the Name of Yahweh; the link—established by Augustine—between Neo-platonic ontology and the Biblical knowledge of God has disappeared. The Biblical meaning of the idea of the "Name of God" now comes into its own. Luther teaches in the Larger Catechism, on the occasion of the explanation of the first clause (in the Lord's Prayer) that the Name of God "*non aliam ob causam nobis revelatum est quam ut utentibus sit fructuosum*", and thus God is glorified. "To be baptized into the Divine Name" means "*ab ipso Deo baptizari*". And the *Augustana* (Müller, *Die symbolischen Bücher der ev. luth. Kirche*, p. 105) says: "*Nomen significat causam quae allegatur propter quam contigit salus.*" Here the personalist meaning, and its connexion with revelation, has been rediscovered as the meaning of the

Idea: the "Name" is the self-revelation which creates communion. In post-Reformation theology it was Chemnitz, in the main, who saw the significance of this idea for the right doctrine of God: *"Deus vult ita cognosci et invocari sicut se patefacit"* ... A theologian of the Cross does not speak of the nameless Majesty of the Absolute, but he clings to the revealed Name of God. *"De Deo non aliter sentiendum quam sicut se seu nomen eius (Christi) dato verbo revelavit"* (Chemnitz, *Loci theologici*).

The Principle of Scripture, rightly understood, is identical with the theology of the revealed Name of God.

Among the Reformed theologians, the perception of the significance of the idea of the "Name of God" is less clear than in the thought of Luther and his closest disciples; this is true in particular of all (Protestant) Scholastics, both Lutheran and Reformed. In the thought of Calvin the tendency to take a rigidly literal view of the Bible, which developed into the doctrine of Verbal Inspiration, comes out in the fact that Revelation and Scripture are regarded as identical; thus the connexion between revelation and the Name of God was lost. In Calvin's thought, too, there was a stronger tendency to lean upon Augustine, which made him less critical of Augustine's Neo-Platonism than Luther was. But—for the whole of post-Reformation theology—it was serious that "Natural Theology" was reintroduced in the sense that the doctrine of God was opened with a chapter entitled *"de existentia et notione dei"*, in which the various Proofs for the Existence of God are classified and discussed. The theology based on revelation once more leans on Natural Theology.

It is strange that even in the revival of Biblical-Reformation theology—whether on the "Biblical" or on the "Confessional" side—there seems little or no understanding of the importance of the Name of God. The only exception, so far as I know—here, too, as at so many other points—is von Oettingen, who begins his work on the Doctrine of God with a chapter on the *Name of God (Lutherische Dogmatik*, II, I, pp. 54 ff.): "The power to know God . . . depends on the fact that God knows Himself, and through His revealed Name . . . which we as human beings can grasp . . . draws near to us" (p. 66). Even with Karl Barth, whose fundamental tendency should have attracted him to this subject, we miss any adequate estimate of the significance of the idea of the Name of God.[1] On the other hand, the increasing tendency among so many dogmatic theologians to

---

[1] Save for a slight suggestion in II, 1, p. 306.

devote their attention to particular names of God in the Bible must be regarded as an unfruitful proceeding.

## (2) THE "NATURAL" KNOWLEDGE OF GOD; THE PROBLEM OF THE "THEOLOGIA NATURALIS"

In recent times, and rightly, the question whether—from the standpoint of the Christian Faith—God can be known outside the historical revelation, is to be answered in the affirmative, or in the negative, is now regarded as a fundamental problem and, like few other problems of this kind, has led to varied and passionate controversies. The very fact of the passionate feeling which has been aroused (a display of emotion which in itself may be deplored) and with which this conflict has been waged, shows that we are here dealing with a decisive question of the first importance. But here, too, the passionate concern for clarity of thought has not always been an advantage; it has indeed led to misunderstandings and misinterpretations which create grave hindrances to the clarification of the problem. Since I myself, by the use of a misleading idea, am bound to admit that I have caused some of the chief misunderstanding, I feel obliged to make yet another attempt to clear up the difficulty.

(i) First of all, we must make a clear distinction between two questions which, unfortunately, are continually being confused with one another: the question of the revelation in Creation, and the question of man's natural knowledge of God. While one side was mainly anxious to deny the validity of a *"theologia naturalis"*, the other side was chiefly concerned to affirm the reality of the revelation in Creation. Now some theologians believed (mistakenly) that their denial of a *"theologia naturalis"* obliged them also to deny the reality of the revelation in Creation; this was due to their mistaken idea that the acknowledgment of a revelation in Creation must necessarily lead to the recognition of a *"theologia naturalis"*. I myself, however, helped to foster this mistaken equation of the revelation in Creation with Natural Theology (which I contested from the very outset), to this extent, that in the first edition of *Natur und Gnade* I described the Christian doctrine of the revelation in Creation by the misleading expression of a "Christian *theologia naturalis*". On the other side, however, it is evident that the correction of this unfortunate phrase, to which I drew special attention in the second edition of this brochure, has not been noticed.

The affirmation of a revelation in Creation has, in itself,

nothing whatever to do with a belief in Natural Theology. A theology which intends to remain true to the Biblical witness to revelation should never have denied the reality of revelation in Creation. All efforts to contest the Biblical evidence for such a revelation must lead to an arbitrary exegesis, and to forced interpretations of the text of the Bible. But even apart from explicit Biblical evidence, the Christian Idea of the Creator should itself force us to admit the reality of a revelation in Creation; for what sort of Creator would not imprint the mark of His Spirit upon His Creation?

(ii) The question whether the "natural man", that is, the man who has not yet been affected by the historical revelation, is in a position to perceive this divine revelation in Creation as such, in accordance with its nature and its meaning, is a quite different question. This question, therefore, has not been answered when we have answered the former question in the affirmative, because between the revelation in Creation and the natural man there stands the fact of Sin.

If it is a mistake, and from the standpoint of the Bible and theology an impossibility, to contest the reality of the revelation in Creation, it is no less mistaken to deny the negative significance of sin for the perception of the truth of the revelation in Creation. Sin not only perverts the will, it also "obscures" the power of perceiving truth where the knowledge of God is concerned. So where a man supports the view of the reality of a *"theologia naturalis"* in the sense of correct, valid knowledge, he is actually denying the reality of sin, or at least its effect in the sphere of man's knowledge of God. Thus, on the one hand, the reality of the revelation in Creation is to be admitted, but, on the other hand, the possibility of a correct and valid natural knowledge of God is to be contested.

(iii) Now, however, the problem is complicated by the fact that when we have said that we must question the possibility of a valid knowledge of God (to the natural man), we have not said all there is to say. There is, it is true, no valid "natural theology", but there is a Natural Theology which, in fact, exists. The place to discuss this, however, is not in connexion with the doctrine of God, for here it has no theological validity, but in connexion with the doctrine of Man; for "natural theology" is an anthropological fact, which no one can deny. Human beings, even those who know nothing of the historical revelation, are such that they cannot help forming an idea of God and making pictures of God in their minds. The history of the religions of mankind provides incontrovertible evidence of this fact. The formation of theological ideas is an empirical fact of the reality of sinful humanity. This fact cannot be denied; all that we can contest is how it should be interpreted. From the standpoint of the Christian Faith, on the basis of the Biblical testimony, how are we to interpret this fact?

(iv) The chief passage in the Bible which deals with this question—Romans 1: 19 ff.—gives the interpretation which alone can stand the test of theological examination. The fact that sinful human beings cannot help having thoughts about God is due to the revelation in Creation. The other fact, that human beings are not able rightly to understand the nature and meaning of this revelation in Creation is due to the fact that their vision has been distorted by sin.

"Sin obscures men's vision to such an extent that in the place of 'God' they 'know' or imagine 'gods' . . . so that God's revelation in Creation is turned into lying pictures of idols" (*Natur und Gnade*, First ed., p. 14). In this sentence I tried to say three things: (a) that the revelation in Creation is a reality; (b) that Natural Theology, as a legitimate possibility, does not exist; (c) that the fact of Natural Theology as an empirical fact, as something which belongs to the nature of the natural man, is understood in its ambiguity. But the doctrine of the Apostle, in spite of its brevity, takes us a step further.

(v) The Apostle cannot be interested in the theoretical question: how are we to explain the *"theologia naturalis"* of the pagan sinful man or woman; but the question which interests him is this: How should we address the man to whom the message of Jesus Christ is to be proclaimed? This question he answers thus: Sinful man is responsible for his sin, because in the revelation in Creation the possibility is given him of knowing God. He is responsible for his idolatry: he is ἀναπολόγητος, "without excuse". Thus, according to the Biblical teaching, the doctrine of general revelation becomes actual in anthropology. Human responsibility is based upon the general revelation.

The quality that makes man "human" is derived from the revelation in Creation, from the relation which God established at the very outset between man and the Creator. Responsible existence—that is, the existence of man in contrast to that of every other creature, is his existence as *person*. Even sinful man does not cease to be a responsible person; this responsible personal existence, which is grounded in the Creation, cannot be lost.

It is very cheering to note that Karl Barth, in his exposition of the narrative of the Creation in Genesis 1: 26ff. has come to the same conclusion. The fact that man has been created in the Image of God (taught in this passage) means responsible existence, the "Thou"-relation with the Creator, which is the basis of the "Thou"-relation with one's fellow man; and *this* fact: namely, that we have been created in the Image of God, cannot be lost (*Kirchl. Dogm.*, III, I, p. 224).

The Fall does not mean that man ceases to be responsible, but that he ceases to understand his responsibility aright, and to live according to his responsibility. Sin, far from eliminating responsibility, and thus *this* vestige of the *Imago Dei*, is, on the contrary, a witness to God-willed responsibility, just as the sinful illusion of idolatry is a witness to the God-given revelation in Creation. The idolatrous images of man—whether they be the massive structures of wood or brass, or the idolatrous abstractions of speculative theology—accuse man, because to him has been given another possibility of the knowledge of God. It is sin which makes idols out of the revelation in Creation.

(vi) This Biblical view of the natural man, and of his *theologia naturalis*, can, and must, be examined in the light of historic facts. What is the result of this examination?

The history of religions shows that mankind cannot help producing religious ideas, and carrying on religious activities. It also shows the confusion caused by sin. The multiplicity of religious ideas of God, and of the "gods", is so vast, and so contradictory, that it is impossible to gather it all up in one positive conception, as the result of research; to reach such a result by a process of elimination is not the task of religion itself but of philosophy. Whither it leads will be shown directly.

Within this welter of religious conceptions of God it is impossible to discover one common denominator. The "higher religions" are contrasted with the primitive religions, and the contradictions are too great to be overcome. There is no common element which could do justice at the same time to the polytheistic personalism of the one, and the monistic impersonalism of the other. (Cf. my *Religionsphilosophie protestantischer Theologie*, pp. 51 ff. and *Offenbarung und Vernunft*, pp. 215 ff.)

(vii) From the beginning of Greek philosophy men have continually tried to reach a clear and certain knowledge of God, not along the path of religion, but by the way of philosophy, by speculative thought, and thus to overcome the irrationalism of the purely religious formation of ideas. These philosophical doctrines of God now confront one another in irreconcilable opposition. Above all, none of them can possibly be combined with the Christian Idea of God. The relation of the "God" of Plato or of Aristotle with the God of the Biblical revelation is that of the Either-Or. The same may be said of every other idea of God which has been attained purely by philosophical speculation. The reason for this will be given in the next chapter: the God of thought *must* differ from the God of revelation. The God who is "conceived" by thought is not the one who discloses Himself; from this point of view He is an intellectual idol. (Cf. *Offenbarung und Vernunft*, pp. 43 ff. and Chapters 20–23.)

## CHAPTER 13

## GOD, THE LORD

WHAT, then, is the "Name", the revealed *Nature* of God, which is disclosed in His revelation? From the standpoint of the revelation in the Bible there is only one answer—primary, fundamental, or possible: He reveals Himself as the LORD. "I am the Lord, thy God."[1] God does not define His Nature: He does not teach us about His Nature. He addresses us as One who is Himself, and this address which begins with "I" is in itself the revelation. The theological doctrine of God, therefore, must not begin with the effort to make an abstract definition of the Nature of God, but with the description of this majestic "I, the Lord, thy God".[2]

"I, even I, am the LORD; and beside Me there is no Saviour"[3] —this is the affirmation of Monotheism as opposed to polytheism. The uniqueness of God, even in the Jewish creed, in the Shema of Israel,[4] is not an independent theme. The fact that He is Lord—or more precisely, the way in which God reveals His sovereignty—implies, as a matter of course, that no other can lay claim to this title. Because, and in so far as, Israel has known the Lord, she has known the uniqueness of God. Monotheism is neither a characteristically Christian view nor even a Biblical one, save as an inference derived from the truth that God is the Lord.

Even to begin with the doctrine of the Godhead would not be in harmony with the testimony of the Biblical revelation. For even this idea is too rational, too little related to revelation, to be used as the central statement of the Faith which is based upon revelation. The only passage where it is used explicitly in the sense of the definition of the Nature (of God) is not connected with the historical revelation, but the prehistorical, that is, the revelation in Creation.[5] In harmony with the historical revelation there is another conception, one which is clearly related to revelation, which contains, it is true, both the fact of "deity" and the truth of His Uniqueness, but

[1] Exod. 20: 2.
[2] It is no accident that in the Bible more than 1,000 sentences begin with this Divine "I".         [3] Is. 43: 11.
[4] Deut. 6: 4. On the exposition of this passage cf. Eichrodt, *op. cit.*, p. 113.
[5] Rom. 1: 20. θειότης. The related idea θεότης is to be understood as an attribute in the only passage where it occurs: Col. 2: 9.

137

which, from the very outset, combines both truths with the "I" who addresses man, containing them as elements in this Self-existence which is proclaimed in the words: God is the Lord.

The translators of the LXX were strictly accurate when they unhesitatingly rendered the Name of Yahweh by the title of "Lord". The Name of Yahweh, as a proper name, was an historical necessity so long as it was necessary to distinguish this Lord, the true Lord of Israel, from the false "lords", from the Baalim of the Near East, which were of no concern to Israel. For Israel the Name of Yahweh meant from the very beginning the God of revelation and of the Covenant, who had revealed Himself to Israel—and to this people alone—as Lord, and indeed as the Lord who was alone in His sovereignty, and only thus to be worshipped. This "Lord" was distinguished from all the Baalim of the surrounding countries by the very fact that He, in His self-originating action, as the One who was not involved in the course of Nature, but Himself was Lord, had mightily intervened in History. In this historical revelation He showed Himself from the outset as One who was quite different from the Baalim, who were essentially connected with the course of Nature, and were thought only to manifest themselves in the processes of Nature. Yahweh is the One who was not "there" already, who was not connected with that which was already given, but the One who elected freely, who Himself established man's relationship with God, who showed Himself in His action in history, and in His self-revelation, as the Lord over all that is "given" and "natural". From His nature which manifested itself more and more in the historical character of His revelation, increasingly His uniqueness, and His sovereignty over the whole of Nature, His Creative Power, became known. Once this had taken place, then His proper name became merely a sign which could finally disappear and, without any danger of confusion with the Baalim, could be replaced by the title "Lord". "I—Yahweh—I am the LORD—and beside Me there is no Saviour", or, as it was expressed later on: "I am the Lord". This absolute and unique "I", beside whom there can be none else: this "I" who alone summons us to "hear" Him, and this "Thou" to whom alone we are to turn for succour absolutely—this is the meaning of "Lord", just as in a remarkable passage in Hosea we read: "It is Thou!" It is from this point that dogmatic reflection must start, from this absolute Lord, not from a neutral definition of the Godhead; to it dogmatics must continually return; to describe this "I" is its sole task.

(1) This implies that God is Subject: addressing us, making Himself known to us.

The God with whom we have to do in faith, is not a Being who has been discussed or "conceived" (by man); He is not an *Ens*, a "substance", like the Godhead of metaphysical speculation; He is not an object of thought—even though in a sublimated and abstract form—but the Subject who as "I" addresses us as "thou". God is the Personality who speaks, acts, disclosing to us Himself and His will.

Philosophers have always raised objections to the use of the ideas of "personality" or "person" for the formulation of the Idea of God, just as they have objected to the idea of the "Name", on the ground that it is "anthropomorphic". "Who", they ask, "gives us the right to take the conception of personality, gained from our own human experience, and to apply it to God?" They contend that to do this makes the Idea of God finite, which is entirely improper; for even though we may intensify the concept of personality to the highest degree possible, this Idea of God still makes Him too human, creaturely and earthly. The "personal God" is a naïve idea, unworthy of the Divinity, a product of the imagination which delights in creating myths. "Personality is the specific form of subsistence of the human spirit or mind as finite."[1] But if we ask: "How, then, should the statement be worded?—What are the alternatives to the idea of the Personal God?"—then all the answers that are given, however they may be expressed, finally say the same thing: God is an "It", not an "I"; He is an Object of thought, something that is constructed in thought, not One who Himself speaks, but a Neuter—an *ens a se, ens subsistens per se, the* Absolute, *the* Inexpressible, the absolute Substance, etc. God is "the Being who is in Himself Being" (Biedermann),[2] "the eternal movement of the Universal which is always making itself subject" (Strauss).[3] These conceptions of God which are supposed to be so "spiritual" are, in fact, the attenuated conception of an "object", weakened by abstraction.

Can we really think that a Supreme Object gained by a process of abstraction is a more worthy conception of God than

---

[1] Biedermann, *Dogmatik.* Para. 716.
[2] *Op. cit.*, para. 712.
[3] *Christliche Glaubenslehre*, I, p. 523.

the concept of Person? The highest that we know is not the "it", the "thing", but the person. We know the person as that which makes itself known to us through speaking to us, through revealing himself in speech. Hence, since God Himself speaks to us, and in so doing manifests Himself to us, the idea of "person" is the only one which is appropriate to describe Him.

Now, however, the question whether the application of the idea of "person" to God is an anthropomorphism, receives a remarkable answer from the standpoint of the Biblical idea of God, such an answer indeed, that it cuts away the ground from underneath the feet of the question itself. The question is not whether *God* is personality, but whether *man* is. It is not the personal being of God which is "anthropomorphic", but, conversely, the personal being of man is a "theomorphism". God alone is truly Person; man is only person in a symbolic way, as a reflection of God, as the *Imago Dei*. God is *only* Subject, He is not also Object; He is the absolute Subject, subject in the unconditional, unlimited sense. Man, however, is a subject which is also an object. The Self of man, indeed, is enclosed in a body, in a material form which fills space; it is therefore "subject" only in a conditional, limited sense. He is a "Self" and an "it"; he is personal and impersonal at one and the same time. Hence man is only "person" in a parabolic, symbolic sense, "person" who is at the same time "not-person", a "thing". God is pure personality; man is not. That which constitutes the nature of the "subject" in contradistinction to that of "object": namely, freedom, positing and not being posited, thinking and not being thought, that which is absolutely spontaneous, that which is only active and not at the same time passive, that which only gives and does not at the same time receive—we cannot infer this from our existence as "subject" or "person" in such a way that we could then "project" it on to God; but we only come to know this truth as the nature of the God who reveals Himself; only when we perceive this do we realize that we—ourselves—as human beings—are addressed by God; we respond to His Call; and in this act of response we become aware that we are responsible persons. In so far as responsibility is the essence of human personal existence as known to us, it already contains that which constitutes the basis of this responsibility, that which creates our responsive, responsible nature, the personal being of God as primary. Human personal existence is the existence which is called into existence by God. That which the natural man in his conscience

feels dimly as the sense of responsibility, only becomes clear
and plain in the encounter with the God who reveals Himself,
and in this revelation lays His demands upon us. The LORD
GOD is the presupposition of our responsible personal being.
Our responsibility springs from His calling; from His self-
revelation as our Lord we have the knowledge of our personal
dignity, of our symbolic personal being, as the reflection of His
self-revealing, unconditioned, personal dignity, of His majesty
as LORD.

Hence it is so essential that in our thinking about God we
should always start from the original situation of faith: God
who addresses us in His revelation of Himself, God who meets
us as the Sovereign "I", and in so doing alone gives us the
dignity and responsibility of persons. This shows us the confusion that is created when the doctrine of God, instead of
starting from this disclosure of His personal Being as Subject,
starts from any kind of neutral definition of being, such as that
of the theology determined by Platonism, Aristotelianism, and
Neo-Platonism. The idea of God of faith is only gained in the
sphere of faith, not in that of metaphysical, neutral thinking,
which only produces neutral "objective" results. True theological thought should never leave the dimension of revelation,
the "I-Thou" relation, in order to pass into the dimension of
the "It". Since *thinking about* God continually leads theologians
to slip into the tendency to regard Him as an *object*, they need
continually to reverse this tendency by moving back to the
original situation: revelation-faith. True theology, therefore,
must not only *begin* with the knowledge of God as the absolute
Subject; its one, its sole task, is to make this clear.

(2) God meets us in revelation as the unconditioned Subject
in such a way that He claims us unconditionally for Himself;
thus He meets us as Absolute Lord. This truth contains two
elements: one ideal, and one actual. The ideal or logical element
is His claim on us; the actual element is the apprehension of us
in actual fact. God reveals Himself as One who has an absolute
right to lay His claim upon us; and He reveals Himself as One
who exercises absolute power over us. We gather up both these
elements in the idea of the Divine sovereign majesty. These
two elements—the Ideal and the Actual—which we distinguish in the process of thought, are one in revelation itself.
Because God has absolute power, He has the absolute right
over us; and in the fact that He lays His absolute claim upon

141

us, we perceive His absolute authority as "Lord". Since God lays His absolute claim upon *us*, who are parts of this world, He reveals Himself to us as absolute Power, the power from which all other power is derived. Only as this power—as the power of the Creator—is He able to assert an absolute right over us. We belong to Him unconditionally, because He has created us. But we do not first of all know that God is Creator, and then, on the basis of this knowledge, acknowledge His sovereignty as Lord; but, because He manifests Himself to us as the absolute Lord, we know both truths at once: His unconditional claim (the Ideal) and His absolute power, His being as Creator (the Actual).

The whole course of the history of revelation bears out this statement. Israel, first of all, knew Yahweh as "Lord"—and then as "Creator", not the other way round. Hence the Biblical idea of the Creator, the one which holds the field in the sphere of faith, is quite different from the philosophical idea of the Maker of the world, the *prima causa*, the πρῶτον κινοῦν, etc. The being of God as Creator is that which is known in and through His Being as Lord. The statement: God is the Creator, is therefore not a theoretical statement about the way in which the world came into existence, but it is primarily a statement about our unconditional responsibility. In revealing Himself as Lord, God reveals Himself as absolute Subject, who has both absolute power and fullness of Being.

(3) Mediaeval theology—and its successors in Lutheran and Reformed scholasticism—describes what we mean by the idea of "absolute Lord" by three philosophical ideas: Aseity, the Absolute, and the *actus purus*. What do these strangely abstract ideas mean?

The idea of Aseity, first used by St. Anselm,[1] that is, of the "*a se esse*", expresses the truth that the Being of God is not dependent, it is not an "*esse ab alio*", but an independent being, an "*esse a se*". There is no objection to this idea, although at first sight it looks so remote and abstract, presupposing, of course, that it is used for a closer definition of the Sovereignty of God, but not for the speculative, metaphysical, artificial construction of the Idea of God. This presupposition, however, is rarely found among the Scholastics—whether of ancient or of modern times. Indeed, they do not start from revelation, thus they do not explain what is given in and with this revelation,

[1] *Monologium*, 6.

but, by means of ontological speculation, by the "Way" of abstraction, they "construct" the Idea of God. Once this has happened, these philosophical ideas tend to obscure the Christian Idea of God, since they weaken the truth of God as Personal Being.

If, however, we begin at the other end, with the self-revelation of God as Lord, then the idea of Aseity—as well as both the other conceptions—may serve to clarify our thinking. In point of fact, the Biblical witness uses expressions which come very close to this philosophical statement, at least to some extent—God is the First and the Last;[1] He is without beginning and without end.[2] He "only hath immortality",[3] and He alone "hath life in Himself".[4] None has created Him, the Creator of all. None has taught Him, the Thinker of all—Providence.[5] As a closer definition of His Being as Lord, of His absolute existence as Subject, the idea of Aseity—however it may be formulated—is indispensable, in spite of the fact that, on the one hand, the construction of this idea of Aseity does not lead us to the idea of God as absolute Lord. The Scholastics say: the "*ens a se*" is the personal, the Lord God. We say, the Lord is, as absolute Subject, "*a se*", independent.

It is the same with the idea of the Absolute. This idea plays a dubiously dual part. The idea of the Absolute, understood as something neuter, is simply the final abstraction of the idea of the object, the "It". We may indeed say that "the Absolute" is the final modification in abstract terms of the idea of the world. Is it not indeed the idea which is reached by a process of "leaving out", by abstraction from concrete being, as the most general conception there can be, beyond all that is particular?

It is, of course, true that modern Idealism believes that it can get rid of this neutral element in the idea of the Absolute gained from Being, since it takes the "I" and not the "It" as the starting-point. That is the meaning of the transition from Spinoza's "substance" to Fichte's "Self". Here, indeed, by the way of speculation, it seems as though the idea of the absolute Subject, and thus of the Lord God, had been attained. But this is an illusion. For since the idea of the Divine Creation—and rightly so, from this abstract, speculative point of view—is rejected as an impossibility for thought ("a creation cannot possibly be conceived"),[6] the being of God and the being of the

---

[1] Is. 44: 6.     [2] Gen. 1: 1; Ps. 102: 23.     [3] 1 Tim. 6: 16.
[4] John 5: 26.     [5] Job 38.
[6] Fichte, *Ausgewählte Werke*, VI, p. 191.

world are equated in this instance from the standpoint of the subject, instead of from that of the object; thus here, too, the idea of the Absolute merges into something which is neuter, an "It", even if this "It" is called "Spirit". Here "Spirit"—because it is not the Creator Spirit—means that which is ultimate for thought, the final attainment of our thinking, the Object of our thought. Hence, also, this idea of the Absolute, in spite of the fact that it starts from the Subject and not from the Object, is impersonal, and the God whom it conceives is an impersonal God, and not "the Lord". Therefore the speculative idea of the Absolute—whether it be conceived in the manner of Spinoza or of Hegel—in the history of modern thought is opposed to the Christian understanding of God, just as it used to work against it in secret, in earlier days.[1]

If, however, the idea of the Absolute is not taken as the basis, but as the means of intellectual clarification of the revealed nature of God's Being, then it is not only useful but indispensable. Indeed, from the standpoint of the revelation of God as Lord, we can say: Only God the Lord is truly Absolute. *The* Absolute, for the very reason that it is something neuter, an "It", cannot be truly absolute.

The neutral Absolute is merely distinguished from the non-Absolute, from the Relative, as the whole is distinguished from the part, or the presupposition from the concrete statement. Being, understood in its totality, is the Absolute; thus the Absolute is never without the non-absolute, *this* "God" is never without the world; or, rather, He is the world as a whole. Or, from the point of view of the Subject: the absolute Self is never without the relative, the empirical human "I" (or Self); God, thus understood, is the "depth of the Self", the "basis of the Self". In both conceptions, however, God is not the Lord of the world, nor is He the Lord of the Self. He is not really above the world and above the Self. In the true sense of the word, the Lord of the world alone is Absolute, He who created the world in freedom, and is still creating it, and therefore is not bound to the world and the Self, but who posits them in His sovereign freedom and binds them to Himself. Only the Free is the Absolute; but this One who is Free can never be known by the way of thought—for only the Necessary can be found thus, but never the Free. God, as the One who is free, as the Lord of the Self, and the Lord of the world, can only be known where, in His free revelation, He gives Himself to be

[1] On this see below, Chap. 17.

known. Only the thought of God which is in accordance with revelation, as the Creator Lord, fulfils that which the concept of the Absolute of thought seems to provide: it alone shows us the truly Unconditioned as the nature of that which is conditioned neither by being nor by thought. Of Him alone can it be said that He is *"a se esse"*. Only where this idea of the Absolute is preceded by the idea of Creator—understood in the Biblical sense—in which the *"a se esse"* and the *"ab alio esse"*, necessity and contingency, are distinguished from each other, can we speak in the strict sense of an *"a se esse"* and of the Absolute. As a clarifying idea alongside of the idea of God the Lord given in revelation, both these secondary theological ideas receive their full meaning, while as fundamental ideas of speculative thought they cannot provide what they promise.

Finally the third, and at first sight the more remote and the most abstract of the three conceptions, that of the *"actus purus"*, certainly ought not to be rejected in connexion with the doctrine of God as Lord. It simply states that in God there is no mere potentiality or receptivity, or need, but that God is the pure activity who posits, creates, gives. Fundamentally, it means the same as the formula: God is Spirit,[1] or to be more exact: God is Pure Spirit: He is not flesh, He is not *Basar*, that is, He is not receptive and receiving Nature.[2]

In so far as God also suffers in the sense of "suffering with" (sympathy); reacts—in the sense of hearing prayer; is "thoughtful" for man—and thus is conditioned in His action, this receptivity springs wholly out of His free willing and positing, out of the fact that He makes Himself finite, condescends to us in free self-limitation, which is based wholly in Himself, in His freedom. Where He does not make Himself passive, God is pure activity, spontaneity, freedom. The corresponding Biblical expression is: the Living God, the God who is the Source of all life.[3] God alone is pure Energy, while all that we otherwise call *energy* also contains the element of indolence, dullness, slackness, in short, that of defective vitality. Only the Spirit, Pure Spirit, is pure Activity, pure Energy. Only the Subject which is wholly subject and in no way object, has unconditional freedom, unlimited vitality, unlimited independence, purely positing, originally creative Power.

[1] Is. 31: 3; John 4: 24.
[2] Otherwise Karl Barth, *op. cit.*, II, 1, pp. 300 ff. in remarkable contrast to the preceding doctrine of the Freedom of God.       [3] Ps. 36: 10.

(4) The sovereign personality of God in the Bible is usually expressed by the idea of "Creator". This means something fundamentally different from those philosophical ideas which are so often taken to be the equivalent of the idea of the Creator; *prima causa*, Prime Mover, the Ground of the world, the Origin. These are all, in their suspiciously neutral character, fundamentally different from the idea of the Creator and Lord. A cause is not a Causer, a Prime Mover is not a Creator, a foundation of the world is not He who calls the world into existence, the Origin is not the One who originates. One cannot replace a Subject, an acting Person, by something neuter without injury.

All these neutral ideas are not only themselves neutral, but they also leave us neutral; they do not make any demand upon us. The fact that we think these ideas does not make us any different. They do not turn a person who prides himself upon being the "captain of his soul" into a "servant of God", into a person who is bound to God in reverence and obedience. We may hold these ideas, and still remain masters of our own fate; since it is indeed we who have conceived these ideas. The Creator-God, whom man has "conceived" in his own mind, the *prima causa*, the Prime Mover, corresponds to the self-determining existence of the "intellectual", just as the fact of the Creator, who is man's "Lord", corresponds to the existence of the believer, of one who loves, receives, and is responsible. Those abstract apparent equivalents for the idea of the Creator show themselves to be in opposition to the true idea of the Creator in the fact that in them God appears to be as much determined by the world as the world is determined by God. Those who use them want to overcome, it is true, the pantheistic equation of God and the world, and to vindicate the priority of God over the world. But they are not successful. The principle of correlation does not permit it. "If the universe is to be understood through God, then also the Nature of God must be understood through the universe",[1] is a characteristic statement of one of these philosophical "Theists". The God who is the result of thought cannot be set free from the thinker and his world. Philosophical Theism, the effort to "think" the Creator and the Creation, always remains a hopeless enterprise.

From this we can understand the protest of the logical thinker: "Hence the positing of a Creation is the first criterion

[1] Pringle Pattison, *The Idea of God*, 1920, p. 304.

of falseness, the denial of such a Creation . . . the first criterion
of truth (sc. philosophical) is the doctrine of religion."

"A creation cannot really be conceived by thought—that is,
by the process of that which we may call genuine thinking . . .
and no human being has ever yet thought thus."[1] To the continuity of thought upon which the argument is based there
corresponds the continuity of that which is thus argued: the
God who is conceived by the world and by man is continuous
with man and the world. The necessity for thought which
posits Him, does not leave Him the freedom which belongs to
the true Creator and Lord. In point of fact, the idea of the
Creator of faith—and in this we must admit that Fichte is right
—for one who recognizes nothing but the necessity of thought
is absurd, or so to speak, a sin against the spirit of pure thought.
That which is not necessarily thought is "not really thought";
it is merely the conception of a fanciful imagination.[2]

The belief in Creation of the Biblical revelation breaks down
the continuity of self-thought by the fact that it is not man,
but God, who posits it. In this positing God reveals Himself as
the free Lord, and His free underived act as the beginning of
all things. Precisely because this is so the world is posited as a
freely posited, irrational, contingent fact. Never can thought of
itself build up the idea of a contingent, non-necessary, freely-
posited world, just as indeed the very idea of contingency was
unknown in ancient philosophical thought.

The Creator alone is the free Lord God, and only in His free,
self-sovereign revelation is He to be known thus. He gives
Himself to be known—thus, and only because He gives this
truth can its content be the freedom of God.

Thus the Creator God and the Revealer God, Creation and
Revelation, belong together: only the Creator, the free Lord,
who "before" the world, and independently of the world,
creates it in freedom, can be the Revealer who in freedom
testifies to Himself in the world; and only upon the basis of,
and in this free revelation can He be known as the Lord God,
who alone is fully free. Only the God who cannot be conceived
by us, but who gives Himself to us to be known, can truly be
known as Creator; and only the Lord who stands over against
His world and our thought in freedom can reveal Himself

[1] Fichte, *Ausgewählte Werke*, VI, p. 191.
[2] This is probably the reason why Plato, when he speaks of a Creator of the
world, uses the form of myth. He cannot accept philosophical responsibility
for this idea.

therein with freedom. Only He who stands free and unhindered above the law of the world, and above the law of thought, is in truth Creator and Lord; and the proof of this His freedom above the law of the world and above the law of thought is His revelation, the "offence" for thought. This His revelation as the Lord is, however, not only the "offence" for *thought*; far more is it an "offence" to the man who wants to control his own life; for this truth makes an end of our self-sufficiency and makes us the servants of God.

(5) But this is not the last word. The highest manifestation of His freedom as Lord is not that God claims our obedience for Himself. The law of the king manifests his rights and his power as king; but still more does this become evident in the fact that where a man is to be condemned according to his law the king acquits him; he has the right to pardon. The highest manifestation of the freedom of God takes place where He sets the sinner free, where He, the King, gives to the rebel soul the life which had been forfeited. He proves Himself as Lord, who stands above the Law which He himself has laid down. Hence the revelation of God as Lord is not fully completed in the prophetic revelation; it is only fulfilled where God, as the generous Giver, in His own Person intervenes in the distorted relation of man with Him, where He, who has royal claims, in royal sovereignty takes the part of the accused, and sets him free from the guilt which separates him, the sinner, from the Creator.

The self-revelation of God in the claim through the Word of the Prophets is not the highest point of the revelation of the Lord, because it is still an indirect revelation which points to something beyond. The prophetic Word is only an indication pointing to the Lord, the Lord is not yet Himself present in person, therefore not in actual sovereignty. This only takes place where the Ruler Himself is present—just as previously His Word was present—in the act of revealing Himself. Where the Βασιλεία τοῦ Θεοῦ ἔφθασεν[1]—where the Ruler Himself is actually present, there alone is the Lord revealed as "Lord". That is why, in the New Testament, the title of "Lord" is transferred to Jesus. He is the κύριος because in Him God exercises His sovereignty in His revealed presence, not merely any longer vicariously and indirectly through the word of the Prophets, but directly and immediately through Him who

[1] Matt. 12: 28.

Himself has royal authority, and can say in His own Person: "I, I am the Lord." "I therefore say unto you . . ."

(6) One final point must be mentioned, in view of the history of theology. At two points we note the perversion of Christian theology, which has been caused by the intrusion of speculative philosophical motives of thought into the thought of revelation: first of all, in the fact that usually the doctrine of the Nature of God precedes a doctrine of the Existence of God. Secondly, in the fact that a distinction is made between the "metaphysical" and the "ethical" definitions in the Idea of God.

(a) In the chapter "de existentia Dei" usually the various Proofs for the Existence of God are formulated. This proceeding is based upon the strange idea that the existence of God must first of all be established before we can speak of His nature as manifested in His revelation. This enigma is solved as soon as we become aware that such thinkers are not dealing so much with the question of the Nature of God on the basis of His revelation, as upon the basis of metaphysical speculative ideas. The doctrine of the "metaphysical" Being of God—that was the second point—is not only by its content, but also by the methods of its metaphysics, not theology. If one has departed so far from the proper path of theology, from the exclusive orientation towards revelation, then the presupposition of the Proofs for the Existence of God, in order to make His existence seem more solid, is not such a great aberration, after all.

Actually, however, behind both these points there lies the same misunderstanding. The existence of God, of which faith speaks, proves itself only as completely sufficient where the Nature of God is manifested: in revelation. In apologetics, indeed, relations may be established between the revealed faith, and rational metaphysics, with its Proofs for the existence of God; but within Christian doctrine itself there is no place for them.

The God in whom we believe cannot be "proved", and the God who can be proved is not the God of faith. We do not want, first of all, to be convinced of the existence of God by Proofs, and after that to believe in the God of revelation. The existence of God becomes certain to us in and with the revelation in which He manifests Himself to us as the Living Lord, and proves Himself to us.

Whatever value the "Proofs" may have, they are of no concern for faith. Faith does not want to hear about them. The God who is "proved" by human reason is not the God who reveals Himself to man as his Lord.

(b) But even the distinction between "metaphysical" and "ethical" statements about God arises from the same misunderstanding. If we have to do with the God of revelation, who is the Lord, the sovereign "I"—where is the possibility of making a distinction between the "metaphysical" and the "ethical"? Is the Sovereign Being of God "metaphysical", or is it "ethical"? This distinction is only possible where one starts from a neutral—actually from a metaphysical, speculative—concept of being, but not where—from the very outset—one has to do with the revelation of the Lord. The Being of God as Lord, if we must use this somewhat dubious distinction at all, is both metaphysical and ethical. Metaphysically speaking, it is the ONE WHO IS who alone gives existence to all other forms of being. Ethically speaking, it is the will of the Lord from which every kind of ethos is derived. Hence we will now take leave of this false, misleading distinction as a rudiment of that "natural theology" with which the Christian doctrine of God is not concerned.

# APPENDIX TO CHAPTER 13

THE PHILOSOPHICAL IDEA OF GOD IN HISTORY

If we wish to examine the question whether the philosophical idea of God is necessarily different from that of revealed religion, historically, then we must first of all note that the whole of Western philosophy, from the beginning of Christianity, moves within the sphere influenced by the Christian tradition. It has never yet been proved that a philosopher who sets out to formulate the philosophical idea of God can deliberately renounce all dependence on the Christian tradition; without himself being aware of the fact, it is at least possible that some of the heuristic principles which guide his thinking, may be derived from the Christian Faith, such as, for instance, the idea of a personal God. It is in this sense, we admit, that the "Christian philosophy" of the Middle Ages is to be understood. "There is not a Christian reason, but there can be an exercise of the reason which is Christian" (Gilson, *L'esprit de la philosophie médiévale*, I, p. 13). The recollection that "the whole Cartesian system depends upon the idea of an Omnipotent Deity" (*op. cit.*, p. 14), that Malebranche was as much Augustinian as Cartesian—one might also add: that Immanuel Kant had enjoyed the advantage of Protestant instruction in preparation for Confirmation, that he knew his Bible well, and that behind his Categorical Imperative lies the narrative of the giving of the Law on Sinai, makes it appear doubtful whether any philosophical system of the post-Christian era would find it possible to disregard the Christian tradition—even when, as, for instance, in the case of Nietzsche, its influence is mainly felt as something in opposition to one's own views. For this reason there are, at least, three groups of philosophies which must be distinguished from one another: (i) those which arose before Christ and outside of Christianity, where there is no question of any Christian influence at all; (ii) the philosophy of the period which was mainly influenced by the Christian Faith; (iii) the philosophy of modern times, which is involuntarily and unconsciously affected by the influence of Christianity.

(i) When we attempt to answer the question: What can philosophical thought, apart from the influence of the Christian idea of God, attain theologically? the classical philosophy of antiquity, down to the time when Christianity arose to rival it, seems to provide the best sphere for our enquiry. Certainly here, too, we would need to examine still more closely the spiritual influence of Judaism in the last century before Christ, in order to be able to say what philosophical thought, untouched by the influence of the Bible, is able to achieve. To this question, the unprejudiced student of Greek philosophy will reply, first of all, that the philosophers of this period—for instance, from Thales to Chrysippus—varied greatly in their ideas about the Divine. Their views range from the grossest materialism, by way of pantheism, up to something which comes very near to Theism. In view of our contention that there is the sharpest contradiction between the Christian and the philosophical Idea of God, naturally the question of philosophical Theism is particularly relevant; for not only the materialist, but also the pantheistic doctrine of God, would from the outset confirm our argument, while Theism seems to make it, to some extent, questionable.

From this point of view Plato and Aristotle should receive chief attention. Yet it would be difficult to find anyone prepared to describe Plato's idea of God as theistic—and to this extent related to the Christian Idea of God. "For if the Universal alone is original and absolutely real, then it is impossible to think that the deity could be conceived otherwise than in impersonal terms" (Zeller, *Die Philosophie der Griechen*, II, I, p. 793). Aristotle, however, seems to offer a more hopeful possibility. It would then be no accident, but an inner necessity, that the Christian philosophy of the Middle Ages should have pre-eminently developed the Idea of God of Aristotle, since from the outset, in the sense of the formula *"gratia non tollit naturam, sed perficit"*, this philosophy seemed most fitting to achieve a philosophical doctrine of God, controlled by Christian heuristic principles.

It now appears, however, that the real Aristotle—not the one of the Thomist interpretation—represents an Idea of God, which, though it may possess certain theistic features, in any case is not only very different from the Christian doctrine, but is also incompatible with it. The God of Aristotle is neither a "Lord-God" nor a Creator, neither the One who freely elects, nor the One who stoops down to man. "According to Aristotle, the Deity stands in lonely self-contemplation outside the world; for man He is an object of awe and wonder, to know Him is the highest task of man's intellect; this divinity is the goal towards which all that is finite aspires, whose perfection evokes man's love; but just as he cannot expect to receive love in return, he cannot receive from this divinity any effect at all that differs from that of nature, and his intellect is the sole means by which he enters into contact with Him" (Zeller, *op. cit.*, p. 791). Man's relation to the deity does not even play any part in the ethical sphere—as, for instance, as a divine law. On the other hand, the relation between the Christian Idea of God and that of Stoic popular philosophy seems much closer—Cicero, Epictetus, Seneca, Marcus Aurelius. But, on the one hand, it is very questionable to what extent we can here speak of philosophical thought at all; and on the other hand, we must not forget that all these thinkers lived at a time when the Hebrew Idea of God was already at work, like leaven, in contemporary thought.

(ii) When we turn to the second period, which is that of Christian philosophy proper, there are two points to note. First, the Fathers of the Church, and the Scholastic theologians, with their rudimentary critical sense, read a great deal into the ancient philosophers which cannot be found there by an unprejudiced reader. Secondly, and chiefly, they in particular have moulded the Christian Idea of God in such a way that, it is true, it made the synthesis of philosophy and theology far easier to achieve, but, on the other hand, it injured the Christian idea of God which was in harmony with revelation. Very early in Christian theology the tendency to "spiritualize" the Idea of God became evident, and thus to bring it nearer to the philosophical idea. This took place, negatively, by eliminating the supposed "anthropomorphism", and, positively, by using the idea of the Absolute, "whereby the influence of Platonism was very evident" (Baur, *Vorlesungen über die christliche Dogmengeschichte*, I, p. 405).

Thus Justin Martyr already develops ideas, in connexion with Plato's words, "God is beyond all existence" (*De Rep.*, VI, 509), which may be in harmony with the Platonist picture of God, but are certainly not in accordance with the Biblical view (*Dial. c. Tr.*, Chap. 4). Still more is the thinking of Clement of Alexandria influenced by the Platonic idea of the Absolute. Clement also gives himself away by showing how he reaches this "spiritualized" idea of God: namely, that he does so δι' ἀναλύσεως, that is, by a process of abstraction, by which the finite ideas about God are gradually eliminated, until finally all that remains is the abstract conception of Unity (*Strom.*, V, 11). Clement does not even wish to admit that God is the One; rather one should say that He is beyond the One and Unity (*The Pedagogue*, I, 8).

The thought of Origen is similar: therefore "*dicimus secundum veritatem Deum incomprehensibilem esse atque inaestimabilem*" (*De Princ.*, I, i, 5). Through these Fathers of the Church, this abstract speculative idea of God entered into Christian theology as a whole; men did not realize that it was in opposition to the Christian Idea of God; still less did they perceive the contradiction between the speculative method and the faith of revelation. After the Platonism of the first three centuries, it was mainly Neo-Platonism, in a modified form in Augustine, and in a highly developed and non-Christian form in the pseudo-Dionysius (the Areopagite) which, together with the Aristotelianism of the twelfth century, moulded the mediaeval doctrine of God.

The mediaeval doctrine itself is a very skilful synthesis of the abstract Idea of God of philosophy, and the personal Idea of God of the Bible, according to the Christian revelation. Modern Protestant thinkers have been fully aware of the disastrous part played by the Idea of the Absolute in this process of fusion. "To identify the Name and the concept of the Absolute with God, means, at bottom, nothing less than idolatry with an adjective", says Fr. H. Jacobi, somewhat too cleverly (*WW.*, III, p. 5). Kähler, too, warns his readers against this idea, which he calls "irreligious" (*Wissenschaft der christlichen Lehre*, p. 247); Cremer does the same (*Die Lehre von den Eigenschaften Gottes*, p. 7). But no one seems to have seen quite clearly what is the basis of this contradiction: the contradiction between the Person as Subject, who discloses Himself, and the object of thought which is attained by a process of one's own thinking.

(iii) In the third period the great contradictions to which speculative thought leads, if left to itself unchecked, broke out. In a way similar to that of the period of ancient philosophy, only in still greater variety and multiplicity, all kinds of systems arose alongside of one another: materialistic, pantheistic, speculative and idealistic, critically idealistic, and theistic. But whereas in the Middle Ages the tendency predominated to approximate philosophy and theology as closely as possible to one another, philosophy—now unhindered by the Christian Idea of God—now goes its own way, and even if it is theistic it still does not evince any particular concern about the question: has its Idea of God any similarity with the Christian Idea of God? A mistaken apologetic, on the side of Christian theology, has always tended to lay as little stress as possible upon the difference between philosophical Theism and the Christian Idea of God. Men seem to have thought that they *must* have the aid of philosophy, hence they had to take the help which it offered, in its own way. An objective examination of the facts of the situation—which, so far as I know, has never yet been accomplished on the part of theology—would probably lead to the following conclusions:—

(*a*) It is a fact that philosophical Theism only prospered (so to speak) in the shadow of the church towers; that is, that philosophers only attained the theistic results of their thinking where the Christian tradition was still comparatively vigorous; whereas in other directions the philosophical metaphysic led far away from Theism to pantheistic Idealism, or to Pantheism proper, or to various forms of Naturalism, to the very verge of Materialism. This fact confirms that *a priori* consideration that there is an unconscious and unwilled influence of the Christian Idea of God on the philosophical doctrine of God, which is not visible in the process of argument, since it is only operative as a heuristic principle.

(*b*) In spite of this, the Idea of God of this theistic philosophy is, as a rule, no less remote from the Christian Idea than is the Aristotelian idea, with which it has the closest affinity. The main intellectual *motif* of philosophical Theism is the greatly varied and enriched Teleological Proof for the Existence of God—the inference from the present existence of the world to a spiritual cause which lies outside the world (especially certain particular phenomena within human natural experience). Here we are not concerned with the value of this argument as a "proof", or with its philosophical relevance. Here we are only interested in the result, and this result corresponds to the process by which it is discovered. The God who is known in this way has no connexion with the Creator Lord of the Bible. It is directly opposed to this Biblical idea.

If God is what this philosophical Theism says He is, then He is not the God of the Biblical revelation, the sovereign Lord and Creator, Holy and Merciful. But if He is the God of revelation, then He is not the God of philosophical Theism. The supposed usefulness of this philosophical Theism within the sphere of Christian theology is based merely upon the erroneous distinction between a "metaphysical" and an "ethical" aspect of the Christian doctrine of God. Once this error has been perceived, once for all we lose all desire to identify the God of philosophical Theism with the God of revelation and faith.

In saying this I do not mean to deny either the value of philosophy or even the value of the philosophical doctrine of God. Its significance lies in the fact that it shows, for instance, that even philosophical thought cannot get away from God, but that in some way or another—and this indefinite phrase is here the only proper one to use—it aims at God even when it does not reach the True God; secondly, in the fact that even in the sinful blindness of reason, the original revelation is shown to be still operative. Theism in particular is thus distinghished above other systems of philosophy by the fact that—even if from afar—it follows the revelation of God in His works of which the Apostle says that in it the divine Godhead νοούμενα καθοράται. It is not the Creator, in the Biblical sense of the word, who is here perceived; but it is still the closest approximation to the idea of the Creator of which reason is capable when left to itself.

## CHAPTER 14

## THE HOLY

FROM the standpoint of revelation the first thing which has to be said about God is His Sovereignty. But this first point is intimately connected with a second one—so closely indeed that we might even ask whether it ought not to have come first: God is the Holy One. "Hallowed be Thy Name"—it is very significant that in the prayer of the Christian Church this clause comes first. The one concern of the Christian Faith is the Holy Name, and the "hallowing" of this Name. Although in the New Testament the idea of the Holiness of God as a Divine Attribute is emphasized somewhat less than in the Old Testament,[1] yet it is everywhere presupposed, and it appears at decisive points, where the whole revealing and saving work of Christ is gathered up as the revelation of the Name: "Holy Father, keep them in Thy Name which Thou hast given me."[2] But the whole of the Old Testament is the revelation of the *Holy* God. What does this mean?

Modern students of religion have come to the unanimous conclusion that the fundamental act of all religion is the worship of the Holy.[3] "The Holy", as Rudolf Otto's beautiful book has shown us in an impressive and conclusive manner, is that to which the religious act is directed. Holiness is the very nature of the Numinous, of that which is divine, thus of that which characterizes "the Deity", "the gods", or the *"mysterium tremendum"*, towards which man, as a religious being, turns. Just as from the subjective standpoint the chief word in all religion is reverence or the fear of God, so from the objective point of view the Holy is the chief word in all religion, the word which alone describes the dimension in which all that is religious is found. In the Biblical revelation, however, we are concerned not with "the Holy" (as an abstract conception), but with the Holy One (as personal). Whereas in the various religions of the world this element, the Holy, may be attached to all kinds of objects, and "the Holy" is therefore the characteristic common to them all, in the Biblical revelation, at least

[1] This modification, however, is more apparent than real, when we reflect that the New Testament lays so much more emphasis upon the Holy Spirit.
[2] John 17: 11.
[3] In addition to Rudolf Otto, *Das Heilige*; cf. G. v. der Leeuw, *Phänomenologie der Religion*, p. 9.

at its highest point,[1] "the Holy" is the very Nature of God, the Lord, who makes His Name known. Yahweh is the "Holy One of Israel".[2] Holiness is that *majestas* which belongs to God alone, which can be ascribed to others only in so far as God Himself "hallows" it, or them, since He makes them vessels and instruments of His Will.

But in order to understand this original word of the Biblical revelation in its own proper sense, it is necessary to consider this word apart from all that has gradually adhered to it, and altered it, in the course of its long history. Originally, the word "holy" had no ethical connotation; it did not mean what we think of when we hear a person described as "holy". Holiness is the Nature of God, that which distinguishes Him from everything else, the Transcendence of God in His very Nature,[3] as the "Wholly Other". Hence Holiness is not a quality which God possesses in common with other beings; on the contrary, it is that which distinguishes Him clearly and absolutely from everything else. To be holy is the distinguishing mark peculiar to God alone: it is that which sets the Being of God apart from all other forms of being.[4]

Even the etymology of the Hebrew word for "holy" (*qādōsh*) suggests this; it contains the idea of "separation" as a fundamental element in the conception.[5] Holiness distinguishes God's nature from every other form of existence. When Otto, with his fine insight, perceived that the essential character of the Holy is the "Wholly Other", in the strict sense of the word, this is true only of the Biblical conception of Holiness. The gods and the divinities of the other religions outside the Bible are most certainly not "*wholly* other".

In the strict sense of the word the God of the Biblical revelation alone is "the Wholly Other", and the word "holy" is used precisely to bring this out.[6] "The" Wholly Other (in the abstract sense of the word) cannot be "wholly Other" precisely because it is an "it", because it is not an "I"; as something neuter it has no real essential transcendence. Its neutral character betrays the fact that "it" somehow or other belongs to the world. Only He who, in the strict sense of the word, is the Lord of the world, the Creator, can be "wholly Other". Only

---

[1] Cf. *Theol. Wörterbuch*, Kittel, I, pp. 89–112.    [2] Is. 43: 3; 45: 11.
[3] On the distinction between Transcendence in Essence and in Being, see below, pp. 175 ff.
[4] Cf. *Theol. Wörterbuch*, I, p. 93 (on Yahweh's "holiness" in contrast to the Creation, both natural and historical).
[5] *Ibid.*, p. 88.    [6] Is. 5: 16; 6: 3; Hosea 11: 9.

the Creator Lord, by His very nature, is different from all other existence, in such a radical and absolute manner as indeed only Creator and creature can be different. The Creator has no trace of "the world" or of "the creaturely" in Himself, and conversely, the creature as such has no trace of "non-creatureliness", of "divinity", and therefore of "holiness". Hence the Being of God as Subject is the logical presupposition of His Holiness; only He who says, "I, even I, am the LORD, and beside Me there is no Saviour"—can be "the Holy One of Israel".

The whole conflict between Yahweh and the Baalim of the Near East raged round this essential Transcendence of God; the conflict raged between the God who is the "Wholly Other" and the nature-gods, who were only hypostasized forces of Nature. That is why the commandment forbidding the worship of graven images was of such decisive significance. It emphasizes the Transcendence of God, the fact that He cannot be compared with anyone or anything else that is creaturely.[1] Whatever may be the value of the idea of the *"analogia entis"*,[2] this, in any case, stands firm, before everything else: that the *Nature* of God as the Nature of the *Creator*[3] must be strictly disinguished from the nature of the creaturely. There is no transition from the creaturely to the Creator, no intermediate being, no demi-gods, no abstract holiness, in which various beings or things could participate. Holiness belongs to God alone, and this means precisely that which He alone possesses. We might, therefore, paraphrase the Biblical idea of Holiness thus: the Divine nature, as it is peculiar to God alone. "I am God, not man; the Holy One in the midst of thee",[4] that is, "I am He with whom none can be compared".

This idea, however, is too static and too logical to give the full meaning of the Biblical word "holy". The Being of God which His Name makes known to us can never be grasped by neutral categories of existence. He is Will. Thus the concept of "the Holy" contains the element of Will, and precisely that Will which is set upon proclaiming Himself as the "Wholly Other". The border-line which separates the Nature of God from all other forms of existence, from that which has been created, is not only a frontier line, it is a *closed* frontier, symbolized by the "mount . . . which burned with fire".[5] God makes this border-

[1] Is. 40: 25; 57: 15.
[2] Cf. pp. 175 ff.
[3] Is. 41: 20; 45: 11.
[4] Hosea 11: 9.
[5] In his vision of the Holy "Isaiah feels the deadly contrast to his own nature". (*Theol. Wörterbuch*, p. 93.)

line; He actively maintains it, and defends it against every infringement on the part of the arrogant creature. God *wills* to be the Only One who is what He IS. He "will not give His honour to another".[1] Hence the idea of "Holiness" is closely connected with that idea of "jealousy" which modern man finds so repellent.

"I, the Lord thy God, am a jealous God."[2] This idea, if rightly understood, not only is not offensive in itself, but for the right idea of God it is central. Certainly it is a parable taken from the sphere of marriage. As the married person rightly guards the exclusiveness of the marriage relation, and will not permit any third person to enter into this relation, which can only be right if maintained between two persons, so God guards the uniqueness of His Divine Being.[3]

He rejects every attack on His sole rights, on that which belongs to Him alone. The Holiness of God is therefore not only an absolute difference of nature, but it is an active self-differentiation, the willed energy with which God asserts and maintains the fact that He is Wholly Other against all else. The absoluteness of this difference becomes the absoluteness of His holy will, which is supreme and unique.

Thus the Divine Holiness is inseparably connected with that character of absolute intolerance which distinguishes the Biblical Idea of God, and differentiates it from all other ideas of God.[4] God will not tolerate the recognition of any other; He opposes those who do not admit His Uniqueness, the fact that He alone is God, and thus His true Nature as God. On the other hand, He emphasizes positively His Being as God, the truth that He alone is the True God. The positive and negative energy of this emphasis is brought out in two equally characteristic words which are of equal value for the Christian idea of God: the Glory of God, and His Wrath. Both ideas have been rendered suspect by a rationalism which does not understand the thought of the Bible; the objection to both ideas is that they savour of "primitive anthropomorphic conceptions", and thus ascribe human passions to God.

In the thought of the Bible—and indeed in all genuine Christian thought—the idea of the "Glory of God" is absolutely fundamental. God *wills* to be recognized as God. To the Zeus of Plato it is a matter of indifference whether man recognizes

---

[1] Isa. 42: 8; 48: 11.     [2] Exod. 20: 5.
[3] The Book of Hosea brings this out particularly clearly and impressively.
[4] Cf. below, pp. 178 ff.

him or not. Unperturbed, he moves on his way in heaven without turning round to see what is happening either behind him or beneath him.[1] The Living God who makes His Name known to us is not indifferent. He wills "that the whole earth be filled with His Glory".[2] He wills that all men should know and confess His Name.[3] He is not a static Being, but the God of revelation, who indeed reveals Himself precisely because He wills that His Name should be made known, in order that He may be glorified, in order that His will should be done. The Holy Name and the Glory of God are inseparable. As the God of revelation He is the God who cares absolutely, to whom it is not a matter of indifference whether the creature does His will, or his own will, whether falsehood or His Truth prevail in the world of men, whether people worship other gods beside Him, or whether they render obedience to other lords. It concerns Him—"it matters" to Him. And indeed it matters to Him that He should be recognized as the Holy One, as the One who is Wholly Other. The Glory of God is the unity of God's sovereignty and His revelation, the revealed visible "glory", the majesty of God as it is seen by His creature, recognized as that which shines forth upon the creature. The revelation of the Holy God has attained its end where the "Glory of the Lord" is "mirrored" in the hearts of believers.[4] This is the meaning of the Biblical idea of the Glory of God.

This leads us inevitably to the second truth: that of His Wrath. It is Holy Wrath, the wrath of the Holy One about the failure to stress the Holy, about man's rebellion against God's holy will, which is the truth. But this wrath is not an emotion which resembles anything we know in human experience; it is the inevitable necessary reaction of the will of God to all that opposes Him. God takes the fact that He is God "seriously"— and this is the only thing that is wholly serious, and from which all that is really serious is derived. "God is not mocked."[5] Both the negative and the positive aspects of the divine energy of will are inseparable from the divine Being of God. What kind of God would He be if He did not care whether people took Him seriously or not? Since God takes Himself absolutely seriously, He gives seriousness to life. If God did not take Himself seriously, what else could be taken seriously?

This "seriousness" works itself out negatively as resistance provoked by resistance, and indeed as resistance which ulti-

[1] Plato, *Phaedrus*.  [2] Ps. 72: 19.
[3] Phil. 2: 10 ff.  [4] 2 Cor. 3: 18.  [5] Gal. 6: 7.

mately is the rock against which all other resistance founders.[1]
The man who fights against God will finally break down at this
point. The resistance of the creature has no possibility of
asserting itself finally against the will of the Creator. The will
of God crushes the will which opposes Him; if the rebel does
not separate himself from the will which is opposed to God, he
himself will be annihilated. This is the Divine Wrath, the
working out of the Divine Glory upon those who refuse to give
Him glory; the working out of the Holiness of God against him
who irreverently, godlessly, does not acknowledge Him. To
speak of all this as "anthropomorphic ideas", of all the references to the wrath of God in the Scriptures as "merely the
crass anthropopathic relics of an uncultured age, which describes
the divine righteousness in terms of the human emotions"
(*Wegscheider*), only betrays the fact that the writer does not
know the God of revelation, the God who makes His Name known
to us, and thus that the very idea of the Holy God and of the
Lord God is unpleasing to him, and that, at the most, he only
recognizes a God who does not claim him by His will. The idea
of the Divine Wrath cannot be severed from that of the Holiness of God.

From all that has just been said it is plain that in the concept
of the Holiness of God there is a twofold movement of the
Divine Will—at first sight a contradictory movement, namely,
a movement of withdrawal and exclusion, and a movement of
expansion and inclusion.

The movement of exclusion refers to the element of differentiation as such. God—alone—is God, the creature is—only—
a creature. Hence the Holiness of God evokes from man an
incomparable sense of distance from Him. God in His Nature is
inaccessible. He dwells "in light unapproachable".[2] The
creature which becomes aware of the Holiness of God recognizes
that he himself is very "far off" from Him. This is that feeling
which Otto describes as "creaturely feeling", which is expressed
by reverent homage. Before God's majesty man sees himself as
nothing: "Woe is me! for I am undone . . . for mine eyes have
seen the King, the Lord of Hosts.[3] "Behold now, I have taken
upon me to speak unto the Lord, which am but dust and
ashes."[4] Man is not equal to God: he is indeed a creature, not
the Creator; he is a dependent, not an independent, person-

[1] This is not only the teaching of the Old Testament, but of the New,
especially in the doctrine of the Last Things.
[2] 1 Tim. 6: 16.          [3] Is. 6: 5.          [4] Gen. 18: 27.

ality. Therefore one cannot stand on a level with God and have
fellowship with Him as if He were just one of ourselves. We
must bow the knee before Him.[1] Reverence is the exact opposite
of that attitude which Hebbel expresses thus:

> To God the Lord it is a triumph
> If we do not faint before Him,
> If we stand upon our feet
> In glorious confidence,
> Instead of falling on our faces
> In the dust. . . .

The creature should bow the knee in reverence before the Holy
God. This humble recognition of the infinite distance between
God and man is the "fear of the Lord": that fear of the Lord
which is the "beginning of all wisdom".[2] This is the expression
of the feeling that we are wholly dependent upon God, and that
He is in no way dependent upon us.

But this movement of exclusion, of keeping human beings at
a distance, is inseparable from a second opposite movement,
which yet at the same time completes the other. God wills that
His Name shall be glorified, that He shall be seen to be the
Holy in His Otherness. Thus He wills that "the whole earth be
filled with His glory".[3] It is precisely unlimited recognition
that He wills, and this *gloria Dei* is His aim. He, the God of
revelation, wills to be known and recognized—that is the
meaning of revelation. But when He is seen to be what He is,
then the glory of His Light illuminates the life of His creature.
The revelation which discloses the distance between the Being
of God and all other existence, also, at the same time, by this
manifestation, removes the gulf between man and God. All
revelation is self-communication, and self-communication is
inclusion, attraction to Himself, "drawing near", a nearness
which wills communion, which, however, where it meets with
opposition may turn into a "consuming fire". But where the
call—"*soli Deo gloria*"—resounds, in a true confession, in
sincere reverence, there is a positive nearness of God; indeed,
there is communion with God: there the creature has become
"full" of God. This is the ultimate dialectic which, as we already
saw at the beginning, lies in the revelation of the Name of God.
It is the dialectic of Holiness and Love. As the Holy One, God

---

[1] In the New Testament the attitude of kneeling as an expression of reverence before the Holy Majesty of God is taken for granted: Phil. 2: 10; Eph. 3: 14; Rom. 14: 11.     [2] Prov. 1: 7.     [3] Ps. 72: 19.

wills to be separate from all creatures; as the Holy One He also wills that all creation should be filled with His glory, and thus should have a share in that quality which is His alone. Thus the Holiness of God is the basis of the self-communication which is fulfilled in love.[1]

This second, inclusive, movement, therefore, is also the source of that which we may call "transitive holiness". God alone is Holy; but since He proclaims His Holiness in His creation, and declares that it belongs to Him, He "hallows" it. Then it is not only God who is Holy, but those upon whom He has laid His claim, and who are "separated" unto Him. In this "secondary" sense, everything that God sets apart as His property and for His service is holy. Hence the "People of God"—Israel, in so far as He has chosen it to be the people to whom He reveals Himself, the people He claims as His "own" —is "holy".[2] The Church is Holy, indeed to use the language of the New Testament she consists entirely of "saints" (ἅγιοι),[3] that is, of those whom God has called unto Himself out of the world to be "His own". Hence the doctrine of *Election*, one of the main themes of the Old and the New Testament, is based upon the Holiness of God.[4]

This idea of being separated to be God's peculiar possession is unintelligible to rational thought. How can any particular individual be "separated" unto God as His special property, since as Creator everything belongs to Him? How can there be anything, which, from the very beginning, does not, as a matter of course, belong to God? Very true, but not all whom God has created acknowledge Him, the Holy One; not all are *de facto* what they are *de jure*—the property of God. Rather, we might say that there are two ways of belonging to God: qualified and unqualified, as property *de jure* and *de facto*. All nations belong to God, for He has created them all. But at first Israel alone was "His people", because He had chosen this people from among all nations, in order that He might, in a special way, set His seal upon it as His own property, because to this people He has made known His Holiness, since it is to it that He has revealed Himself. All human beings belong to God; but "His own", in the qualified sense of the word, are only those who "receive" Him in His revelation.[5]

---

[1] The first to perceive the oneness of the Holiness and the Love of God was Hosea. The testimony to this unity comes out most impressively in the Second Isaiah; the Holy is, as such, the Saviour. (Is. 41: 14; 43: 3; 47: 4.)

[2] Ps. 34: 10; 89: 6.    [3] Cf. I Cor. 1: 2; I Pet. 2: 9.

[4] The "holy" are the "elect" (Col. 3: 12).    [5] John 1: 12; 10: 14.

Once more we see the close connexion between God's Nature and His revelation. Because He is, and wills to be, the Holy One, He reveals Himself, He is to be known as the Holy, and the creature to whom He reveals Himself becomes His hallowed property, a creature upon whom the Creator has specially laid His Hand, thus enabling him to know God as the Holy One, and himself as God's property. In His revelation the otherwise hidden being of God is expressed. In what sense God is the Holy One, only comes out where His Holiness manifests itself as electing revelation and revealing election. Thus the position is not that first of all God is "something", and then, later on, reveals what He is; rather, we may say that it is God's very nature to want to reveal Himself, since it springs from His Holiness. God's Holiness is the will to possess His creatures, therefore it is the will to reveal Himself. Revelation is not something which is *added* to His Nature, it is part of His very Nature. God is the God of revelation; He is the One who seeks man, the God who wants to have man for Himself, the God whose very nature it is to be sovereign Will. It is part of the very Nature of God as the Holy One that He is concerned to be known by His creatures, and to possess them in a qualified sense as His own possession, that is, as creatures who recognize Him as their Lord. The Nature of God is not rightly described if it is not described as *Will* directed towards the sovereignty of God. As One who creates a "people for His own possession" God is the Holy One.[1] Here we merely suggest a thought which we shall be developing in its whole breadth and depth later on, namely: that it is of the very Nature of God, of the True God, of the God who manifests His Name, to care for the creature whom He has created to stand "over against" Him. God does not ignore the will of His creature; He cares intensely for His creature, He wills, infinitely seriously, to be known by this creature as that which He is. In infinitely divine passion He is Will turned towards man: He is the θεάνθρωπος θεός.

Only now can we understand the connexion with the *moral* idea of the Holy. As in the religions outside the world of the Bible, so also in the earlier stages of the witness of the Old Testament, the idea of Holiness is non-ethical, if not a-moral. The Numinous, the *"mysterium tremendum"*, has at first nothing to do with the ethical element. God does not only "hallow" persons, but also animals, places, times, vessels.[2] But by the time of the Prophets this ethically neutral idea of Holi-

[1] John 17: 4.   [2] Cf. *Theol. Wörterbuch*, I, pp. 88 ff.

ness disappears; in the New Testament it has completely vanished. The Holy One is at the same time the Moral, and the Moral has become entirely the Holy. "The Holy God proves that He is holy through righteousness."[1] It is not, however, a synthesis which has been achieved,[2] but what has happened is this: the deepest nature of the Holy, and the deepest nature of the Moral, have here become evident in their original and natural unity. For in the most profound sense of the word, what is the so-called "Moral" element? It simply means to be determined by the will of God—to belong to God. Behind the Moral Law, behind the Categorical Imperative, behind the commandments of God, there stands in the last resort simply this: "You belong wholly and entirely to God." Hence, both in the ethical, and in the religious sense, the person who knows he wholly belongs to God is "holy".

There is no such thing as "the Moral" in itself—as the "autonomous" ethic says there is—that is, something which is "Moral" in and for itself, that which is "morally Good", understood as independent of the Will of God. That which is morally "good" is identical with that which is determined by the will of God. The only "good" will is one that wills—utterly and entirely—only what God wills, and one which wills this—simply and utterly—because God wills it. The fact that the content of this Good is the will to do good to one's fellow-man, to help him to further everything which will contribute to the well-being of man and to remove all that is evil, thus that it wills love of our neighbour, consideration for others, justice, etc.—all this, on the other hand, is not something separate and secondary. For all this is rooted in, and derived from, the will of God.

The illusion of a supposedly "independent" morality or ethic is due to the fact that our natural processes of knowing begin first of all with this relation to the well-being of others, and the fact that this is rooted in the will of God is only regarded as a sanction, afterwards applied, for this social imperative which already exists. Actually, the very opposite is the case. To will the good of our neighbour is a Moral Imperative because the God to whom we belong wills this good of our neighbour. The will is good not because it wills the good of our neighbour, but purely and simply because, and in so far as, it wills the good of our neighbour as that which God wills. The truly good will is the holy will, that is, the will which is wholly controlled by the will of God.

Hence the Moral is an integral element in the Holy. What we

[1] Is. 5: 16.     [2] Cf. Otto, *Das Heilige*, pp. 21 and 82.

call the Moral is only one side of "belonging" to God, the side
which is turned towards man. But to belong to God is the
result of the claim that the Holy God lays upon us as our
Creator. So long as this Holy Will of God is not rightly known,
a contradiction between the content of the Moral Law—the
law which commands us to seek the good of our neighbour—
and the will of God can exist; thus religious obedience and
moral obedience may come into conflict with one another, and
therefore there can be non-ethical religion and non-religious
morality. But the morality which is severed from the will of
God always tends to become superficial, as, on the other hand
—apart from revelation—there is always a tendency towards
ethical indifference.[1]

But wherever the will of God is known as the will of the
Holy, as the will of the Lord and Creator who is bent upon
asserting His rights over us, there is no possibility of a conflict
between the religious and the moral elements. What God wills
—the sovereignty of God—is the foundation of all true morality;
conversely, all morality which is directed towards the good of
our neighbour has its basis and its deepest motive in obedience
to the Will of God. Thus the "saints", in the sense of those who
are designated as such because they are the possession of God,
become "saints" in the sense that they are those who are completely obedient to the will of God, and whose will is identical
with the will of God. In the Christian revelation alone the
Divine and the Human are one.

Now, however, how can we combine the statement of the
Holiness of God, which expresses and works itself out as consuming wrath, with the other statement—that His Holiness is
one with His love? To put it quite simply: what is the relation
between the truth—taught in the Bible—of the Love of God
and the equally Scriptural truth of the Divine wrath? It is
obvious that the conception of the Divine Wrath not only
causes great embarrassment to a rationalist of the Enlightenment school, or to a theologian like Schleiermacher, with his
pantheistic tendencies, but it is also true of those theologians
who are greatly concerned to keep close to the teaching of
Scripture in their theological work.[2] Where they are dealing

[1] Thus, on the one hand, there is the dull bourgeois morality of utility, and
on the other hand, that a-moral "Numinous" which we perceive, e.g. in the
cult of Shiva.

[2] That even Karl Barth, in his present doctrine, finds himself in this quan-
dary, comes out most plainly in his present conception of Predestination; cf.
below, pp. 346 ff.

with Judgment and the Wrath of God they turn away from the Bible. But it is precisely here that we stand at the decisive point in the whole Christian doctrine of God; hence here we need to give very careful consideration to the whole subject, and especially to pay great attention—in a spirit of reverent obedience—to all that the Bible has to say.

No modern theologian, perhaps no theologian at any period in the history of the Church, has grasped so profoundly the contradictory ideas of the wrath and the love of God as Luther; this is probably due to the fact that no other theologian has had such a profound experience of the annihilating Holiness of God as he. All the lines of the Reformation understanding of faith converge at this point, which is designated in the teaching of Luther by the contradictory pair of ideas, *Deus absconditus*, *Deus revelatus*, the hidden and the revealed God. We cannot, I suppose, do a greater service to the clarification of the actual problem than by a short summary of Luther's ideas upon this cardinal question in theology. Such a survey is necessary also, because, so far as I can see, all previous expositions[1]—with the single exception of Theodosius Harnack[2]—have not been able to reach any real clarification at this point.

The understanding of the doctrine of Luther has been made more difficult by two facts: firstly, that in his younger days he taught the doctrine of a double predestination which later he gave up; secondly, that he speaks of the "hidden God" in two different senses. Why he does so, and what he means in both instances by the formula "the Hidden God", can be made clear quite simply and plainly if we begin at the right point.

We must begin with the statement that the true, valid knowledge of God can only be gained in His revelation, in Jesus Christ. Through all the phases of Luther's theological development, and in all the aspects of the development of his teaching, that is the one constant and clear element. Why, alongside of this, there is yet a certain valuation, a conditional place given to the natural knowledge of God in Luther's thought,[3] will become clear to us in a moment. In Jesus Christ alone, however, God makes Himself known as He really is. In Him God shows Himself to us as "an abyss of eternal love".[4] The revelation and the communication of this love, the work of free grace

---

[1] Cf. Kattenbusch, *Deus absconditus bei Luther* (*Festgabe für J. Kaftan*), 1920; Blanke, *Der verborgene Gott bei Luther*, 1928; Schlink, *Die Verborgenheit Gottes, des Schöpfers, nach lutherischer Lehre* (in the *Festschrift für Karl Barth*), 1936.  [2] *Luther's Theologie*, I, New ed. 1927.
[3] Cf. *e.g. W.A.*, 44, 591 ff.; 667 ff.  [4] *Ibid.*, 36, 426.

is "God's proper work", His *opus proprium*.[1] For through this, His reconciling, redeeming work, His work in Christ, God creates faith, and through faith He receives His glory. Thus, if it is the will of God to receive His glory, His Holiness, then both His Holy and Loving Will are fulfilled in faith. "Faith gives glory to God."[2] Here, then, the Holiness and the Love of God are one.

But this faith presupposes that the sinful man confesses and repents of his sin. This, however, only occurs where he places himself under the judgment of God. Before God can give love, life and grace, He must first of all kill the old Adam. "*Si Deus vivificat, facit illud occidendo.*" "These, then, are two works of God, much praised by the Scriptures, that He kills and makes alive, wounds and heals, destroys and helps. . . ."[3] Men do not like to admit that they are sinners, "they do not want to have their old Adam killed, for this reason they do not attain to the proper work of God, which is justification, or the Resurrection of Christ".[4] Thus, if God is to do "His own" work, He must do a "strange work", an *opus alienum*. "Nevertheless"—so Luther puts the words into the mouth of God—"this is not My Own work, but it is a strange work".[5] It is a "strange work" because it does not spring from the essential will of God, but because it is forced upon Him by the sinful resistance of men, "*quod contra suam naturam (Deus) suscipit, cogente malitia hominum*".[6] Sin, the resistance of man, is the reason why God must do this "strange work", why He must show Himself and express Himself as the wrathful God. Sin obliges Him "to turn his back on man",[7] to do His work "on the left hand",[8] instead of His work of grace "on the right hand". Indeed, the Cross of Jesus Christ itself, as a death of this kind, as a result of the wrath of God, when we look at this aspect of the "slaying" of the Son of God, is a "strange work" of God,[9] while on the other hand, where it attains its end, in the repentance and faith of the sinner, it is in very deed the most characteristic work of the Grace of God.

This change, however, does not always take place. A man may not be willing to repent; he may not want to admit that he is a sinner; hence he rejects the grace of God in Jesus Christ. Upon such a man there "abides" "the wrath of God"[10] as a terrible reality.[11] Thus the wrath of God, even if it does not

---

[1] *W.A.*, 5, 63 ff.     [2] *Ibid.*, 40, I, 360.     [3] *Ibid.*, 7, 658.
[4] *Ibid.*, I, 112.     [5] *Ibid.*, 25, 190.     [6] *Ibid.*, 42, 356.
[7] *Ibid.*, 46, 672.     [8] *Ibid.*, 46, 669.     [9] *Ibid.*, I, 112.
[10] John 3: 36.     [11] Luther, *ibid.*, 40, II, 342; 378.

correspond with God's "proper" will, is nevertheless a divine reality. It is not that the doctrine of the wrath of God is an error, or a human misunderstanding. The wrath of God is something terrible; indeed, it is an infinite reality, "as great as God Himself", "eternally immeasurable, infinite, irrevocable—an incomprehensible *infinitum*".[1] Because God takes Himself, His Love, infinitely seriously, and in so doing also takes man infinitely seriously, He cannot do otherwise than be angry, although "really" He is only Love. His wrath is simply the result of the infinitely serious love of God.[2] Because it is true that Jesus Christ alone is the Light and the Life, it cannot be otherwise than that outside of Christ there is darkness, death, destruction.[3] "Therefore there is at all times enmity between man and God, and they cannot be friends and agree with one another; and where the two persons come into conflict with one another, there must man be broken to pieces, for he cannot stand against God."[4] Faith, however, is that turning-point where man submits to the Divine judgment, abandons his resistance, and flees from the God of wrath to the God of Grace, where men "flee to God from God", where "they break through His wrath" and call upon Him, "appealing from His Throne as Judge to the Throne of Grace".[5]

Where this does not occur, where this has not yet taken place, that is, in the whole sphere of the "natural man", and therefore also in the whole sphere of the natural knowledge of God, and of the natural course of the world, God is the Wrathful One, there *man stands under the wrath of God.* In this sphere, in this knowledge of God, therefore, man has to do with the *Deus absconditus.* Hence, the *Deus absconditus* is above all the God of natural, philosophical speculation about God, of the philosophical knowledge of God.[6] He who wants to know God thus, does the opposite of that which alone leads to the knowledge of the True God; he begins with the sublime knowledge, with the hidden majesty, with God as He is "in Himself", because—as the God of speculation—He is not the God of revelation, the God who is "for us".[7] Luther calls this speculative doctrine of God "clambering up to the Divine Majesty". In so doing, God becomes an *"objectum,* namely, the God who is not revealed".[8] There are only these two possibilities: either the natural knowledge (of God) with its *"objectum",* the *Deus*

[1] Luther, *W.A.*, 40, II, 3.
[2] *Ibid.*, 19, 167 ff.
[3] *Ibid.*, 18, 779.
[4] *E.A.*, 13, 313.
[5] *Ibid.*, 5, 204; 19, 229; 36, 366 ff.
[6] *Ibid.*, 44, 591 ff.
[7] *Ibid.*, 40, 11, 315 ff.; 37, 43.
[8] *Ibid.*, 43, 458 ff.

*absconditus*,[1] or the knowledge of God given in revelation. But the *Deus absconditus* and the way to Him, as the God of wrath, as the naked Divine Majesty, is a consuming Fire.[2] Hence the warning is given: *"scrutator majestatis opprimitur a gloria"*, and Luther adds: *"ego expertus scio"*.[3] It is—and this is only another equivalent for the *Deus absconditus*—the *Deus absolutus*, not the God who has revealed Himself to us, but the God who, in Himself, is mystery. Of Him it is true: *"Deum absolutum debent omnes fugere, quia humana natura et Deus absolutus sunt inter se infestissimi inimici nec potest fieri quin a tanta majestate humana infirmitas opprimatur."*

The natural knowledge of God leads to no other end than this. As it is the natural knowledge of the reason, so also is it the knowledge of the law. The heathen indeed have the knowledge of the law, the reason has *"cognitionem legalem"*,[4] the knowledge of that righteousness of God which only gives and demands law. Therefore it is a truth whose final result is condemnation, the annihilating judgment of God on sinful man.[5] The wrath of God and this law—that *Nomos* of the Epistles to the Galatians and the Romans—belong together. Finally, it is an uncertain knowledge,[6] for as He is in Himself, in His naked majesty, God cannot be known.[7] He can only be known with certainty in His revelation, where His terrible Majesty is graciously veiled, where He makes Himself finite and knowable for our sakes.[8]

We have now reached the point at which the idea of the "Hidden God" acquires a second meaning, which is diametrically opposed to the first one.[9] The revelation of God, from the standpoint of that absolute, non-revealed *"majestas"*, is a gracious veiling of that devastating Majesty. In this connexion we must understand the new pair of opposites, *Deus nudus*, *Deus velatus*. The *Deus nudus* is that naked Majesty, the sight of whom is intolerable for the sinful creature, "God merely and apart from Christ".[10] Over against this God the sinner" is without protection or shade in the blazing sun".[11] It is only the gracious veiling of this terrible Majesty in the human Person of the Redeemer "which protects us from the heat, which comes from the contemplation of the Divine Majesty; this shade gives

---

[1] *E.A.*, 43, 458 ff.      [2] *Ibid.*, 25, 106.      [3] *Ibid.*, 40, 1, 78.
[4] *Ibid.*, 46, 671.      [5] *Ibid.*, 40, I, 75 ff.      [6] *Ibid.*, 40, II, 386 ff.
[7] *Ibid.*, 42, 294.                               [8] *Ibid.*, 42, 294 ff.
[9] Blanke, in his otherwise excellent work, does not discuss this twofold use of the formula "Hidden God".
[10] Luther, *E.A.*, 42, 494 ff.                    [11] *Ibid.*, 25, 106.

us coolness, so that the thoughts of wrath pass away".[1] God has graciously descended to our level *"ad captum infirmitatis"*; He deals with us *"per aliquid volucrum"*,[2] He has so veiled Himself —*"velatum tali persona . . . quae nobis attemperata est"*.[3] Thus it is precisely the gracious revealed God who is "veiled", because, and in so far as, He becomes known to us, not as the unveiled naked Majesty, but only in this veiled form as Love. Hence "he who does not wish to fall on this stone and be broken to pieces, let him beware, and not deal with God 'nakedly' apart from His Word and His Promise. For human nature and God in His naked Majesty (*Deus absolutus*) cannot get on with one another, nor can they be compared. For it is impossible that human weakness should grasp and be able to bear the High Majesty of God".[4] This *Deus velatus* is also the *Deus revelatus*. The form of the *velatio* is precisely the possibility of the *revelatio*. This concealing is therefore not a real hiding of God's Face, but it is indeed the real unveiling. Therefore, Luther does not speak in this connexion of the *Deus absconditus*. The *Deus absconditus* is the really Hidden God, He who is really not to be known in His true Being, the *Deus absolutus*, the God of wrath. He is the God, as we have Him outside of Christ, hence He is also the God of the Law, "which is intolerable for the conscience".[5]

In the conception of the *Deus nudus* or *absolutus* Luther gathers up several ideas, which must first of all be disentangled and distinguished from one another; but they all have this common element: they all refer to God apart from Christ. First, there is the idea of the Irrational, the Numinous, before which man sinks down in his nothingness, which awakens in him absolute fear, that "creaturely feeling" in the presence of the Holy. Secondly, there is the Absolute, which is the *"objectum"* of speculative thought, that empty absoluteness in which all definitions disappear, and alongside of which an independent creature and its freedom has no room, thus in which the human person is reduced to absolute nothingness. Thirdly, there is the God of the Law with its demands, who only *demands* righteousness, but who does not give, whose verdict therefore crushes sinful man.

However far, at first sight, these three ideas differ from one another, and correspond to quite different experiences, they are at the same time at one in the fact that they represent the

---

[1] *E.A.*, 25, 107.    [2] *Ibid.*, 72, 294.    [3] *Ibid.*, 40, II, 329 ff.
[4] *Ibid.*, 40, II, 329 ff.    [5] *Ibid.*, 40, I, 75.

"God outside of Christ", the God whom we encounter in the natural sphere. They are also one in the fact that in their effect upon us they are all negative, destructive. Hence they correspond to the wrath of God, under which man stands, so long as he has not entered into the sphere of grace of Jesus Christ through revelation and faith. This, then, is certainly God, it is not a mere imagination; but it is God as He is, and remains, outside of Jesus Christ.

Hence—and here we come to the conclusion of this line of thought—it is God as He meets us in Nature and in the natural course of the world.[1] *God is thus*—in the world, outside of Christ. He who wishes to understand God from the point of view of the world cannot help seeing Him thus. God meets sinful man in the world as the wrathful God, as the Majesty which condemns and destroys. All that we know naturally in the world, in the course of this world, in the visible divine governance of the world, is the God of wrath; thus the course of this world, as we see it naturally, apart from Jesus Christ, is therefore also a "strange work" of God, and this "strange work" of God reaches its culminating point in the Cross of the Son.[2] Precisely in this highest manifestation of the wrathful God, however, is it possible—and here alone—for faith to "break through wrath", and to see in that which is "strange" the work of God, which is most peculiarly His own, reconciliation through Jesus Christ, in which the inmost being of God is disclosed as the abyss of Love.

In his earlier days, until 1525, Luther believed that one ought to see a double decree of God in the reality of the wrath of God which shows itself most manifestly in judgment on the godless, just as at that time he thought that he had to ascribe completely objective truth to the idea of naked majesty, of the "*potestas absoluta*". He did not yet see clearly that the inmost Being of God, that which He is in Himself, must be identical with that which He is for us.

But even then he was certain that God was not to be regarded in His double predestination, but solely and simply in Jesus Christ and His Grace. Thus there was still a great gulf between his objective understanding of the Supreme Truth, and his religious and pragmatic understanding of the same Truth.

Later on, Luther abandoned this dualism without ever being quite clear about the break he had made. This comes out in the fact that he now ascribes the will of God expressed in wrath

[1] E.A., 42, 295 ff.    [2] See above on p. 169.

solely to the guilt, the *malitia* of man, and that in the Love of Christ, in the Holiness which is identical with it, the true Nature and Mystery of God is known. "Just as one must say of a pious Prince and Lord: the Prince is purely love and kindness to everyone . . . none the less he must make use of the sword, the pike, the halberd, and he must have executioners and jailers in his service, in order that he may act with vigour in his territory, and crush those who try to resist his rule and his peaceful government, or to do harm to his people. But in his hall and in his castle there is nothing but mercy and love. . . . Thus, too, there is no wrath and harshness in God, and His Heart and His Thoughts are full of love and nothing else."[1] Through faith in Jesus Christ and only through Him do we know "what is going on within the highest Majesty and most secret Being. . . .",[2] "what God is in Himself. . . ."[3]

But even this truth of faith is only perceived where the truth is taken seriously, that outside of Jesus Christ, outside of faith, outside the refuge of His reconciliation, God is really the God of Holy wrath. That is why Luther contests the "Pelagian" spirit "which imagines something for itself, does not regard the wrath of God, constructs for itself such a God who is merciful, as now the world is accustomed to do".

[1] *E.A.*, 36, 427 ff.   [2] *Ibid.*, 17, II, 313.   [3] *Ibid.*, 49, 328.

# APPENDIX TO CHAPTER 14

(1) TRANSCENDENCE OF ESSENCE AND OF BEING, AND THE
   "ANALOGIA ENTIS"

IN modern theological discussions there has been a great deal
of unnecessary controversy about the idea of Divine Transcendence; this is due to the fact that the ideas of transcendence
of essence and transcendence of being have not been clearly
distinguished from one another. Transcendence of essence
means that God is God alone, and that His "Godhood" is
absolutely and irrevocably different from all other forms of
being, as the essence of the Creator differs from the essence of
the creature; thus God and the world must be kept absolutely
distinct from one another. Transcendence of Being, understood
in the absolute sense, would mean that God is not immanent in
the world in any sense at all, but that He is quite separate from
the world. While the former idea is necessarily connected with
the Biblical idea of God, the latter represents the statement of
an extreme Deism. The Biblical statement about the relation
of God to the world which He has created occupies a middle
position between a Deistic doctrine of Transcendence and a
Pantheistic doctrine of Immanence.

Hence in modern times (K. H. Krause, Lotze, etc.) some
have used the phrase "Pan-entheism" and have supported this
term by appealing to Acts 17: 28: "For in Him we live and move
and have our being". But this formula does not adequately
express the Biblical idea, because it is too static, and not
sufficiently dynamic. God's presence in the world, and His
nearness to man, are not correctly described by the formula
"being-in", because God's nature is "*actuositas*", "being-in-
action". In the second volume of Dogmatics this subject will be
treated more fully.

With the assertion that God is the Wholly Other, the problem
is stated of the relation of likeness or unlikeness between God
and His creation. The assertion of a likeness between the
creature and the Creator has led in Catholic theology to the
formulation of the doctrine of the "*analogia entis*", which Karl
Barth has called an invention of Anti-Christ and against which
he has inveighed with controversial vehemence (*K.D.* I, 1, 3rd
ed. Preface, p. viii). Now, in so far as the Catholic doctrine of
the "*analogia entis*" is connected with Neo-Platonist ontology,
and with the Natural Theology which is based thereon, Barth's

attack would command our complete assent. There is, however, not only a Neo-Platonist, but also a genuinely Biblical doctrine of a likeness between the creature and the Creator, namely, the doctrine that God, the Creator, has stamped the imprint of His nature upon His creation. But what this "likeness" means cannot be understood from the standpoint of Natural Theology, but only—rightly—from within the historical revelation. Revelation is the basis of the *knowledge* of the right doctrine of "likeness"; but within this knowledge based on revelation we now perceive that this "likeness" imparted by the Creator to the creature determines the *being* of creatures, so that they *are* thus, whether it is recognized or not, whether it is rightly understood or wrongly interpreted. Hence the doctrine of the "*analogia entis*"—in the Biblical sense—cannot be contrasted with an "*analogia fidei*". Faith is certainly the presupposition of right knowledge; but the analogy itself, since, and through, the Creation, is in the creatures themselves.[1]

For us, however, this raises the question: How can we reconcile this statement of a "likeness" between the Creator and His creation with the statement that God is the Wholly Other? To this we may give the following answer:

1. As the One who alone is Creator, God stands "over against" His creation, because it does not participate in His Being as Creator—the "Wholly Other". The fact that God is the Wholly Other refers to that which distinguishes Him as Creator from the creature. He alone is Lord, He alone is the Source of all life; He alone is the Giver of every good and perfect gift. He alone is "*a se, non ab alio*". Thus there is no "way" between the creaturely and the divine; between both there lies the absolute gulf: that outside of God there is only that which has been created, outside Him who is "*a se*", only that which is "*ab alio*"; thus outside the One who is entirely independent, there is only dependent being, the creature. This difference is greater than all other differences of any kind; this is the absolute transcendence of essence of Him who alone is God.

2. Now, however, God has created a being outside Himself, a being who stands "over against" Him: a created, creaturely being, creatures, and creaturely relations. In that He creates

---

[1] The reader of the latest volume of Barth's *Dogmatik* (III, 1) will be pleasantly surprised to note that Karl Barth himself now speaks of an "*analogia relationis*", which constitutes *that* "*imago Dei*" which has not been affected by the Fall (pp. 224 ff.).

them at the same time He imprints in and upon them something of His own Nature. He manifests in and through them "his everlasting power and divinity" (Rom. 1: 20). As the highest creature—in this connexion we are not considering the angels—He creates Man. He, the Absolute Subject, creates a being which is also "subject", and in this "existence or being as subject" is "like" God; but Man is absolutely unlike God in the fact that he is a created, conditioned, limited subject, whereas God is absolute Subject. He creates in man a creative nature, and one which is capable of dominion, and fitted for dominion—once more, like God. But man is absolutely unlike God in the fact that his creative activity is always connected with that which is *given* him, and that his dominion is always limited by his responsibility towards Him to whom he owes an account for the use he makes of his powers. In all that makes man like God, man remains absolutely unlike Him, in the fact that all that he has, he has received from God, and that for all that he does he is responsible, so that his very freedom can only be realized in absolute obedience to God; thus human freedom itself shows both man's "likeness" to God, and his "un-likeness"—an "unlikeness" which is an abiding fact.

3. The fact that man possesses the power of speech, that he can use and understand words, is connected with his being as subject. That, again, is a similarity with God, who indeed is Himself *Logos*, who has created all by His Word. God speaks —man also speaks; who could deny this similarity?[1] But, once more, this similarity also expresses an absolute "unlikeness", which consists in the fact that man can only speak truth as one who has received it, thus that he can only speak on the basis of that which God has already said. Secondly, the "unlikeness" consists in the fact that God's Word is always more than a word: namely, the Son, to whom the Word simply bears witness. (See above, Chap. 4.) Were the human word—the word of witness—not like the Divine Word, it could not bear witness at all. The similarity of the human word to the Divine is the presupposition of the fact that it can bear witness to the Word of God. But were it not only similar, but identical, then Christ the Son would not be the Word of God. The "being-as-

---

[1] Thus even Karl Barth says: "Speech, even as Divine Speech, is the form in which reason communicates with reason, person with person . . . primarily analogous with the process in the natural-corporeal sphere of creation." (*K.D.*, I, 1, p. 139.)

subject" which resembles the divine, the personal being of man, is the presupposition of the fact that God's revelation can take place in the Incarnation of the Son;[1] the human word which is like the divine is the presupposition of the fact that it can be the bearer of the Divine Word. This "likeness" which does not exclude absolute "unlikeness", is thus the possibility of revelation, and of the knowledge of God.

All this, however, can only be understood on the basis of the event of revelation, in faith. The "likeness" is, therefore, not the basis of a *theologia naturalis*, because the sinful reason always understands this "likeness" in a wrong way, without perceiving the radical "unlikeness" at the same time, which is rooted in the fact that God alone is God, that He is Creator and Lord. In particular, the Neo-Platonist doctrine of the "*analogia entis*" is a misunderstanding of this kind, in so far as it is based upon a speculative ontological theory of a hierarchy of being, but not upon the Biblical idea of the Creator and Lord. Only where this Neo-Platonist theory lies at the basis of thought can one believe that it is possible to achieve the knowledge of God by the way of abstraction; only then can one hold the view that in absolute being, thus in the abstract conception of "object", in the "*ens*", in that of "absolute substance", we have grasped what faith calls "God".

## 2. THE "INTOLERANCE" OF GOD

In recent times the tolerance of the Indian religions—including Buddhism—and of mysticism in general, has often been praised at the expense of the "intolerance" of Christianity. If tolerance is taken to mean simply that the propagation of one's own belief and its defence must be carried on without any resort to coercion of any kind, then a right view of the Christian doctrine of God would necessarily demand the most complete tolerance. The God who gave His own Son for the redemption of the world, and whose glory has been revealed in the Cross of His Son, does not will that the message of His Name should be propagated by fire and sword, the burning of heretics, or by compulsory baptism. For His kingdom is not of this world (John 18: 36). Nothing shows so plainly how far historical empirical Christianity has fallen away from the Gospel than the growth of the use of force in support of the Word of God.

[1] Cf. Luther, "*Quia conditus est (homo) ad imaginem invisibilis Dei, occulte per hoc significatur, Deum* se revelaturum *mundo* in homine Christo. (*W*., 42, 66.)

178

But if tolerance means the "toleration" of a different belief, to the extent of not laying any stress on the truth of revelation against the one who does not share this belief, then "tolerance" has almost come to mean a "relativist" outlook which does not believe that absolute truth exists. This relativism (which lies behind Lessing's parable of the Three Rings), is, in the last resort, the renunciation of Truth and the Good. Truth itself is intolerant: *"Verum judex sui et falsi"*. And the Good is intolerant; for it wills that evil should not exist. It is therefore no accident that the highest spiritual religions are intolerant—namely, all those which acknowledge God as Lord—and, above all, that faith which alone knows the Holy Lord is in the highest degree intolerant. But because this Holiness is identical with Love, this sovereign will with self-surrender, a genuine faith in Christ can only preserve its "intolerance" in the loving missionary spirit which renounces all dependence on force, even for its own protection.

The tolerance of the Indian religions and of mysticism is intimately connected with the lack of the personal idea of God. "The" Absolute has no power to reject, and no will to conquer; therefore it is not exclusive. Likewise, mysticism is always determined by the idea that the Ultimate is inexpressible; hence everything, even the most contradictory statements, can be conceived as symbols of this Ultimate. Mysticism does not mould the will, and it has no vigorous purpose; the idea of struggle and of victory is foreign to it. It is satisfied that the individual should become "one with the Infinite", without enquiring what is happening to humanity as a whole. Its non-historical character precludes any goal of history at which man has to aim, an aim which necessarily excludes all other aims. This is the reason for the weary resignation, the secret despair of achieving the True and the Good, which dwells within mysticism.

On the other hand, certainly it is very easy for sinful man to misunderstand faith in the God who alone wills to be Lord in the sense of practical intolerance. Sinful man believes that he ought to help the truth of God by forcible means. This confusion, especially this confusion of truth and violence, characterizes the "Yahweh"-religion of pre-prophetic Israel, Islam, and *per nefas*, empirical Christianity after Constantine. This false "theocracy" is in opposition to the Gospel of the Feet-washing and the Cross; there has been no more terrible misunderstanding of the Cross than the Crusades.

## 3. THE GOOD AS HOLY, AND THE GOOD AS AUTONOMOUS

The philosophy of Positivism (Comte, Spencer), with its purely natural explanation of the Moral, expresses a very ancient view, in its extremest form: namely, the conception of the autonomy of the moral consciousness: the view that there is an ethic which is independent of God. This view, which has been continually re-formulated since the days of the Sophists, and has been defended with varying degrees of intensity, has a certain basis of fact. As at the present time there are many people who will admit the existence of a Moral Imperative, but who will not admit that there is a Divine Will, so also the history of mankind shows a widespread independence, both of morality from religion, as well as of religion from morality. The history of religions shows numerous and impressive manifestations of the Numinous, which are not only ethically indifferent, but which must indeed be called immoral and contrary to morality; on the other hand, we see moral ideas which develop independently of the given religion, and indeed which even develop in opposition to it. From the historical, empirical point of view there is no clear, positive connexion (and often none at all), between the Moral and the Religious. Now a certain philosophical ethic has taken this state of affairs as the starting-point of its thought, and has produced the idea of the "autonomous" ethic, which, for its part, has found its most logical secular expression in the philosophy of Positivism. While at the beginning of the Enlightenment, in the thought of Herbert of Cherbury, and still more in that of John Locke, the Moral was never thought of apart from the Will of God, and while even Kant (although not very clearly, in spite of his insistence on the "autonomy" of the Moral), to some extent still admits this connexion, in the post-Kantian philosophy the idea of an "autonomous" ethic begins to be taken seriously; the Moral Law, however, is still regarded as something mysterious, and transcendent; only no one now ventures to take the step of anchoring this Moral Law, from the point of view of religion, in the Will of God. Positivism, however, eliminates even that last relic of the religious background of ethics, the mystery of the Transcendent, and "explains" the Moral from the psychological and biological point of view, as "necessary" for human life in community.

And yet there still lingers an element of the mystery of the Divine, even if not in the form of explicit theory, yet in the actual moral consciousness, in connexion with the idea of responsibility; the "thou shalt not . . ." still retains a semi-numinous quality; it suggests that there is a limit beyond which it is not right to pass; this prohibition has an almost "sacred" character. This comes out most clearly in the elementary phenomenon of "conscience". Even where this is explained on entirely "natural" grounds, in practice, man feels intuitively that there is something mysterious about conscience; it is like a voice from another world, speaking to us here and now, checking us, accusing us, and making demands upon us. The "unwritten law" fills even the unbeliever with a kind of religious awe, even when he does not want to admit this, and in theory denies it.

This phenomenon suggests the connexion between the Will of God and the Moral. From the standpoint of revelation this is a clear indication of truth; we might indeed regard this fact as a kind of "proof of Christianity", since only here do we see how intimate is the connexion between religion and ethics; here it is clearly and plainly defined. Here Religion is wholly ethical, and ethics is wholly religious. The love of God revealed in Jesus Christ, *Agape*, is both the sole norm and the sole content of moral behaviour. Existence-in-love is both perfect piety and perfect morality, since even Jesus Christ, while He reveals the Nature of God, at the same time reveals, and fully expresses in His life the perfectly Human. Pure Humanity is also perfect divinity; the true *Humanum* is present where the true *Divinum* reveals itself.

All this, however, shows that the separation between a religion which is indifferent to ethics, and an ethic which has no use for religion, and thus the phenomenon of an ethic which is supposed to be "autonomous", is a profound misunderstanding of truth. Man's sinful blindness comes out in the fact that instead of honouring a Holy God, he pays homage to an ethically neutral or even immoral Numinous. The fact that he believes in an autonomous ethic, and thus regards the Moral Law as severed from the Will of God, and the Law of God implanted in his reason as the law of his reason, as "autonomy", is due to his self-willed alienation from God. A "religion" which respects no "law", and an ethic which has lost all sense of the Holy, are both products of the Fall: both show what happens when man is severed from his Creator. This would also be true, if it could be proved to apply to that which is known in the scale of development as "primitive religion". In actual fact, however, it is precisely the "primitive" religions which show a remarkable union of ethical and religious elements in the phenomenon of Taboo, which erects barriers which are both "numinous" and "ethical". This does not mean that this "primitive" element could be equated with that which might be described in theological terms as the "primal" or "original"; for even this primitive unity of religion and morality, when measured by the truly Moral and the truly Religious, is both non-moral and non-religious. The "Original", in the sense of the Revelation in Creation, cannot be classified under any historical heading, nor under any theory of development, any more than this is possible for the Fall. (On this point see my theological anthropology, *Der Mensch im Widerspruch*, pp. 121 ff.)

## CHAPTER 15

## GOD IS LOVE

THE statement "God is Love" points to the very heart of the message of the New Testament, of the Christian Gospel. As in the Old Testament everything turns on the Holiness of God, so in the New everything turns on the Love of God. Here the main concern is with the love of the *holy* God; hence the truth of the Holiness of God is not only historically but actually the first to be perceived; but the Holiness which the Bible teaches is the Holiness of the God who is Love, therefore the truth of the Holiness of God is completed in the knowledge of His Love. This indissoluble connexion between Holiness and Love is the characteristic and decisive element in the Christian Idea of God. Thus, in this paradoxical dualism of Holiness and Love, God reveals His Name to us; it is thus that He wills to be known and worshipped. It is thus that He reveals Himself, simply and solely, in the Bible, in Jesus Christ.

The message that God is Love, is something wholly new in the world. We perceive this if we try to apply the statement to the divinities of the various religions of the world: Wotan is Love, Zeus, Jupiter, Brahma, Ahura Mazda, Vishnu, Allah, is Love. All these combinations are obviously wholly impossible. Even the God of Plato, who is the principle of all Good, is not Love. Plato would have met the statement "God is Love" with a bewildered shake of the head. From the standpoint of his thought such a statement would have been utter nonsense. "One only loves that which one does not possess, and that which one lacks. . . ."[1] Whoever would dream of desiring that which he already possesses." "A god does not have any intercourse with men."[2] The idea of love, and the humanly-conceived idea of the god who is entirely self-sufficient are mutually exclusive. Although from the point of view of the Platonist, Aristotelian, or Neo-Platonist philosophy, it is true that it is quite proper to say that man can, and indeed must love God,[3] yet it is equally clear that to introduce the statement "God *is* Love" into their systems of thought, would be completely nonsensical. Rather, this statement is the supreme point of the Biblical

---

[1] Plato, *Symposium*, p. 200.      [2] *Ibid.*, p. 203.
[3] Exactly the same may be said of the *"amor intellectualis Dei"* of Spinoza, who denies the love of God, but desires love to God.

revelation alone, and only in this connexion is it possible and intelligible. The God who makes Himself known to us in His revelation, who, above all, discloses His Name to us in the Incarnation of the Word in Jesus Christ, is the God whose whole revelation is one sole movement of gracious condescension to man, an act of saving Mercy.

This connexion between the revelation[1] and the incomprehensible Mercy of God is proclaimed for the first time by the Prophet Hosea. The "Unfathomable"—the love that is not based upon any quality in Israel, but solely in the election which is rooted in the will of God—expresses the eternal love of God. God's faithfulness to His unfaithful people springs out of an incomprehensible love, for which the "foolish" love of Hosea for his unfaithful wife is both the most daring parable of the love of God and also one which is chosen by God Himself. In the later testimony to revelation, too, in the writings of Jeremiah,[2] and in the Book of Deuteronomy, the Covenant of God with Israel is the outflow of His eternal Love.[3] It is not because there is anything special about Israel—for it was a particularly unfaithful people—that from the very beginning and all through its history, with its repeated apostasy, God has continually drawn it back to Himself, and continually saved it.[4] The promise of its final redemption, and the fulfilment of the Covenant with God is based upon this divine love alone, not upon the fact of Israel's repentance.[5] Thus already in the Old Testament the witness to the love of God shines forth.

But it is only in the New Testament, in the testimony to the love shown to sinners by the Saviour, Jesus Christ, "who came to seek and to save that which was lost",[6] that this Love of God becomes the dominant theme, and indeed the central theme of the revealed truth which is proclaimed to man. The sending of the "Son of His love",[7] the surrender of His "own Son" to the death on the Cross, the act of reconciliation which proceeds from God alone, all this—and this alone—shows us what the love of God means; this, too, shows us why it is the real meaning of the whole of the divine revelation, and thus that in this revelation God discloses the secret of His being. "Herein is love, not that we loved God, but that He loved us."[8] To reveal this love, that is the Mission of Jesus, that is the content of the New Covenant. Only now is it possible to express

[1] Cf. *Wörterbuch zum N.T.*, I, pp. 30 ff.
[2] Jer. 12: 7–9; 3: 19; 3: 4; 4: 1.   [3] Deut. 6: 7 ff.
[4] Hosea 14: 5.   [5] Is. 65: 1 ff.
[6] Luke 19: 10.   [7] Col. 1: 3.   [8] 1 John 4: 10.

the most daring statement that has ever been made in human language: "God IS Love".[1] This implies that love is not a "quality" or an "attribute" of God; God does not share with other beings the quality of being "loving". Rather, Love— that is, the love of which the Bible speaks—is the very Nature of God, so that we can say: "He that abideth in love abideth in God.[2] It is not that God is "loving", but that He is, as Luther says, "a furnace and blaze of such love that it fills heaven and earth".[3] "If a man tried to paint such love, he would have to make a picture that would not really be human or angelic or heavenly any longer, but it would be a picture of GOD HIMSELF."[4]

This becomes clear when we try to say what is here meant by love. For when we try to make this intelligible, all that we can say, at its best, is in the form of parable. It is not that we already know what "love" is, and can then apply it to God; if this were so, love would be really a "quality" of God, but not His Nature, as Holiness is His Nature. Rather, the situation is this: that the *idea*, the understanding of love— the *Agape* of the New Testament—can only be understood from what *happens* in revelation. The story of revelation, Jesus Christ, the Crucified, defines *realiter* the meaning of the new conception: Love, which is *Agape*. Love is the self-giving of God: love is the free and generous grace of the One who is Holy Lord.

We can approach this understanding of *Agape* (in order to avoid misunderstanding we will in future use this term for love) by comparing it with what is usually meant by the word "love". Let us take as our starting-point the Greek idea of *Eros*. When the Greek speaks of Love he means and says *Eros*.[5] This does not mean only the desire of the senses, the desire which is connected with the sex-life of man. We interpret *Eros* in the broad, and at the same time sublime, sense in which the word is used in Plato's *Symposium*. *Eros*, so it is said in this work, is the son of Poros—superfluity, and Penia—poverty.

Eros is the desire for that which we do not possess, but which we ought to have, or would like to have. *Eros* is therefore directed towards a particular value; we love something because it has value, because it is worthy to be loved. Thus *Eros* is that love which is derived from, and evoked by the beloved. It is

[1] I John 4: 8, 16.     [2] I John 4: 16.
[3] Luther, *W.*, 36, 424.     [4] *Ibid.*
[5] Cf. Nygren, *Eros v. Agape*, 2 vols.—and *Theol. Wörterbuch zum. N.T.*, I, pp. 34 ff.

the movement which aims at the fulfilment of value, the appropriation of value, the completion of value. The character of the values which attract us, and thus evoke "love" from us, is, it is true, a very significant and important question, but it does not concern us here. This variety of values, at which *Eros* aims—whether natural or spiritual, high or low, etc.—may indeed create different sorts of *Eros*; but this shows all the more clearly the element common to all these varieties, namely, that the love which is *Eros* is the desire for value, and the will to appropriate such value. In all cases *Eros* is based upon, motivated by, the belovéd, therefore it is perfectly intelligible and transparent.

This, however, is true of all the love with which we are familiar, whether it be the love of which the poets sing, the love which draws man and woman together, the love which is kindled by the sight of beauty, the love of the fatherland, mother love, the love of friendship—all this is love which is based upon something which has been "motivated", which is kindled by its object, and which makes it desire and strive for, or to enjoy and maintain, union with that which it loves. Whether the object loved is material or non-material, vital or non-vital, concrete or abstract, neutral or personal—it is always something which is known to contain *value*, something "lovable" which is loved.

The Love of God, the *Agape* of the New Testament, is quite different. It does not seek value, but it creates value or gives value; it does not desire to get but to give; it is not "attracted" by some lovable quality, but it is poured out on those who are worthless and degraded; in the strict sense of the word this Love is "unfathomable", and "passeth all understanding". This Divine Love turns to those for whom no one cares, because there is nothing "lovable" about them—people whom we would instinctively shun or even hate. The highest expression of this *Agape*, therefore, is loving fidelity to the unfaithful, the love of the Holy God for those who desecrate His sanctuary, the love of the Holy Lord for one who is rebellious and disobedient— that is, the sinner. The contrast between Divine and human love also comes out very clearly in its aim. This love (*Agape*), does not seek to transfer a value from the belovéd to the one who loves, it does not seek the fulfilment of value. Here the One who loves does not seek anything for Himself; all He desires is to benefit the one He loves. And the benefit He wants to impart is not "something", but His very Self, for this Love is self-surrender, self-giving to the other, to whom love is directed. "For God so loved the world, that He gave His only-begotten Son, that whosoever believeth on Him should not perish, but should have eternal life."[1] And this indeed took place "while we were yet sinners",[2] for "while we were yet weak . . . Christ died for the ungodly . . .[3] while we were enemies."[4] This Love is truly unfathomable, unmotivated, incomprehensible; it springs solely from the will of God Himself; that is, from His incomprehensible will to give His very self to us.

*This* kind of Love we do not know. From our human point of view we can only understand that other kind of love, which is based upon, and motivated by, the worthiness of the object to be loved. Because the pre-Christian philosopher only knows this sort of love, he cannot proceed to formulate the idea that God could love. The purer and the more spiritual his idea of God becomes, the more firmly must he reject the idea that God can love, or that He is love. God has indeed all that He needs; He is in Himself perfect, therefore He is self-sufficient. He desires nothing outside Himself, hence He does not love. He can, of course, *be loved*, for the sake of His perfection, eternity, and blessédness, but He Himself cannot love; for only one who needs fulfilment can and must love; love is indeed the fulfilment of value, or rather the striving after the value which will lead to completion. Hence wherever God is conceived as the Absolute the Love of God is unthinkable.[5] There is nothing in the Absolute which could move it to give itself, and to seek *communion* with a being which is not absolute. The Absolute is sufficient to itself, and does not go out of itself. The God whom we "think" for ourselves, the God of human thought, cannot love.

Only now do we understand why love and revelation belong to one another. Love is the movement which goes-out-of-oneself, which stoops down to that which is below: it is the self-giving, the self-communication of God—and it is *this* which is His revelation. The idea of self-communication gathers up into one the two elements love and revelation. The distinction between a "formal principle" and a "material principle", between "revelation" (Bible) and "grace" (Justification) is a misunderstanding. Revelation is gracious love and grace is revelation. Jesus Christ is the revelation; He is the Love of

[1] John 3: 16.  [2] Rom. 5: 8.  [3] Rom. 5: 6.
[4] Rom. 5: 10.  [5] Cf. below, pp. 201 ff.

God in Person. Only when we understand love as this self-communication of God do we grasp it as groundless and generous, as freely-electing, as incomprehensible love, as that which the Bible calls *Agape*. To know this love means to know His self-communication. From our end, from our natural experience of love, the nature of *Agape* is not intelligible, in so far as all natural self-giving has its deepest foundation in an attraction to the beloved. Hence the perception of this love is bound up with the event of revelation, or, as we have already said, this love does not define itself in intellectual terms, but in an Event.

From what we have just said it is also clear why this love is not a "quality" of God, but is His Nature, like Holiness. For this love is nothing other than the desire to impart Himself, the will of God to reveal Himself. God's Nature is this capacity to impart Himself, just as it is His Nature to will to be Lord and to assert and maintain His claims. Revelation is not only the means through which God shows us Himself, as He is; but revelation is the flowering of the Divine Nature itself; by His very Nature God is one who wills to reveal Himself; for this very reason, too, He is the One who loves.

To go forth from Oneself, to impart Oneself—this is the Nature of the Living God, in contrast to the self-sufficient Being of the Absolute of thought. Hence revelation is not only a means, it is the "thing itself". The God of revelation, that is, the God whose Nature it is to impart Himself, can only be known in this event of self-revelation; a God who cannot be known *thus*, is *eo ipso* not this God. Likewise: only in the actual process of this self-communication do we experience that God is One who loves; and only in this self-communication do we learn what this Love is—this Love which is fathomless, generous, free, and without "motive".

This brings us to the question of the relation between Love and Holiness; for just as there is an essential and necessary relation between Love and Revelation, so also, as we have already seen, is there a similar relation between Holiness and Revelation. What, then, is the relation between this self-giving Love and the Holiness of God?

First of all, there is a sharp and essential contrast; for Holiness creates distance, but love creates communion. Holiness erects barriers, love breaks through them. Holiness is the will which asserts its rights, and claims glory, recognition, sovereignty. The Holy God speaks thus: "I will to have all for

Myself; claim everything for Myself." But love is the very opposite of all this. Love says: "all for thee, nothing for me". Love is surrender, sacrifice, renunciation of one's own claims, service.[1] Above all, however, the contrast becomes clear when we look at Holiness in its negative form: as the wrath of God, which annihilates resistance, and finally crushes those who resist Him. This contrast must not be glossed over or weakened, for if we do either we make it impossible to understand either Holiness or Love. The question, however, is this: How, then, can both exist together? Is there not a danger that if we do hold them both, by asserting that both are the Nature of God, our Idea of God may be infected with an element of tension which must inevitably destroy its unity?

First of all we must recognize that Holiness is the *presupposition* of the Love that gives itself freely. To use a parable from human life—as the love of a human being only has value if he has some self-respect, if he has some care for his own honour, so only the love of the *Holy* God is truly free and generous love. Only the God who in Himself possesses all Perfection, who is perfectly self-sufficient and needs no other, thus only the God who is absolute Lord, sovereign personality, can love in freedom, can love unfathomably. One who needs another loves the other with *Eros*, not with *Agape*. Only He who owes man nothing, because He is Creator and Lord, in whose Presence all human claims are stilled,[2] because all from the very outset belongs to God, can love truly generously. So then also the verdict of God upon sinful man, namely, that he is an enemy of God, a rebel, one who is godless,[3] is the presupposition of that highest love, which loves the sinner, and gives peace to the rebel. One who is a sinner in the light of the Holy Will of God, who has been condemned by the Holy Law of God, is the one whose sin is forgiven, and to whom mercy and grace are freely given. Only where the Holiness of God and the judgment on man which is its necessary result, are taken very seriously, can we begin to see the unfathomable nature of the forgiving love of God, and thus can love be understood as *Agape*.

But the connexion between Holiness and Love is still more intimate. We have already seen that Holiness contains the two-fold movement away from God, for He is Holy—and

[1] Matt. 20: 28; John 13: 1 ff.; 10: 11; 15: 13.
[2] Jer. 18: 6; Rom. 9: 20 ff.                    [3] Rom. 5: 8 ff.; 8: 7.

attraction to Him, for He is Love. As the Holy One, God, wills that His Holy will shall be realized in the whole of His human creation, by the fact that He is freely and willingly obeyed. Thus God wills that the creature should become full of His own nature—and that is the same as His will to impart Himself, His love. God's Holy will is fulfilled in the creature as perfect communion with Him, the Holy One, and this is His Love. The perfect rule of God is only realized where His Love breaks down all resistance, and where His own love streams back to Him from the hearts of His own people. Only in the fact that God gives Himself wholly in His Son do those who are His own wholly become His property.[1] Thus Holiness merges into Love, and thus becomes complete. Conversely, the self-communication of God is only achieved where the creature is wholly united with the Holy Will of God, and is a mirror of His holy nature; where, loving Him, it glorifies Him. In Jesus Christ, in the perfect communion of the redeemed with the Redeemer, and of the redeemed with each other, both are gathered up into one: the rule of the Holy God, and the self-communication of the merciful God.[2] There both are one: the complete δόξα, the reflection of Holiness in the creature, and complete communion and salvation.

For us human beings this is a combination of two opposite elements which is quite beyond our understanding; Holiness and Love must, first of all, be sharply contrasted, and indeed set in opposition to one another, and yet Love completes Holiness, and is only fully Love in the fulfilment of Holiness. It is thus that Hosea, who was the first to proclaim the unfathomable and boundless and incomprehensible love of God, saw the Love of God: "How shall I give thee up, Ephraim? how shall I deliver thee, Israel . . .? mine heart is turned within Me, My compassions are kindled together. I will not execute the fierceness of Mine anger, I will not return to destroy Ephraim: for I am God, and not man; the Holy One in the midst of thee: and I will not come in wrath."[3] The Second Isaiah, likewise, emphasizes the redemption of the people of Israel from the point of view of "sanctification". As the Holy One, Yahweh expiates man's guilt.[4] It is thus, however, above all, that Jesus Christ Himself is the Holy One. In Him God accomplishes His rule; that is why He is called CHRIST; in

---

[1] This is the thought which lies behind the Biblical phrase that believers, through the death of Christ, have become His "purchased possession", or have been "bought with a price" (1 Peter 1: 18; 1 Cor. 6: 22; Titus 2: 14).

[2] John 17: 22.   [3] Hosea 11: 8–9 (R.V. marg.).   [4] Is. 48: 9; 43: 25.

Him, also, through the Atonement, He creates perfect communion with Himself. It is on the basis of this communion that Christian believers are called "the saints". The acquittal of sinners and the blotting out of their guilt is at the same time their sanctification.[1] It is the *Holy* Spirit who unites them, and makes them holy. Those who are "called to be saints" are sanctified in Christ; they are "brethren beloved of the Lord . . . God chose you from the beginning unto salvation in sanctification of the Spirit".[2] The most wonderful testimony to this final unity between Holiness and reconciling Love is found indeed, at the close of the Farewell discourses of Jesus in the Gospel of John: "Holy Father, keep them in Thy Name which Thou hast given me, that they may be one, even as we are . . . that the world may know that Thou didst send Me, and lovedst them, even as Thou lovedst Me."[3] The whole passage is a symphony, in which the themes of Holiness, Glory, Communion, and Love constantly recur and blend in perfect harmony. The *"gratia"* is fulfilled in the *"gloria"*, and the *"gloria"* itself is simply perfect communion.

Upon what ground can we—may we—must we say: God is Love? We have already answered this question by saying that the foundation of this statement can, may, and must be revelation. We have already rejected the misunderstanding that the revelation is merely the means of the disclosure through which we learn that God is Love. For were this the case, there would be only an indirect, instrumental relation between Love and revelation, like that which exists between a gift and the one who transmits the gift. Rather, revelation as the self-communication of God, is the act of Divine Love. As the One who reveals, namely, as the One who reveals Himself, God is One who loves.

In the traditional works of dogmatics, both the Holiness and the Love of God are treated under the heading of the doctrine of the "Divine Attributes", and indeed, they are treated after the "metaphysical attributes" have been discussed, under the heading of the "ethical attributes". This arrangement shows the influence of those metaphysical and speculative ideas derived from Greek thought, which is so utterly opposed to that of the Bible. The Bible really means that Love is God's *Nature*, and not merely His "temper" (or disposition). Just as sovereignty is His Nature—the Being who is Absolute Subject —so also, to put it in an abstract way for once, so also His

[1] I Cor. 6: 11.  [2] 2 Thess. 2: 13.  [3] John 17: 11 ff.

Being as Subject is "for-some-end", it is Being which goes forth from Itself, Being which communicates Itself. To use a parable: We cannot grasp or describe the nature of radium without speaking of radio-activity. Radium is the radiant element—that is its very nature. Even so the nature of God is to shine forth in His Glory, communicating activity, personal being, which wills communion. There is nothing "more metaphysical" in the doctrine of God than this: that God's Nature in Himself is precisely His Being-for-us. If the doctrine of God as He is "in Himself" is the philosophical formula of "Being-Subject", then the Christian formula for the Being of God is "Being-for-us", or, as we have just said: "Being-for-something" (for some purpose). To think that it is correct *first of all* to deal with the metaphysical Being of God, and *then* with His Love, as His "ethical attribute", means that the decisive element in the Biblical Idea of God has not been perceived. That is why it is so important to know the Love of God not as an "attribute", but as the fundamental Nature of God. God's Nature is the radiation of spiritual energy, an energy which is the will to impart Himself. In contrast to all other forms of existence, this is the Nature of God: the will to impart Himself. This is Christian ontology, this is the doctrine of the Being of God, and this is fundamentally different from that of speculation.

Only now do we see clearly the connexion between revelation and the Nature of God. Because God's Nature is radiating spiritual energy, the will to impart Himself, therefore He is the God of revelation. And because He is the God of revelation, He can only be known *through* and *in* His revelation. Hence all other "knowledge" of God is an idolatrous materialization of God, however "spiritualized" and abstract it may be. Hence the line of thought represented by this speculative, human way of thinking, which came into the life of the Church from the Platonist doctrine of God of the Early Church, can only be injurious to the understanding of the Biblical Idea of God. How can He whose Nature it is to radiate energy be known otherwise than in this spiritual radiation? Thus, how can the God whose Nature it is to will to impart Himself, be known otherwise than in this self-impartation? On the other hand, when man tries to understand God in a different way, by a process of abstraction from Nature, as the Absolute, it is inevitable that he should miss the meaning of His Nature; thus there arises that fatal compromise between Greek speculative thought and Biblical thought, which we see in the traditional doctrine of the Love of God as an "ethical attribute"!

At first sight, however, the idea that God's "metaphysical" Being is not only "God as He is in Himself" (Subject), but also God as He is "For-us", is objectionable, because it seems to suggest that such a relation of God to His creation should be reckoned an integral part of the Nature of God, which, indeed, is unthinkable. In point of fact, we are here concerned with something quite different, namely, that it is only from this "God as He is in Himself" that creatures come into being at all. The first effect of this Being of God "for us" is the Creation; this therefore is both the manifestation of His Nature and the revelation and the work of His Love: the gracious, kindly Creation of the Lord who in Himself is Perfect, who desires to have an "other" alongside of Himself, and to have communion with him, who wishes to impart Himself to him. Moreover, we must now consider the different forms of the revelation of God, as the manifestation of His love.

The Original revelation in the Creation already possesses this "forth-going" character. God might, indeed, have existed without creating; He does not need a creation. He is sufficient unto Himself. But He does not will this; He wills to impart Himself; He wills to give Himself to another, "over against" Himself, to whom He can impart something of Himself. This comes out most clearly in the fact that He has created man "in His own image". It is His will that His own quality, His own Holiness, should be reflected in the face of Man. The first truth this reveals is that the basis of the fact that Man is "made in the Image of God" is Holiness. As the Holy One, God wills that man's whole personality should be stamped with the "Image" of the Creator, as *His* property. This reflection, however, can, and should, take place only in the fact that God gives Himself. It is the Love which God gives which streams back to Him as a return of love from man, that love which is to make man like God, that self-giving love which has no other reason than that it is love itself, "that ye may be sons of your Father which is in heaven", who "maketh His sun to rise on the evil and the good, and sendeth rain on the just and the unjust".[1] The man who has been created to be like God is one who has been created in love, and for love, and this is the quality of such a love: "We love, because He first loved us."[2]

[1] Matt. 5: 45      [2] 1 John 4: 19.

193

This is man's destiny in Creation, which remains his destiny, in spite of sin, but which is actually destroyed by sin, and can only be realized by redemption in Christ: "But we all, with unveiled face reflecting as a mirror the glory of the Lord, are transformed into the same image, even as from the Lord the Spirit."[1]

Similarly the Old Testament Covenant revelation derives its origin and its meaning from this self-giving love. It is the election of the people of Israel, which, from the human point of view, was so worthless, and in no way worthy of love, with which it begins.[2] It is the making of the Covenant between the Lord who stoops down to His people, and the people which has nothing but its sense of need, in which this election takes historical form. The Holy One of Israel is the God of the Covenant who wills to have complete fellowship with, and in, His people.[3] Even where God's wrath is revealed, this revelation is not made in order to annihilate Israel, but in order to remove its resistance, to lead it to repentance and obedience, in order to create real union with God.[4]

Thus, too, the Promised Messiah is not only One who will establish the Rule of God, but One who is also the Servant of the Lord, who takes upon Himself the sins of the people,[5] and His rule, the Messianic Kingdom, is the state where God and people truly become one.[6] The Messianic era is also the era of the New Covenant, where sin will be forgiven, and the will of God will be implanted in the hearts of men.[7]

Thus the New Testament, the actual Coming of the Promised Messiah, is both the fulfilment of the revelation, and the fulfilment of the establishment of communion, the dawn of the rule of God, and the realization of communion with God. Jesus Christ, the Crucified, is the perfect self-communication of God to His sinful creatures. In the Cross of Jesus two things take place: the Lord God comes into His own, and the Love of God is completely expressed.[8] It is the final element in the descending movement, the "stooping-down" of God to man—and in the Resurrection this proves to be the victory of the Holy God over the whole rebellious world.[9]

Thus, also, the *witness* to the revelation, whether it be the primitive witness of the Apostles or the witness of the Church

---

[1] 2 Cor. 3: 18.     [2] Cf. Ezek. 16: 4 ff.; Hosea 13: 5; Is. 5: 1 ff.
[3] Exod. 19: 5 ff.; Jer. 7: 23; 3: 19 ff.     [4] Hosea 6: 1 ff.
[5] Is. 53.     [6] Ezek. 36: 26; 34: 23 ff.
[7] Jer. 31: 31 ff.     [8] Rom. 3: 25.     [9] Col. 2: 15.

which is based upon this testimony, is itself both a service and an act of divine Love: "The love of Christ constraineth us."[1] All preaching is not only the message of the love of God, but it is a message and a service which is rendered out of love: it is both readiness for community and the creation of community: it means drawing others into the communion which we have with Christ and through Him.[2]

There is still one point to be cleared up, which militates against the full understanding of Love as the Nature of God. If love, in the sense of *Agape*, generous, self-sacrificing love, and even the love of our enemies, is what God expects from man, and is indeed laid upon him as a command, how can something which man is *commanded* to do be the Nature of God? And how can we maintain that something which is the sum-total of the Moral Law can only be understood through revelation— through the self-surrender of God in the death of His Son on the Cross? If this Moral Law exists, is there not also a possibility of understanding what love is without the revelation of God's grace? In point of fact, one of the deepest roots of the mis-understanding of Love as merely a "quality" or "attribute" of God, and thus that love is like other familiar qualities which we know in our own experience and can then transfer to God, springs from the reflection that love is the New *Commandment*. Thus we must try to make quite clear the difference between *Agape* as a "Command", and the *Agape* which is revealed to us in Jesus Christ, and their relation to one another. From the point we have now reached in our argument, it will not be difficult to show that all the problems connected with the fact of the commandment of Love, can be solved.

(1) The controversy between those who maintain that the summons to love our neighbour—that is, *Agape* as a Command-ment—is known to all men, and those who deny this, is very ancient, and it is still undecided. Obviously both those who deny this fact and those who assert it have good reasons for their point of view.[3] This is the actual situation: that among all peoples, and at all times, there has been some knowledge of a moral law of responsibility for others, and consideration for their welfare, or a form of the "Golden Rule".[4] This fact can be proved historically as well as from reflection upon the Moral

[1] 2 Cor. 5: 14; 1 Thess. 2: 7 ff.      [2] 1 John 1: 3.
[3] Cf. Bultmann, *Das christliche Gebot der Nächstenliebe* in *Glauben u. Verstehen*, pp. 229 ff.      [4] Matt. 7: 12.

Imperative. The "Golden Rule" is found in many places, quite apart from the Biblical revelation.[1] But who would care to maintain that this Golden Rule already contains the whole mystery of self-giving Love (*Agape*)? Even the recognition of the duty of loving our enemies is a very rare phenomenon in the history of the moral views of many nations. Still less, however, is the radical sense which Jesus gives to the requirement of love in the Sermon on the Mount generally known. But the fact that this Commandment contains the whole Law, that all the Moral Law, or the Divine Command, is summed up in *this*, but "this", meant with that absoluteness which Jesus teaches—indeed, even compared with the moral teaching of the Old Testament, this is[2] something new.

(2) Is the Commandment of love to be understood in the sense of self-giving love at all? He who knows love merely as a command, does not really know what love is.[3] It is in the nature of law that it demands something which the man who is only acquainted with law cannot do. But this impotence is in the last resort also a form of ignorance. The man who only knows *Agape* in the form of the Law does not really know what *Agape* is. The Law only gives him a glimmer of it, and this is the reason why the Law is powerless to move the will to that which is truly the Good. Indeed, ultimately the form of the Commandment is opposed to the content of *Agape*. How can love be *commanded*! Love is precisely that which cannot be commanded—for who could love at the bidding of another? And yet at the same time it is the one thing which must be commanded. This is the tragic element in the Moral Law of which St. Paul speaks in the Epistle to the Romans,[4] which every Christian knows.

(3) In point of fact, the Moral Law of the love of our neighbour does not stand by itself, but it is the result of the original relation between the self-giving, creating God, and the man who has been created by Him and for Him. The first element is man's relation with God is not the Law, but the self-giving love of God; but this generous love of God claims the will of man for Himself. The love which God has first of all given to

[1] Cf. Westermarck, *Christianity and Morals*, pp. 70 ff.; Spooner, "Golden Rule" in the *Encyclopaedia of Religion and Ethics*, VI, p. 311.

[2] In the Old Testament the command to love our neighbour (Lev. 19: 18) is *one* among many others.

[3] Cf. "The Dialectic of Law" in my book *Man in Revolt*.

[4] Rom. 7: 14 ff.

us is to be given back to God and our neighbour in our loving. Actually, the Moral Law does not come first, but second. It does not come before, but *after* the love which is given to us. Its original form is that which is expressed in the words: "We love . . . because He first loved us"; the truth is that moral obedience is man's response to the Love which he has received as a gift.

But man, in his sinful perversion, has transposed this order; or, rather, all he has retained of the original revelation of the Divine Love is the abstract Moral Law, and this in an ambiguous form. The Law is not the original element, but it is something which has "slipped in between".[1] But to sinful man it now seems to be the primary element, that is, until he has learnt to know the revelation of Christ. The world before, and outside of, Christ, therefore, knows the Law of God only as the Moral Law of the love of our neighbour, but not as the command of the love of God. The twofold Commandment[2] is exclusively of Biblical origin, and—as it is expounded by Jesus—can only be understood within the context of the divine revelation of Love. Jesus does not teach an abstract "law in itself", but He proclaims the living law of the divine Rule which He reveals and brings with Himself. Hence the meaning of *Agape* as the demand of God only becomes intelligible to one who knows the fulfilment of this law from the standpoint of Jesus Christ, in the surrender of Christ Himself; that is, only to one who receives the divine gift in Jesus Christ in faith. Thus the real knowledge of what is meant by the command to love our neighbour agrees with the experience of the love of God which has been given. Thus it confirms this fact: only one who knows the revelation of the love of God knows the true meaning of the words "the love of our neighbour"; a phrase which he may, it is true, have always known as an abstract law, but whose meaning always remained hidden from him. What the love that is commanded *is*, only he can know who has *experienced* the love which has been given.[3]

From the days of the Enlightenment the mistaken view has been widespread that the essential element in Christianity is the "command to love our neighbour". The fact that Kant equated the Categorical Imperative with the Sermon on the Mount[4] did a great deal to extend this idea. In this moral

---

[1] Rom. 5: 20.    [2] Matt. 22: 37, 38.    [3] Rom. 8: 39.
[4] In *Religion innerhalb der Grenzen* . . . IV, 1, 1: *Die Christliche Religion als natürliche Religion.*

teaching the moral task is totally severed from the divine gift, and in this religious teaching the idea of God has been so entirely defaced that it has become the idea of a moral Law-giver. The consequence is, not only is the truth of the self-giving grace (of God) eliminated, but also the command to love one's neighbour is misunderstood. The Categorical Imperative can never command men to love their neighbours, all it can do is to urge men to respect one another.[1] Respect for other men is a great thing; but it is not the love of one's neighbour. Kant, however, was absolutely right when he said that respect alone could be commanded, but not love. The Biblical Commandment of the love of one's neighbour cannot be understood, nor is it intended to be understood, as an isolated commandment.

The Biblical commandment of the love of our neighbour, both in the Old and in the New Testament, springs from the proclamation of the divine generous love which comes first. To put the command, the task, first—*that* is the misunderstanding. In the message of the Bible the gift comes first and the task second. Thus only where the commandment is understood as coming second does the rational principle of respect for human persons become the religious commandment of the love of our neighbour. For only there can love be understood as the love which gives, and man as the neighbour who needs this love. Between the Categorical Imperative of Kant and the Biblical commandment of the love of one's neighbour there lies the same gulf as that which stretches between his doctrine of the autonomy of the transcendental reason and the Biblical faith in the Creator.

This moralistic sterility of the Moral Law in the Enlighten-ment would not, however, have been possible had not the Church, on the other hand, in its ecclesiastical orthodoxy, misunderstood the nature of faith (by regarding it as belief in Verbal Inspiration and in a body of doctrine), and thus des-troyed love. As against an orthodoxy which had become ethically sterile the moral sentiment and seriousness of the Kantian Enlightenment was as much justified in its attitude as, measured by the standard of the Bible, it was mistaken about the indissoluble union of faith and love. The Bible knows nothing of that "orthodox", ethically sterile, literalist view of Biblical Inspiration. It only knows of "faith which worketh through love".[2] Faith is indeed simply being grasped and held

[1] Kant, *Kr. d. prakt. Vernunft*, I, 1 B, III. "Love cannot be commanded" (Cf. *Offenbarung v. Vernunft*, pp. 326 ff.).　　　　　　　　　[2] Gal. 5: 6.

by the love of God in Jesus Christ. It is *that* which makes man a "new creature"[1] which comes to pass when a man is "in Christ", that he may no longer "live unto himself".[2] The self-communication of God to man does not end in "knowing something about" faith, but in the actual communication of His self-giving love. Hence the final word of the Biblical revelation is not "faith" but "love". Faith is indeed simply the vessel which receives the divine love.[3] It is not *faith* which "never faileth"[4]—for it disappears with the earthly conditions of life—but *love*; for this love is: God Himself. God is not faith, but God is love. The fact that God is love is the quintessence, the central word of the whole Bible. The God of revelation is the God of love.

Hence, because God is the Holy One, and because He is Love, He wills to impart Himself. His Nature, His inmost secret is self-communication. Thus within Himself, "before all worlds", He is the Self-Communicating One. This brings us to the mystery of the doctrine of the Trinity. This doctrine tells us that the God who reveals His Nature to us is the same as the Son who reveals the divine Nature, and that they are both the same God, and yet distinct, as the Revealer and the Revealed. The doctrine of the Triune God contains the truth—which we have already perceived to be the decisive element in the Biblical doctrine of God: the unity of God's Nature and of His revelation. If we ask what is the Name in which God reveals to us His Nature, then the answer of the New Testament is: It is the threefold Name of the Father, the Son, and the Holy Spirit.

[1] 2 Cor. 5: 17.  
[2] 2 Cor. 5: 15.  
[3] Rom. 5: 1 and 8.  
[4] I Cor. 13: 8.

# APPENDIX TO CHAPTER 15

To describe the pre-Christian world—and in this sense, too, the non-Christian world—as "a world without love" (Uhlhorn: *Geschichte der christlichen Liebestätigkeit*, I, pp. 3–39), may seem to some to be an unfair statement, and to others to be true and fitting. Outside the Christian sphere of influence there were, and are, mother-love, the love of friendship, the love of country; there is even a well-known doctrine and practice of the love of enemies (Cf. Hans Haas, *Idee und Ideal der Feindesliebe in der ausserchristlichen Welt*; *see also* the references to the literature of the subject in Westermarck, *op. cit.*, p. 78).

Nor can we deny that in the non-Christian religions there are ideas of divine goodness, divine good-will, of a disposition to help and to forgive. Alongside of "evil", destructive, hostile, divine forces, there are also those which give life generously, who do good to man, and care for his needs. There is even a "gracious" God (Cf. K. Hutten, *Die Bhakti-Religion in Indien und der christliche Glaube*). But the fact that God is Love, and thus that love is the very essence of the Nature of God, is never explicitly said anywhere, and still less is it revealed in divine self-surrender. The God of the *Bhakti* religion, which is often regarded as a parallel to the Christian Faith, is "essentially —in his relation to the World—wholly uninterested. This springs directly from the fact of His isolation and His sublimity" (*op. cit.*, p. 36). He is not a Subject who goes forth from Himself, who gives Himself freely.

Thus the God of Epictetus is, it is true, a kindly Father, and it is our noblest duty to thank and praise Him (*Gespräche, Ausg. R. Mücke*, pp. 49 ff.). But here there is no trace of the love of God who desires to give Himself to His creatures. When, however, we try to formulate an answer to this question, on the basis of the Comparative Study of Religion, then we must say that non-Christian religion does not know the God of love; this means that here the nature of Love itself, as the reply of man to the self-revealing love of God, has not been understood. Even the love of enemies which we find here is something quite different from the *Agape* of the New Testament: "Thus when the Sage exercises love, and, it is true, even to his enemies, he does so, not out of interest in the individual, but only because he has the whole in his mind, and does not think it is worth while getting excited about one individual" (R.G.G., III, Sp. 1636).

Hence the pre-Christian world, the world outside the Bible, does not know what the New Testament calls *"Agape"*. But as we have already seen, this was already known by Hosea, and indeed in a strict and indissoluble connexion with the revelation of the merciful and gracious God: namely, as an answer to His generous love. *Agape* thus belongs to that sphere in which God is shown to us as He stoops down to man, which is completed in Jesus Christ. in His self-surrender on the Cross.

Hence, *Agape* is sharply opposed to that whole idea— peculiar to later Hellenism—of the ascent of the soul to God, of that "Alexandrine world-scheme" which began with Aristotle (Cf. Nygren, *Agape and Eros*, I, pp. 163 ff.), which reached its fullest development in Neo-Platonism, where its influence was most extensive, both in religion and in philosophy.

Theology—and philosophy—are indebted to Anders Nygren not only for the clear way in which he has worked out the contrast between *Eros* and *Agape*, but also for the proof (which he carries out in the second volume of this work) of the powerful influence exerted by the *"Eros-motif"* in the formation of the patristic and the mediaeval idea of Love. As Nygren moves through the history of the theology of the Early Church and the Mediaeval Church, conducting a searching investigation into the purity of the idea of *Agape*, on the one hand, and the influence of the *Eros-motif*, on the other, he arrives at a critical distinction between the Christian and the non-Christian elements in the theology of the Fathers of the Church and of the Scholastic theologians, which runs exactly parallel with our own, which starts from the contradiction between the theology of revelation and the speculative theory of the Absolute. The enquiry into the validity of the one criterion yields results which apply equally well to the other.

Thus it appears that Irenaeus, the early theologian who thinks most purely in terms of revelation, and not in terms of speculative theology (*see* my remarks on Irenaeus in *Der Mittler*, pp. 219 ff.), is also the one who develops the idea of *Agape* which is least influenced by the *Eros-motif*: "Nowhere in the Early Church do we meet the idea of *Agape* worked out so clearly as in the thought of Irenaeus" (*op. cit.*, p. 208). On the other hand, we see that Origen, who was greatly influenced by Plato, also confuses *Agape* and *Eros*. In the thought of Augustine, his blending of speculation on the Absolute with the theology of revelation corresponds also to an idea of love which represents a compromise between *Eros* and *Agape*: the idea of *Caritas*, an idea which was destined to have an immense influence on all who came after him.

It was only to be expected that Dionysius the Areopagite, in his Christian dress, whose purely Neo-Platonist philosophy is only superficially coloured with a Christian tinge, also has an idea of love which bears the features of *Eros* rather than of *Agape*. In point of fact, this test case does not break down. Nygren thus sums up his extremely careful analysis of the idea of love in the thought of the Areopagite thus: "So we see him . . . even formally, replacing *Agape* by *Eros*." The Areopagite was not satisfied with the compromise of Origen between *Agape* and *Eros*, but "he went so far as to contest it actively" (p. 410). "*Eros* is diviner than *Agape*", says the Areopagite himself (*op. cit.*, p. 413).

A classical example, and characteristic of the Golden period of the Middle Ages, and also powerful in its after-effects, is Bonaventura's *Itinerarium mentis in Deum*, this—when looked at from the formal point of view—wonderful little book of doctrine, which, like scarcely any other, shows the permeation of mediaeval theology and piety with the spirit of Neo-Platonist speculation and mysticism. "God is love; but Bonaventura conceives the divine love in the manner which had become usual after Augustine and Dionysius, as equally meaning the love of God for Himself . . . in virtue of which the divine Being eternally contemplates Himself and is turned inwards upon Himself" (*op. cit.*, p. 450). Hence the motif of "ascent"—the *Itinerarium ad Deum*, the "Alexandrine world-scheme"—dominates the thinking of this great mystic, who quotes no "Father of the Church" so often and so reverently as he quotes the Neo-Platonist, Dionysius the Areopagite.

On the other hand, by this criterion, also, the Reformation shows a return to the Biblical understanding of God. Luther indeed regarded the Areopagite as one who had done much harm: *Admoneo vos, ut istam Dionysii mysticam theologiam . . . detestimini tamquam pestem aliquam"* (*Disp. against the Anti-nomians*, Drews, p. 294; *W.A.*, 39, I, p. 390). He is aware of the connexion between this kind of mysticism, speculative ontology, and the idea of Merit. Grace is the descent of God, not the ascent of man, the *Itinerarium* of the obedient Servant of the Lord to the death of the Cross, not that of the ascent of man to heaven: "*Ipse descendit et paravit scalam.*" "He will not have thee to ascend, but He comes to thee, and has made a ladder, a way and a bridge unto thee" (*W.A.*, 16, p. 144). Here, therefore, the pure idea of *Agape* breaks through the mediaeval *Caritas-Eros* tradition. "*Amor Dei non invenit, sed creat suum diligible, amor hominis fit a suo diligibili*", occurs already in the *Heidelberger Disputation* (*W.A.*, I, p. 354). It is the gracious love which makes its free choice, which loves for no "reason", which, therefore, since it is "given", does not seek that which is "*diligibile*" in man, but as a love which is "shed abroad" turns towards the man who is not worthy of love. (Cf. Nygren, p. 551.) We must admit, that of all the Reformers it was Luther who saw and felt this contrast most plainly, while in Zwingli—especially in his work on Divine Providence—the Neo-Platonist ideas of the "*summum bonum*" and the "*summum esse*" have a disturbing influence; Calvin's witness to the love of God was hindered by his doctrine of Predestination, and his idea of Love was somewhat rationalized by the influence of Stoicism.

The doctrine of the Love of God was terribly meagre among the Protestant scholastic theologians, who, in their doctrine of the Divine Attributes, revert entirely to the mediaeval metaphysic. The doctrine of God's *Nature* is confined to the statement of His "*infinitas, spiritualis essentia*"; among the Divine Attributes "Love" is scarcely mentioned in comparison with "*unitas, simplicitas, immutabilitas, infinitas, immensitas,*" etc., as well as "*sanctitas*" and "*justitia*". Love is—so to say—an outflow of His "*bonitas*". But what *is* said of it—in this connexion, in the doctrine of God—is strongly influenced by the Neo-Platonist *Eros-motif*: "*exemplar perfectionis creatae; allicit quoque aut movet in sui tanquam summi boni amorem ac desiderium*" (Baier, in Schmid, *Dogmatik der ev. Luth. Kirche*, p. 82). According to Reformed doctrine the Love of God is a "*propensio quaedam benevola et benefica versus creaturas*"—but that could have been said by a sage like Epictetus (cf. Heppe, *Dogmatik der ev. ref. Kirche*, p. 49).

On the whole, the later dogmatic theologians follow the erroneous tradition, until—here, too, once more—von Oettingen as the first, finds his way back to the truth of the Bible as taught at the Reformation, and teaches the Holiness and the Love of God ("God, the Holy Love") as the Nature of God, which are to be distinguished from His Attributes (*Lutherische Dogmatik*, II, pp. 140 ff.). In the thought of Schlatter, who is usually so close to the thought of the Bible, his brief teaching on the love of God culminates in the strange sentence: "This is for us the final word that we can attain about God, because *in us* nothing deeper can be found than the good will." On the other hand, the observations of Kähler, the other great "Biblical" theologian, are excellent (*Die Wissenschaft der christlichen Lehre*, pp. 230 ff.). Here he works out clearly both the nature of love as well as the connexion between revelation and the knowledge of love.

Equally excellent are Karl Barth's observations on God's Being as the One who loves in freedom (*Kirchl. Dogm.*, II, 1, pp. 288 ff.). "His inmost Self is His self-communication" (*op. cit.*, p. 31). The critical remark: "If we seek the goodness of God behind His Love, in a '*summum bonum*', which differs from His Love, then in the effort to define this *summum bonum* it would be difficult to avoid falling back into the idea of pure unmoving Being" (*op. cit.*, p. 311)—shows that he is aware of the contrast between his own doctrine of God and the ontological speculative doctrine of the God of the Scholastic tradition. Yet his love for the Reformed scholastic thinkers prevents him from being fully aware of the Neo-Platonist injury they have inflicted on the Idea of God, in spite of his apt remarks about Polanus and Quenstedt, p. 313.

The doctrine of the love of God, the heart of the Gospel, obscured by the disastrous Neo-Platonist doctrine of the *summum bonum*, was re-discovered by the Reformers, but in their followers it was once more hidden by scholastic speculation, and in spite of much excellent preparatory work we shall need a great deal of intellectual labour based on the truth of the Bible, before this doctrine can once more gain its full New Testament depth.

## CHAPTER 16

# THE TRIUNE GOD

WHEN we turn to the problem of the doctrine of the Trinity, we are confronted by a peculiarly contradictory situation. On the one hand, the history of Christian theology and of dogma teaches us to regard the dogma of the Trinity as the distinctive element in the Christian Idea of God, that which distinguishes it from the Idea of God in Judaism and in Islam, and indeed, in all forms of rational Theism. Judaism, Islam, and rational Theism are Unitarian. On the other hand, we must honestly admit that the doctrine of the Trinity did not form part of the early Christian—New Testament—message, nor has it ever been a central article of faith in the religious life of the Christian Church as a whole, at any period in its history. Thus we are forced to ask: Is this truth the centre of Christian theology, but not the centre of the Christian Faith? Is such a discrepancy between theology and faith possible? Or, is this due to an erroneous development in the formation of the doctrine of the Church as a whole?

Certainly, it cannot be denied that not only the word "Trinity", but even the explicit idea of the Trinity[1] is absent from the apostolic witness to the faith; it is equally certain and incontestable that the best theological tradition, with one accord, clearly points to the Trinity as its centre. However, there is a third point to be noted, namely, that the re-discovery of the New Testament message at the Reformation did not re-vitalize this particular theological doctrine; the fact is, the Reformers did not touch or alter this fundamental dogma of the ancient Church, but rather, so to speak, "by-passed" it, than made it the subject of their own theological reflection. The statement of Melanchthon,[2] "*Mysteria divinitas rectius adoraverimus quam vestigaverimus*", is characteristic of this attitude. Calvin expresses himself in the same way; he regards the doctrine of the Trinity from the following point of view only; namely, that through its conceptions, which differ from those of the Bible, the opponent of the divinity of Christ—who is the enemy of the Christian Faith—is forced to throw off

[1] On the triadic passages in the N.T., see below. The only trinitarian passage which is found in some ancient versions of the Bible (1 John 5: 7) is regarded as not genuine.　　　　　　　　　　　　　　　[2] *Loci. com.* Introduction.

his disguise, and to fight in the open, instead of concealing his hostility under a cloak of Christianity.[1]

How are we to explain this strange situation? Here I anticipate the result of the following enquiry, and state it in the form of a thesis: The ecclesiastical doctrine of the Trinity, established by the dogma of the ancient Church, is not a Biblical *kerygma*, therefore it is not the *kerygma* of the Church, but it is a theological doctrine which defends the central faith of the Bible and of the Church. Hence it does not belong to the sphere of the Church's message, but it belongs to the sphere of theology; in this sphere it is the work of the Church to test and examine its message, in the light of the Word of God given to the Church. Certainly in this process of theological reflection the doctrine of the Trinity is central.

## (1)

The starting-point of the doctrine of the Trinity is, naturally, not a speculative one, but the simple testimony of the New Testament. We are not concerned with the God of thought, but with the God who makes His Name known. But He makes His Name known as the Name of the Father; He makes this Name of the Father known through the Son; and He makes the Son known as the Son of the Father, and the Father as Father of the Son through the Holy Spirit. These three names constitute the actual content of the New Testament message. This is a fact which no one can deny.

Our God is called the "Father in heaven". This is the Name which the Christian Church gave Him from the very beginning. The fact, however, that she gave Him this Name was not her own discovery, nor was it due to her own caprice. It was taught by the Son, by Jesus Christ. The fact that Jesus Christ is the Son, the μονογενής[2] or the ἴδιος υἱός,[3] "the" Son, not "a" son, alongside of other sons or children of God, is the decisive central confession of faith of the Primitive Christian Church. Its creed therefore speaks of Him who makes His Name known as the Name of the Father, and of Him who makes this Father-Name known as the Son. But the Church speaks of this disclosure of the Name of the Father through the Son not merely in the sense of something historical in the past, but also in the sense of a present reality. The Father and the Son are present in the Church—through the Holy Spirit. If the Name "Father" designates the origin and content of the

[1] *Institutio*, I, 13, 4.   [2] John 1: 14, 18; 3: 16–18.   [3] Rom. 8: 32.

revelation, the Name of the "Son" designates the historic Mediator, and the "Holy Spirit" the present reality of this revelation. These three Names sum up the whole of the New Testament message. People may reject this view, but no one can deny that this is the message of the New Testament,[1] which contains everything that belongs to the Gospel: the Kingdom, the Atonement, Redemption, the final consummation of the Rule of God. These three Names—Father, Son, and Holy Spirit, in their unity and in their difference, are the content and the meaning of the New Testament.[2] The Primitive Christian Church lived on the fact that through the Son it had the Father, and that it was united with the Father and the Son through the Holy Spirit. This does not need to be proved, but, admitted by everyone, may be taken as the starting-point. The problem does not consist in the fact that there are these three Names, but in the question: What is their relation to each other?

The God who makes His Name known, is the God who wills to be called "Father". *This* is the Name by which He wills that we should call upon Him: "Our Father, who art in heaven." Jesus has made this Name known to men; in the knowledge of the *Father* the historical movement of the revelation which culminates in Jesus Christ, reaches its goal. He came in order to show us the Father,[3] and the flowering of faith in the heart of man, effected by the Holy Spirit, is expressed in the cry: "Abba", "Father".[4]

"That we may know the mystery of the Father",[5] that those who believe in Christ "may have the name of His Father written in their foreheads"[6]—this, and this alone, is the one thing that matters. Jesus Himself says the same thing: "No one knoweth the Son, save the Father; neither doth any know the Father save the Son, and he to whomsoever the Son willeth to reveal Him."[7]

The Father-Name for God is not, however, as such, the new and distinctive element in the Biblical revelation. Zeus, indeed, was called "Father", and the name of "Father" was often used to designate the Supreme Being. It is not the name of

---

[1] It is also plainly that of the Synoptic Gospels. The fact that, even if in a veiled way, it is the message of Jesus Himself, has gradually been admitted by Biblical critics since Albert Schweitzer.

[2] Explicit confirmation is contained in passages like Matt. 28: 19; 2 Cor. 13: 13.

[3] Matt. 11: 27; John 16: 25; 17: 1 ff.      [4] Rom. 8: 15; Gal. 4: 6.

[5] Col. 2: 2—this is what is meant, even if the reading "God" is more strictly accurate.      [6] Rev. 14: 1.      [7] Matt. 11: 27.

"Father" in general, but *the* Name of Father, which the Bible teaches us to say, which constitutes the content of the revelation. Hence we must take special note of the fact that the Father-Name for God is not in any way prominent in the Old Testament. When He is called "Father" in the Old Testament (which rarely occurs) the allusion is chiefly to His Creative Power and His Providential Care, but not to that which is the real meaning of the title of Father in the New Testament: the Nature of the Holy and the Merciful God in its unity.[1] Holiness and Love, not confused with one another, yet absolutely united, the Holy *"majestas"* with His right over all creation as its Author, and the merciful love which stoops to the lost: only in the New Testament Name of "Father" are both these aspects of His Nature gathered up into a unity. It is the paradoxical unity of One who creates and wills absolute distance from the creature, and yet absolute communion with the creature.

But this knowledge of the Father is far from self-evident; rather it is the great and glorious new truth given to mankind in Jesus Christ; this is shown above all in the fact that God is not only "the Father", absolutely, but that He is called the "Father of our Lord Jesus Christ".[2] Through Him, in Him, He is our Father. He becomes *our* Father through the fact that the Son, who alone knows Him, "wills to reveal Him to us". We know God as our Father through the fact that we know Him first of all as the Father of this Son, Jesus, and through the fact that we know this Jesus as the Son of the Father. Our υἱοθεσία, our status as children of God, is both revealed, and made a reality, through Him who from the very outset is the Son, and who therefore is called the ἴδιος υἱός or the μονογενὴς υἱός.[3] Hence the terms which the New Testament uses when speaking of "the Father" are quite different from those which describe a general, rational, timeless idea of the Fatherhood of God, as, for instance, in the theology of the Enlightenment. The knowledge of God as our Father is the work of the Son, and is the counterpart of the truth that Jesus is the Son of the Father.

Similarly, it is far from obvious that we know the Son as the ἴδιος υἱος, as the μονογενὴς παρὰ τοῦ πατρός.[4] How could anyone

---

[1] The only passage which has an affinity with the N.T. use of the Father-Name (Ps. 103: 13) does not *call* Him "Father", but *compares* God with a father.    [2] 2 Cor. 1: 3; 11: 31; Eph. 1: 3, etc.
[3] See above, p. 206.    [4] John 1: 14.

perceive in the Crucified One on Golgotha "the glory as of the Only-begotten from the Father, full of grace and truth?"[1] When Jesus received for the first time—from the lips of Peter —the confession: "Thou art the Christ, the Son of the Living God", He Himself emphasized the miraculous nature of this statement. "Blessed art thou, Simon Bar-Jonah: for flesh and blood hath not revealed it unto thee, but my Father which is in heaven."[2] The proclamation that Jesus was the Son of God, the promised Messiah, has indeed, from the very earliest times down to the present day, been more often rejected than accepted. "To reveal His Son *in me*":[3] Saul, the erstwhile persecutor of the Christians, knew that this was the work of the Holy Spirit.[4] The witness within my heart which enables me to appropriate to myself the truth which the Bible or the Church proclaims to me from without, is the *Testimonium spiritus sancti*.

Thus two events had to take place before the mysterious, unknown God could be revealed as the Father: He had to come forth from His Mystery, enter into history, and "show" Himself as Father in the form of man, in the Son; and He had to enlighten the darkened heart of men through the Holy Spirit, that in the form of the Man Jesus we might be able to see the Son, and in the Son the Father. That is the first intelligible connexion of the three Names in the testimony of the New Testament. This connexion does not yet formulate a doctrine of the Trinity, but it provides the starting-point. In these *three* Names—Father, Son, and Holy Spirit, the *One* God makes *His* Name known to us.

(2)

In the centre of the controversies about the Trinity stands the name which is also the centre of the New Testament witness: The Son. *This* was indeed the characteristic element in the community of disciples, in contrast to the Jews and the pagans; they confessed Jesus as Lord, and called upon His Name in prayer. In the New Testament itself the Name of the Son has first of all a functional or official character. The idea behind this term is not that of a *"generatio"*, but it is a title of dignity. The Messianic *King* in Psalms 2 and 110 (which are constantly quoted in this connexion) is called "Son". The phrase "this day have I begotten thee",[5] does not mean a

[1] John 1: 14.　　　　　[2] Matt. 16: 16 ff.　　　　　[3] Gal. 1: 15.
[4] 1 Cor. 12: 3.　　　　　　　　　　　　　　　　　　　[5] Ps. 2: 7.

physical or metaphysical process of procreation, but an investiture with royal dignity. How the Son proceeds from the Father?—at first this question was not even asked; what *is* said is this: that the Son, endowed with the authority of the Father, "represents" Him upon earth, and establishes His royal dominion. The original Christology was entirely concerned with *action*; indeed, we might say that its essential idea could only be expressed in verbs and not in nouns. All that matters is what Jesus *does* as the Christ. From this we learn what and who He *is*. At first the statements about His *work* far outweigh those about the mystery of His *Person*, His *Being*. Indeed, the mystery of His Being itself, where it becomes a special point of interest, is gathered up in ideas which point to His Work. Who is He? He is the Revealer, the Reconciler, the Redeemer, the Lord, the Liberator, the One who brings in the Kingdom of God. He is the One in whom God becomes present, Immanuel, God with us. "God was in Christ, reconciling the world unto Himself."[1] He is the active, personal Presence of God, the personal God at work, the Word of God become Person, and the Act of God become Man. In Him God deals with us as the Mediator. Or, as John puts it so simply: It is He in whom the Father shows us who He is. "He that hath seen Me hath seen the Father."[2]

It is thus that Jesus bears witness to Himself in His own teaching, which is historically intelligible. He avoids, it is true, the actual use of the name Messiah for Himself. But again and again, in many different ways, He implies that with Him the new Age, the era of the new Covenant, the Messianic Age, has dawned.[3] He is the One who ushers in this turning-point in the history of man. As such He is endowed with divine authority. That is why He who had learned the wisdom of the Law and the Prophets, dared to confront the whole authority of the written revelation with the great claim: "But *I* say unto you . . ." That is why He says that with Him the period of the Prophets is past, that the last and the greatest of the Prophets, John the Baptist, was less than the least in the Kingdom of heaven,[4] because with Him, Jesus, the Kingdom of God has not only come near, but has "arrived" or dawned.[5] That is why He speaks of the fact of His own coming in a way no prophet ever spoke of himself. This phrase "I am come"[6]

---

[1] 2 Cor. 5: 19.  [2] John 14: 19.
[3] Cf. Kümmel, *Verheissung v. Erfüllung*, 1945.  [4] Matt. 11: 11.
[5] Matt. 12: 28.  [6] Luke 12: 49; Matt. 20: 28.

points towards the dimension of transcendence. As the Prophet proclaims and emphasizes the Word of God which has *come* to him, so Jesus is the *One who has come*, who proclaims the Rule of God, and invites men to communion with God. When He, Jesus, goes into the house of Zacchaeus, the tax-gatherer, that day the promised Messianic salvation has come to that house.[1] When He shows Himself the Friend of publicans and sinners, He proves that He is the Good Shepherd, who, in His loving compassion, seeks the lost sheep of the House of Israel.[2] When, in the course of bringing in the Rule of God He is met by the resistance of the usurping masters of the vineyard, He experiences this as "the Son", whom the Father sends, as previously He had sent His servants.[3] Thus the witness of Jesus to Himself is the witness to His Messianic dignity, to the Messianic presence of God in Him. Jesus Himself bears witness to Himself —without actually saying so, in words—as the Immanuel of prophecy, and all His acts—according to the unimpeachable witness of a scholar who is not an orthodox Christian believer—are "acts of the Messianic self-consciousness of Jesus".[4]

But His disciples, who not only knew His life and His work, but had also experienced His death on the Cross and His Resurrection, could proclaim His Messianic authority and His saving significance with greater certainty and clearness than He Himself could, or ought to do.[5] This is the reason for the relative difference between the Christological message of the Apostles, and the witness of Jesus to Himself. Only gradually does the whole fullness of the knowledge of Christ develop in the Primitive Church and in the Apostolic teaching. But one point, and that the central one, was clear from the very outset, and was simply expanded in detail later on: He is the Lord, to whom prayer is offered: "Come, Lord Jesus", *Marantha*. Thus His dignity is not that of a creature, but it is that of the Holy, who stands "over against" His whole creation. These first Christians, who gave Him the title "Lord", were no polytheists; that is, they were not people to whom it would be easy to ascribe divine dignity to any human being. They were Jews, men who had recited the Jewish Creed every day of their lives, from their early childhood; "Hear! O Israel! the Lord

[1] Luke 19: 9.     [2] Matt. 18: 12; Luke 19: 10.     [3] Matt. 21: 37.
[4] Albert Schweitzer, *Geschichte der Leben-Jesu Forschung*, p. 415.
[5] The view that there is a contrast between the "Synoptic" and the "Pauline-Johannine" Gospel can only be maintained so long as one does not perceive that the Message of Jesus Himself is disguised "Messianism".

our God is One Lord",[1]—Jews, for whom there were no demi-gods, no transitional beings between the creation and God. When they addressed Jesus as "Lord" in their prayers, they intended to give Him the dignity of the One God. In the presence of this one phrase or word, *Maran* (Lord), (which in its Aramaic form was current in the very early days of the Jewish-Christian Church, and was adopted by the Greek-speaking Church as part of the primitive Christian liturgy), all the theoretical views of a contradiction between a "Christo-logical" and a "non-Christological" Primitive Church, between Paul and the first Christian community, or between the Synoptic Gospels and the Fourth Gospel, must disappear. As Jesus, according to the oldest historical testimony, knew that He was the Messianic Lord, so, still more, did the witnesses of His Resurrection know it. The progress, the development of the ideas about the nature and the significance of this dignity of Christ as Lord, takes place *within* this common original confession of faith, and does not alter anything in its original content. The most primitive Christian Faith of the Early Church and the developed Christology of Paul and John is *one* in the confession: "Jesus is the divine Lord." The simple prayer "Maranatha" and the confession "Christ is Lord", raise the *problem* of the Trinity. This Jesus is the Lord who is to be invoked as God; that is one side of the problem. But there is only one Lord to be invoked as God, the Lord who has created heaven and earth; that is the other side of the question. The Son is God, of equal dignity with the Father; there is only one God.

The first question which forces itself upon our minds is this: What is the relation between the Son whom we invoke as Lord, with the Father whom we invoke as Lord? Even the Apostles were aware of this question. In different ways they tried to answer it, and their answers—as primitive testimonies to the Christian Faith and experience of the Early Church—are of decisive importance. But none of their doctrinal formulas is the truth itself. Paul mainly emphasizes the significance of the *work* of Jesus Christ. Jesus is the Lord, to whom the Highest Name of God Himself is given.[2] He is the "Son of His love", through whom we are "delivered from the power of darkness" and "translated into the Kingdom of His dear Son".[3] He is the revelation of that "righteousness", which is yet so generous and gracious, which makes an end of the righteousness of the

[1] Deut. 6: 4.　　　　[2] Phil. 2: 9.　　　　[3] Col. 1: 13.

Law.[1] It is He in whom we receive the love of God as a gift,[2] who reconciles and redeems us,[3] who, as the Head, unites us with Himself in one Body,[4] who breaks the power of sin, of the law and of death,[5] who gives us a share in eternal life,[6] and who sheds abroad in our hearts the Holy Spirit as the first-fruits and the pledge of eternal life.[7] It is He who Himself is the true Image of God, who transforms us into this image of God.[8] We must understand the Christology of Paul from the point of view of the work of Christ, as something which, essentially, can only be expressed in *verbs*, not in *nouns*, in historical, and not in metaphysical terms.

And yet there are some passages in Paul's Letters which explicitly point beyond that which is given in history—while the others only do it implicitly—passages which reveal the eternal background of the story of Jesus. He whom we know in the form of a servant, obedient unto God, of a human being in sinful flesh, has "taken on Himself" this "form of a servant". "Before" He did this He was "in divine form", which belonged to Him by right of His nature.[9] In Him "dwelleth all the fulness of the Godhead bodily".[10] For our sakes He *became* "poor", although He was "rich", with the wealth of God.[11] He is the "image of the invisible God",[12] "through whom are all things, and we through Him".[13] Thus He is the One in whom all things, things in heaven and things on earth[14] have been created— "for all things have been created through Him and unto Him".

While Paul's thoughts do not move for long at this height of transcendence, but constantly return to the historic centre, the saving work of this Christ, in "John" that meta-historical aspect of the Person of Christ is more fully developed, yet without ever losing the relation with the historical work of Christ. Jesus is above all the Revealer, in whom "the Word" through whom all has been created "became flesh".[15] He shares the full Divine Godhead;[16] He possesses explicitly that predicate of deity which we called "His own glory": He has "life in Himself".[17] Therefore He and the Father are one, and He that seeth Him seeth the Father.[18] He therefore is Himself the Truth, the Life, the Resurrection.[19] From all eternity He has a share in the

---

[1] Rom. 3: 21.    [2] Rom. 8: 32.    [3] 2 Cor. 5: 19.
[4] Eph. 4: 15.    [5] Rom. 8: 2.    [6] Rom. 16: 23.
[7] Rom. 8: 23; 2 Cor. 1: 22.    [8] Rom. 8: 29; 2 Cor. 3: 1.
[9] Phil. 2: 6.    [10] Col. 2: 9.    [11] 2 Cor. 8: 9.
[12] Col. 1: 15.    [13] 1 Cor. 8: 6.    [14] Col. 1: 16.
[15] John 1: 14.    [16] John 1: 2.    [17] John 5: 26.
[18] John 14: 9.    [19] John 11: 25; 14: 6.

glory of the Father;[1] hence, in contrast to all of us, He is the One who is "from above",[2] who has come to us "from the bosom of the Father";[3] therefore, in contrast to all those who come to sonship through Him, He is the only begotten Son[4]— Paul, meaning the same thing, calls Him God's "own" Son.[5]

All these expressions clearly mean the same thing: Jesus Christ, as the Son of God, is θεός, God. He has a share in the divine Being, He stands over against us who are creatures as the One who is Uncreated,[6] who has Himself shared in the Act of Creation.[7] He shares in that Life and that Glory, in which we only participate in the eternal life of God through Him, in the eternal redeeming, reconciling, new-creating Love and Holiness of God.[8] It is He through whom God imparts to us this life; He is the Mediator of the divine self-communication, in its twofold sense of revelation and salvation, truth and grace, light and life.

In all these varied expressions, reflecting the thought-world from which they come, the Apostles are only trying to say *one* thing; but if this "one" thing is to be said at all, it has to be said in many ways; this is what they mean: that "the Son" is He in whom God discloses Himself to man, as the Holy One, and as Love, as the Holy, Merciful Father. The Son is the revelation of the Father; when we call upon Jesus as Lord we call upon Him who from eternity is Lord alone, whom, however, we only know in Jesus as He wills to be known, and whom we possess as He wills to give Himself to us.

### (3)

The dynamic element in the formation of the doctrine of the Trinity is the Son. The conflict rages round the question of His divinity. The problem of the "Third Person", of the Holy Spirit, has been much less acute, and has caused far less upheaval within the Church. This corresponds to the fact that the earliest creed of the Church only referred to the Son.[9] The point at issue was this: that in the *Son*, and in Him alone, we have the Father, and that through the Son—and only through Him—we receive the Holy Spirit; thus that only from the standpoint of the Son do we know the Father and share in the life of the Spirit. If this central point is right, then everything

---

[1] John 17: 5.     [2] John 3: 31; 8: 23.     [3] John 1: 18.
[4] John 1: 18.     [5] Rom. 8: 32.     [6] John 17: 5.
[7] Col. 1: 16.     [8] John 17: 24.
[9] Cf. Cullmann, *Die ersten Christlichen Glaubensbekenntnisse*, 1943.

else is right. Only he who has the Son has the Father; only the Spirit who witnesses to the Son is the Holy Spirit.[1] Hence, it is not at all surprising that the doctrine of the Holy Spirit—as part of the doctrine of the Trinity—should be far less prominent than that of the Son. Even outside the Christian Church, indeed, men speak of God as "Father", and of the Spirit of God. The specifically Christian element was the new knowledge of the Father given through Jesus, the Son of God, and the life in the Holy Spirit mediated through the Son. To think aright about "the Son" meant that, in essentials, men also knew how to think of the Father and the Spirit.

In itself, however, the doctrine of the Holy Spirit is just as important as that of the Son, and the witness of the New Testament to the Spirit is as rich as that to the Son. But whereas faith in Jesus is proclaimed as a creed, witness is borne to the Holy Spirit as an experimental reality. For the Holy Spirit, contrasted with the historical revelation, is the inward revelation, and the personal Presence of God Himself. Belief in the Son means that God has intervened in history, revealing, reconciling. Belief in the Holy Spirit means: this *historical* revelation of God is the source of the *inward* personal presence of God, through which we, as individual believers, and as a community, participate in the life-renewing power of God, and indeed only in this way does the historical revelation become truth for us. The New Testament testimony to the Holy Spirit is therefore plainly directed towards Christ. The Holy Spirit teaches us to understand Him, His truth and His work;[2] through Him the Love of Christ becomes our portion and our possession,[3] indeed, through the Holy Spirit Christ Himself, as "Christ-for-us", becomes "Christ-in-us".[4] The self-communication of God is not only accomplished in the Historical and the Objective; He seeks us, our very self, our heart. The self-communication of God wills *our* sanctification,[5] the self-communication of the God who is love sets us within His love,[6] and pours His love into our *hearts*.[7] Sanctification and communion in love[8]—this is the work of the Holy Spirit, the self-communication of God, whose nature is Holiness and Love. The Spirit who dwells within us is indeed the Spirit of God, and what He effects can therefore be nothing less than the manifestation of the life which is His own. To have the Holy Spirit does not mean possessing

---

[1] I John 2: 23, 21.  [2] John 16: 14 ff.  [3] Rom. 8: 15, 23.
[4] Gal. 2: 20; 4: 19; Col. 1: 27.  [5] I Pet. 1: 15.
[6] Col. 1: 13.  [7] Rom. 5: 5.  [8] Eph. 2: 22; I Peter 1: 2.

"something", but "Himself", and in Him we have eternal life.[1]

Hence there can be no question whether the Holy Spirit also is *Person*; in the New Testament such a question cannot arise; it would indeed be tantamount to asking whether God Himself were Person. The misunderstanding which lies behind such a question may perhaps be explained by the fact that in some passages in the New Testament, especially in the *Acts of the Apostles*, certain manifestations of the Holy Spirit, and the Holy Spirit Himself, are not clearly distinguished; thus the "gifts" of the Holy Spirit, which are really "something" and not Himself, are equated with Himself.[2] This somewhat "neutral" way of speaking of the Holy Spirit is, however, not that of the Pauline and Johannine testimony, but must be regarded as belonging to a more primitive level. The mighty *reality* of the Holy Spirit in the Primitive Church was so overwhelming that the *doctrine* of the Spirit only gradually became clear. But in the writings of the great teachers of the Primitive Church, in Paul and John, there is no doubt at all about the personal character of the Holy Spirit. Indeed, John does not shrink from placing this personality on a level with the psycho-physical personal reality of the Lord as a parallel in the form of the Paraclete.[3] This, however, is only intended to emphasize the truth—which is the common and decisive element in the whole of the witness of the Primitive Church: that the Holy Spirit is God Himself, is therefore, like God Himself, Subject, not "something"; He is the Giver, not only a gift; a personality, who speaks, creates, judges, guides, and plans. The Spirit bears witness,[4] teaches,[5] punishes,[6] works,[7] imparts,[8] wills,[9] prays,[10] He can be blasphemed,[11] He can be grieved.[12] He sighs in and with the soul in prayer; He represents us. The fact that He is "given *to* us" is no more difficult to believe than that the Son has been "given *for* us". The fact that He is "sent" is exactly paralleled by the fact that the Son has been "sent". Indeed, Paul seems to go even further, and to identify the Spirit with Christ: "The Lord is the Spirit."[13] But this does not mean that the difference between the historically objective and the inwardly subjective form of the revelation has been eliminated; what it means is this: that in so far as Jesus Christ is in us He is so in the way

---

[1] Rom. 8: 10 ff.
[2] Cf. Acts 4: 31; 8: 39; 10: 44; 19: 2 ff.
[3] John 14: 16, 26; 16: 7.
[4] Rom. 8: 16.
[5] Rev. 2: 7, etc.
[6] 1 Cor. 12: 11.
[7] John 16: 8.
[8] 1 Cor. 12: 11.
[9] 1 Cor. 12: 11.
[10] Rom. 8: 26.
[11] Matt. 12: 31.
[12] Eph. 4: 30.
[13] 2 Cor. 3: 17–18.

in which the Holy Spirit is within us. Taken in isolation, this passage is as easy to misunderstand as—on the other hand— it is to speak of the Paraclete as the "representative" of Jesus Christ.

(4)

This, then, is the Biblical evidence—not for the Trinity, but evidence which points in the direction of the doctrine of the Trinity. The God who communicates Himself, the God of Holiness and Love, makes Himself known to us in this three-fold Name—Father, Son, and Spirit. These three Names stand, as designations for God as He communicates Himself, in this definite, irrevocable order: from the Father through the Son to the Spirit. The theology of the Early Church, as we shall see, did not, it is true, alter this order, but since it had very little idea that this order "mattered", its teaching suggests three "persons", side by side; this had a disastrous effect upon the doctrine of God. To a certain extent, of course, it is true that there are several passages in the New Testament where the "triad" of names is used in such a way that they seem to be "side by side", passages where the three Names—Father, Son, Spirit—evidently are placed alongside of one another con-sciously and deliberately as in a formulated Creed;[1] but the Biblical doctrine does not go further than this. The idea of a "Triune God" does not form part of the witness and message of Primitive Christianity. Through the Biblical evidence, how-ever, the Trinitarian *problem* for theological reflection was raised in such a way that it could not be evaded. This brings us to the theological, dogmatic task of the doctrine of the Trinity.

In order to understand the seriousness of this task, and the passion which theological controversy about the doctrine of the Trinity aroused, that is, to understand what, and how much, was at stake in this conflict, we must not stop short at the Biblical factual evidence, but we must go further and enquire into the ground for this evidence. From our previous enquiry we may thus sum up the results of the Biblical evidence: only through the Son do we have the Father; only through the Son do we have the Spirit; only through the Spirit do we have the Son. But in all the One God reveals and gives Himself to us.

In Jesus Christ the Holy and Merciful God meets us: reveal-ing, reconciling, redeeming; through the Holy Spirit, all that He has given in historical events is translated into our inward

[1] Matt. 28: 19; 2 Cor. 13: 13; 1 Cor. 12: 4–6; 1 Pet. 1: 2.

experience, which He creates within us. Why does this article of faith include—in the fullest sense of the word—the confession of the *divinity* of Christ? Why must we understand the phrase "God was in Christ"[1] in this way and in no other? Two lines of thought are at our disposal, and the evidence of the Scriptures points equally to both: the "theological" line—the understanding of the reconciling revelation from the Nature of God—and the "anthropological" line—the understanding of the reconciling revelation from the situation of man "without God, and without life"; in other words, there is the "theocratic" line of thought, and the line of soteriology.

(i) *God is the Holy Lord, and God is self-giving Love.*

(a) God, as the Lord, wills to rule over us. Therefore He wills to put an end to our rebellion, to sin. This is not accomplished by the Law of God; the Law simply brings sin to a head, without being able to overcome it. But even the prophetic word of promise is not able to do this; it merely promises, it does not usher in the Kingdom of God. It promises the Coming of God in the Person of the Messiah, in order to establish the Rule of God. This Promise was fulfilled in Jesus Christ. His Coming is not merely a Word from God—as it came to the Prophets—but it is God's coming in His own Personal Presence. In Him the Holy One Himself is present and creates obedience to Himself, since He—through the Holy Spirit—takes possession of the heart of man. He Himself, the Holy One, is personally present.

(b) God, who is Love, wills to give Himself to us—that is, He wills to give us this love, which is Himself. He does not do this through His Law; for there He *demands* love. Nor does He do this through His prophetic Word; for there He *promises* His love. He does this in His own Presence, as the promised Immanuel, "God-with-us". God's merciful love only lays hold of us *realiter* as His loving Presence in the Person of Him who really stoops down to sinners, and really gives Himself to death for us. The Cross of Jesus is the culmination of this process of "coming down",[2] of the infinitely gracious coming of the loving God in His own personal presence. When this love—which is God's own love—lays hold of us, it destroys our pride, and banishes our fear, and—through the Holy Spirit—we are inwardly "apprehended" by God, and filled with His Love. He Himself who is Love, in His personal presence, achieves this miracle.

(ii) *Our human situation is that of the creature who has become*

[1] 2 Cor. 5: 19.          [2] Exod. 3: 8,

*sinful. Through sin we are in a state of self-deception or of blind-ness to truth; and through sin we are in isolation, due to the fact that we are separated from God by His wrath.*

(*a*) As those who are deceived, we cannot perceive God's truth by our own efforts. We can perceive the truth of God only in the fact that He gives Himself to us to be known. This truth of God, however, is Himself, His personal mystery. This personal mystery cannot disclose to us any doctrine; no "Word-about-Him", not even a prophetic word, can give this to us. It can only be given to us through the fact that He, the Truth, Himself gives Himself to us, as Person, as He Himself is Person.

(*b*) Since we are in a state of sin and guilt, we cannot have communion with God. We cannot of ourselves bridge the gulf between ourselves and God, created by the wrath of God, our sinful will, and our bad conscience. We cannot of ourselves come to God. If He is to be with us, then He must Himself come *to us*, to us in our lost condition, into the wrath and curse which separate us from God, and so He must establish communion with us. Just as certainly as it is only God's personal presence which discloses to us the secret of His Person, so, too, it is only the fact that God gives Himself to us which enables us to have communion with Him. Only if it be true that "God"—Himself —"was in Christ", is it true that He has "reconciled us to Himself". Only when that becomes true *to us* are we reconciled; it is only the fact that He Himself, in His forgiving Love, comes to us personally, that enables us to have genuine communion with Him.

Now let us sum up: Only the true personal presence of God, only the Incarnation of the Word, and the coming "in the form of a servant" of Him who was in divine form, can establish the rule of the Holy Lord, and create communion with Him who is love; only God truly present, Himself in Person, can truly reveal God to us, and truly reconcile us to Him. The revelation in the "Word-about-Him" is not able to do this. The Prophet as person is not the presence of GOD, and the Prophetic Word is not the presence of God in *person*. Only the identity of the Revealer with that which is revealed, of the "Bearer" with that which He "bears", can do this. Neither the Prophet nor His word are God Himself speaking and acting. The prophetic Word is revelation, it is true, but it is an incomplete, provisional revelation. Only the personal Presence of God, speaking and acting, is the perfect revelation and reconciliation. And this has taken place in Jesus Christ. "God was in Christ reconciling the world unto Himself."[1] "The Word became flesh, and we saw His glory—full of grace and truth."

These statements do not say "something"—they say all there is to be said about the Christian Message as a whole. The whole point is the True *God*, whose Nature is Holiness and Love, and that true *revelation* and *reconciliation* which is nothing less than the self-communication of the True God. What matters is the *reality* of this self-communication, which is only true reality if it is the Presence of God in Person. Only in this self-communication, which is the personal self-manifestation of the presence of God, do we perceive what it means that God is Holy and that He is self-giving Love. All that we have been saying in the last two chapters about the Nature of the God who makes His Name known to us is the *"ratio essendi"* of the Christian revelation—and reconciliation. But this revelation itself is the *"ratio cognoscendi"* of that knowledge.

### (5)

This unity of the *nature* and the *revelation* of God is what is meant by the doctrine of the Trinity. This doctrine itself, however, developed out of the process of defending the truth against certain doctrines which would eventually have destroyed this unity of the Nature and the Revelation of God. Here the Church had to fight for her existence tooth and nail, for the question was one of life and death; the whole Gospel was at stake. Whether the doctrine which finally emerged from these conflicts was really in accordance with the truth it desired to defend, is another question.

In the following pages we shall be discussing this question. I shall try to show that we can only answer it in the affirmative in a very restricted sense, and why this is so.

(i) Very early the Christian Church had fixed the main content of its faith in a threefold "triadic" baptismal formula as a kind of creed. The naïve way in which the three Names were placed alongside of one another was bound to meet with opposition on the part of those who realized the all-importance of the Unity of God. In a polytheistic world the preservation of the Divine Unity was a concern of paramount importance. The danger of conceiving the three Names as a little Christian Pantheon was not remote. Hence, before everything else, the truth had to be stressed that—beyond all doubt—there is only *One God*. This emphasis on the Divine Unity, however, took

[1] 2 Cor. 5: 19.

such a form that it endangered the reality of the revelation itself; this danger was present in both forms of *Monarchianism*. The first of these forms—that known as "Dynamic" Monarchianism—we may describe briefly as the free-thinking, Unitarian theology of the Early Church. Jesus Christ is not truly God, but—in spite of the Virgin Birth, which is not attacked[1]— merely a human being inspired by God and filled with His Spirit, who, because of His specially high degree of obedience to God, was adopted by God as His Son, either at His Baptism or after His Resurrection. The Revealer is different from that which is revealed; fundamentally, here we are still on the plane of the Old Covenant.

In the second form of Monarchianism, known as "Modalism", the situation is different. Here both elements of truth are maintained; the unity of God and the divinity of Christ; but here, too, the identity of the Revealer with that which is revealed is lost. The *"unicus Deus"* has incarnated itself in Mary, and as such is called "Son". Thus there has only been a Son since the Incarnation, but this "Son" is truly God. This makes Christ a kind of theophany, and God the Father Himself suffers the pangs of death. Whether this was really the doctrine held by the Sabellians, or whether it is merely a caricature created by the theologians who triumphed over them, cannot now be determined with any precision. The provenance of this Modalism from Asia Minor, however, rather suggests that here was a type of doctrine which was still close to the thought of the New Testament, but was already being misunderstood by the Church, and was therefore distorted, and—in this form— rightly contested. But if the presentation of the antagonists be correct, then certainly this doctrine, which denied the eternity of the Son—even though it does not deny His divinity— should be attacked with the utmost vigour.

(ii) The Logos doctrine was now utilized as a weapon against this mistaken effort to preserve the Divine Unity. The Son is identified with the Logos, and the latter is no longer regarded as the Impersonal Divine Wisdom, but as an hypostasis, as something which has independent being. This defended the super-historical character of the Revealer over against Modalism, and His divinity over against Adoptionism. Now the question is: What is the relation of the Son as Logos to the

[1] Neither Paul of Samosata nor Arius, these two extreme opponents of the doctrine of the Church, denied the Virgin Birth. (Cf. Loofs, *Dogmengeschichte*, pp. 218 and 236.) This shows how little the doctrine of the Virgin Birth is able to protect the doctrine of the Divinity of Christ.

Father? Immediately a new form of error appeared: Subordinationism.

The Logos is pre-existent, it is true, but is not eternal. The Logos—not the historic God-Man—the Eternal Son of God who has not yet become Man, is thus a divinity, who is at the same time a creature. This Logos conception of Arianism brought Christian doctrine into the sphere of polytheistic mythology. This constituted an attack on the first article of the Biblical creed, namely, that there is no intermediate being between God and His creatures. This doctrinal error therefore had to be rejected still more decidedly than the others, and excluded from the doctrine of the Church as "arch-heresy".

(iii) Thus after a conflict against heresy, lasting two hundred years, in which the Church had defended the positions of the full divinity of Christ, and the unity of God, she herself had to make the effort to express the central mystery of the Christian Faith in doctrinal form; so she created the doctrine of the Trinity. At first, however, this was not so much the actual doctrine of the Trinity as a clearly expressed doctrine of the Divinity of the Son, as expressed in the Nicene Creed: "Christ, the μονογενὴς υἱὸς, begotten of His Father before all worlds, Light of Light, true God of True God, begotten not made, of one substance with the Father." It was not until the Athanasian Creed was formulated a century later that the final step was taken, and the standard formula for the Triune God was formulated (at least for the West) in the following terms:

*Deum in Trinitate et Trinitatem in Unitate veneremur, neque confundentes personas neque substantiam separantes.*

Henceforward this was the orthodox ecclesiastical Idea of God of the Roman Catholic Church, which was also adopted by the Churches of the Reformation.

### (6)

Now, we may ask, is this formula of the Trinity, of the *"tres personae"* and the *"una substantia"*, really in accordance with the centre of the message of revelation, the unity of God's Nature and His Revelation? So much is certain: every formulation of the mystery which either removes or attacks the identity of the the Revealer and that which is revealed—revelation and the Nature of God—endangers the decisive message of the Bible. If God Himself did not become man in Jesus Christ, then His Revelation is not revelation, and His Atonement is not atonement. "Nothing created can unite the creature with God"

(Athanasius).[1] "God alone can unite the creature with God." "No one could make us the children of God save He who is the true and essential Son of the Father" (Athanasius).[2] The Reconciler must be God Himself, "because by no other means than that of an eternal Person could we be rescued from our terrible fall into sin and eternal death; such a Person alone could have power over sin and death, to expiate our sin, and to give us instead righteousness and eternal life, no angel or creature could do this, but it must be done by God Himself" (Luther).[3] The "event" of revelation and reconciliation, both understood in the sense of complete reality, means: the breaking through of the creaturely barrier which irrevocably separates God and the creature, the "entrance-into-history" of Him who stands above all history. If Jesus really is the Revealer and the Reconciler, then in Him we meet God Himself. On the other hand, in so far as in Jesus Christ God Himself is present and deals with us in His form of Being as Revealer, He differs from Him who is Revealed. Jesus is God, He is not a $\phi i\lambda o s$ $\overset{\prime}{\alpha} v\theta\rho\omega\pi os$, a mere human being who is endowed with the Spirit of God. He is the *True* God, not a *created* "God". But as the revealing Son He is different from the revealed Father. Thus we are forced to consider the formulas of the doctrine of the Trinity. Yet there are weighty considerations which raise misgivings about them.

(i) In the Biblical testimony to Jesus Christ the historical revelation occupies the dominant position in the centre of interest. The main concern is with the work of Christ, with that which happens through Him for us and to us. We must not allow our gaze to move away from this historical centre to look at the realm of transcendence; or rather, from the historical centre we can better see into the realm of the Transcendent. This historical centre, this work of revelation and reconciliation, which takes place in the Person of Jesus, has a background of eternity, apart from which it is not what it is. Christ's Origin is an integral part of His Nature. Belief in His pre-existence or eternity forms part of our whole belief in Him who is the Revealer and the Reconciler. But this article of faith must always be based on the historical centre, and must never be severed from it. Through the Spirit we see the Son as the Son of the Father, and through the Son we see the Father as the Father of the Son, and as Our Father. The three Names do not stand alongside of one another but after one another. The

[1] C, Ar., II, 69.    [2] C. Ar., I, 39.    [3] W.A., 21, 51.

background can only be seen and understood as the background to this foreground.

From the time of Origen's doctrine of the Logos, however, speculation was rife in the sphere of theology; thus men's interest was deflected from the historical centre to the eternal background, and then severed from it. People then began to speculate about the transcendent relation of the Three Persons of the Trinity within the Trinity; they were set alongside of one another, and the fact that there was an order in the Three Persons was forgotten. The transcendent relation of "Three Persons" became the dominant theme, the real subject of theological interest. The result of this placing of the "Three Persons" "side by side", so to speak, was the formula of the classical doctrine of the Trinity.

(ii) Not all the theologians of the Church, however, devoted their attention to metaphysical speculation. In the Church there was another line of religious and doctrinal tradition in which the main concern of the Bible, that of the history of salvation, was maintained. This tradition arose in Asia Minor, and by way of Ignatius to Irenaeus, and from Irenaeus to Marcellus, represented a school of thought with which Athanasius had much sympathy.[1] He protected Marcellus when others were eager to label him a Sabellian and a heretic. Typical of this kind of theology is the absence of philosophical formulas derived from the Logos doctrine of the Apologists and of Origen; further, another characteristic was the tenacious hold on the historical centre, and the "order" resulting from that of Spirit, Son and Father: through the Spirit the Son, through the Son the Father; finally the renunciation of the attempt to make any more exact definition of the transcendental relations within the Trinity, the refusal to formulate a doctrine of the "Three divine Persons". This tradition of "saving history"—Irenaeus—shows itself here—as at other points—as one that is purer than the more or less classical doctrine of Origen, and has preserved more fully than the latter the connexion with the Biblical *kerygma*.

(iii) This does not mean that the doctrine of an "economic" Trinity is played off against that of an "immanent" doctrine. We have no desire to lay exclusive emphasis upon the historical as such, and to ignore the background of eternity. We would repeat: the Origin of Christ is an integral part of His Nature.

[1] Cf. Loofs, *Dogmengeschichte*, pp. 139–51, etc., and the article on *Marcellus* in *PRE*, 3, 12, pp. 259 ff.

Only when we know that He has come to us from "the bosom of the Father", from the eternal mystery of God, from the realm of Transcendence, do we know who He is and what He does. But what matters is not *whence* He comes, but the *movement* from the one sphere to the other. We must see this movement, in order to understand the gracious act of "stooping-down" to man, and thus the revealing and reconciling self-communication of God. Therefore our understanding likewise must trace this movement back to its starting-point, and come to the belief in the pre-existence and transcendent nature of Christ and thus to confess Him as the Eternal Son. But this article of faith should be the final term in this process. But if this be the case, to make the mutual relation of the Three Persons within the Trinity a subject of theological discussion becomes impossible; the question is of no interest to us; indeed, it is not allowable, for to do so means, as it were, placing the Three Names as Three Persons "side by side", and thus creating a speculative truth, which is really an illusion.

(iv) But when we speak of the "Persons of the Trinity" as if they were "in a certain *order*", we do not mean an *historical* order. This was the error of the Sabellians—at least, so it seems if the polemical views of the orthodox teachers of the Church are correct. However that may be, we mean the "order" which is implied in the movement of the divine self-communication, which therefore has no other aim than to express this one, central truth: Jesus Christ is God in His revelation, God in His Self-communication.

If we understand it thus, then one point becomes clear which is only obscurely expressed in the classical doctrine. The revelation of God is truly His self-communication. Jesus Christ is truly the Personal Presence of God. He who reveals to us the True God, is indeed wholly God, but this revelation does not *exhaust* the whole mystery of God. In saying this we must refer to a truth which we mentioned at the very beginning, the truth of the dialectic which lies in the nature of revelation itself, namely, that the revelation does not remove the mystery of God; on the contrary, the revelation deepens the mystery of God. The revelation issues from the mystery of God; it reveals to us the heart of God. But all that can be said about God, all that the Son can disclose to us of the Nature of God, still leaves a residue of mystery: something which can never be said; something unfathomably mysterious. Even the revealed God remains a hidden God, and He wills to be worshipped as the one

225

who is Hidden and Unfathomable. "God dwells in Light unapproachable"—this applies not only to the time before, but to
the time after, the revelation through Christ, and in spite of it.
*Pater est fons totius Trinitatis.* The Mystery of God stands at
the beginning and at the end of revelation.

(v) It was never the intention of the original witnesses to
Christ in the New Testament to set before us an intellectual
problem—that of the Three Divine Persons—and then to tell
us silently to worship *this* mystery of the "Three-in-One".
There is no trace of such an idea in the New Testament. This
·*"mysterium logicum"*, the fact that God is Three and yet One,
lies wholly outside the message of the Bible. It is a mystery
which the Church places before the faithful in her theology, by
which she hampers and hinders their faith with a heteronomy
which is in harmony, it is true, with a false claim to authority,
but which has no connexion with the message of Jesus and
His Apostles. No Apostle would have dreamt of thinking that
there are the Three Divine Persons, whose mutual relations and
paradoxical unity are beyond our understanding. No *"mysterium logicum"*, no intellectual paradox, no antinomy of
Trinity and Unity, has any place in their testimony, but only
the *"mysterium majestatis et caritatis"*: namely, that the Lord
God for our sakes became man and endured the Cross. The
mystery of the Trinity, proclaimed by the Church, and en-
shrined in her Liturgy, from the fifth or sixth century onwards,
is a pseudo-mystery, which sprang out of an aberration of
theological thought from the lines laid down in the Bible, and
not from the Biblical doctrine itself. At the beginning of this
chapter we said that the doctrine of the Trinity was a theological doctrine formulated in order to protect and preserve the
centre of the Biblical message, but it was never meant to be
the *kerygma* itself. In so far as the Church has made it part of
its *kerygma*, it has given a false direction to faith. This was what
the Reformers meant when they warned people against in-
dulging in Trinitarian speculations, and urged them to return
to the simplicity of the Bible. *Hoc est Christum cognoscere, bene-
ficia ejus cognoscere.* Thought of this kind is in harmony with
the history of salvation; it is loyal to the centre of Christian
thought, and does not attempt to turn the background of this
centre into the religious foreground.

(vi) This view, however, means that we must give up the
endeavour to construct a doctrine of the relation between the
"Trinitarian Persons". As soon as we try to do this—an effort

which reason is ever urging us to make, we step out of the
Biblical line of "saving history" and place the Father, the Son
and the Holy Spirit "side by side". The terms used in the
Athanasian Creed, and from this source incorporated into the
traditional doctrine of the Trinity taught by the Church, *"una
substantia, tres personae"*, must sound strange to us from the
outset. What room is there for the idea of *"substantia"* in
Christian theology? Indeed, it represents that intellectual
aberration which substitutes speculative and impersonal thinking for the line of thought controlled by revelation; thus "God"
now becomes a neutral *"ens"*, "the Absolute", instead of God
who is "Lord" of heaven and earth. The idea of *"substantia"* of
the Athanasian Creed helped to foster the unfortunate speculative aberrations of mediaeval theology.

But even the idea of "Three Persons" is to be regarded with
misgiving. It is indeed impossible to understand it otherwise
than in a tri-theistic sense, however hard we may try to guard
against this interpretation. To analyse the truth of revelation,
that the Lord God reveals Himself to us as the Father through
the κύριος χριστός, the Son, as a "tri-unity" of "persons" is a
temptation for the intellect, to which we ought not to give
way, but which we ought to resist—just as we ought to resist
the temptation to infer that the eternal divine election implies
an equally eternal divine rejection.[1] We have the Father
*through* the Son, *in* the Son; but we do not have the Father
*alongside* of the Son, and the Son *alongside* of the Father. We
have the Son through the Spirit, in the Spirit; but we ought not
to have the Spirit alongside of the Son, and the Son alongside
of the Spirit. This rightful attitude of reverent silence before
the mystery of God is not served by inventing, by the use of
concepts of this kind, a *"mysterium logicum"*, but rather by
renouncing the attempt to penetrate into a sphere which is too
high for us. and in which our thinking can only lead to dangerous illusions.

(7)

On the other hand, from what has just been said, we may
draw two conclusions of the utmost importance. The first
comes from the statement that the Revealer and Him who is
revealed are one. God the Father is really He who reveals
Himself in Jesus Christ. When Jesus Christ, in His Holy and
Merciful authority, speaks to us as "I", the Holy and Merciful

[1] Cf. Chap. 23 below.

God Himself is really speaking to us. God is the One who reveals Himself in Jesus Christ as the God *for us*. The love of Jesus is really the love of God. Thus God is not merely the Loving One in His relation to us, but in Himself He is Love. He is not only loving in relation to the world which He has created; He did not begin to love "only when there was a world", but He loves "from before the foundation of the world",[1] "from all eternity"; He "is Love".[2] This highest and most daring word of the New Testament, and of human speech as a whole, is only possible if the love of God is really "before the foundation of the world", if therefore God is in Himself the One who loves.

Only when we see this do we perceive that the distinction between God and the world—but not the separation—is an absolute one; this means, however, that only now has the possibility of Pantheism been for ever eliminated. God is only the absolute Lord of the world if He is wholly independent of it; thus if it is wholly a work of His freedom. But He is only wholly independent of it if He is what He is "from before all worlds", and not merely "since" the world began, and, through the world. Only if, in Himself, from all eternity, God *is* the Loving One, no world is needed for Him to be the Loving One. On the contrary, the world as creation is the work of His Love. Only when this statement is fully accepted is that other finally denied, to which our natural thinking continually urges us; namely, that there is a necessary correlation between God and the world, so that, since we cannot conceive the world without God, we cannot conceive God apart from the world. God and the world are not in the relationship of correlation like *left* and *right*. The relation between God and the world is one-sided: the world is derived from God, through God; He is its Source. The world is determined by God; God is not determined by the world. This statement, however, is only true if it be true that, apart from the world, God is also the One who loves, who loves "before all worlds". From all Eternity He loves His Son, and therefore through His Son He creates the world.

Secondly, this truth alone maintains the distinction between *Eros* and *Agape*. *Agape* is the love which is not determined by its object, but wholly by the loving subject, the love which is not kindled by something *diligibile*, but which creates that which is *diligibile* for itself. Only of God Himself is love from all eternity, is His love really *Agape*, and not *Eros*. The world did not come into being because God felt a *need* for fellowship

[1] Eph. 1: 4.  [2] John 4: 8–16.

or completion, but it arose wholly out of His own incomprehensible *will* to create communion. God does not *need* a world; He wills it, and He wills it because He wills to give Himself. The being of the world and its manner of existence is not the ground, but the work of His love. This applies primarily to the creature fresh from God's creating hands, not to the creature perverted and defaced by sin. But God's freely-creating, freely-electing love reveals its highest glory when it confronts the sinful creature, which has lost every element of attractiveness, and is indeed far from being *diligibile*.

Finally, only through the identity of the Revealer and that which is revealed is it possible to conceive the strictly personal idea of God. If God were not in Himself Love, but only became so through His relation to the world, then only in relation to the world would He be personal; in Himself He would be impersonal. The personal being of Jesus Christ is not merely a πρόσωπον of God, a personal theophany, but the personal being of Jesus Christ is the personal Being of God Himself. The "I" of God who speaks to us is the eternal "I" of God; His Self-existence as an "I" is not an historical manifestation, but it is His eternal Nature. From all eternity, before there was any world at all, God is the One who speaks and loves; the Word does not arise first of all as a means of communication to the world; from all eternity it is an integral part of the Nature of God. Only when we have thus traced the Biblical Idea of God back to its ultimate source can we finally eliminate that Hegelian idea—so dear to the thought of the natural man—of the God who only "becomes personal" within the sphere of History. Yet all this is already implicit, if not explicit, in the simple statement of faith: God, the Father of our Lord Jesus Christ.

(8)

The second conclusion leads in the opposite direction, since it proceeds from the second article of the doctrine of the Trinity, namely, that the Father and the Son are not identical. If we take this second idea seriously, we find that this leads to conclusions which are of the greatest practical significance, even for our attitude towards social and ethical questions. Jesus Christ does say, it is true: "I and the Father are one",[1] "He that hath seen Me hath seen the Father";[2] but the Scriptures never say: "The Father is the Son and the Son is the Father." Now this distinction between Father and Son is particularly

[1] John 10: 30.  [2] John 14: 9.

important in view of what was said at an earlier point about the Hidden God; but the traditional form of the doctrine of the Trinity has never been fully able to express the conclusions to which this leads, because the fact that "Father and Son" were set alongside of, instead of after one another, prevented it.

God IS the One who is revealed in Jesus Christ. As such He is the Word, the Light, and the Life, Salvation, Love. In Jesus Christ we perceive God in His "own proper work". But we know that there is also a "strange work" of God, which He does *"cogente malitia hominum"*. This "Work" is not Salvation, it is not Life, it is not Light; this is the Work which He does where He is not known, not loved, not trusted, not recognized. There, too, He is the Holy God; but His holiness does not express itself as love, but as wrath, as consuming Fire.[1] Where He is *thus* present, as the wrathful God, there He is not present in Jesus Christ, but outside of Him. The witness of the New Testament confronts us unmistakably with this alternative: either in Christ, the love of God, or outside of Christ, wrath. To be "in Christ", from the subjective point of view, means "faith", and from the objective point of view it means "salvation". The God whom we have in Jesus Christ is Life and Salvation; and the God whom we have in Jesus Christ is He whom we have in faith, in obedience to His Word. But the God whom we have in unbelief, outside of Jesus Christ, is the angry God who does not prepare salvation for us, but judgment for doom.

Thus God acts in a twofold sphere: the sphere where God is as He reveals Himself in Jesus Christ, as Salvation, Light, and Life; and the sphere where He is not present in Jesus Christ, namely, as consuming wrath, which destroys, annihilates, and works in darkness. These two spheres are reality; the one is the reality in *Christ* in which we are set by the saving Word and saving faith;[2] the other is the reality *outside of Christ*, the world of doom and darkness, out of which we are rescued by Christ,[3] in so far as we believe in Him.

The reality and the seriousness of decision depend upon the reality of these two spheres. Upon this fact, too, rests the reality of redemption as being rescued from actual doom. The denial of this twofold reality may end in the denial of reality, that is, of the reality of redemption. If this takes place, then revelation is not salvation, but merely the removal of error.

[1] Heb. 12: 29.      [2] Col. 1: 13.
[3] 1 Thess. 1: 10; Rom. 5: 9; 1 Cor. 1: 21.

The seriousness of being rescued is just as great as the serious-ness of the danger from which we are rescued.

And not only are these two spheres real, but God also is real in these two spheres, as the Loving One in the one, and as the Wrathful One in the other. It is possible, by remaining in unbelief, or by turning away from faith, to fall away from Jesus Christ and the salvation revealed in Him—that is what makes the summons to believe so serious. But we cannot finally escape from God by unbelief and disobedience. Even in Hell, God is present, not as the God revealed in Christ as Love, but in His wrath, which is a Consuming Fire. Where Jesus Christ is, there is Light and Salvation; where Light and Salvation are not present, Jesus Christ is not present. But GOD is still there, as the God of wrath. "He that believeth on the Son hath ever-lasting life: and he that believeth not the Son shall not see life; but the wrath of God abideth on him."[1] This is the testi-mony of the whole of the New Testament.

We may try to deny this distinction—which is repellent to the monistic type of thought—by rejecting either the reality of destruction and doom or the fact that God is at work in destruction. The former is the radical doctrine of Apokatastasis, which leads ultimately to a denial of judgment. If there is no doom outside of Christ, then to remain in unbelief is not a serious danger, then "in any case" everything will come right in the end, with or without faith; then the decision of faith loses its seriousness, and the same applies to the message of rescue through Jesus Christ. We shall be dealing with this point later on in connexion with the doctrine of Election. The second way out of this difficulty is suggested in the view that although doom undoubtedly exists, because it lies outside the sphere of Jesus Christ, it also lies outside the sphere of God. But this would lead us directly into a metaphysical dualism; there would then be a power of darkness which is not subject to God, a devil who is not an instrument of the wrath of God, but another "God"—an enemy of the True God. This doctrine is in opposition both to the Biblical idea of God and the clear witness of the Bible. Even darkness, doom, death, ruin, lies within the sphere of God's working; it is the working out of the divine wrath.

The Biblical truth of the Holy God forces us to this con-clusion: where God is known and recognized in His revelation, where obedience is rendered unto the Son, there Holiness is one

[1] John 3: 36.

with the Love of God; but where God is not recognized, where the Word of Holy Mercy is not received, there the Holiness of God works itself out as His wrath. God sometimes exercises His sovereignty in a way which is not His "own proper work", His work in Christ, but His "strange work". Thus God is present where Jesus Christ is not present with His Light and Life, in the darkness, as the God of wrath. Thus there are works of God which as such are precisely not works of the Son. This non-identity of God and the Son is based upon the fact that God alone is Creator, but that the Son is called simply and solely the mediator of the Creation. In the New Testament the Son, or Jesus Christ, is never called the Creator. This title is given to the Father alone.[1] It is He who has "granted unto the Son to have life in Himself".[2] God *gives* to the Son deity from all eternity, as it is the Father who sends the Son to be the Redeemer of the world. This "Subordinationism", which does not eliminate the ὁμοούσιος, is inseparable from the Biblical testimony and the Biblical idea of God. God freely determines Himself for the Son, for community, and for love; hence, also, He is free to determine His Holiness as wrath, and—*cogente malitia hominum*—to work doom. This freedom of God, to effect salvation and doom, light and darkness, life and death,[3] is the unfathomable mystery of God, which even in the revelation of the Son remains a mystery. The mystery of God is not exhausted by the Son; for *"pater est fons totius trinitatis"*; God *can* be other than the One revealed in Jesus Christ as Light and Life, namely, the Hidden God, who as such operates not in the Word and its light, but in that which is not "word" or "knowledge", in darkness. This is the *Deus nudus*, who does not veil Himself in the form of the Son of Man—the terrible Majesty, which is "intolerable to all creation".

From all this, then, we can understand why it is that wherever natural life and events are severed from their relation to their "end" in Christ—hence where the natural sphere of this world as such is in question—the Bible speaks, it is true, of *God*, but not of Jesus Christ, not of the Son. Certainly, even the natural creation, even the natural course of events has its *goal* and its *meaning* in the Son, in the Kingdom of God.[4] Everything is to be gathered up in Christ, just as the keystone of the arch locks all the stones of the vaulting together, and thus

---

[1] The Psalm-quotation used in Hebrews 1: 10 should not be used as an argument against the explicit doctrine of 1: 2.
[2] John 5: 26.　　　[3] Is. 45: 7.　　　[4] Col. 1: 17; Eph. 1: 6.

sustains the whole.[1] Creation is intended to be perfected, and this perfecting takes place in the Son of His Love, in the Kingdom of God, in the fellowship of love between the creature and the Creator.[2] But not every creature reaches this goal, and not everything in the natural order is directed towards this end. There is therefore a *separation*, a κρίσις, at the end of the age, a Judgment. But the elements which will then be separated are even now present—even though invisible—like tares mingled with the wheat.[3] Something is ripening, not only towards the fullness of harvest but towards ruin. This is the sinful natural element and the natural course of this world, in so far as it is, and remains, outside of Christ. As such it is the "sphere of wrath", which stands under the "Prince of this world", in which the wrath of God is supreme.

God's governance in the State also belongs to this natural course of events in this world in which God is also at work. In the New Testament this sphere is clearly and explicitly assigned to a plane which comes under the wrath of God, and therefore nowhere is it related to the activity of Jesus Christ. It is not the Son, who has "ordered" this sphere of retributive justice but "God".[4] Pilate has not received the power to kill Christ from the Son; it is given to him absolutely "from above".[5] Indeed, from one point of view, is not the Cross of Christ, in its destructive effect, God's "strange work", effected by those who worked against Christ, through the betrayal of Judas, through Pilate's judicial murder, through the blasphemous verdict of the Jewish religious authorities? To this extent it is not a mistake to perceive, behind the powers which crucified Christ, the demonic angelic powers.[6]

In so far as this is the case, the wrath of God is at work, the wrath of God, which the God-Man suffers in place of man. All this is the *opus alienum Dei*, therefore it is not the work of Christ, because, and to the extent in which the distinctive quality of Christ, *Agape*, is not evident. It is the God who in the Judgment separates those who belong to Christ from those who do not, the Father who has "prepared eternal fire for the devil and all his angels",[7] that fire which consists precisely in absolute alienation from Christ.

The result of all this is, that we see how necessary it is to make a clear distinction between the works which God does in

[1] Eph. 1: 9–10.   [2] Eph. 1: 20 ff.; 3: 19.   [3] Matt. 13: 30.
[4] Rom. 13: 1 ff.   [5] John 19: 11.
[6] 1 Cor. 2: 8. Cf. Cullmann, *Christus und die Zeit*, p. 90.
[7] Matt. 25: 41.

and through the Son, from those which He does outside the Son of His Love. The statement which, from the point of view of Trinitarian theology has been laid down as a "rule",[1] and which has been repeated countless times: *opera trinitatis ad extra sunt indivisa*, must therefore be used with extreme caution. There are works of the Father, which are most certainly not the works of the Son. For the Scriptures never speak of the "works of wrath" of Christ, but only of the wrath of God. But the foregoing statement becomes a disastrous heresy if it is used without the "Augustinian Clause"[2]: *servato discrimine et ordine personarum*.[3]

If, however, this clause is forgotten, then one feels justified in transferring all that is said of the working of the Father to that of the Son, by which the whole distinction between the sphere of doom outside of Christ and the sphere of salvation in Christ becomes blurred. The failure to make this distinction then produces a Christian Monism which leaves no room either for the wrath of God or for Judgment; this means that the seriousness of decision is removed from life, and necessarily leads to a non-Scriptural doctrine of Universalism.

The Biblical message contains in itself the dialectical tension between Wrath and Mercy, between the Holiness which is identical with Love, and the Holiness which, as the wrath of God, is in opposition to it. Human thought, however, is always trying to evade this dialectic. It desires and demands an obvious unity. For this there are two possibilities: Calvin's doctrine of the "double decree" of God, or the opposite doctrine of Universalism. Neither the one nor the other is in accordance with the teaching of the Bible. There is no "double decree", but only the one which is revealed in Christ. There is, however, also no soothing doctrine of Universalism, because there is a sphere which lies outside of Christ—abiding under the wrath of God.

This Biblical view, however, is connected with the distinction between the works which the Father does in the Son, and those which He does in the sphere which is darkness and death, which thus has no part or lot in the Son, who is Light, Life, and Salvation. Thus the web of the true doctrine of Election is inextricably entangled with the correct doctrine of the Triune God.

---

[1] K. Barth, *Kirchliche Dogmatik*, I, 1, 395.
[2] Luthardt, *Kompendium der Dogmatik*, 11, p. 130.
[3] Cf. Augustine, *De Trinitate*, I, 4.

# APPENDIX TO CHAPTER 16

(1) ON THE PLACE OF THE DOCTRINE OF THE TRINITY AND ITS
    HISTORY

In contrast to other aspects of the Doctrine of God, the historical development of the doctrine of the Trinity has been treated so often and so thoroughly, and it is also such a favourite subject in the History of Dogma, that there is no need to devote a long section to it. In order to supplement what has already been said in the text, therefore, I will only deal with some specific points.

Karl Barth, as everyone will readily admit, has rendered a great service to theology by re-emphasizing the decisive importance of the doctrine of the Trinity within Protestant theology; he has been the first to do so, and it is to him that we owe the renewed sense of its significance (cf. also my work: *Der Mittler*, 1927, pp. 233-52). In his view, the outstanding, and indeed the absolutely decisive importance of this doctrine lies in the fact that in it he sees the basis for his main concern, the contrast between the speculative *"theologia naturalis"* and the theology which from beginning to end, in accordance with revelation, is orientated towards Jesus Christ alone. The Triune God is the God of revelation, not the God of the philosophers. Hence he sets the doctrine of the Trinity at the beginning of His work and has no use for a theology in which the Being of God in general—and that can only mean with speculative philosophical categories—is dealt with first of all. Indeed, he places the doctrine of the Trinity not merely at the beginning of the Doctrine of God in his *Dogmatics*, but at the beginning of his Prolegomena to the *Dogmatics*. For if the Prolegomena are to be a theological Theory of Knowledge, how can they help dealing with revelation? And if they deal with revelation, then certainly they must deal with the Triune God.

The vigour and force with which Barth lays stress on this his main concern has had such a salutary effect upon the whole development of theology that I would gladly abstain from criticism. But Barth, in the defence of his main concern—with which we are in entire and unhesitating agreement—in his great "spring-cleaning" has cleared out and thrown away a great deal that had nothing to do with Natural Theology, but was an integral part of the truth of the Bible; owing to the one-sided way in which he has defended his cause, he has injured the legitimate claims of Biblical theology, and has thus created unnecessary hindrances for the promulgation of his ideas.

(a) From the standpoint of method, it seems strange that the most important part of the doctrine of God is not treated here, but in the Prolegomena. Certainly, the Prolegomena deal with revelation, and thus with the God who reveals His Name to us in Jesus Christ. But either the Prolegomena are what their name says—and then its theme is a formal and not a material one—or, to put it still more plainly, that which is treated *materially* in the *Dogmatics* proper, should be here presented from the *formal* point of view, or there are no Prolegomena at all. The theme of the Prolegomena is certainly revelation, and that implies the "Triune God". What should now be done, however, is to deal with revelation from the formal point of view—with revelation, that is, as *"principium cognoscendi"*; revelation should not be treated as *"principium essendi"*, as the content of the doctrine of God. It is the formal theology of revelation, and is only thus to be distinguished from material dogmatics. Prolegomena in which the most important part of dogmatics is anticipated, and dogmatics in which the most important element is absent—this certainly is not the classical way of building up theology.

(b) Now, however, this structural anomaly is connected with a defect in the content of his doctrine of the Trinity, and this is the reason why this must be mentioned here. Barth does not distinguish between the *problem* of the Trinity which is set us by the message of the Bible, and the *doctrine* of the Trinity. He does not see that the doctrine of the Trinity is the product of reflection and not a *kerygma*. The *kerygma* is the God revealed in Christ, Christ, the genuine revelation of God. The doctrine of the Trinity itself, however, is not a Biblical doctrine, and this indeed not by accident but of necessity. It is the product of theological reflection upon the problem, which is raised, necessarily, by the Christian *kerygma*. The Bible also speaks of the Holy God, of the God who is Love, of the Almighty, etc.; the theme of these theological doctrinal elements is itself Biblical. But the Bible does not speak of the "Triune God"; this theme, as a theme, is a product of reflection on the truth given in the revelation, upon the problem which the revelation, the *Kerygma*, has raised.

Thus Barth assigns an importance to the Doctrine of the Trinity which does not legitimately belong to it, but only to the revelation itself. This means that more weight is given to the doctrine of the Trinity than the actual message of the Bible warrants.

(c) On the other hand, as compared with Barth, we have to justify the fact that we do not begin our study of the doctrine of God with the doctrine of the Trinity, but with the doctrine of the Holiness and the Love of God. From all that has just been said, it is easy to see what our reply will be. Here we are most certainly not reverting to the *theologia naturalis* or the speculative doctrine of God, which Barth, rightly, rejects with such horror. On the basis of the Biblical revelation, there is indeed sufficient ground for clear teaching about the Nature of God. To teach the truth concerning the Nature of God means nothing but the God who is revealed in Jesus Christ; but this does not mean that without further ado, and first of all, we begin by speaking of the problem of the unity of the Revealer with that which is revealed. On the contrary, the doctrine of the Trinity only becomes really intelligible when first of all, and indeed in harmony with revelation, we speak of God's Holiness and Love. For the revelation flows from His Holiness and His Love. His Revelation is *rooted* in the *Nature* of God; but from the revelation we come to *know* His Nature. The doctrine of the Trinity, however, springs from reflection upon this process; it is—so to speak—the product of reflection on the unity of the *ratio essendi* and the *ratio cognoscendi* of revelation. The Christian revelation is only to be understood from the standpoint of the Holiness and the Love of God, but both are to be understood, not as "attributes", but as the very "Nature" of God, although we only know the Holiness and the Love of God through revelation.

(d) The question of the place of dogmatics, therefore, proves to be a criterion for the clarity of the distinction between that which is "given" in revelation, and reflection upon it. Because Barth does not make a clear distinction here, and thus gives a bias to the doctrine of the Trinity which it ought not to have, he also fails to make a clear distinction between faith and theological reflection, and to this extent falls into *"theologismus"*.[1] Owing to this over-emphasis, theological thought acquires an importance which cannot be ascribed to it from the faith contained in the Scriptures. This high estimate of the doctrine of the Trinity is a legacy from Catholicism, and certainly cannot be derived from the Reformation.

Far more clearly than Barth, the Reformers distinguished

---

[1] The error of substituting theology for personal faith. (TR.)

between faith and theological reflection, while the failure to make this distinction is derived from the Catholic idea of faith. Moreover, Barth's concern—which is so entirely Scriptural and Reformed—to eliminate the *"theologia naturalis"* from the doctrine of God, is endangered by this. A further result, which can only be mentioned in passing, is the fact that even in the formulation of the content of his doctrine of the Trinity, Barth penetrates too far into the speculative sphere, and does not use that necessary reserve which springs from the centrality of the *history* of salvation in Biblical thought.

(*f*) Finally, from this view of the problem of the Trinity there arises also a certain, even though very limited, justification for the opposition to the ecclesiastical doctrine of the Trinity. The stumbling-block for thought which it provides, is not the stumbling-block and "foolishness" of the Gospel, but, if I may put it so—an artificial stumbling-block. It is not the Unity of the Three Persons which is the mystery of the Christian Faith; rather, *this* stumbling-block is the result of the process of transferring the interest from the realm of salvation to that of transcendental speculation. It is therefore intelligible that it is precisely those theologians whose thinking is entirely controlled by the thought of the Bible who have had little sympathy with the doctrine of the Trinity. I am thinking of the whole school of "Biblical" theologians. This has nothing to do with hostility to the doctrine on the part of Socinian and Rationalistic thinkers, save that perhaps even the Socinians must be credited with having a certain understanding of this position. The rationalistic rigidity of the theology of the Enlightenment, like many other peculiar features of the Enlightenment, is not to be ascribed wholly to the pride of man's reason, but also to the lack of understanding displayed by so many ecclesiastical theologians. How often, and at how many points, has the doctrinaire temper of orthodox theology driven men into Rationalism, who would perhaps otherwise have been ready to listen to a truly Biblical theology.

## (2) THE ORTHODOX DOCTRINE OF THE TRINITY

In order to judge the orthodox doctrine of the Trinity aright, as presented in the Athanasian Creed, it is necessary to consider what was the point at issue at that time.

Nothing less was at stake than the rejection of polytheist mythology (Arius) on the one hand, and the retention of the Divinity of Christ and the reality of revelation on the other

(Monarchianism). To put it in other terms, what was at stake was whether Christianity should become either Paganism or Judaism, or whether it should remain Christianity. We cannot be sufficiently grateful that the Fathers of the Church saw this danger, and that they did all that lay in their power to avert it. Had Arius conquered, it would have been all over with the Christian Church.

But that is only one side of the question. The ecclesiastical doctrine of the Trinity is not only the product of genuine Biblical thought, it is also the product of philosophical speculation, which is remote from the thought of the Bible. The idea of *"una substantia"* has had a particularly disastrous influence. It greatly facilitated the development of the Ontologism of the Middle Ages. To conceive God as Substance is the very sharpest contrast to the Biblical idea of the Absolute Subject. We may refine the idea of substance as philosophically as we will: it is, and it remains, the idea of the Object. That this fatal idea entered into the *Credo* was a real disaster.

Similarly, the idea of the Three Persons is more than questionable. Even Augustine felt this (cf. *De Trinitate*, V, 9). K. Barth seems to share this misgiving (*Kirchl. Dogm.*, I, 1, p. 703). We may order people to think thus: "Thou shalt think these Three Persons as One", but it is no use: there still remains an uncertain vacillation between Tritheism and Monotheism. Not only the idea of "substance", but also this idea of "Person", was much too wooden to express the mystery of the unity of the Revealer and that which is revealed. The fact that the Three Persons were conceived as "side by side" was, however, the result of the fact that Biblical thought, with its emphasis on the *"history* of salvation", was no longer understood. Theological attention was devoted to the transcendent background of revelation in itself, and the life of the relations within the Trinity was made the main subject of consideration; this is the profoundly non-Biblical element in the ecclesiastical doctrine of the Trinity. Finally, the ecclesiastical doctrine of the Trinity aided the growth of the mistaken understanding of *Agape*, the confusion between *Agape* and *Eros*. Since the life of God within the Trinity was severed from the history of Salvation, the *Agape* of God came to be understood as His love for Himself.

This alone "legitimized" the confusion between *Eros* and *Agape*. If Love be *Eros*, then naturally God can do no other than love Himself; for He alone has value for Himself; He alone—to use Luther's phrase again—is *"diligibile"*. To this extent, but really only to this extent, we can agree with Nygren's criticism of the doctrine of the Trinity. It is true that already in Augustine this confusion of *Eros* and *Agape* finds some support in his understanding of the Trinity (Nygren, *Eros und Agape*, II, pp. 358 ff.) and Nygren shows clearly that the mediaeval doctrine of the Trinity in particular serves to support the *Eros motif*. But when Nygren finds a certain tendency to move in this direction even in the Gospel of John (*ibid.*, I, pp. 126 ff.), because here the Love of God to His Son is the archetype of all love, there is certainly some confusion of thought. Nygren, too, admits that love is the Nature of God, and that John wished to express this in particular in his Trinitarian "metaphysic" (I, p. 131). But it would be an exaggeration of the contrast between *Eros* and *Agape* if God were said to be able only to love the sinner and the lost, in order that He might only love that which was unworthy. The love which God has for His Son is certainly not His love for sinners; but it is and it remains self-giving love. For it is the Father who "gives" to the Son, "to have life in Himself". Here too the character of love as self-communication is preserved. The essence of love within the Trinity is not "self"-love but self-communication, and in harmony with this, the love of the Son is the "giving-back" of that which has been received.

Nygren's criticism of the problem of the Trinity, however, remains a criterion and a warning to this extent, that it shows how dangerous it is to allow our thinking to be mainly concerned with the Nature of the Triune God, apart from the historical revelation of God in Christ. When we do this we are not far from the Augustinian error. The fact that Karl Barth has not fallen a prey to this temptation testifies to the strength of his Biblical thought.

## CHAPTER 17

# THE PROBLEM OF THE "DIVINE ATTRIBUTES"

WHILE the Biblical revelation naturally ascribes certain qualities or "attributes" to God; He is Almighty, Righteous, Omniscient, Omnipresent, etc.—in the sphere of theology the idea arose very early that the notion of "attributes" was dubious, that it was something which detracted from the purity of the Idea of God. The question was raised: Does not this way of thinking shake our belief in the Absoluteness of God? Does not each "attribute" mean that God is made finite? Even among the very early theologians of the Church, among the Apologists,[1] men's minds were influenced by the recollection of Plato's words that God exists without defining "how" he exists; He is not merely unlike man: ἄποιος γὰρ ὁ θεὸς, οὐ μόνον οὐκ ἀνθρωπόμορφος.[2] For He is indeed above all being ὑπερούσιος, ἐπέκεινα τῆς οὐσίας.[3] In later times it was mainly the thought of the absolute "simplicity" of God that prevented the ascription of definite qualities to God. Involuntarily we think of Spinoza's *Omnis determinatio est negatio*, when we already read in Arnobius:[4] *Quis enim Deum dixerit fortem, sapientem, constantem, quis probum, sobrium? Quidquid de Deo dixerimus, in humanum transit.*

And since Augustine once said:[5] *Quidquid de Deo digne dicitur non qualitas est, sed essentia*, criticism of the idea of the Divine Attributes has never ceased. Even the Protestant scholastics see themselves forced to try to solve this idea in Nominalist terms, *Si proprie et accurate loqui velimus, Deus nullas habet proprietates* (Quenstedt).[6]

What is the origin of this striking contrast between theology and the witness of revelation? Can it be really true that the Prophets and the Apostles speak of God in a way which is not *"digne"* or *"proprie"*? Is their naïve way of speaking of the Divine Attributes really a *transire in humanum*? Or can it be that here, at this decisive point, there is perhaps an actual contradiction between two ideas of God, which, in point of fact, cannot be combined, two views which may be described as the philosophical and speculative Idea of God on the one hand, and

[1] Cf. Justin, *Apology*, II, 6.     [2] *Leg. alleg.*, I, 47.
[3] *De rep.*, I, 509, casually quoted by Justin, *Dial.* c.T.c. 3.
[4] "Adv. gent.", III, 19.     [5] *De Civ. Dei.*, VIII, 6.
[6] *Theol. did. pol.*, I, C. 8, Sect. 3.

on the other, one which is based upon the thought of God in revelation?

In any case, from the standpoint of Biblical thought, in reference to the God of revelation, the use of the Platonic phrase: ἄποιος γὰρ ὁ θεὸς οὐ μόνον οὐκ ἀνθρωπόμορφος, arouses our misgivings; for this is the language of those who, when they speak of "God", mean "the Absolute" of philosophical speculation. "God" cannot be reached by rational thought save through a process of abstraction, carried out to its logical climax, for which no statement on "being" can be abstract enough. This "God" is certainly ἄποιος, ἐπέκεινα πάσης οὐσίας. Measured by this ideal of the "pure" Idea of God, certainly all that in any way reminds us that God is Subject or that He is Person, must look like anthropomorphism. For thought of this kind, however, it is not enough merely to avoid such "anthropomorphic" expressions; rather, every definite statement about the Nature of this Absolute comes under the judgment of the *omnis determinatio est negatio*. As an Ultimate, all that here remains for us is that which is not determined, that which is completely unspeakable (ὑπὲρ λόγον), "the Absolute", in the final sense of the word.

Anyone who knows the history of the development of the doctrine of God in "Christian" theology, and especially the doctrine of the Attributes of God, will never cease to marvel at the unthinking way in which theologians adopted the postulates of philosophical speculation on the Absolute, and at the amount of harm this has caused in the sphere of the "Christian" doctrine of God. They were entirely unaware of the fact that this procedure was an attempt to mingle two sets of ideas which were as incompatible as oil and water: in each view the content of the word "God" was entirely different; for each view was based on an entirely different conception of God.

They did not perceive the sharp distinction between the speculative idea of the Absolute and the witness of revelation, between the "God of the philosophers" and the "God of Abraham, Isaac and Jacob", of which Pascal became so clearly aware in that decisive experience of his life. From the standpoint of speculative thought about the Absolute every Christian statement about God must inevitably end in an *"in humanum transire"*, it must seem an unfitting "anthropomorphism", something which is *"non digne loqui"*. But this contradiction does not first emerge when confronted with the Biblical language about the Attributes of God, it occurs as soon as fundamental

242

definitions of Being are formulated. The God who is without all qualities, who is above all Being, is never the God who makes His Name known, never the Father of our Lord Jesus Christ, whose Nature is Holiness and Love.

This obliviousness of so many early theologians accounts for the extensive influence of this point of view—(the speculative way of thinking which could not be combined with the Biblical revealed religion)—on the development of the doctrine of God, but above all on the doctrine of the Divine Attributes. The extent of this *influence* is absolutely amazing. It is hardly an exaggeration to say that the theological doctrine of the Divine Attributes, handed on from the theology of the Early Church, has been shaped by the Platonic and Neo-Platonic Idea of God, and not by the Biblical Idea. The proof of this statement will be produced directly. But first of all we ask, how was such a fantastic distortion of thought possible? We find the answer in a fact to which Ritschl was the first to draw our attention, in his criticism of the development of the dogma of the Early Church, but which, for his part, he was unable to stress sufficiently clearly, because his own theological knowledge (far more than he himself was aware) was affected by the influence of that which he himself called: "the Hellenization of Christian Thought". In point of fact, we are here confronted by the decisive element in this process; here, in the sphere of the doctrine of the Divine Attributes, we see it operating, so to speak, *in flagranti*. The theologians of the Early Church were all more or less educated in Greek philosophy—and no intelligent person will blame them for this, or even suggest that there was anything wrong in it! But in their eagerness to present the Christian Idea of God in "pure", "exalted", and "spiritual" terms, they failed to notice the contradiction between the speculative method of the Greek thinkers and the way of reflection prescribed for the Christian theologian by that which has been "given" in revelation. Thus, without realizing what they were doing, they allowed the speculative idea of the Absolute to become incorporated in the *corpus* of Christian theology.

In the earlier stages of the theology of the Early Church (which extends from the Apologists to the Nicene Fathers), this influence was still limited; in essentials the doctrine of God was still determined by revelation and the history of salvation; thus it was still Biblical; some of the Fathers, such as Irenaeus, and even Athanasius, reveal scarcely a trace of the speculative bias in comparison with the Biblical foundation. But when the ideas of Neo-Platonism began to stream into the Church, especially from the time of the Pseudo-Dionysius (whose addition of the name of "Areopagite" gave him an almost apostolic authority), and began to influence theology, and when, from the time of Scotus Erigena onwards, throughout the whole of the Middle Ages, it acquired an almost unlimited reputation, and an almost canonical authority, infinite havoc was wrought in the sphere of the theological doctrine of God.

Here, again, we must use the word "obliviousness". Anyone who comes for the first time from the Bible into the world of Scholastic Theology feels himself in a foreign world. At every turn he is confronted by quotations from the Areopagite which have the authority of proofs. No Father of the Church, not even Augustine, is quoted so often, nor has exercised such an influence upon the theological thought of the Middle Ages, as this Neo-Platonist with the Biblical pseudonym, with his speculative thought of the Absolute tinged with Christianity. Along with the "Donation of Constantine" and the Pseudo-Isidorian Decretals, the writings of the Areopagite are one of the most impressive examples of the sinister influence of a pseudonym on world history.

There is the further fact that in addition to the work of Dionysius, the writings of Augustine also provided another channel for the infiltration of the Neo-Platonist idea of the Absolute into mediaeval and post-mediaeval theology. At the same time, we must admit that the Neo-Platonist element in the thought of Augustine—at least in his later works—is not so strong as it is in the writings of Dionysius, but must be described as one which is entirely subordinate to the faith of the Bible. To complete the picture we must recollect the Platonism of the earlier Fathers of the Church—such as Clement, Origen, Gregory of Nyssa and Gregory Nazianzen—through whom, although to a lesser extent, the speculative idea of the Absolute entered into theology. No one has yet computed the final result of the devastation wrought in the "Christian" theological Idea of God by these three elements, which all point in the same direction; once this is perceived, however, amazement will never cease.

After this historical digression, which is justified in view of the importance of the subject, we return to our particular theme: the problem of the doctrine of the Attributes of God. The aberration introduced by the speculative and philosophical

Idea of God appears mainly in the method by which the theological idea of the Attributes was acquired. The fact that anyone ever came to speak of the Divine Attributes at all is not, indeed (according to those voices to which we have just been listening), a matter of course, but it could not be avoided if one wished to remain in contact with the Biblical doctrine. Thus a compromise was made: properly speaking we cannot talk about the Divine Attributes, but we do it nevertheless, since the Biblical and Church tradition forces us to do so; but we do it in such a way that it agrees with philosophical, but not with Biblical thought. This way is the method of the *"viae"*.

This concept and this method is derived—characteristically —from the Areopagite.[1] The method of the *"viae"* in the doctrine of God corresponds exactly to the "method" in the practice of mysticism. In both cases a "way"—a method, a *via*—leads from man to God, in the one case—in the theological doctrine of the Attributes—a way of thought, in the other— in mysticism, a spiritual exercise. The first and the most important of these "ways", the *via negationis*,[2] is in exact accordance with the practice of mystical Neo-Platonism. The process of abstraction of the thinker is paralleled by the self-emptying of the mystic, his gradual emancipation from all that is earthly. In so doing the mystic reaches—as the goal of this self-emptying —union with the Godhead, the "liberation from all images", through the experience of ecstasy; the thinker, at the close of his process of abstraction, attains the idea of the Absolute, that which cannot be named.

The second "way" is the *via eminentiae*. The process here consists in moving from the creaturely analogy, by a process of gradual ascent, to the Infinite, to positive statements about the Attributes of God. We might, therefore, also call this process the way of Analogy. Man is mighty, the angels are mightier, God is Almighty. Man knows, the angels know more in a higher sense, God is All-knowing. The inclusion of the Angels which gives a dynamic to this argument, is in entire harmony with the role assigned to superhuman, and yet creaturely beings in

---

[1] *De div. nom.*, VII, 3. Certainly here there lies behind his thought the idea of Clement of Alexandria, *e.g.* that through abstraction one must eliminate the finite elements in the thought of God, till all that remains is the Idea of Unity (*Strom.*, V, 11).

[2] Like this method of the *"viae"* in general, so also this specifically Neo-Platonist *"via eminentiae"* was followed by the Protestant Scholastic theologians. Cf. B. Hollaz, *Examen. Theol.*, p. 190.

mediaeval thought from the time of the book published by the Areopagite on the *tres hierarchiae.*

The third "way" is the *via causalitatis.* From that which is given in the experience of the world through the causal idea we work back to the author of this "given" element, in accordance with the principle: the effect presupposes the cause. Thus, too, one gains certain positive statements about the Nature and the Attributes of God, possibly even, as philosophical Theism shows us, to a positive valuation of the Personality of God. If, however, the latter is once presupposed, then in this way it is possible to set up such a sum-total of qualities that to some extent they agree with that which has been said above about thought controlled by revelation, questionable as the application of the idea of causality to God may be.

All these "ways" are possibilities of knowing "God" in a human manner; they are natural, rational theology.[1] How far these methods are justified as ways of thinking need not be discussed here; this is a subject for philosophical criticism. All this has nothing to do with the Christian Idea of God, and with the way in which faith, on the basis of the divine self-revelation concerning God, knows of His Nature and His Attributes. All this is rational metaphysics, it is not Christian theology; it is *theologia naturalis,* not *theologia revelata.*

If, however, this speculative rationalistic process of the *viae* in the sphere of a Christian doctrine of the Divine Attributes is forbidden to us once for all, on the other hand a purely literalistic Bible statement is also insufficient. It consists, like all other "biblicist" procedure, in collecting Bible passages, arranging them in some kind of order, and then summing all this up. Although this process is not so dangerous as the speculative method, yet it is very unsatisfactory, because it is so arbitrary. The Biblical statements about the Attributes of God are, however, not parts of a whole which only need to be fitted together. Such a use of the Biblical testimony contradicts the nature and intention of this testimony. The very fact that the Bible uses so much poetical, pictorial language should suffice to warn us not to follow this line of thought. In so doing the theologian both makes his own task too easy, and does violence to the Bible. Dogmatics does not consist in constructing a system of Biblical statements, but it is reflection upon revelation, on the basis of the religious evidence of the Bible.

[1] This is why the comparatively mild verdict on the method of the *viae* by Karl Barth is somewhat surprising (*Kirchl. Dogm.*, II, 1, pp. 390 ff.).

What, then, in the legitimate formation of theological concepts, can be meant by the "Divine Attributes"?[1]

We return once more to that sentence of Augustine, where he says that all that we say *"digne"* about God is not an "Attribute" but His "Nature". This statement, in spite of the fact that it is untrue, has founded a "school" of thought, and has even led good theologians astray. The Nature of God is that which God makes known to us of His revelation about Himself, about the mystery of His Person, about what He is "in Himself". But now on the basis of this self-revelation of God we have to make statements about His Being not only as He is in Himself apart from this created world, but as He is also in relation to the world He has created. God in Himself is the Holy One; that is His Nature, His sovereignty and freedom from the world, the fact that He is in no way conditioned by the world, that in Himself He is wholly self-sufficient.

In Himself, however, God is not the Almighty, the Omniscient, the Righteous One; this is what He is in relation to the world which He has created. Or, to put it more correctly, in the statements which refer to the "attributes of God" we express (on the basis of His self-revelation) God's Nature, as it works itself out and is made known to us in view of the world which has been created by Him. The ideas of divine attributes, which we encounter in the Bible in poetical or in childlike non-reflective forms as direct testimonies of faith, all point back to God's Nature, but they express this Nature of God in relation to different particular aspects of the created world. This shows clearly the line which the theological doctrine of the Divine Attributes should follow; its task is to reflect upon the basis of the Biblical revelation in relation to certain definite aspects of the created world.

[1] We prefer this idea to that which Barth has taken over from the Protestant Scholastics of the "Perfections" of God, because the latter is too closely related to the tradition of the *viae*.

## CHAPTER 18

## GOD, THE ALMIGHTY

IF we turn from the Bible to a work of mediaeval or post-Reformation theology on the idea of the Divine Omnipotence, our first impression is one of astonishment at two facts. First of all, the doctrine of God's Omnipotence is not placed first, as we might have expected, but it usually appears near the end of the list of Divine Attributes;[1] secondly, the teaching on the subject is very meagre. The "Attributes" which come first are those which a theologian who is accustomed to test all doctrine by the touchstone of revelation would not regard as legitimate subjects at all; chief among these qualities is the "simplicity" of God. The development of the doctrine of God has been determined, not only by mediaeval theology but also in post-Reformation theology—and thence to a large extent even in modern Protestant theology—by the ontology of Neo-Platonism: God as Being, the *Summum Bonum*, the *One* who cannot be named. Hence the primacy of that doctrine of the "simplicity" of God, a doctrine which, almost more than any other, shows very clearly the difference between the speculative and the Biblical Idea of God. If God be defined as "Being", then that which the Bible understands by the Omnipotence of God can only be of secondary significance.

Then, too, the way in which this teaching is arranged is characteristic of this fundamental contradiction. The Latin word *omnipotentia* is here closely related to the speculative tendency in theology. Revelation, as we shall see directly, teaches nothing about *omnipotentia*. The Biblical conception means God's power over the whole universe; but *omnipotentia* means the abstract idea that "God can do everything". It is based upon the idea of "being able", which is entirely absent from the Biblical idea. This is no accident, but it is necessarily derived from the speculative ontological starting-point, *God = Being*. A more exact analysis of its content would show that it is a compromise between the Neo-Platonist, Dionysian concept of "Being" and the Biblical Idea of God; that is, the result of the effort to achieve a point of contact with the very different Biblical doctrine of God from the standpoint of the speculative idea of All-Being and All-existence, of the All-One.

[1] See below, pp. 294 ff.

It is from the idea of *omnipotentia* that all those theoretical, curious, fanciful questions arise, which are included in this idea that "God can do everything", and "what He cannot do"— a process of questioning which characteristically begins with Augustine, and in Thomas Aquinas[1] leads to long disquisitions on such questions as "whether God could make the Past not to have existed" or whether He "can make that which He does not make", or "whether God could make that which He does make still better", which finally ended in those absurd problems in sophistry which Erasmus treats with such scathing mockery.[2] Once more: this is no accident; it arises inevitably out of the idea of *omnipotentia*, which would be impossible for a genuinely Biblical system of thought.

The connexion between the idea of Being and the Idea of God in speculative theology, however, brings with it a still more dangerous set of problems, which may end in confusing the Omnipotence of God with the *potentia* or with the *potestas absoluta*. For if the Omnipotence of God be understood as *potestas absoluta*, then this idea swallows up all creaturely independence. God, the Almighty, becomes the One who alone can effect anything, which again leads logically to the idea that He is the Sole Reality, and this means Pantheism, or "Theopanism".[3] The fact that this theology derived from the Areopagite was a serious menace, can be proved by the existence of the most outstanding work of theology of the early Middle Ages, *De Divisione naturae* by Duns Scotus; other instances are the early chapters of Zwingli's *De Providentia*, and several parts of Luther's *De servo arbitrio*. The theology of the Church was clear, however, that it must not follow this path. Hence it rejected the idea of "sole Reality", and to a large extent also the idea of the "sole" working of God; but this was only achieved with difficulty so long as it retained the equation *Deus = Esse*. The result of this effort is the distinction between the *potestas absoluta* and the *potestas ordinata*. In more recent times we find a similar compromise-solution in Schleiermacher, in the transition from his system of identity to the idea of God as the "source of absolute dependence". This compromise is contained in his definition of Omnipotence:[4] "The conception of the Divine Omnipotence contains two ideas: first, that the entire system of Nature, comprehending all times and spaces, is founded upon divine causality, which, as eternal and omni-

---

[1] *Summa Theol.*, I, 25, 4 ff.    [2] In the *Epistolae virorum obscurorum.*
[3] Cf. *Revelation and Reason*, p. 224. (TR.)    [4] *Glaubenslehre*, para. 54.

present, is in contrast to all finite causality; and, second, as affirmed in our feeling of absolute dependence, is completely presented in the totality of finite being, and consequently everything for which there is a causality in God happens and becomes real." Therefore, he goes on to say,[1] if we want to define the idea of Omnipotence still further, there is no need "to go beyond the natural order". We will now show that the Biblical conception of God as Almighty means exactly the opposite. But it was necessary, first of all, to show the problem created by the theological tradition, in order to be able rightly to understand the Biblical conception of Omnipotence which is of an entirely different order.

These problems, created by the idea of the *potestas absoluta*, do not arise in the Biblical view. The Biblical teaching about Divine Omnipotence is concerned with the relation of God to that which He has created. Briefly, this is what it says: that God has power "over all". Hence it is an Attribute, not a conception of being. God is not, in Himself, "the Almighty"— such a statement would be meaningless for the thought of the Bible, since the power that God possesses—in contrast to that abstract idea that "He can do everything"—always means exercising power over *something*. The idea of "Omnipotence", however, like that of all other "attributes", is rooted in the Nature of God, namely, in the fact that God is Free and Sovereign Lord, whose power cannot be limited by anything or anyone. In His unrestricted freedom He creates the All, over which He, because He is its Creator, has complete authority. The subject of the Biblical idea of Omnipotence is not that of the Absolute *Ens* to that which relatively exists, but that of the Free Lord and Creator to that which He has created. Its content, too, is the exact opposite of that which is suggested in Schleiermacher's definition: namely, that God, because He *is* the Creator-Lord, is not bound by the creature, but disposes of him freely. God is free to take the course of nature which He has created into account or not, to preserve it, or to bring it to an end. What the Bible means is especially this freedom of God from the course of Nature, the non-identity of His will with that of the causality of Nature. God is the God who can work miracles if He wishes, who can preserve and maintain the course of Nature, or can suspend it, or do away with it entirely, if He wills. The fact that God is Absolute Lord over His own creation is an integral part of His Nature, as the Living God.

[1] *Glaubenslehre*, para. 54: 2.

The course of Nature in the created universe has, it is true, some connexion with certain limitations to God's power, and this is the second important element in the idea of Omnipotence; namely, that God *limits Himself* by creating something which is not Himself, something "over against" Himself, which he endows with a relative independence. Thus it is God Himself who creates this limitation—hence He is also free to remove it. He creates it, He limits Himself, in order that a creature may have room alongside of Himself, in whom and to whom He can reveal and impart Himself. Thus from the very outset the Biblical idea of God as Almighty is related to revelation. It can only be understood in its correlation with this divine self-limitation which lies in the nature of His Creation. For this very reason it is entirely free from the problems raised by that idea of *potestas absoluta*, which makes all other forms of existence appear as nothing, which takes from them every vestige of independence, and above all leaves no room for the freedom of the creature.

While the idea of the *"potestas absoluta"* necessarily leads to determinism, within the thought of the Bible the problem of freedom in connexion with the idea of God as Almighty is never actually raised. In the Bible there is no metaphysical problem of freedom, but only an ethical one, because the idea of the divine Omnipotence always implies the independence of the creature. Because this Omnipotence is that of the Lord and Creator, who makes Himself known to us in His revelation as One who wills to communicate Himself, it is a power which does not eliminate creaturely independence, nor, above all, the freedom of the creature endowed with reason, of Man, but, on the contrary it establishes it. Compared with the *potestas absoluta*, it is a limited power, limited, that is, by that freedom of the creature which is willed and established by the Creator. But this limitation is freely self-imposed; God wills the existence of an independent being alongside of Himself; thus in the last resort this limitation springs from the love of God. Thus there is no limitation from without; the limitation comes from within, and is imposed by the sovereign will of God alone. This idea of Omnipotence, however, means that this self-limitation of God, because it is the act of His own will, does not erect any barrier to His power or His authority. God remains in authority over the universe which He has created. This excludes both errors: Pantheism and Deism. The independence granted to the creature does not mean that it can erect barriers against the will of God. The creature, in spite of its real independence, remains so entirely at God's disposal that at any moment He could annihilate it.[1] Accordingly, the whole order of Nature which He has ordained is such that it only exists and functions so long as God allows it to exist and to function. Thus God remains free, over against the universe He has created, and its order; He has authority over it; He is Almighty. In the Biblical revelation the Divine Omnipotence means that He is free to deal with the Universe He has created when and how He wills. This is an unlimited Divine authority, which does not remove the independence of the creature, but does bind it wholly to the life of God; and it is a limitation of the power of God, based solely and simply in His will as Creator and Preserver; which thus not only does not infringe His freedom, but on the contrary asserts it to the full.

In this sense alone does the Bible speak of the Omnipotence of God. The word "Omnipotence" does not occur in the Bible, and the word "the Almighty" only occurs at one point: παντοκράτωρ.[2] But the truth itself is expressed in a variety of ways. God is El Shaddai;[3] He is the Lord of Lords;[4] He is the only Lord.[5] He does what He wills;[6] "He spake and it was done; He commanded, and it stood fast";[7] hence "with God nothing is impossible".[8] All that is, has been created by Him; nothing happens and nothing exists apart from His will.[9] Not even the least thing happens apart from His will,[10] God is, above all, the God who works miracles, who freely disposes of His creatures. God can do what He wills, without any limitations at all.

Moreover, the Biblical idea of Omnipotence is completely free from that fanciful, argumentative, experimental element which is inevitably connected with the idea of the *potestas absoluta*, which leads to those typically scholastic explanations about the extent of the divine Omnipotence. We are not concerned with an "Omnipotence in itself", but with the unrestricted freedom of the God who has made His nature and His will known to us in His revelation. There is no room here for the question: What *could* God do, if He *would*? He reveals Himself as the One who *can* do all that He *wills*. The Bible is speaking of something quite different from that abstract idea

---

[1] "Heaven and earth will pass away" (Matt. 24: 35): this, like the Creation, is one of the fundamental truths stated in the Bible.

| | | |
|---|---|---|
| [2] Rev. 1: 8. | [3] Gen. 17: 1. | [4] Ps. 115: 3. |
| [5] 1 Tim. 6: 15. | [6] Ps. 115: 3. | [7] Ps. 33: 9. |
| [8] Luke 1: 37; Matt. 19: 26. | [9] John 1: 1 ff. | [10] Matt. 10: 29. |

of Omnipotence when it says: "For He spake and it was done; He commanded and it stood fast." This means: that no difference exists between what God *wills* and what He can *do*, that His will already contains its realization. *This* is His power over the All: that it is always at His disposal.

But this will is that which He has revealed to us. Hence the Omnipotence of God is nearly always mentioned only in connexion with His work of revelation and redemption. This comes out plainly in the way in which the Bible speaks of miracles. In miracle, in the freedom of God over the course of Nature which He Himself has ordained and ordered, we are meant to see chiefly the "All-power" of God in the Biblical sense of the word; yet the idea of "miracle" is to be understood in its specifically Biblical sense, and not in a general sense. While in heathen religions the miraculous power of the "gods" is expressed in all kinds of curious and sensational ways, in the Scriptures, both of the Old and of the New Testament, miracles are more or less closely connected with the history of the Covenant.[1] The God who reveals Himself as the Holy Lord and as Love, is also He who in this revelation shows Himself as the Almighty. "Miracle in itself" is no more part of the right idea of Omnipotence than the idea of "Omnipotence in itself". The miracle stories of the Bible—apart from some exceptions —are "theocratic" or "connected with salvation"—that is, they are means through which the plan of God is realized.

Through this close relation between the revealing and the redeeming activity of God, however, this idea of Omnipotence shares in the paradoxical unity of revelation and hiddenness, which is bound up with the nature of the true revelation. As the Holiness and the Sovereignty of God merge into Love, which finds its highest expression in complete self-giving, so is it also with Omnipotence. God shows His Omnipotence in highest sovereignty where the impotence of the Crucified, the defeat of the Son of God, must accomplish the work of revelation and reconciliation. Yes, here in particular the specific nature of the true Omnipotence in the Biblical sense, in contrast to all rational ideas of omnipotence, becomes plain. Even of Omnipotence it is true to say: "Truly Thou art a God who hidest Thyself."[2] That One who has suffered defeat in the service of God, whose enemies crucified and mocked Him, One who out of the depths of dereliction cried aloud to God, could reveal the Almighty

---

[1] In the N.T. this is always the case; even in the O.T. it is almost always so (cf. Eichrodt, *op. cit.*, II, pp. 83 ff.).　　　　[2] Is. 45: 15.

power of God—what human understanding, or what human imagination would have conceived such an idea?

At the beginning of this chapter we said that what distinguishes the Omnipotence of God from the *potestas absoluta* is the self-limitation of God through and for His creation. Here, in the Cross of Christ, where the decisive saving Act takes place, this self-limitation reaches its climax: God surrenders Himself in His Son to the contradiction of men, and in so doing reveals the incomparable character of His Omnipotence as compared with all that the human mind could conceive. God orders the course of the world in such a sovereign way that even, and especially through the maximum of resistance to His will, He makes it the means of His revelation, and the instrument of realizing His sovereignty.

There is a Divine Omnipotence which is exercised in compulsion—His work in the realm of Nature, and in that which man experiences absolutely as Destiny. But there is also a Divine Omnipotence where man decides in freedom, and this is His "Omnipotence" proper, that which most clearly expresses His sublime divine Nature: His Nature as the Holy Lord, and as the Loving Father. God *so* wills to be "almighty" over us, that He wins our hearts through His condescension in His Son, in the Cross of the Son. No other Almighty Power of God could thus conquer and win our hearts. The heart is the one sphere which cannot be forced. No love can be forced— God the Creator makes us so free that even *His* coercion could not force us to love Him. But He has indeed created us so free because He wills to reveal Himself to us as love, because our free love is the highest that He desires. If we would describe the Omnipotence of God, we would have to do it in the way in which Rembrandt depicts the Passion. Everything which might otherwise be described as "Omnipotence" would have to be left wholly or half dark, and all the light would be concentrated on this One point: the love of the Crucified—which, as the only power that can do so—subdues our pride, conquers our fears, and thus wins our hearts. The turning of the rebellious despairing heart of man to God as the result of His turning to man, man being dethroned from his position of likeness to God by the stooping down of God from His Throne—that is the supreme proof of the divine Omnipotence, because it is His most difficult work. At its highest the Omnipotence of God is one with His Holiness and His Love.

Thus so great is the distance between the Biblical idea of

Omnipotence and the speculative idea of *potestas absoluta*, that it is at its greatest where also the freedom of man is at its height. For man is never so free as where in faith He allows himself to be apprehended by the love of God. In this faith—to use Luther's phrase—man becomes a free Lord over all creation. In this faith there is no coercion, no unwillingness; here we see how free God wills man to be. And precisely where this freedom is greatest, God also gives the highest proof of His royal freedom. Indeed, it is this royal freedom of God that makes men free. While the *potestas absoluta* of speculation excludes freedom to such an extent that it even absorbs into itself all independent being, all being that is not God Himself, the true divine Omnipotence includes the highest freedom of man, the willingness of love.

## CHAPTER 19

# THE OMNIPRESENCE AND THE OMNISCIENCE OF GOD

THE words used to describe the Divine Attributes which are most important for the Christian Idea of God all begin with the word "all"; this is not a linguistic accident. All these words are closely connected with one another, and each emphasizes a particular aspect of the absolute freedom of God over the "All" which He has created. We are almost tempted to say that the Omnipresence and Omniscience of God are only special modes of Omnipotence. But it would not be wise to give way to this temptation, because it springs from the failure to distinguish sufficiently clearly between the conception of the attribute of Omnipotence and the concept of the nature of sovereign self-determining personality. Keeping strictly to the theological canon we will only speak of that God who makes His Name known to us, and this will show us that the theological treatment even of these ideas has been biased by the speculative method, that is, by the Idea of the Absolute.

## (1)

If we understand the idea of the Omnipresence of God from the metaphysical and speculative standpoint, then Pantheism is practically inevitable. The Divine Immanence in His Creation then becomes the Sole Reality of God, the creatures become merely "disguises" or "masks" of God;[1] this means, not only that the central idea of the independence and reality of the creature, but also the specific element in the Biblical doctrine of the Presence of God has been misunderstood. In order to estimate this aright, we must begin with the observation that in the Bible many different kinds—and even different degrees —of the Presence of God in the world are mentioned. This means that the idea of the Presence of God loses that neutral quality which is usually ascribed to it in dogmatic treatises. Above all, however, it shows clearly its connexion with the event of revelation. In the witness of the Bible it is not so much that God merely reveals that He is Present; rather the

[1] These expressions are derived from Luther, and show that some of his ideas verge on Pantheism (cf. Blanke, *Der verborgene Gott bei Luther*).

revelation itself is one of the ways in which He is present, and indeed it is the most important and decisive one.

At first, certainly, we have to begin with the apparently neutral idea of the Presence of God, that is, with the spatial conception; as a rule when we speak of "Omnipresence" this is what is intended. Here, the point is the sublimity of God, and the fact that He is highly exalted, far above all spatial distance and separation. While it is inherent in created existence to be localized—it is "here" and not "there"—it is inherent in the Being of God that He who appointed this limitation for his creature Himself transcends it. God "fills" the whole world of space; there is no place in the world where God is not. The explanation of the difficulties which this idea causes to our imagination, does not come within the sphere of the present work; it belongs rather to a work of Christian philosophy. All these difficulties arise from the fact that our imagination is connected with space, but neither for the Christian believer nor for the thinker are these difficulties of very great moment. The important point, however, is the fact that in spite of this absolute infinity of the Divine Being in the Biblical revelation, the thought of the Bible never even hints at the pantheistic elimination of the independence and reality of the creature. God is everywhere, but it is God Himself who gives to this space, and the creatures it contains, the character of reality, and of—limited—independence. That which creates a sense of distance is real for us, but not for God; because He appoints it, it is real, and because it is *He* who does so, for Him it does not exist. In the Old Testament, it is true, there are traces of a primitive anthropomorphism which thinks of God in the localized sense, which, therefore, can only imagine that distance—in the spatial sense—can be transcended by human methods of "presence"—that is, by going from one place to another.[1] As a rule, however, the anthropomorphic expressions, God "dwells in Heaven", "He looketh down upon the children of men"— have a quite different origin and meaning. They are the expression of that sovereign glory of God who is Himself the mighty Lord of the universe, for whom there is no spatial "distance". The "coming down", the "coming" of God, does not belong to the sphere of primitive anthropomorphism but is intended to express the truth that God "intervenes" in the life of history.

[1] These are the primitive anthropomorphic expressions on which a rationalist philosophy loves to base its arguments against the Christian and Biblical Idea of God: *e.g.* Gen. 2: 18 ff.; 3: 8; 11: 5, etc.

The Commandment forbidding the worship of "graven images" is based on this idea of the sublimity of God exalted above the realm of space. Only that which is spatially limited can be seen. The God who is worshipped in an image is localized, limited by space. The protest against making an image of God does not only mean that He is unlike the world, but also that He is not tied to space. "The Lord of heaven and earth dwelleth not in temples made with hands",[1] any more than He dwells in a graven image. He indeed fills the heaven, "the heaven of heavens cannot contain" Him.[2] The earth is only "His footstool",[3] but "heaven is His Throne".[4] These phrases are poetical and childlike expressions of the truth that God is infinitely High, above all the limitations of space; "heaven" means the essential Transcendence of Him who is immanent within all that is created, whose "footstool" is the earth.

And yet, God is not present to all in the same way. Beyond this extensive Presence of God there is one which is intensive and qualitative. It is only against the background of this qualitative differentiation of Presence that the Biblical language about the Omnipresence of God is rightly understood. There is a "distance" and there is a "nearness" of God. One may be "near" God, and one may be "far" from him. Therefore God may "come near" and He may "go away", and we may "come near" to, and "move away" from Him.

We ought not to raise the objection that in these statements the Bible is only using parabolic language. It is not simply a parable when Jesus says: "I am come." It is true, of course, that this phrase, like all human language about God, is parabolic. But it does mean a real Presence, just as the promises of Christ: "Where two or three are gathered together in My Name, there am I in the midst of them",[5] or: "I am with you always, even unto the end of the world"[6] mean what they say. Here a real presence is meant, although it is not a presence which can be understood in spatial terms. In addition to spatial distance there are other forms of distance, therefore there are also other forms of nearness, and other forms of "presence". There is the distance between the Creator and the creature, the "inaccessibility" of God. There is the distance between the sinner and the Holy God, distance from God, man's departure from God, on the one hand, and the withdrawal of the wrathful

---

[1] Acts 17: 24.
[3] Is. 66: 1.
[5] Matt. 18: 20.

[2] 1 Kings 8: 27.
[4] Is. 66: 1; Ps. 123: 1; 115: 3.
[6] Matt. 28: 20.

God, on the other hand. This "distance" is removed by revelation and by the establishment of communion between God and man; the final goal of this "movement-towards-us" is the act of "beholding, face to face", the full unrestricted presence in person. It is due to our creaturely limitations that we cannot conceive this revealed Presence otherwise than in spatial terms, that is, through the idea of "presence", of "being-here" or "being-with-us", so that when we try to do without this expression, in losing the expression, we lose the reality itself.[1]

Now in order to understand God in accordance with revelation it is of decisive importance that this qualified presence—which includes equally a qualified non-presence, or distance from God—is also determined by time. The movement consists of Space and Time together. Hence the basis of the Biblical doctrine of God is the "coming" of God. In pagan mysticism, as well as in metaphysical speculation, the presence of the deity is always known in the same way. If there be movement, if there be distance and the removal of distance, then, according to this view, it is all on the human side, and is due to the limitations of man's knowledge by his senses. True knowledge, then, is that there is no distance, that there never has been any such distance, and never will be, that all that separates is only to be ascribed to our own erroneous and imperfect knowledge. Hence for mysticism and for philosophical theology there is no idea of God revealing His Presence, by His own Act.

On the other hand, the presence of God Himself in person, the Coming of God, is the central article of the Biblical confession of faith. God comes. The whole Bible, the Old, as well as the New Testament, simply aims at saying this one thing. Hence the revelation reaches its climax in the coming of the Messiah (Emmanuel), of whom, in whom, and through whom, God is "with us", and in whom—through this "coming"—the Indwelling of the Holy Spirit has been made both possible and actual. This presence, the Christ in us, is the real goal of the historical revelation, of the history of the Covenant and of salvation. Through this "dwelling-in-us" of the Holy Spirit, that distance, that remoteness from God has been overcome, which most sharply divides us from God. This is His presence in salvation, His presence tempered to our need.

Here, too, the distinctive element in the Biblical doctrine of God becomes evident: the connexion between the Glory of God

[1] On the significance of the doctrine of the Real Presence of Christ in the Eucharist for the doctrine of Omnipresence, see below, pp. 298 ff.

and the Love which wills and preserves the independence of the creature. For this "nearness" of God comes, it is true, only through the movement of God, through His self-revelation and self-communication, but it takes place with full consideration of the freedom of the creature. For the "nearness" of God realizes itself only through the repentant and believing acceptance of the revelation and the self-communication of God. "Repent and believe"—that is the condition on which alone the presence of God in Christ becomes real to man. Without this movement of the heart Christ does not mean nearness to God but rather the very opposite, distance from God. "He came unto His own, and they that were His own received Him not. But as many as received Him, to them gave He the right to become children of God, even to them that believe on His Name".[1] The Epistle of James has given clearest expression to this personal correspondence, to this Divine movement to which the human movement corresponds—indeed so strongly does he put it that it might easily be misunderstood—when he says: "Draw nigh to God, and He will draw nigh to you."[2]

Indeed, in the negative sense, even the nearness of God, which here means the distance, is primarily dependent on man, not on God. Sin, apostasy from God, is distance from God, for which man, not God, must bear the responsibility, even though God, moved thereto by the sin of man, withdraws Himself from him, by "hiding His Face", in that He sets His wrath between Himself and man. The wrath of God is the reaction of the Divine Holiness to the apostasy of man from His Creator. Thus the conception of the Presence of God is qualified as personal in a twofold sense, and therefore is also determined historically in a twofold sense. In accordance with the act of apostasy the "becoming present" of God also must be an act, a history, a quite definite historical event which corresponds to the universal event of sin, but one which is to be appropriated by the individual, although it is universal.

Now that we have reached the end of our course of reflection, we perceive that even that apparently neutral idea of Omnipresence, namely, the exalted position of God above Space, thus that which is usually meant by Omnipresence, is not the starting-point but the end, in so far, namely, as the right understanding of that exaltation of God above spatial distance can only be fully understood from the standpoint of the God who makes His Presence known to us in this revelation of Himself.

[1] John 1: 11–12.      [2] James 4: 8.

Even that Presence is presence in revelation and in grace; if not in the historical sense, then in the "pre-historical" sense of revelation and grace in general. God's Omnipresence is not only His sublime height above Space, but far beyond this it is His gracious presence with His Creation. As the French speak of making an *acte de présence*, so the Presence of God is an *acte de présence* of God, a gracious "Being-with-the-creation" of the Creator which cannot be taken for granted.

In our effort to think out the idea of Omnipresence, therefore, we have come to the conclusion that even this idea is insepar-ably connected with the event of the revelation of the Holy and Merciful God, and indeed, that in the last resort, it is one with Him. For the perfect Presence of God is identical with His perfect revelation and self-disclosure. In other words, we can only understand the Biblical teaching about the Presence of God along the following line: that the whole of the story of salvation, the Creation, the Fall, the Old and the New Covenant, the Fulfilment, is reflected in the various "modes" in which the Presence is made known. In all this, the spatial Presence of God lies on the outermost fringe of the Divine Mystery, and is already filled with a richer content in the sphere of the Know-ledge of Creation. God's Presence in His creatures is more than His mere existence; it is the abiding basis of their being, their life, and indeed of their life as it is determined in particular forms. God is present in a stone otherwise than in a plant, differently again in an animal, and again in man quite differently from His Presence in all His other creatures—quite apart from sin and redemption. God's Presence, in whatever form, is always the principle of the possibility of existence, and of the—very varying—fullness of being of that which has been created. These are thoughts which should be developed further in a Christian ontology; for they throw light on a wholly new aspect of the problem of being, and of the planes of existence as a whole.

(2)

No less significant is the difference between thought deter-mined by revelation, and by speculation, in the understanding of the divine Omniscience. This idea is intimately related with that of Omnipresence, as indeed the *locus classicus* of this doc-trine, the 139th Psalm, shows—indeed, we might even say that it reveals the ideal aspect of Omnipresence. Hence from the very outset we have to expect that here, too, we shall have to reckon with a differentiation of different kinds of divine knowledge. First of all, here, too, there is an apparently neutral kind of knowledge, one which includes equally every kind of knowing; the fact that God knows everything. When Schleiermacher maintains that "divine thinking is the same as the divine will",[1] when he thus equates Omnipotence and Omniscience, from the point of view of the thought of the Bible we must be ready to protest. For behind this assertion there lies the pantheistic idea of the Absolute, which makes the independence of the creature an illusion. If the creature is real it is other than God, then we must make a very clear distinction between the Divine thinking which creates and that which reflects His activity. The fact that God knows about His creature is not the same truth as that He creates it. He knows about it as a created reality, which stands over against Him. He knows of an action of the creature which is not His own action. He knows above all about the free activity of that creature to which He has granted the freedom to decide for himself.

But the Divine Knowledge is not bound to Time and Space, to perception and inference, as ours is. All stands in eternal presence before the eyes of God—and yet as a knowledge of something which is not Himself. The activity of the creature which takes place in freedom is enclosed within this knowledge. From the foreknowledge of God men have drawn the false conclusion that the creature has no freedom. Augustine already proved that this was a wrong conclusion.[2] We certainly can only know beforehand to the extent in which something does not happen in freedom; for our knowledge is bound to Time and Space. The future can only be known by us in so far as it is contained in the present, as it necessarily follows from that which now is. The freedom of the Other is the border-line of our knowledge. For God this limitation does not exist. His knowledge of the future is not a knowledge based upon something that exists already in the present, but it is a knowledge which lies outside the boundaries of temporal limitations.

As we know the *present* not only as something that is necessary, but also as something that is accidental, contingent, so also God knows the *future* as something contingent. The future stands equally directly before Him as the present stands before us. God knows that which takes place in freedom in the future as something which happens in freedom. This kind of knowing is beyond our powers of imagination, and it is unintelligible;

[1] *Glaubenslehre*, Section 55, 1.    [2] *De Civ. Dei*, V, 10.

but it is directly implied in the idea of the sovereign freedom of God, of the self-sufficient Personality in which He reveals Himself to us.

Now, however, the Biblical testimony to revelation shows that this neutral, "objective" ability to "know everything" is not the actual subject of this article of faith. Here, too, where the Knowledge of God is mentioned, as in the case of His Power and His Presence, everything is viewed in the closest connexion with His aim in revelation and in redemption. Certainly, God knows everything that happens in the world of Nature—He knows "the ordinances of the heavens";[1] He knows the "rising and the going down of the sun";[2] He knows "the balancings of the clouds";[3]—but all this is not at the centre of the Biblical point of view, but at the circumference; at the centre there stands all that refers to the realization of His purpose for the Kingdom. God's knowledge is not objective and impersonal but "interested". "I know the thoughts that I think toward you";[4] thus "saith the Lord, who maketh these things known from the beginning of the world".[5] "In Thy book were all my members written . . . when as yet there was none of them."[6] His knowledge is the expression of His sympathy, His care, His planning,[7] and His love. He "knows what we have need of before we ask Him"; He also knows the day and the hour of the Parousia.[8]

This becomes very plain in the mode of knowledge which we call "knowing". When the Bible says that God "knows" anyone it means that He loves him. "The Lord knoweth them that are His."[9] When He calls a man by name He has chosen him, as is the case with one whose name "is written in the Lamb's book of life".[10] The idea of "knowing" merges into that of "election". Yahweh says, through Amos, "You only have I known of all the families of the earth."[11] This "knowing" means being known as a member of His Kingdom. Hence the meaning is always a positive one. It is said of one who is rejected that God "knows him not".[12] This "knowing", then, is the expression of His will for communion, of His electing, generous grace and love.

We could, of course, try to explain this Biblical phrase as peculiar to the primitive life of community, where to "know"

| | | |
|---|---|---|
| [1] Job 38: 33. | [2] Ps. 104: 19. | [3] Job 37: 16. |
| [4] Jer. 29: 11. | [5] Acts 15: 18. | [6] Ps. 139: 16. |
| [7] Matt. 6: 8. | [8] Mark 13: 32. | [9] 2 Tim. 2: 19. |
| [10] Rev. 21: 27; Dan. 12: 1. | | [11] Amos 3: 2. |
| [12] Matt. 25: 12; cf. Ps. 18: 44. | | |

anyone is primarily connected with the mutual familiarity within the primitive society. We still have a relic of this phraseology in our everyday speech. To "know" a person means that we recognize him as belonging to our community. But to do this would be to miss the chief point in the idea of the Bible, that is, the sovereign freedom and unfathomable love which are expressed in this "knowing", and its creative character. All whom the Lord "knows" as "his own" He makes "His own". In this sense, and in this connexion, certainly Schleiermacher's phrase: "with God to think is to effect (something)", is apt. Here "to know" is the same as the eternal purpose which precedes the Creation and gives it its direction.

Hence Paul is able to say "that if any man loveth God, the same is known of Him".[1] For our love to God is the fulfilment of the destiny which God has given us in His love. We understand this connexion best if we introduce that middle term which, even in the Biblical testimony, lies in the centre between election (being known) and love: the idea of "the Calling". Man is what he is—as man—as one who is "called". The ground of our personal existence is the Call of God, the call of love, to love. This call gives us our responsibility, and in this responsibility our freedom. Therefore the fact that God knows us, and knows about us, always means two things: an expression of sacred responsibility, and an expression of the love of God. Our true freedom and our true humanity therefore are realized where we freely experience the call of God, and His free and generous love in Jesus Christ. Through Him we become His own, whom He knows, His own, whom He has chosen from all eternity.

This knowledge which God has of us, on this highest plane of the witness of revelation, is the very opposite of all neutral objectivity, hence, too, it is the very opposite of that kind of knowledge which simply means to "know about . . .", it is the highest, freest, creative act of the loving God. But it is at the same time a "knowing" which claims from us—to the highest degree—our own free act of decision. It is therefore not something "effected" in Schleiermacher's sense, but something "effected" *sui generis*, which both establishes, and claims, the highest independence of the creature as liberty to make decisions. Thus once more the Biblical idea of an Attribute scatters all rational and metaphysical definitions to the four winds like chaff. This connexion between knowing, creating, loving and

[1] 1 Cor. 8: 3.

choosing cannot be discovered along the line of speculative thought. This "knowing" is rather the highest point that is, and can be, reached in the knowledge of faith which is granted to us in the revelation of the Holy and Merciful God.

Once more, however, the apparently neutral statement about the Omniscience of God from which we started is illuminated afresh, and is placed within the context of the highly qualified or qualitative statement of the doctrine of Election. Even the way in which God knows about all things, the things of nature and their order, is, when seen more closely, not a purely neutral objective process. Even this Omniscience of His is enclosed within His loving interest; it, too, is connected with His comprehensive plan for His Kingdom and for Redemption. For these things, too, have all been created in the Logos, in the Son, and "In Him all things cohere".[1] But even here God does not know these things in a cool, objective way; His knowledge is not that of a record office, but it is the knowledge of Him who wills to glorify Himself in this Creation, and to have fellowship with it. The ancient contradiction between thinking and being, knowing and reality, is here overcome; for all that is, is because it is known and willed by God. But what He thus knows, because it is not merely known, but also willed, and indeed willed as something which is an integral part of His saving purpose, is not an illusion, and its independence is not illusory but real, and is to the highest extent respected by Him, the Creator.

[1] Col. 1: 17.

265

## CHAPTER 20

## THE ETERNITY, UNCHANGINGNESS, FAITHFULNESS, AND RIGHTEOUSNESS OF GOD

(1)

THE Omnipresence of God means His exaltation above space; His Eternity and His Unchangeableness mean His exaltation above time. Once more we raise the question: Are we not here dealing with a statement about the Being of God in Himself, not merely with an "attribute", that is, with a statement concerning the Nature of God in view of the created universe? Is not God in Himself the Eternal just as He is the Lord and the Loving One? Is not the Idea that God is Eternal and Unchangeable already implied in the idea of His Sovereignty, of that Being which is *a se*, which is not derived from any previous source, and, therefore, can have no beginning and no end? This question, too, confronts us with a decision of the greatest significance. The question at issue is this: Is Time created or not? Just as the idea of God as the Almighty, understood as a description of being, equates Omnipotence and *"potestas absoluta"*, and leaves no room for the independence of the creature, so the idea of Eternity, understood in the same way, carries with it the consequence that Time becomes an illusion, the "μὴ ὄν" of Platonism.

As the Idea of Omnipotence, conceived as *absoluta potestas*, has slipped into Christian theology through the speculations of Platonism and Neo-Platonism, so also the Platonic idea of eternity, which understands eternity as timelessness, is a legacy of Greek thought. Its starting-point is the timelessness of the Ideas. Truth, in the sense of the truth of the Ideas, has no relation with Time. Where the Ideas are concerned the question "Since when?" or "Till when?" has no meaning. Twice two "are" four, in timeless truth, in an objectivity for which time has no significance. It is "static" truth. This static truth now becomes the model for the theological idea of eternity. It stands in the closest connexion with the speculative idea of the Absolute. This "Eternity" is the negation of Time, as the Absolute is the negation of the finite. It makes Time an illusion, which has no share in timeless truth. Time must be depreciated, denied, as the creaturely must be depreciated and denied. The eternal godhead of Plato has no relation—or at least a merely negative one—to all that "is becoming" within Time.

Within the sphere of the Christian revelation the idea of Eternity is entirely different. It can only be understood from the statement that Time has been created.[1] But because Time has been created, it is not negative, but it is positive, like all the divine Creation. The temporal as such is not intended to be regarded negatively: the negative view only applies to that "time" which has been altered by death and sin; just as we do not regard the Creation as such, from a negative point of view, but it is only the created universe which has been perverted by sin and death which is to be regarded negatively. It was the Platonist Origen who lit upon the idea of conceiving Time as the product of the Fall, as it was he, too, who placed the bodily state of the creature under the same negation.[2] This way of thinking is not in accordance with the Biblical understanding of revelation, where Time is conceived as the Temporal, which is a creaturely phenomenon, and thus belongs to the created universe. God's attitude towards Time and growth is not negative but positive. God *gives* Time.[3] He posits, or "launches" time from Himself. He wills that Time should exist, just as He wills that the creature should exist; He wills creaturely "becoming". He wills that in Time something shall become ripe, that something shall be fulfilled. God's purpose is not the negation of time,[4] not timelessness, but a state of being in which the full significance of time is conserved. In the sphere of the mathematical, timeless Truth of the Ideas nothing happens, and nothing is meant to happen; mathematics, ideas as a whole, are an abstraction. But in the sphere of Creation something does happen, and is intended to happen; for the Creation is a reality established by God.

Hence the relation of God to Time and to temporal development is not negative but positive. God is infinitely "interested" in the time-process. It is precisely this which distinguishes the Living God from the absolute Godhead of speculative thought. God takes part in temporal happenings, indeed He even

---

[1] Only thus is it possible to say πρὸ τῶν αἰώνων (1 Cor. 2: 7); for the direct evidence, cf. Heb. 1: 2.

[2] *De princ.* III, 5, 4.    [3] Thus explicitly, Rev. 2: 21.

[4] Cf. W. Schmidt, *Zeit und Ewigkeit*, p. 299. The important work of Cullmann, *Christus und die Zeit* (which appeared just before this book went to press), rightly emphasizes the *positive* valuation of Time in the New Testament; on the other hand, it retains the unresolved contradiction between the thought that God is Lord of Time, and that He Himself has a share in the temporal form.

involves Himself in the temporal; He reveals Himself in historical time; He becomes Man. God is not, as in Platonism and Stoicism, a θεός ἄπαθος, but He is One who is infinitely concerned. He follows the creaturely happenings in the movement of Time with an absolute interest, with a Holy and Merciful "sympathy". The tension which indwells human life, the tension of being directed towards a goal, is also a divine tension. It is the tension of One who says: "I am come to send fire upon the earth; and how am I straitened until it be kindled."[1]

Hence God the Holy and the Loving One is—in a certain sense—not unchangeable. If it be true that there really is such a fact as the Mercy of God and the Wrath of God, then God, too, is "affected" by what happens to His creatures. He is not like that divinity of Platonism who is unconcerned, and therefore unmoved, by all that happens upon the earth, but goes His way in heaven without looking round, without taking into consideration what is happening on earth. God does "look round"—He does care what happens to men and women—He is concerned about the changes upon earth. He alters His behaviour in accordance with the changes in men. God "reacts" to the acts of men, and in that He "reacts", He changes. God says: "I will not cause my countenance to fall upon you."[2] He "hideth His Face",[3] He withdraws Himself—and again: He draws near, He discloses Himself, He "makes His face to shine upon thee".[4] The strongest expression in the Bible for this fact that God "changes" is the one which says that "The Lord repented concerning this".[5] Is not this a gross anthropomorphism? But if we have once seen what lies behind this objection to "anthropomorphism", and the end to which it leads—when we have perceived that this objection is not only raised against the phrase: "God repented Himself", but that it is directed against all expressions which suggest personal being, and that it nullifies not merely the idea of person, but every definite statement about God, *omnis determinatio est negatio*—then from the outset we shall hear these objections to the Biblical phrase "God repented Himself" with hesitation and mistrust. Does it not belong to the same category as the objection to God's "jealousy", which ultimately culminates in a denial of His Holy will as Lord, of His will to be the Sole Sovereign? Behind the expression "God repented Himself", there lies, in

---

[1] Luke 12: 49.  
[2] Jer. 3: 12 (R.V. marg.).  
[3] Job 34: 29; cf. Is. 64: 7; 54: 8.  
[4] Num. 6: 25.  
[5] Amos 7: 3, 6; cf. Jer. 42: 10; 1 Sam. 15: 11, etc.

point of fact, nothing less than the fundamental Biblical idea of the relation between God and the world: namely, that God wills the independence of the creature, and therefore, since He limits Himself for his sake, He enters into the life of His creatures. God enters into the activity of man, and acts accordingly. There is a personal correspondence. God's behaviour alters according to the behaviour of man. For this very reason He is the Living God, in contrast to the divinity of abstract thought.

If the expression "God repented Himself" arouses hostility, then, on the other hand, the assurance that God hears prayer[1] shows the significance of this hostility very clearly. The God of revelation is the God who hears prayer. The God of Platonism does not hear prayer. To hear prayer means to be concerned about that which ascends to God from the world; it means that God is interested in what happens upon earth. The Biblical revelation confronts us with this tension, namely: that we may say of God that He is the Sovereign Lord, from whose will all proceeds, and also, that He is the Merciful God who hears prayer. In so far as He hears prayer, in so far as "He repents Himself", in so far as He is concerned about man, God is not the Unchangeable. He is not Unchangeable because, and in so far as, He has created Time, and takes part in temporal happenings.

But this is only one side of the question. The fact that He shares in what happens upon earth does not, in any sense, mean that idea which is so dear to modern man: the God who "becomes". The idea of a "God who becomes" is a mythological and unreal idea. Were God Himself One who is "becoming" then everything would founder in the morass of relativism. We can measure nothing by changing standards; changeable norms are no norms at all; a God who is constantly changing is not a God whom we can worship, He is a mythological Being for whom we can only feel sorry. The God of the Bible is eternally Unchangeable. He shares in Time as the One who is high above the Temporal. He is the Same from everlasting to everlasting, the First and the Last, the Alpha and the Omega; He is the Lord of Time. The Kingdom of God *comes*; and God is infinitely concerned about its Coming. But He Himself stands high above the sphere of becoming; for Time is His creation. God stands above Time because He is its Creator and Lord. The God who creates Time, who makes a beginning, who "allows" time, and

---

[1] Put most bluntly in Luke 18: 1 ff.

who will one day say: "Now it is ended!"—this God is not Himself involved in the Time-process.

We cannot understand this without reflection upon the Divine *Agape*. God's love is not like *Eros*; in His loving He seeks nothing for Himself. His loving is not like that of *Eros*, "Son of Penia", of need. His love does not arise out of a vacuum but out of fullness. So also His sharing in Time does not mean His dependence upon Time, but it is the expression of His sovereign freedom. He gives Himself to Time as He gives time to us. The fact that He is affected by events within Time is not the result of dependence, but is solely the result of His free love. So, too, His interest in the happenings within the sphere of Time is also an act of His freedom, of His Love and Holiness. He gives Himself to Time because He wills to fulfil the Temporal.

His Eternity, then, is something quite different from timelessness: it is a sovereign rule over Time and the temporal sphere, the freedom of Him who creates and gives us Time. As for the Creator, the limitations and laws of the created world do not limit Him, because it is He who posits them and creates them, so also for Him the barriers of the temporal—the separation into past, present, and future—do not exist. God includes and comprehends Time within His Presence; He does not eliminate it, but He fulfils it. God's Being is not timeless; but it is full of time, fulfilling time; all that is temporal is present in Him in the same way, or, to put it more correctly: He is present in the Temporal as a whole as He wills. If we take seriously the idea that God has created Time, that Time "lies within His hands",[1] that He gives Time, then we see that the statement about the Eternity of God is concerned wholly and entirely with His relation to *created* Time, and thus that it is a concept of "quality", not of "being". God's Nature is not Eternity, but God's Nature is Sovereignty, which, as such, is not related to Time. The eternity of God—this simply means His Lordship over the Time which He has created. There is no better expression for this truth than that of the Psalmist: "For a thousand years in Thy sight are but as yesterday when it is past."[2] All statements about God's eternal *Nature* lead inevitably to the Platonic idea of timelessness. The question of the temporal or the non-temporal cannot touch the divine Nature. The most we could say would be to speak of God as above time—were it not that this expression suggests a connexion with the idea of

[1] Ps. 31: 16.　　　　[2] Ps. 90: 4.

timelessness. We will simply confine ourselves to saying that the idea of eternity means the sovereignty of God over Time which He has created; we shall then remain true to the Biblical line of thought, which combines the idea of the freedom of God above Time with that of His entry into Time, just as it combines the idea of Omnipotence—as the sovereignty of God over the world which He has created—with that of His freedom, and at the same time of His free self-limitation.

(2)

In the Bible itself the idea of the *faithfulness* of God is of fundamental significance, but in the traditional doctrine of the Divine Attributes it plays almost no part. This is not accidental; but the cause is similar to that which we suggested about the traditional conception of Omnipotence. Where, namely, the speculative idea of the Absolute, with its timelessness and unchangingness, has taken the place of faith in the Living God, there is actually nothing left to say about the faithfulness of God. This word is now regarded as only a popular and imaginative expression for that unchanging quality which is involved in the idea of the Eternal. Truths concerning ideas *are* unchangeable; to speak of their "faithfulness" is meaningless. If we may put it so—the truth of ideas *can* only be unchangeable. It has no relation to happenings in time, it has nothing to do with the temporal process, it does not "react" to it. Its unchangeableness is obvious, as part of its very nature. So many theologians speak about the Unchangingness of God as of an abstract, intellectual truth, because they are not thinking of the Living God of revelation, but in terms of the *"Esse"*, the Absolute, Substance, etc. The God of philosophical speculation is *"per definitionem immutabilis"*.

The whole situation is quite different where the Living God of revelation is concerned. The Living God does not, like the divinity of Plato, stand above the changing temporal process, but He enters into it, indeed He even steps into History. As the Holy and the Loving One He takes part in the historical process, with an infinite interest in what men do and leave undone. If He directs His will towards the realization of His purpose with an infinitely holy passion of wrath and love, then also through these events He is determined in His will. Hence His faithfulness, the holding fast to His plan of creation, and its final accomplishment, is very far from obvious. The Biblical language about the faithfulness of God is therefore

271

everywhere the expression of a great and joyful amazement;[1] to the Prophets and Apostles the certainty of this faithfulness is the most important thing that they have to say, the new good tidings which they have been empowered to proclaim to the world. Thus once more, in the doctrine of the Divine Attributes, we see how great a gulf extends between a knowledge of God which springs from speculation, and that which arises from revelation.

In order to understand this aright, we need to go back to that dialectic which was disclosed to us in the knowledge of the Holiness of God. The Holiness of God can indeed, precisely in its unconditional constancy and logic, develop in two opposite directions: as wrath, which destroys resistance to the Divine Will, and as Mercy, which overcomes resistance by means of incomprehensible love. The prophets of Israel learned to reckon with the possibility that God might reject and annihilate His Chosen People.[2] In virtue of their divine commission they had to proclaim to their people this possibility first of all as a threat, and then as certain judgment.[3] In this situation the philosophical idea of the unchangingness of God was completely meaningless; what mattered to them was to know whether it was the wrath of God or His mercy which would determine the destiny of Israel. The same applies, in a still more radical way, to the New Testament. Here what is at issue is not merely death or life, deliverance or destruction, but eternal death and eternal life, absolute ruin and absolute salvation. Both could be deduced equally from the fact that God is unchangeable. Because God wills the Good unchangeably, He must destroy evil; because God wills the Good, He must, by grace, change the hearts of the wicked, He must lead them to conversion and redemption. Hence there is no point in speaking of the Unchangingness of God. It can only seem to be part of a satisfying knowledge of God if one ignores the actual situation, and the reality of the relation of God to this actual situation.

The Biblical witnesses, however, do not ignore these two facts: the revelation of the Living God points to them directly, and in this situation revelation makes known something new and unheard-of, something which could never have been foreseen: namely, that God is faithful, that for those who trust in this faithfulness, deliverance, not deserved ruin, not the righteous judgment of condemnation, is certain.[4] Thus this

---

[1] Ps. 138: 2; Is. 49: 7.      [2] Hosea 1: 9; 4: 6.
[3] Is. 5: 5; 6: 10.      [4] 1 Cor. 1: 9; Hosea 2: 20; Rom. 3: 21 ff.

faithfulness of God is nothing which could have been predicted from our knowledge of His Nature; it is a divine decision which answers the false decision of man, which for its part could not be deduced from the nature of man. Hence the faithfulness of God—if we may put it so—is the historical quality of God which can only be known from the historical revelation. This word "faithfulness" gives the answer to that otherwise unanswerable question: How are we to think of God in view of this twofold possibility: how does God Himself solve this dialectic of Holiness and Love? Only from this knowledge of the faithfulness of God is the Biblical idea of *faith* to be understood, namely, as a trust which responds to this faithfulness.

Thus the idea of the faithfulness of God shows very clearly the fundamental contrast between the philosophical doctrine of God and the Biblical doctrine of God based on revelation. All speculative knowledge of God is not only non-historical because it is not related to the historical revelation, but also because it has no relation to the real situation of man. It wills only to work with constants, with that which it is "in accordance with nature" to predicate of God and man. But the Biblical doctrine starts from the point that something has been altered in that which is "in accordance with nature". Something has happened, man has fallen; he has become a sinner. And this historical element, this which is not in "accordance with nature", this which is not a "constant", which cannot be understood by means of any general conception, is now decisive in our relation with God. This has indeed altered our relation with God; that which used to be positive has now become negative. Hence in view of this historically determined situation all natural, timeless, ideal conceptions of truth fail. Quite simply expressed, what matters is how God "reacts" to the new situation, how He behaves to man who has become sinful. Nothing can be said about this from the point of view of human nature, because the human relation with God has been destroyed. The gravity of this situation is shown in the fact that man has lost all power to know himself, that God's disclosure—in historical terms—is necessary, if we are to know the one thing that matters, namely, how God will react in this new historical situation, created by man. This disclosure has to take place in the shape of an *event*, it must be historical; the irrational outbreak of sin must be matched by an equally irrational act of self-manifestation on the part of God—or there will be no answer.

The fact that this answer did come, and that it came in such a way that, in spite of the irrational outbreak of sin, the Original element still persisted—that is what is meant by the Biblical language about the faithfulness of God. In spite of sin God held firmly to His plan of Creation, to His aim of self-communication—on the one presupposition, that man will believe this of Him, that he will trust to this incomprehensible faithfulness, and indeed that he will trust and believe because God says so and proclaims it.[1] In the New Testament, and especially in the teaching of the Apostle Paul,[2] this state of affairs, and indeed precisely the relation to that dialectic which lies in the nature of the Holiness of God, is expressed by the idea of the "revelation of the righteousness of God",[3] and that of the "righteousness of faith".[4] I must, however, briefly mention another idea which is particularly important for the understanding of the "historical attribute" of the faithfulness of God, namely, the *long-suffering* of God.

This idea represents, so to speak, the highest point of contrast with the abstract and speculative Idea of God, since it contains the element of Time as its main characteristic. It must therefore appear completely irrational, and the critics in particular, scorn it as an "anthropomorphism". In reality it has no connexion with "anthropomorphism", but it expresses the truth that God has an infinite concern for the time-process. The long-suffering of God is nothing less than the *possibility of history*.[5] Without detracting from His Holiness God could make an end of sinful man. But if an end must be made, if the book of History must be closed, and the hour of judgment must strike, then why not *now*? Why not much earlier than this? Why not at the beginning of sinful humanity? To this question there is no other answer than this, that God's Mercy gives this breathing-space to the human race in order to give it "a last chance", the possibility of repentance and amendment.[6]

The long-suffering of God, however, is closely connected with that "historical" answer in which God Himself answers the question which—from the human standpoint—could not be answered: How does He feel towards sinful humanity? that is, with the historical revelation of the long-suffering of God. This historical revelation is only accomplished where God shows His Mercy in such a way that His Holiness is not misunderstood,

---

[1] 2 Cor. 1: 18 ff.
[3] Rom. 3: 21.
[5] Cf. Rom. 9: 22 and Gen. 6: 13 ff.

[2] Cf. also 1 John 1: 9.
[4] Rom. 4: 13.
[6] Rom. 2: 4.

thus where the revelation of His forgiving and redeeming love cannot be misused by human frivolity, and the revelation of wrathful Holiness does not lead to despair—in that very revelation of the "righteousness of God" which takes place in the Cross of Christ. The long-suffering of God extends the time of the possibility of decision within history to that point where man can perceive the full answer of God to the question which through the Fall was unanswerable.[1] In the full sense, here alone does faith become possible, faith which reposes upon the amazing faithfulness of God, that faith which "justifies".

(3)

Like the Faithfulness of God, so also the *Righteousness* of God signifies the constancy of the Divine Will, and therefore, at least in the actual use of language in the Bible, can often scarcely be distinguished from the latter. Now, however, we must make it quite clear to ourselves that the *idea* of righteousness in revelation (as a whole) does not coincide with the content of the Biblical word for righteousness. When we speak of the Righteousness of God—if we are not Biblical scholars— what we mean is something quite different from that which was intended by the pious Israelite, or the Christian of Jewish ancestry in the Early Church when he used this word. This raises a problem for theology which can scarcely be solved to our satisfaction. In the language of the present day there is no exact equivalent for the Biblical word "*ts'daqa*" or δικαιοσύνη. If we translate it—as indeed we must—by "righteousness", then if we leave it thus, without a commentary, it gives a misleading rendering. If we say: God is "righteous", we mean something entirely different from the real meaning of these two Biblical words.

The Righteousness of God in the Old Testament means the constancy of God's Will in view of His Purpose and Plan for Israel. Hence this Old Testament word "righteousness" contains meanings which at the present time we would never dream of trying to express by this word: Because God is Righteous or just He helps,[2] He saves,[3] He forgives sin.[4] Likewise the Old Testament idea, when applied to man, contains meanings which our word can never express: the "righteous man" is the man who is in covenant with God, he is

---

[1] Rom. 3: 25.
[3] Cf. Ps. 31: 2; Is. 45: 21.
[2] Zech. 9: 9; Ps. 145: 17.
[4] 1 John 1: 9.

merciful,[1] kindly;[2] in contrast to the godless man, he is truly religious.[3]

This specifically Biblical idea of Righteousness reaches its zenith in the Pauline doctrine of Justification. When Paul speaks of the Righteousness of God, the δικαιοσύνη θεοῦ,[4] he does not mean what everyone who hears the present German word—and this applies to many other languages as well—understands by it. The "Righteousness of God", in the sense in which it is used in the Epistle to the Romans, can only be understood as the fulfilment of the Old Testament word *ts'daqa*, namely, the working out of God's purpose in His gracious dealing with us in Jesus Christ.[5] In Jesus Christ God realizes His will to save; thus God achieves His purpose, and comes into His own. Through the Atonement on the Cross of Christ God realizes in sinful man, and in sinful humanity, His Holy and Merciful plan for humanity as a whole. That is the "Righteousness" of God[6] in Jesus Christ. Hence it is not only futile, but dangerous—from a mistaken idea of loyalty to the Bible—to try to regain for our word "righteousness" this rich wealth of meaning, which is moreover quite alien to our usual line of thought in this connexion; this is a futile proceeding because it can never really succeed; it is dangerous, because it inevitably leads to continual misunderstanding.[7]

The translator of the Bible may continue to render δικαιοσύνη θεοῦ as the "righteousness of God", leaving it to the Biblical commentator to explain later on what seems at first difficult to understand—but the dogmatic theologian has a different task. When he speaks of the "Righteousness" of God, he must begin where the modern conception of "righteousness" begins to-day. He is dealing with the idea of a "righteousness" which certainly does *not* forgive sins, but punishes them; which does not *give*, but which makes demands; which does not place "grace" before "right" or "justice", but—on the contrary—stresses the right of the Lord and Owner to His own possession, the rights of God over His own creation. This conception, which is what *we* mean by "righteousness" (understood as "justice") is also found in the Bible; indeed, this, too, is

[1] Ps. 112: 4; Prov. 12: 10.    [2] Prov. 21: 26.
[3] Ps. 92: 13; 1: 5.    [4] Rom. 1: 17; 3: 21 ff.; 10: 3.
[5] Cf. the excellent article on δίκη in the N.T. *Wörterbuch*, by G. Schrenk.
[6] Rom. 3: 21 ff.; 2 Cor. 5: 21.
[7] The linguistic problem would be much easier to solve if, as in English, we had the two words "justice" and "righteousness"; the former corresponds to some extent to the narrower modern idea, and the latter to the more comprehensive Biblical idea of "righteousness".

expressed by the phrase, the "Righteousness of God,"[1] but it constitutes a subordinate element within the paradoxically rich idea of *ts'daqa*, δικαιοσύνη. When *we* speak of the Righteousness of God, we mean the constancy of the divine will, which in the Law demands the Good, and punishes the transgression of the Law, dealing with man strictly "as he deserves". For this is the essence of Righteousness (or justice)—of that which everyone means by "justice": the rule of equality according to "desert"—giving every man his due; for instance, equal wages for equal work, equal punishment for equal wrong-doing, equal treatment in the same circumstances. A "just" man is one who logically and impeccably acts according to this rule; thus the Just (or Righteous) God would be primarily the God from whose will this rule is derived, and whose own dealings are the expression of this rule.

The question, then, in this connexion—that of the Christian doctrine of God—in contrast to that which is treated within the exegesis of Scripture—is this: Is God, in this contemporary use of the word, "just" or "righteous"?

May we, and should we, state this to be an attribute of God on the basis of His revelation? Is this principle of equal dealing according to equal merit really derived from the Will of God?

This question must be answered, quite plainly, in the affirmative. The righteousness of God in judgment, in particular, which is an integral element in the body of revelation, is of this kind. God punishes like the just Judge,[2] without respect of persons.[3] There is a correspondence of guilt and retribution which is based on equality. "God is not mocked: for whatsoever a man soweth, that shall he also reap."[4] The idea of Divine Judgment, which is the presupposition of the central message of the Bible—deliverance from condemnation—is determined by this idea of righteousness. Here as elsewhere behind the idea of Judgment lies the idea of the Law, according to which judgment and the idea of the divine demand is the natural consequence to which the law gives expression.[5] But the demand of God is based upon His Sovereignty. Because God is Lord, because the creation derives its life from Him alone, thus because it belongs wholly to Him, His will is its law. The Law, the *"lex aeterna"*, which precedes all legislation according to the historic revelation, is given with the Creation. Since man derives his life from God, he also receives his orders regarding

---

[1] Cf. I Sam. 26: 23; Ps. 72: 2.       [2] Ps. 72: 2.
[3] I Peter 1: 17.       [4] Gal. 6: 7.       [5] Rom. 3: 19.

the lines on which he is to use this life according to the will of Him who gives it. The gift comes first; but the gift implies the task; the generous word comes first, but the generous word is followed immediately by the word which makes demands on man. God claims man for Himself. He wills that man should be, and live, and act—both in his own life and in his dealings with others—in a particular way, and not otherwise. And this will of God, which demands so much of man, is unchangeable and immutable. This is the divine Righteousness.

Righteousness, therefore, is simply the Holiness of God, as it is expressed when confronted with the created world—the creation which has been created in and for freedom. The Nature of God which is Holy, manifests itself over against His creature as the divine quality of Righteousness. Behind the irrevocable demand of the Law stands the Holy Will, but the expression of this Holiness over against the creature is the constancy of the divine demand—the Law—and the consequence of its assertion, judgment and punishment, and this is the Righteousness of God, understanding the world in its present-day sense. Because God means His demand seriously, and emphasizes it without any intention of ever revoking it—this is why there is judgment and punishment for him who disobeys the divine Law. If there were no retribution, then God would not take His own Law seriously; then He would not be rigidly firm and constant in His will which makes such a demand upon men; then He would not be Righteous (or just). It is not merely the way in which the judgment is given—without respect of persons, impartially, objectively—which is the expression of the divine Righteousness, but the very Fact of Judgment as well.[1]

The element of equality which is characteristic of the idea of justice in the contemporary sense of the word, is based on the fact—on the one hand—that the life of the created being is intended to be in harmony with the Divine Will—and on the other hand, on the fact that the same response is required from all human beings because, in principle, the same life and the same destiny has been given to all. The fundamental law of life is this: Love God and your neighbour. This fundamental law clearly expresses the fact that there is a "correspondence" between God and Man, namely, that God, the Loving One, desires man's love in return—and nothing less than this. "*Dilige et fac quod vis!*" And this one demand is made upon all

[1] Acts 17: 31.

because all have been created in, and through, and for, this
Love. But this is the only "equality" which may be included
within the idea of the Divine righteousness. There is only one
claim of God upon His creatures; but there is no equal claim of
the creatures on God. The inequality in the lot of human beings
does not contradict the fact of the divine righteousness, for
the Creator is under no debt to His creation. The idea of
righteousness in revelation, therefore, is strictly limited to that
which is connected with the claim of God upon us, and never
merges into a claim of man upon God. God alone has rights over
against man; man has no rights over against God, although, it
is true, that in virtue of a divine arrangement he has rights over
against his fellow-man, original rights, human rights. But
this question does not belong to this subject, but to the sphere
of ethics.

This aspect of the divine will, expressed in the idea of
righteousness, is the rational element within the doctrine of
God. Even the reason has been created by God. The rational
element, however, is that which is in accordance with law, that
which can be conceived by law, and which corresponds with
law. Therefore *this* understanding of the divine righteousness
which is designated by the ideas of God's demand, of Law,
Judgment and Punishment, is that in which the two elements
in the doctrine of God meet: the element of revelation and the
rational element. Outside the sphere of the Biblical revelation,
too, there is a conception of God as a just Law-giver and Judge,[1]
as, on the other hand, there is an idea of a human righteousness
which consists in the fulfilment of the divine Law, which we
find in the non-Christian ethic. The special element in the
doctrine of God in revelation is not this conception of righteousness in itself, but the way in which, through its connexion
with the other, it, itself, becomes modified. This shows how
this linguistic problem arose, which consists in the fact that the
Biblical word "Righteousness", although it contains this
idea of judgment and law, also has quite different meanings,
from which its characteristic meaning is derived.

In contrast to the rational element the idea of God in revelation is determined by the Freedom of God. God is not the
Law, and the Law is not God. God is the LORD—even of His
Law. The Law, therefore, is not an independent entity, and it is
not an ultimate, as it is within reason. The Law has always
been established by *God*. As the Lord of Creation and its

[1] *Zarathustra.* Cf. also, Plato's *Gorgias.*

"orders" stands above the Creation and its orders, and manifests Himself as such in miracle, so the righteous God stands above His Law and judgment and manifests His sovereign freedom by setting men free from the punishment demanded by the law, through forgiveness. We must go deeper still. We have already seen that God's Holiness, in spite of the fact that in some way it differs from His Love, is yet fulfilled in love, and that it is precisely in this unity and yet non-identity of Holiness and Love that the decisive element in the Idea of God in revelation consists. This is worked out in the understanding of the Righteousness of God in the fact that the divine righteousness finds its paradoxical fulfilment in the pardon, or "justification", of the sinner. This fulfilment cannot be understood from the standpoint of the rational, general, idea of righteousness, as expressed in the conceptions of law, judgment, punishment, and indeed as equal law, just judgment and just punishment; from this point of view it seems wholly unintelligible. But, on the other hand, if—as we must—we understand the Law to have been established by God, in His own free way, in a freedom which means that, if He chooses, He has a perfect right to ignore the Law and to act freely in another way, just as a king ignores the law when he grants a royal pardon, we then begin to see that here the most profound meaning of the idea of "righteousness" is disclosed.

For what is the inward intention of Law and Judgment? Surely it means that God should have His own rights, that His unlimited sovereign right as Lord should be emphasized. But how can His sovereign "rights" be more plainly emphasized than in the fact that He graciously forgives sin, that He, the King, pardons the rebel and in mercy receives him back again into favour, without executing upon him the just sentence of death? As God's Holy will fulfills itself in the fact that He rescues the sinful creature by His merciful love, creates him anew, and sanctifies him, so His righteous will is accomplished in the fact that He exercises His supreme right, His right to pardon. God comes to His right in that through His forgiveness, through His reconciliation, He turns, changes the whole outlook of his rebellious child, breaks down his resistance, and gives freely to the loveless that love which the law required in vain.[1] This is the Biblical witness to the Righteousness of God, and this witness culminates in the doctrine of the Justification of the sinner through Jesus Christ.

[1] Rom. 8: 3 ff.

But this is not all. The Holiness of God is fulfilled, it is true, in His merciful love, but it is not absorbed into that Love of God; it still remains distinct, and must be recognized by us as part of the Nature of God. So also the just penalty which is pronounced upon the sinner is not simply swept away by forgiveness. God does not simply ignore His own law. He uses His right to pardon simply by confirming the validity of His judgment and therefore of His law. Hence He who came to give to us God's merciful love, took upon Himself the "curse of the law",[1] and Himself went to the death which was appointed for sinful man. The Cross of Christ, the atoning Passion[2] of the Righteous One, Holy and Loving, is both the manifestation of the irrevocable will of law, and the seriousness of judgment and of merciful pardoning love, thus of the Holiness of God in contrast to love, and the Love of God as the fulfilment of Holiness.[3] Thus the paradoxical righteousness which God's Law effects in the act of pardon includes the non-paradoxical rational righteousness which consists in the correspondence of guilt and expiation. The Cross of Christ took place to show His righteousness,[4] as the confirmation, and at the same time as the transcending of the just judgment of God through the Divine Act of Atonement. He Himself, the God who comes to us, "pays the debt"[5] which we could not pay, so that the twofold truth shines out: how great God is in Judgment, and how wonderful in Mercy. "The Lord, the Just One, pays all His servant's debts."

[1] Gal. 3: 10, 13.  [2] Is. 53: 5.  [3] Rom. 3: 25 ff.
[4] Rom. 3: 25.  [5] Matt. 20: 28; 1 Peter 1: 18; 1 Tim. 2: 6.

## CHAPTER 21

# THE WISDOM AND THE GLORY OF GOD

## (1)

THE conception of the Righteousness of God has already forced us to look at the relation of God to the reason. Even if it is clear from the outset that the God of revelation cannot be grasped by means of any rational categories, on the other hand we have no right to construct a contradiction between God and the reason. The very fact that in the Bible so much is said about the divine Wisdom should militate against such a mistake. Actually, too, there is this further consideration against such a view, namely, that all truth, even the truth acquired by the reason, is derived from God. As the Righteousness of God also includes within itself that righteousness (or justice) which everyone, by means of his reason, can recognize as justice— the justice that treats every human being equally, according to his deserts—so also the Wisdom of God includes within itself everything that can be known through the reason as true and valid. The higher divine righteousness includes the rational righteousness; this is the only right order. So also the divine Wisdom includes the truth of reason, and not the other way round. The reason does not grasp God, but the reason is derived from God, and possesses its own divine justification.

That is why the Bible frequently speaks of God as performing rational acts which are like our own: God "knows", God "judges", God "decides", God "counts", God "calls by name". That which is regarded as rational among men upon earth is also recognized as valid in heaven; there is no reason to doubt that mathematical truths and the laws of logic are also recognized by God as valid, not indeed that they belong to a sphere which is above God, but because they are the overflow of the divine thought and will. The same God who guides the heavenly constellations on their way and "counts the number of the stars",[1] in addition to their path and their number, has also established the truths of mathematics, just as He has established the orders of Nature. Kepler was not mistaken in believing that he ought to praise God for having allowed him, by means of his astronomical researches, to "think His thoughts after Him". The Logos of reason is not, as such, the *"verbum*

[1] Ps. 147: 4.

*Dei"* in whom all things have been created; but it is not alien to the Word of God, but is included within it.[1] The Reason of God is infinitely greater than what we usually call "reason" and "rational"; but the truth of reason which we do know has a share in the divine truth.

God's works in Creation are therefore both revelations of the divine Wisdom, and are recognized as such by the reason. Νοούμενα καθοράται, God's creation is, it is true, not rational but it is accessible to reason; it is only because this is so that we have the knowledge of Nature, laws that can be perceived, order which can be presented with mathematical exactness. Hence the Bible often speaks of God's Wisdom in connexion with the order of the world.[2] Certainly, in all this the emphasis is not so much upon its accessibility to reason for our thought, as on that which transcends all our thinking, the Wisdom of the Works of Creation which can never be fathomed nor penetrated by us; thus the emphasis is not so much upon the fact that they are accessible to reason as on the fact that they are supra-rational. We shall have more to say about this in connexion with the doctrine of Creation. The Wisdom of God, as it is manifested in the Creation, might be described as the ideal aspect of the Divine Omnipotence[3] with which it is often classed. For this Divine Wisdom is the Power of God in its absolutely unlimited spiritual creativity, a creativity which is perpetually flowering into new forms of life, based upon profound and impenetrable depths of infinity—these are the signs of the Divine Wisdom at work, which distinguish its operations from all human activity.

In the New Testament, however, the idea of the Divine Wisdom is found more frequently in connexion with God's governance in History than in connexion with the Creation. This implies that the Wisdom of God is the fundamental category of a Christian philosophy of History. It is the absolute mastery of the Architect who builds the City of God, the absolute planning of God, above all that is accidental and frustrating in the course of this world.[4] In all the apparent meaningless of this process of history, in all theories of teleology *and* dysteleology, in good and in evil, in the beautiful and in the ugly, in that which leads to death, and in that which leads to life, in that which is significant, and in that which has no

[1] Cf. Calvin's observations on John 1: 9; *Wke.*, 47, 8 ff.
[2] Ps. 104: 24; Jer. 10 : 12.
[3] "Wisdom and Might", Job 12: 13; Prov. 3: 19.
[4] Eph. 3: 10; Rom. 11: 33; in connection with Chs. 9–11.

meaning, God controls and rules all by His Wisdom, and He weaves all these various threads—so different in kind and in origin—into His tapestry; He uses all these strange materials as stones for His building, for the final establishment of His Kingdom—as yet still hidden and secret, but one day to be revealed to all men.

If Hegel's philosophy of History is built upon the idea: all that is real is rational, the Christian philosophy of History is based upon the idea: everything that happens is a means of the Divine Wisdom. Hegel's thesis breaks down when confronted by what is obviously irrational and contrary to reason. Thought controlled by revelation includes all this in the Divine Wisdom. It is able to do this because its centre is the "folly of the Cross", in which God reveals His Wisdom,[1] and the plan for the world which He has made on these lines. The irrational and contra-rational elements in that event, the fact that it is against all common sense, that the Holy One of God should be condemned as a criminal blasphemer and executed—this is the decisive method in the Hands of God for revealing His Holiness and His Love. From this centre we can also perceive the same law at work at other points in the history of redemption, that is, that God takes the very things which seem most contrary to His Purpose and uses them to accomplish His Will. This was already the view of the Prophet of the Exile: the Servant of the Lord, the true Israel, bears the sickness and guilt of the people.[2] It was also the view of the Apostle Paul: the present rejection of disobedient Israel is the means by which God makes room for the heathen nations in His Kingdom, in order that He may finally include rejected Israel within it, too. In face of this revelation the Apostle breaks out:

> O the depth of the riches both of the wisdom and the knowledge of God! How unsearchable are His judgements and His ways past tracing out![3]

But this wisdom is only accessible to faith: it can only be perceived *"sub contraria specie"* in the folly of the Cross.[4] God's wisdom is unsearchable", His "ways are past tracing out";[5] the reason of God is not our reason, therefore it cannot be reached by our own efforts of rational thought.[6] To call the ways of God in history "wise" and "rational"—does not lie in the sphere of natural judgment, based on perception and logic;

---

[1] I Cor. I: 21 ff.     [2] Is. 53.     [3] Rom. 11: 33 (R.V.).
[4] I Cor. I: 24.     [5] Rom. 11: 33.     [6] Is. 55: 8.

this is only possible παρὰ δόξαν, against appearances, against all the natural evidence, upon the ground of that revelation which conceals the Glory of God in the "form of a servant". When the Evangelist says: "We saw His Glory," this "seeing" is a supernatural act; it is "seeing" with the eyes of faith.

(2)

Both in the Old and in the New Testament the "Glory"—the "*Doxa*"—of God is frequently mentioned. Once again we are confronted by the question: Are we here dealing with the concept of the Nature of God, or with a Divine Attribute? Can it not be said that "Glory" should be ascribed to God as He is in Himself? Does not "Glory" mean particularly that which is characteristic of God's manner of Being, in contrast to that of the Creation? We must certainly be on our guard against letting ourselves be led astray by the German word *Herrlichkeit* (glory), by connecting it directly with the thought of Him as *Herr* (Lord). This connexion is alien to the thought both of the Old and the New Testament (*i.e.* both the "*Kabod*" of the Old Testament and the "*doxa*" of the New). But is there not an *actual* relation, even though it is not a verbal one?

Since we are here dealing with an idea which is in a very special sense a Biblical one—so Biblical, indeed, that outside the language of the Bible it is difficult to find an exact equivalent—it will be advisable to begin with some lexicographical observations.[1] The Old Testament word *Kabod*, which the Septuagint usually renders as *doxa*, means literally "difficulty", "weight"; but where it is used of God, it is first applied to certain majestic phenomena of the Divine Presence of a natural character, *e.g.* thunderstorms, supernatural light, illuminations of a special kind, by which the Israelites knew that Yahweh was present. Later on this idea acquired the more abstract meaning of "Honour", the majestic self-manifestation of God, with a strongly eschatological tendency; it is used to describe the radiant signs of the Presence of God in His Creation at the end of the Ages.

The Greek word δόξα, on the other hand, has an entirely different linguistic origin. The word is evidently derived from the subjective cognitive sphere, and means, first of all, the "opinion"—akin to "dogma"—which one holds about something or someone; then it means the "respect", "reputation", or "fame" which someone enjoys. "When, for the first time,

[1] See the article on δόξα in *Theol. Wörterbuch zum N.T.*, II, pp. 236–57.

a translator of the Old Testament hit upon the idea of rendering *kabod* by *doxa*, a linguistic change took place which was of unusual significance. The Greek word began to be modified and re-shaped to an extent which cannot be exaggerated. From an idea which denoted 'thinking' and 'meaning', which implies the subjective element, with all the variations in human thinking and 'wondering' that this involves, we now have a massively objective idea, which denotes the absolute reality of God."[1] "Divine Glory, Divine Majesty, Divine Power, the visible radiance of the Divine Light"[2]—in the New Testament these are the varying shades of meaning which merge into one another as attempts to explain this mysterious, almost incomprehensible word. Some of this feeling still clings to the Latin phrase "*gloria Dei*", which has paved the way for most later translations of *doxa* in Christian terminology. What is the actual problem which lies behind this linguistic one?

The idea of the Divine Glory is in itself both objective and subjective.[3] It designates something in God, and yet again something which does not mean God's Being in Himself, but rather God's Being as it becomes visible in His revealed Presence for the eye of faith: "Glory of revelation."[4] Glorification is the aim of the divine revelation, the aim of the God who as the Holy One must assert Himself, and as the Merciful and Loving One wills to be near to us, and to bring us into communion with Himself. God's Glory, then, is not "in Himself", but in the world He has created, in so far as He communicates Himself to it, and in it is fully recognized. It is, moreover, the reflection of the Being of God from the Creation back to Him, the Creator, and to the eyes of those who are illuminated by this reality of His revelation. "Let the whole earth be filled with His Glory";[5] and the glorification of the Son, and of those who belong to Him, is the aim of the mission of Jesus.[6]

Hence "glory" is not one of those concepts which describe the Being of God as He is in Himself; nor does it form one of the ideas of the "Attributes", each of which expresses His relation to the created world in a particular way; the Glory of God is the sum-total and the unity of all that God shows forth, in the fullness of His revelation, of the realization of His

---

[1] *Theol. Wörterbuch*, II, p. 248.　　　　　　　　　　　[2] *Ibid.*, p. 251.
[3] Hence expressions like "the knowledge of the Glory of the Lord" (Hab. 2: 14) and "the knowledge of the Glory of God in the Face of Jesus Christ" (2 Cor. 4: 6).
[4] Cf. expressions like "the glory of the Name"—to "show honour to", etc.
[5] Ps. 72: 19; Is. 6: 3.　　　　　　　　　　　[6] John 12: 28; 17: 5, 24.

sovereignty. This idea is so fundamentally Scriptural, because it expresses the whole of the Biblical knowledge of God, as knowledge of the revealing and communicating God. This also shows why this word always contains such a strong eschatological element. It designates above all the perfect revelation at the end of the Ages—the manner of Divine Being, as it will be when the sovereignty of God, and communion with God, will be perfect, God with us and God in us, in its perfection.[1] God's Nature or Being, His Holiness and His Love are one thing, His Glory is another. God's Holiness and Love are always there, quite apart from the existence of the world. But God has His "Glory", in the sense of δόξα, with and in His creation, perfected by Himself.

Therefore δόξα should be translated by the objective idea of the shining of a light, as well as by the subjective-objective idea of Honour. Glory as Light, because it is Divine reality, the divine Presence which one day will be seen "face to face";[2] Honour, because the Presence of God is not merely objective but it is also subjective-objective, the full recognition of His sovereignty and the full affirmation, the exultant praise of His Presence and His Love on the part of His Creation.[3] This Glory proceeds wholly from God's Being; it is based solely in Him, and that not merely as His work, but in His Presence. And yet it is not His nature in itself, but His nature in His revelation, the will which has accomplished its purpose, the realized and completed Presence of God. The idea of δόξα, therefore, expresses the most characteristic element in the Biblical Idea of God; that God is One who desires to communicate Himself, that revelation is of His very Nature, and that this can only be perceived as it is in the final accomplishment of the revelation.

(3)

In dogmatics it is usual to speak of the Bliss of God. This phraseology is alien to the thought of the Bible.[4] The question is: Is this "strangeness" accidental? Or is it an integral part of the whole question? The Bible does not speak of the "Bliss" of God because it knows nothing of the θεὸς ἀπαθος of abstract speculation. The God of revelation is passionately "interested"; there is a Divine Wrath and a Divine Mercy, the wrath of the

[1] Rom. 8: 18; 1 Cor. 15: 43; Col. 1: 27; 1 Peter 5: 1, etc.
[2] 1 Cor. 13: 12.
[3] Hence all "doxology", "on earth and in heaven". Rev. 1: 6, etc.
[4] The only exception is 1 Tim. 1: 11 and 6: 15; but both passages have no particular emphasis; they are used formally.

Holy, the Mercy of One who is Love. That God in Himself is Bliss or Joy, within the truth about Him determined by revelation, can only mean that God does not love because He desires something which He lacks, but because He Himself has, and is, "Fullness" itself. But it is not for us to reflect upon that about which the Bible is silent, not merely because the Bible is silent, but because we know why it is silent. Unlike some theologians of the past and of the present,[1] the Bible says very little about the Beauty of God. For our human feeling and thinking Beauty is so closely connected with visible form, that we would not know how to apply this idea to God. God creates the beautiful; He allows us to have pleasure in Beauty. But of Him who is the Original Image of God it is said "there is no beauty that we should desire Him".[2] This is said, it is true, of the Son "in the form of a servant". But when the Scriptures speak of His form in its perfection, they do not speak of "Beauty", but of "Glory"—δόξα. We might, of course, put it thus: the "Glory", the δόξα, is the Beauty of God, and no other word is large enough to express this. Beauty, in the ordinary sense of the word, is an earthly parable of the Divine Glory, and at the same time a substitute for the δόξα which is lacking. It is precisely this ambivalence which is characteristic of it. This is why it is not mentioned in connexion with the Biblical knowledge of God.

Finally, the "Perfection" of God: there is a very famous Biblical passage which speaks of the Perfection of God: "Ye therefore shall be perfect as your Father in Heaven is perfect."[3] But in this context a quite particular kind of Perfection is intended, namely, love in its fullness. Otherwise the Bible does not speak of the Perfection of God. Not indeed because there could be any imperfection in God, but because the idea of Perfection is not suitable for God. It only expresses the formal element that nothing is lacking. In order to make this statement there must be a standard by which one measures whether anything is lacking. Thus this conception presupposes that there is a standard which one can apply to God, and the result of this measurement would be that there is nothing lacking in God! This whole intellectual procedure is alien to the thought of revelation. It is far more in harmony with that kind of

[1] Cf. Delitzsch, *Biblische Psychologie*, pp. 34 ff., and von Oettingen, *Luther's Dogmatik*, II, pp. 259 ff.  [2] Is. 53: 2.
[3] Matt. 5: 48. According to Professor J. Hausheer, however, it seems possible that this is a mistranslation of the Aramaic, and that the original reading was: "Therefore you must forgive, as your Heavenly Father forgives."

thinking which follows the *"via eminentiae"*, but not with that which starts from the idea of the Absolute Lord. But what can be lacking in One from whom alone we receive all we can know! What could be lacking in Him who is the Source of all Norms, the Lawgiver who has given all laws! Even to put the question at all is foolish. Even that great idea of Anselm, that God is He *"quo majus nihil cogitari potest"*, is not fitting for the God of revelation. It also, like the related idea of the *Summum bonum*, does not belong to the sphere of Biblical thought but to that of speculation. All these conceptions imply that God is the last link in a chain; or the highest step on a ladder; they co-ordinate Him into a hierarchy where He can be compared with others who are like Him, and in so doing they miss the Idea of God according to Revelation, namely, that God cannot and should not be compared with anything at all; that all abstract thinking which indulges in such comparisons does not reach *God*, but only the Idea of the Absolute, which is only the shadow cast by the reality of God on to rational thought.

# APPENDIX TO SECTION ONE

# APPENDIX TO SECTION ONE

## ON THE HISTORY OF THE DOCTRINE OF THE DIVINE ATTRIBUTES

As we have already shown in Chapter 17, the metaphysical, speculative perversion of the Doctrine of God comes out particularly clearly in the dogmatic treatment of the Attributes of God. This general statement will now be emphasized and illustrated in the following pages by some actual examples.

### (I)

### (1) THE SIMPLICITY AND IMMUTABILITY OF GOD

It is characteristic of the speculative tendency, even within Protestant Scholasticism, that among the "Attributes" with which it deals, that of the "Simplicity" of God stands at the head of the list, and is explained and expounded with much detail and vividness. This idea of the *"simplicitas Dei"* is inevitable if we make the abstract idea of the Absolute the starting-point for our thought. This is simply the undifferentiated *Monas* of Neo-Platonism modified by Theism. It was only from the time of Dionysius the Areopagite that this subject became a characteristic theme of dogmatic consideration, although even some of the later Fathers of the Church used this idea, on occasion, in their effort to solve the problem of the Unity and the Trinity of God (cf., for instance, Cyril of Alexandria: *De sancta et consubstantiali Trinitate dialogi* in *Rouët de Journel*, 2081; and other passages in the same work). To "think" the Absolute necessarily leads one to the idea of undifferentiated Unity. In so far, however, as something definite must be said about this undifferentiated One, that is, attributes must be predicated, then the idea of *"simplicitas"* forms the necessary transition; it expresses the truth that that which is to be differentiated cannot be broken up into its component parts, so "that whatever is thought in God is God Himself, and thus the most absolute identity exists between the Divine Being and His Attributes" (Heidegger, *Corp. theol.*, III, 30). The identity of substance and attributes, the absence of anything that can be conceived as "built up" or "divided", constitutes the logical apparatus with which the Scholastic theologians of the Middle Ages and of the Post-Reformation period operated (cf., *e.g.*, Johann Gerhard, *Loci. theol.*, I, pp. 305 ff.).

But when a man like Johann Gerhard, in accordance with his Reformation outlook, also enquires into the *usus practicus* of the doctrine, then his answer shows—in its futility and its evasiveness—that here there is really no *usus practicus*, that he is here dealing with a speculative *theologumenon* or *philosophumenon*, which has nothing at all to do with the God of the Christian Faith. Here we are not dealing with an Attribute of God at all, but with the fact that the idea of the Absolute permits no differentiations.

The situation is similar in the case of the idea of *"immutabilitas"*, the Changelessness of God. Anyone who takes seriously the definition given by (*e.g.*) Quenstedt (I, 288): *"immutabilitas est perpetua essentiae divinae et omnium ejus perfectionum identitas, negans omnem omnino motum, cum physicum, cum ethicum"*, has ceased to think of the Living God of revelation; once more he is thinking of the undifferentiated Absolute. If he thinks that it is possible, at one and the same time, to think of this abstract idea of the undifferentiated Absolute with which it is identical, and the Being of the God of revelation, then we cannot offer him any better advice than to study the *Dogmatics* of David Friedrich Strauss, who, with the aid of this idea of the Absolute, completely destroys the Biblical, Christian, Idea of God. If there be no *"motus"* in God, then there is neither wrath nor love in God; then most certainly there is no "heartfelt mercy", but the most rigid immutability of the self-sufficient idea. It is therefore cheering to see that more recent Protestant theology —here true to the revelation in Scripture—has given up perpetuating the doctrine of these Scholastic ideas of the Divine Attributes of the Dionysian tradition. Hermann Cremer, in particular, has rendered us a great service—as founder of the *Theologisches Wörterbuch zum Neuen Testament*—in his outstanding small book, *Die christliche Lehre von den Eigenschaften Gottes*, as the first to have pointed out the contrast between the traditional doctrine of the Divine Attributes and the Idea of God in the Bible. Karl Barth also follows in his track (see *Kirchl. Dogm.*, II, 1, pp. 291 ff.). Twenty years ago, when I began to teach dogmatics, it was Cremer, too, who opened my eyes.

## (2) THE IDEA OF OMNIPOTENCE

The thought of the Fathers of the Church about God is dominated by the problem of the Trinity, so that their doctrine of the Divine Attributes is not highly developed. The outstanding Platonists among them—Clement of Alexandria, Gregory Nazianzen and Gregory of Nyssa, Origen, and above all Augustine, emphasize the speculative idea of the Absolute, and the Neo-Platonist ontology leads Augustine to make statements which sometimes seem to verge on Pantheism. Once one has accepted the Neo-Platonist idea, *"Deum nihil aliud dicam esse nisi idipsum esse"* (*De moribus ecclesiae*, XIV, 24) it is difficult to make room for an *"esse"* alongside of God. But in the works of Augustine this Neo-Platonism is continually permeated with the Biblical Idea of God. Of course, the situation is different when we come to the writer whose thinking dominated the Middle Ages: Dionysius the Areopagite. For him the one statement about God that matters is this: God is "the One", or the "Divine One" (ἐν καὶ πᾶν). By the *via negationis*, which the Areopagite describes in his own classic way (*De div. nom.*, 7, 3) by abstraction, one reaches this undifferentiated "Alone", which may equally well be described as the "All" or "Nothing". Thus all concrete representation, all definite statement, even that about Omnipotence, is only a subjective reflection of the "Alone" in our consciousness.

This idea is developed by Duns Scotus with ruthless logic in the pantheistic sense. The doctrine of the Church did not follow this line. It was an event of great significance when Anselm asserted the existence of the Divine Subject over against the abstract idea of Existence, and so, by means of the Biblical idea of God, arrested the development of speculation on the Absolute. In accordance with this view, he rejects the axiom that the Attributes of God can only be distinguished in the human subject. (*Dico, quod non tantum haberi potest conceptus naturaliter, in quo quasi per accidens concipitur Deus, puta in aliquo attributo, sed etiam aliquis conceptus, in quo per se et quidditative concipiatur,"* Sent., I, dist. 3.)

This means that the idea of Omnipotence as a relation of God to a created existence becomes possible. In the main period of Scholastic theology—as in later Protestant and Catholic scholasticism—by means of the idea of the *potestas ordinata* a compromise was sought between the Biblical idea of God as the Almighty and the idea of *potestas absoluta* derived from Neo-Platonism; here the main problem of discussion is whether what God can do goes beyond that which actually is. The subtle and often ridiculous explanations about all that God could do "if" He wanted to do so, play an important part in this kind of thinking (cf. on this Gieseler, *Kirchengeschichte*,

II, 4, 5, pp. 324 ff.). On the other hand, in this line of thought, the decisive element in the Biblical Idea of God as "Almighty" is absent: the relation to the fact of Redemption.

Luther's idea of Omnipotence is inconsistent, and even contradictory. But this inconsistency is due to the profound changes which took place in Luther's thought after he had published his work, *de servo arbitrio*. In this work, as indeed during his early period as a whole, Luther does not expound the Biblical idea of Divine Omnipotence, but that of the *potestas absoluta*, even though he gives it a turn of his own. Not the *"esse"* but the *"velle"* of God is absolute. Here the idea is that "God does anything" (*Allwirksamkeit*), which leaves no room for any kind of creaturely causality, but explicitly denies it. This is why it is connected with the idea of the *"mera necessitas"*: *"Deus nihil praescit contingenter, sed omnia incommutabili et aeterna infallibilique voluntate et praevidit et proponit et facit"* (*W.W.*, 18, 615). This idea of a God who "does everything" (*Allwirksamkeit*), with its complete determinism, is opposed to the Biblical idea of Omnipotence, as has already been shown. Later on, when he was trying to correct his doctrine of double predestination Luther saw this, but he never reached a clear re-formulation of the idea of Omnipotence; rather, later on, he seems to have thought that the solution lay in the sphere of the *Deus absconditus*, and that the idea of Omnipotence belongs there, with the Divine wrath, which, in so far as it is understood as *potestas absoluta*, is quite right (see above, p. 170), but this would have led to a different conception of Omnipotence, and to one in accordance with revelation. Luther uses ideas like these, it is true, in his preaching, but he did not develop their theological interpretation.

Zwingli's Neo-Platonist Idea of God, in his work *De Providentia*, will be dealt with later on (see below, p. 321). But it would be a mistake to think that Zwingli only followed this line later in his career. Already in the *Commentarius de vera et falsa religione* he adopts the traditional Platonic exposition of the "Name of Yahweh", and infers from this: *"Illud ergo esse tam est bonum, quam est esse"* (III, pp. 644 ff.). But alongside of this speculative idea Zwingli also uses the Biblical idea of Omnipotence. Calvin's conception—in spite of the views ascribed to him by tradition—comes nearest to the Biblical idea of Omnipotence. Where Calvin explicitly teaches the *omnipotentia* he limits it strictly to the Divine Creation, and rule of the world, and by means of the idea of Providence he connects it with the divine plan of salvation. He firmly rejects the scholastic idea of Omnipotence, and all the sophistry which indulges in questions about what was possible and what was not possible for God to do. God *"censetur omnipotens non quod possit quidem facere, cesset tamen interim et desideat* (the idea of power as being able merely 'to do anything') . .. *sed quia sua providentia coelum et terram gubernans, sic omnia moderatur, ut nihil sine eius consilio accidat"* (*Institutio*, I, 16, 3).

The Protestant Scholastic theologians, on the other hand, follow the mediaeval scholastics; on the whole they tend to follow most closely in the steps of St. Thomas Aquinas: as, for instance, when Quenstedt (*L.I.*, 293) explicitly says that he does not wish the idea of the divine Omnipotence to extend only to that which God wills, but also to that "which is in any way possible", by which he means everything which contains no contradiction within itself. Maresius (*Syntagma theologiae*, p. 24) says likewise: *"Multa plura potest facere quam fecit . . . omnipotentia ad omnia possibilia extenditur."*

We have spoken already of Schleiermacher's idea of Omnipotence, which, of course, is entirely on Dionysian lines. Of later theologians, Rothe (*Dogmatik*, para. 32) develops the idea of Omnipotence in the direction of the Biblical conception: "that the relation of God to the world is that of His absolute freedom over against it" (*Dogmatik*, I, 123), and once more it is von Oettingen who formulates the decisive idea of the divine self-limitation: "Omnipotence which sets up its own limitations for itself, is not only thinkable, but is necessary for thought, if human freedom is not to founder on the rocks" (II, I, p. 259).

Upon the whole, in the treatment of the idea of Omnipotence in modern theology, there are hopeful signs of an increasing influence of Biblical exegesis, and accordingly an abandonment of speculative scholastic thinking. I have already alluded to the achievement of Cremer in opening up the path for this development; characteristically, in Biedermann's *Dogmatik* there is no positive statement about Omnipotence at all (cf. para. 713).

## (3) OMNIPRESENCE AND OMNISCIENCE

The history of the doctrine of God's Omnipresence and Omniscience bears very clear traces of the disastrous influence of the speculative metaphysical doctrine of God. What the theologians say about this shows that there is almost no connexion at all with faith in the God of revelation; without always being aware of it, of course, their disquisitions are natural theology, pure and simple.

In the *doctrine of Omnipresence*, this comes out particularly clearly in the fact that the subject of the doctrine is simply that which we have already described as the neutral idea of Omnipresence: the relation of God to extension in space, thus the problem: How can the God who is non-spatial be everywhere present within space?

"The Divine is not confined to one place, but neither is it absent from any place; for it fills all things, passes through all things, and is outside all things and in all things" (Cyril of Alexandria, *Commentary on the Gospel of St. John*, 14: 9)—this is an idea which was certainly not calculated to attract any great theological interest, so long as theology is at least to some extent aware of its purpose. Hence the idea of Omnipresence lies on the outer rim of the circumference of theological explanation. How very different would have been their outlook if these theologians had really considered the *locus classicus* for the Divine Omnipresence, the 139th Psalm; this would have opened up new vistas to them! How wonderfully the Psalmist's vision comprehends both the Presence in space and in saving personal communion: "Thou hast beset me behind and before, and laid Thine hand upon me."

It is characteristic of the further development of this doctrine that the statement of Omnipresence became a mere inference from the "Infinity" of God, which, for its part, was an inference from the idea of absolute Being. Thus St. Thomas Aquinas (*Summa*, I, qu. 8) develops the doctrine of the ubiquity of God (Art. 2–4) as a purely metaphysical problem of being, without any consideration of what the Bible says about it. The only passage from Scripture which he quotes is, characteristically, a passage from the Book of Wisdom, allegorically explained. A new, genuinely Biblical movement only entered into this whole sterile metaphysical business at the time of the Reformation, through the discussions about the Presence of Christ in the Sacrament of Holy Communion. Even if Luther's doctrine of ubiquity is fantastic, still it is the expression of a genuine Biblical concern: the point at issue is the real Presence of Christ with His own. Following in the steps of Luther, the Lutheran scholastic theologians supplemented the mediaeval idea of the *omnipraesentia essentialis*—which shows the connexion with the idea of "being"—with the idea of the *omni-praesentia operativa seu gratiosa*, and thus they came at least within sight of the Biblical idea of the Presence of God. But this did not lead to a re-formulation of the doctrine, and later systems of dogmatics lost sight even of this link, and, so far as I can see, almost without exception the neutral problem of Space still occupies all their attention. (On K. Barth, see the next section.)

So far as the next point—the *idea of Omniscience*—is concerned, the situation is somewhat better. Something, indeed, was needed to connect the Neo-Platonist idea of God as *"esse absolutum"* with the central Biblical idea, that God is "knowing Subject". We have already pointed out the significance of Anselm in this connexion (see above, p. 295). Is the Omniscience of God recognized—on whatever grounds the doctrine may be based—then, of necessity, problems arise which at least point in the direction of the Biblical statement, in connexion with the Divine Decree, with Providence, and with the Divine Plan of Salvation. Even St. Thomas had to ask the question (I, qu. 14, Art. 9) whether, and how, God can know the future, whether, and how, He knows Evil, and how this knowledge is related to His will. But, now, instead of at last recollecting the Divine Plan in the Scriptures, this problem is solved by means of the Platonic Theory of Ideas (qu. 15).

In the period of the Reformation the situation changed. The idea of Omniscience is considered in connexion with that of Providence, and this latter idea is understood in the Biblical sense as loving sympathy, loving forethought, and finally as Election. In the great Reformers themselves, in any case, this connexion is clear and predominant, even though it is over-shadowed in the teaching of Luther (during his earlier activity), Zwingli, and Calvin by the doctrine of a double predestination. Among the later scholastic theologians, on the contrary, to a large extent the doctrine of Omniscience (in the doctrine of the Divine Attributes) was ignored—and has been so ever since. Thus Rothe, with evidently polemical emphasis, underlines his statement: "This, and nothing further—namely, the neutral idea that God knows everything—is what the idea of Omniscience contains" (*Dogmatik*, I, p. 123). The majority of modern theologians evince no interest in the problem. Schleiermacher's detailed treatment of the subject (*Glaubenslehre*, para. 55) is an honourable exception to this statement, but in the sentence: "The Divine thinking is one with the Divine Will, and Omnipotence and Omniscience are the same" (55, 1), the pantheistic background of his thought shows through very clearly. Von Oettingen rightly attacks this statement as "pantheistic"; for God knows that which He does not will; God's knowledge of the created world is different from His will which brings it forth (*Luthers Dogm.*, II, 1, p. 258). But he, also, like other modern theologians, fails to perceive the connexion between Omniscience and the Plan of Salvation, and thus the distinctive Biblical doctrine of the Knowledge of God. Strangely enough, in Karl Barth's *Dogmatik* there is no mention of the idea of Omniscience, and even the doctrine of Providence is nowhere fully developed. On the other hand, his observations on the Divine Omnipresence are to a large extent similar to those expressed in this book, although his dependence upon the Scholastic tradition shows itself in the fact that here, too, the abstract problem of Space predominates, and that Barth— with St. Thomas—conceives Omnipresence as the consequence of the Infinity and Simplicity of God (*Kirchl. Dogm.*, II, 1, para. 31, i).

### (4) THE RIGHTEOUSNESS OF GOD

We have already shown in detail that traditional Dogmatics completely ignores the idea of the *Faithfulness* of God, which is so central in the Scriptures, and why this is so. In so far as it is mentioned at all, this occurs under the heading of *Veracitas*, which, however, is discussed without connexion with revelation, and moreover, as an idea of a divine ethical virtue. In Protestant theology there occurs now and again a suggestion of the *constantia Dei in servandis promissionibus*, which at least opens a small window in the direction of that which the Bible understands by the Faithfulness of God.

On the other hand, the idea of the *Righteousness* of God everywhere plays a considerable part. But here, in particular, in this idea there also appears the widespread influence of the speculative perversion, in the fact that the "Righteousness of God" is regarded entirely as the rational idea of righteousness; that is, the idea of retribution, and expecially the *legalistic idea of equality*.[1] *Deus non solum est in praestando benignissimus, sed etiam in vindicando justissimus* (Augustine: *De. Lib. arb.*, II, 1). Pre-reformation theology does not reveal any trace of the New

[1] *I.e.* the notion of desert—reward and punishment correspond exactly. (TR.)

Testament idea of the "Righteousness of God", the δικαιοσύνη θεοῦ. Its re-discovery was indeed the most decisive act of Luther. Luther himself was conscious that his vital experience at Erfurt, when the true Biblical meaning of Romans 1: 16 ff. dawned upon him, was the moment when the Reformation was born. But the fact that Luther always related this righteousness only to faith, and not to God Himself, thus that he always translated "δικαιοσύνη θεοῦ" by "the righteousness which counts in the sight of God", meant that the newly discovered idea of "righteousness" had no influence upon the doctrine of God. Hence the "righteousness of God" was still regarded as that "*justitia*" which is contrasted with grace: the righteousness which demands the keeping of the Law, and which punishes all falling away from the law. Thus Johann Gerhard, for instance, (*Loci theol.*, I, 346) formulates the Righteousness of God as *aeterna constans et immota voluntas suum cuique tribuendi*—the influence of the idea of the Law of Nature, from Roman law, is unmistakable. So, too, that decisive passage in Paul, Romans 3: 21 ff., especially "for the proof of His righteousness", is understood in the sense that the Atoning Sacrifice of Christ has done enough to meet the divine demand for righteousness, in entire agreement with Anselm's doctrine of "satisfaction". No theologian of those days noticed that in the thought of Paul everything in the Christian revelation was included under the conception of the "righteousness of God", that in the thought of Paul the point at issue was precisely *not* that in the Cross the contradiction between righteousness (or justice) and mercy had been removed, but the identity of both (cf. on this point the excellent presentation of the orthodox doctrine of the penal sufferings of Christ in Ritschl (*Rechtf. u. vers.*, I, ch. 6). Thus the real Biblical doctrine of the Righteousness of God was not understood, even by orthodox Protestant theologians. The reason for this can only be perceived when we look at the whole tradition of the doctrine of God. The traditional idea of righteousness is part of the *theologia naturalis*, of speculative theology, which dominates the whole doctrine of the Divine Attributes. Only gradually, above all under the influence of modern Biblical exegesis, does an understanding begin to dawn of the difference between this rational idea and the Biblical idea of righteousness. The essay of the Old Testament scholar Diestel, "*Die Idee der Gerechtigkeit im Alten Testament*" (*Jahrbücher für deutsche Theologie*, 1860), a pioneer effort in this direction, even though the Biblical research of later days had to moderate, to some extent, the extreme swing of the pendulum represented in Diestel's thesis against the "juridical" idea of righteousness (cf. on this point the article by Schrenk already mentioned on δίκη and δικαιοσύνη in the *N. T. Wörterbuch*). Diestel saw that the Old Testament, when it speaks of the Righteousness of God, means something which is not in dialectical opposition to His grace, but that, on the contrary, more or less it means the same thing, and that this relation—which cannot be grasped on rational lines, is intelligible from the standpoint of the Covenant, or of the Kingdom of God.

And yet even that rational element of retribution is contained within the idea as a whole; hence it also contains that element of "juridical" punitive "righteousness" which is what we mean by "justice" at the present day. This retributive justice operates wherever the "righteousness" of grace is not accepted. This second element—which corresponds to the idea of the divine wrath in Holiness—was hidden from Diestel.

It is now essential that we should try to carry the process of definition further, till the Biblical idea of righteousness (justice) is really understood. This, of course, involves abandonment of the old rational idea of justice. Yet this exegetical truth has scarcely borne any fruit yet within dogmatics. In the thought of Karl Barth, it is true, the fundamental adjustment to revelation is present (*Kirchl. Dogm.*, II, pp. 413–57); but the tension between the rational, and the revelation idea of "righteousness" (justice) is not brought out clearly. A good deal of work still needs to be done, until at last, in the science of *dogmatics*, we take the idea of God's Righteousness seriously, which has already been perceived in Biblical studies. We must not forget, however, that the Biblical scholar has an easier task than the systematic theologian, since the problem which is raised by the present-day use of the word "righteousness" does not trouble him.

## SECTION TWO

# THE WILL OF GOD

### CHAPTER 22

## THE ETERNAL DIVINE DECREES AND THE DOCTRINE OF ELECTION

Is it not presumptuous to think man can discuss the eternal Divine Decrees? Should we not be dissuaded from such an undertaking, particularly from the standpoint of the Biblical revelation, since the Holy Scriptures so decidedly and so plainly direct our attention to the historical revelation? For this surely implies that we ought to remain content with what God has shown us within the sphere of our human experience, and not even wish to know the eternal mysteries which God keeps to Himself? Is not a doctrine of the Eternal Decrees rather like that attempt to "clamber up the steep ascent to the Supreme Majesty", against which Luther warned us so urgently, when he said: "*ego scio, ego expertus sum*"? Thus is not the very attempt to formulate a doctrine of Predestination something to be condemned out of hand, even before it has been begun?

### (1)

The history of the doctrine of Predestination itself teaches us that with the question of the Divine Decrees we have entered the danger-zone, in which faith may suffer severe injury, and theological thinking may easily stray into disastrous error.[1] And yet the attempt cannot be renounced, not because our thought itself drives us to it, but because the witness of revelation in the Scriptures forces this subject upon our attention, for theological consideration. It is not merely the—comparatively meagre—mention of the "Divine Decrees", which moves us to this, but the fact that Election constitutes the centre of the Old and the New Testament. The content of the divine revelation in Jesus Christ is simply the "mystery of His Will";[2] that which is disclosed to faith within earthly history, in the Incarnate Word, in the Crucified Son of God, is nothing less than the eternal Will of God. "Having made known unto us the

---

[1] See below, pp. 340 ff.　　　　　　　　[2] Eph. 1: 9.

mystery of His will, according to His good pleasure which He purposed in Him unto a dispensation of the fulness of the times, to sum up all things in Christ, the things in the heavens, and the things upon the earth; in Him, I say, in Whom also we were made a heritage, having been foreordained according to the purpose of Him who worketh all things after the counsel of His will."[1] When God reveals Himself, He reveals eternity: the eternal Origin and the eternal End, that which "was" before all history, and that which will be behind, or after, all history, this (from our standpoint) twofold eternity, between which hangs our earthly historical existence like a suspension bridge between two pillars, supported by them as it sways in mid-air over the abyss of Nothingness.

Jesus Christ came in order to reveal this eternity, and to integrate our life within the dimension of this twofold eternity, in order that our life should not be lost in nothingness. For apart from this integration into eternity "we pass our years as a tale that is told".[2] Apart from this foundation in eternity, and this goal in eternity, the whole history of humanity is a mere nothing, which is swallowed up in the whirlpool of the temporal. Without this firm foundation in our eternal Origin, and without the firm goal in the eternity at the end of the ages, man literally lives "for the day"; he is like a mayfly which lives for a day, and then disappears; his life is played out on the surface of the finite. Only through his relation to eternity does he acquire depth; the "surface" is the finite, the temporal, eternity alone is "depth". And this dimension of "depth" is the same as the dimension of "meaning". Either life has an *eternal* meaning or it has *no* meaning at all. For what is meaning, if it can be finally swallowed up in meaninglessness, and annihilated? And what sort of "meaning" would there be without an eternal foundation?

It is not only the Christian Faith which places human life— and life as a whole—within the dimension of eternity. This takes place also in non-Christian religions. It occurs above all in that school of thought which, alongside of the Christian message, has influenced the spiritual and intellectual life of the Western world most deeply and permanently, the idealistic philosophy of the Greeks. Even the philosophy of Plato teaches man to seek and to find meaning in eternity. This eternity of the world of the Ideas is, however, of such a kind that it depreciates the value of the Temporal and the Historical, so that all

[1] Eph. 1: 9–11. (R.V.)        [2] Ps. 90: 9.

that has a share in "becoming", by this very fact becomes more or less an illusion. As a crowd of human beings seems small and insignificant, if viewed from a great height, so there is a view of eternity which assigns no decisive value to temporal happenings, because temporal events and eternity cannot be connected by means of the idea of the "decisive event". Where eternity is conceived from the human end, there is no decisive event, no event which unites us with eternity, there are merely ideas which conceive timeless, eternal truth, and in so doing contrast the Timeless and Eternal, as true Being, with that which is merely temporal and transitory. Temporal events with the quality of a "time of decision" only exist where eternity itself has entered into time, where the Logos who became Man enters into History, and reveals to man, lost in the temporal, his origin and his eternal end, and makes these the goal of his decision of faith. Only through this revelation of eternity does our history itself acquire a share in eternity.[1]

Thus it is this revealed eternity alone, through which, and in which, I, this individual human being, this individual person, receive eternal meaning, and my individual personal existence is taken seriously. One who only knows an Eternity which is intellectually conceived—an eternity of Ideas, an eternity of intellectual truth and of spiritual values—finds his personal existence merged in the life of the All;[2] in the Christian revelation of eternity, however, my eyes are opened to perceive the truth that God, *My Lord*, regards *me* from all eternity, with the gaze of everlasting love, and therefore that my individual personal existence and life now receive an eternal meaning. Through the fact that my eye of faith meets the gaze of the Eternal God, that I know that I am being "looked at" by His everlasting love—"Thine eyes saw me when as yet there was none of me"[3]—I myself acquire an eternal dignity. The call that is addressed to me through Jesus Christ from all eternity calls me to my eternal destiny. To be called from the eternity of God to eternal communion with God—that is the Gospel of Jesus Christ. Briefly, that is the meaning of the New Testament message of eternal election. How, then, can we not see that this message of election is the same as the good news of "sonship" and of the Kingdom of God?

---

[1] In the Old Testament both the revelation of Eternity and the decisive character of Time are equally provisional and incomplete.

[2] We should not quote the Platonic doctrine of Immortality as a counter-argument. In so far as it is personal and individual, it is religious myth; in so far as it is philosophical it is impersonal.  [3] Ps. 139: 16.

(2)

On the other hand, how terrible and paralysing is all talk of predestination, of a decree of God, by which everything that is to happen has already been established from all eternity. Is there anything more devastating for the freedom and reality of decision than this idea that everything is predetermined? Does not this reduce all history to something which has already been determined, and is being carried out on these preconceived lines? and thus that all decision and all freedom is an illusion? Such a view makes human history a mere game of chess, in which the human figures are moved about on the board by a higher unseen Hand, or like a piece of tapestry of many colours, into which the many destinies of mankind are woven, but woven without the assistance of men, a tapestry already prepared from all eternity, which is merely unrolled in time. In such a view is there any room for that element which alone gives meaning and dignity to human life, the element of responsible, freely-willed action?

Finally—if everything is predetermined by the Divine decree, how could any other court of appeal be responsible for this happening than His who had predetermined it? If everything is predetermined, evil as well as good, godlessness as well as faith, hell as well as heaven, "being lost" as well as "being saved", if it is predetermined, by God's eternal decree, that not only the temporal, but also the eternal destinies of men are assigned unequally, so that some, from eternity, are destined for eternal death, and others for eternal life—is it possible to call the One who has promulgated this *decretum horribile* a loving Father of all men? If *this* hidden decree of God lies behind the revelation of Jesus Christ, what meaning has the call to faith, repentance, and thankful trust? Does not this doctrine menace the whole meaning of the message of the love of God, and the seriousness of the decision of faith?

If there is any point at which it is urgent that the Church should re-examine the content of the Christian Message, it is certainly at the point of the doctrine of the Divine Decree, and of Election.

(3)

Reformed theologians usually make a distinction between a decree of Creation and a decree of Election.[1] The Scriptural

---

[1] Cf. Wolleb, *Christ. Theol. Comp.*, p. 20.

evidence offers no support for this view; in any case the ideas which characterize the eternal decree in the New Testament are not applied to the Creation.[1] This is not due, as we shall see, to any accident of language, but to a strictly observed order. There can, however, be no doubt that the origin of the Creation is simply and solely the thought and the will of God.[2] The world exists, because God wills it; the world is as it is because God wills it so. Hence it is the expression, manifestation, revelation, of His thought and will. Because thought, God's thought, God's wisdom, lies at its foundation, there is in it an order which can be perceived; that is why it is accessible to knowledge, that is why it has a logical rational aspect. To use the language of the ancients, it is "comprehensible to reason". But because it has been created by the free will of God it is "contingent", not necessary. The idea of the *contingentia mundi* only became a subject for philosophy through Christianity.

This is the first great difference between the Greek theory of the cosmos and the Christian doctrine of Creation. For Greek philosophical thinking the Cosmos is not only accessible to reason but it is rational, because it has not been created by means of the will of God, but because it proceeds, with timeless necessity, out of the Eternal Logos. For speculative thought there is no Creation, because it has no freedom to create or not to create. As the effect springs from the cause, so the world issues from the Logos. In this view there is no room for the irrational element of will. The world comes from eternity because it has no beginning. But it is precisely the doctrine of Election which understands the world as something which was not there "at the beginning", but that it is something which was preceded by something else. Almost always, wherever the doctrine of Election is mentioned, it is emphasized that this took place "before the Creation of the world".[3]

The second fundamental difference between the idea of the Cosmos and the idea of Creation is connected with an idea which at first sight seems to be a common element to both: the Logos. The Cosmos is pervaded by the Logos, it issues from the Logos. This Logos is the ultimate, fundamental presupposition of thought. It is the necessary principle of necessary thought, hence it is the firm support for the whole of philosophy. As

[1] The προ in: πρόγνωσις, πρό-θεσις, προ-ωρισμος, everywhere means: πρὸ καταβολῆς κόσμου.
[2] In spite of the mystical flavour of the phrase "without form and void", this is the meaning of Gen. 1: 1 ff.—expressed still more strongly in Rom. 4: 17 and Heb. 11: 3.     [3] Eph. 1: 4; 1 Peter 1: 20; Matt. 25: 34.

such, it is an abstract impersonal idea. But the Biblical idea of Creation is based upon a different Logos, upon that Word which "was in the beginning", "without whom nothing has been created",[1] and is identical with the Son of God. In Him who is the "Image of the invisible God", the "firstborn of all creation"—"in Him all things are created", "for through Him, and unto Him, are all things, and He is before all things, and in Him all things cohere".[2] Not an impersonal Logos of thought, but the thought and will, the loving will of God, who meets us in the Person of Christ, the "Son of His love",[3] is the foundation and the origin of all existence.

In this connexion the truth which we have already seen acquires new significance, that the world, it is true, was created *through*—διά—the Son, but not *by*—ὑπο—the Son, that it has been created *in* Him and *unto* Him, but that He Himself is never called the Creator. It has pleased God the Creator to create the world in the Son, through the Son, and unto the Son. The fact that between the Creator and the Creation there stands the Mediator of creation means that the world is an act of the freedom of God, that it does not proceed from the Logos. The Son is the meaning of the world, for whom God in free decision determines and creates the world. If it be the Eternal Son, yet it is also the free resolve of God, that He creates the world in the Son and for the Son.[4] The self-revelation of God as the Origin and End of all creation is God's free act. Hence the Scriptures suggest that "God" alone is the Subject of Creation—not the Son, although He "gave unto the Son to have life in Himself". The freedom to design and to create, and the content of that which has been thus planned, must be distinguished from one another, if the Creation is to be an act of freedom. God's free act is the plan of the world "in Jesus Christ".

(4)

The Creation of the world is connected with the decree of Election by the fact that the mediator of both is the Son, the Son whom God "loved before the foundation of the world".[5] He is the Son-Logos, who, as the Incarnate One, gives us both the knowledge of Election and the knowledge that the world has been created *through* the Son, *in* the Son and *unto* the Son. Thus the origin, meaning, and purpose of the world are only to

[1] John 1: 1.     [2] Col. 1: 15–17.     [3] Col. 1: 13.
[4] Eph. 3: 9.     [5] John 17: 24.

be perceived where faith in the historical revelation of the love of God, in the calling to Divine sonship through the Crucified, becomes the assurance of eternal election. The truth which concerns the Creation is—both in point of time and of fact— subordinate to the truth which concerns Election. This is the reason why the Bible does not speak of a decree of Creation. The Creation is subordinate to Election, it is neither co-ordinated with it nor super-ordinated above it. The way of truth proceeds from the historical revelation to the eternal Election, and only through that to the Creation. This is of decisive importance for the understanding of Election itself.

The first truth which the doctrine of Election contains is not the general one, a *"decretum generale"*,[1] as the formula of the theologians is worded—dubiously—which is then followed by the *"decretum speciale"* of personal Election. In the Bible, most emphatically, this is *not* the way in which Election is mentioned. For this order of ideas is based upon a mistaken idea of faith. In the New Testament faith is not directed to something general, but to something personal. Faith is the encounter between me, as an individual person, and Jesus Christ; it is not faith in a general statement, in a doctrine. Since the individual, sinful, human being meets the gracious, generous will of God in Jesus Christ the Crucified One, and through Him is "rescued from the power of darkness",[2] from the wrath of God, and is raised to the plane of sonship, he gains an insight into the background of eternity; he experiences and hears the word of the historical calling as the word of eternal Election. Faith is, first of all, a "Thou-relation", and only after that is it knowledge of God's relation to the world, to Creation. The truth revealed to the believer—as one to whom the word of justifying grace and sonship in Jesus Christ has been granted—is, first of all, that which "was before the foundation of the world", and only after that does he learn the other truth: that the world as a whole derives its origin, its meaning, and its preservation, from the very Son whom he has learned to know as "the Son of His love". Faith is directly related to the eternal, to the will of God directed to the person, with His decree of election "before the foundation of the world", not with the created world itself. The individual human being, the one who is "called", possesses his direct relation with the God who "elects", and with His will, which precedes everything else—so personally, and so

---

[1] In the thought of the Reformed theologians the *decretum generale* is identical with the Decree of Creation.  [2] Col. 1: 13.

intensely is all this directed to the "Thou". The truth of Election is not the result of a deduction from a general statement; faith is, and remains—even where its content is the eternal election—a direct, immediate, personal relation, which is the exact opposite of a general theory.

Faith possesses this character owing to its historical origin. This alone is the starting-point, to this all must be referred, if —in contrast to that which the theologians call "predestination" —we are to understand what the Bible means by Election. Israel experienced its election as an historical event: "For thou art an holy People unto the Lord thy God, and the Lord hath chosen thee to be a peculiar people unto Himself, above all peoples that are upon the face of the earth."[1] Through Moses and the Prophets this people became aware that Yahweh was speaking to it in the events of history, as God's incomprehensible, free, unfathomable act, an act which is also a Word.[2] Its election is the same as the peculiar course of History by which God leads this People—and this people alone, among all nations. The Election of Israel, indeed, consists in this historical encounter in which the Holy and Merciful God manifests Himself to it as "the Lord *thy* God", and thus makes Israel His own People, and in so doing singles it out from all other nations upon earth.[3] The fact that this election is based solely upon the free election of God, upon the unfathomable love of Yahweh, and not upon any quality inherent in Israel itself, is brought home to it in the fact that Yahweh can, and may, reject and cast out His chosen People.[4] The basis of election never lies in the one who is chosen, but exclusively in the One who chooses.[5] Election means precisely this: that Israel knows itself to be wholly dependent upon the grace of the One who has chosen her, and that she ought to live in this attitude of continual dependence. The historical character of the fact of election, and the freedom of God in election, are one and the same thing. "The Lord hath taken you, and brought you forth out of the iron furnace, out of Egypt, to be unto Him a people of inheritance. . . .[6] For this historical fact of election is truth which cannot be deduced by arguments: it is God in action, Unique and Unfathomable.

All this, however, is only fulfilled in the historical events of the revelation in Christ. There alone does the Historical be-

[1] Deut. 14: 2.          [2] Amos 2: 3.
[3] Cf. the excellent remarks by Quell in the *N.T. Theol. Wörterbuch*, IV, 163 ff.
[4] Amos 3: 2; Jer. 5: 12; 7:4      [5] Deut. 7: 6 ff.      [6] Deut. 4: 20.

come the Unique in the strict sense of the word, there alone is
the absolutely unfathomable character of the divine Act of love
fully manifested—in the "folly of the Cross",[1] in the justification of the sinner, in the vicarious suffering of Him who, as the
Holy One, had every right to be angry and to condemn. Election here takes place through the fact that the love of God
enters into the curse which sinful humanity has drawn down
upon itself.[2] At the Cross of Christ that "nevertheless" of the
Divine Love takes place, so that it is not the sinner who is
annihilated, but the curse of sin which separates man from God.[3]
At the Cross we hear the call of God, a call which has only one
condition: that we should hear it as the unconditional call that
it is, that is, that we should believe.[4]

Thus, as Israel perceived and received its election in the
Historical "Act-Word" of God, so the sinful human being perceives and receives his own election in the historical "Act-
Word", in the Incarnate Word of God, Jesus Christ, through
faith: "Mine art thou, My son." "Thine am I, Thy Father."[5]
Here, too, primarily election is the same as in the Old Covenant
the encounter with the God who calls in love, the God who calls
us to Himself. The "elect" is the "one who is called", one who
in faith accepts the call to sonship with God, and to communion with God. Only the individual can perceive this call as
a call addressed to him personally, just as Israel had received
and perceived it as the truth, "I am the Lord Thy God". *Now*,
however, this call is not addressed to a nation, but to the sinful
individual person, for this call desires that which the individual
person alone can give: personal decision, the obedience of
faith.[6]

But in order that this call should be really perceived as the
call of the Eternal God, since the Son is known as the Eternal
Son of the Father, as the one who has come from beyond all
that is created, as He in whom the eternal secret of the Father
is manifested, it is understood as a call from eternity, and the
encounter with it in historical reality becomes the encounter
with the Eternal will of God.[7] In that I know myself as belovéd
in the Eternal Son, I know that I have been loved from all
eternity. The ἐκλογή, the eternal election, opens the door to
the κλῆσις. But as in our knowledge of the Son it is not the

---

[1] 1 Cor. 1: 18.  　　　　　　[2] Rom. 8: 3.  　　　　　　[3] Col. 2: 14.
[4] Rom. 3:22:"unto all them that believe"; 3: 26:"him that hath faith in Jesus".
[5] Rom. 8: 15.
[6] Rom. 1: 5. Directly connected with Election: 1 Peter 1: 2.
[7] Eph. 1: 5–

pre-existence of the Son which predominates, but His historical act, and we gaze beyond that at the eternal background, for a moment as it were, but we do not stay there—so is it here. The truth of eternal election is seen by the eye of faith, but it does not stay there,[1] because it is fitting to dwell on the historical encounter. If this background becomes the foreground, then it is almost inevitable that the idea of faith should become speculative, and then perverted, by trying to deal with matters which are too high for it, which only leads to the production of illusory "truths" of the most dangerous kind.

If the starting-point remains firmly established at the historical centre, and if faith continues to perceive that the "call" of Jesus Christ is the call of God, then it is impossible that there should be any contradiction between election and responsibility. One who knows that he has thus been "called" by God as son, and has been placed within the ranks of "His own", knows that in so doing he is called into the service of the Holy God, as a "slave of Jesus Christ", as one who no longer belongs unto himself, but to Him who has called him out of darkness "into His marvellous light".[2] He knows that he has been called "to be conformed to the image of His Son",[3] to die with Him who calls him—as the "old man"—and to rise with Him—to a new life.[4] Hence the evidence of the New Testament does not contain a trace of that whole complex of problems connected with the doctrine of Predestination, dealing especially with moral freedom and responsibility. Thus the tormenting and insoluble problems raised by an erroneous belief—Predestination—e.g. how can fore-ordination and freedom, predestination and responsibility co-exist?—not only do not constitute any problem for the New Testament, but are regarded as truths which are naturally and inseparably connected. As the election of Israel to a covenant-relation with God constituted an obligation to service, and indeed was based upon an exclusive relation to the service of Yahweh, and since the whole unique *ethos* of the people of the Old Covenant is based upon this election, so the election in Jesus Christ constitutes the foundation of the special *ethos* of the Christian Church. Indeed, we might even call the Christian ethic an "ethic of election".[5] It is the respon-

---

[1] The passages which deal with the eternal election, like the allusions to the Pre-existence of the Son, are few compared with those which deal with the historical Work of Christ.

[2] 1 Peter 2: 9.  [3] Rom. 8: 29.  [4] Rom. 6: 5 ff.

[5] In spite of Eph. 1: 11 and 2: 10, however, this is not actually said. Perhaps it would be better to describe it as an "ethic of the calling".

sibility of those who are "called to be saints," who in their κλῆσις experience both the eternal election and the call to service in love. This connexion comes out particularly plainly in that passage where the eternal election is expressed with special emphasis and meaning: "He chose us in Him before the foundation of the world, that we should be holy and without blemish before Him in love . . . for we are His workmanship, created in Christ Jesus for good works, which God afore prepared that we should walk in them."[1]

Not only do election and freedom not cancel each other out, but freedom is based upon the fact of election. Only he who knows that he is elect, who accepts his election in Jesus Christ, is truly free. As already—to use this analogy on the natural plane—the Moral Law, according to Kant, is the basis of moral freedom, so the fact of belonging to the Holy and Loving God in Jesus Christ, that is, the eternal election, existence in the Good, freedom from the compulsion of sin, and thus genuine freedom, are all based on faith. "If therefore the Son shall make you free, you shall be free indeed."[2] "Where the Spirit of the Lord is, there is liberty."[3] The only true freedom is to know that from all eternity we have been destined, through the Son, for communion with God.

(5)

Now that we have defined the right approach to the true doctrine of Election, which is in accordance with revelation, there are still certain misunderstandings and misinterpretations which we must discuss; for their own sake, and owing to their— to some extent—disastrous consequences, they need some attention. One of them, which is very recent, and therefore has not yet had any widespread influence, can only be mentioned briefly. To the question: Who elects and who is elected?—each time the answer is, Jesus Christ.[4] Now it cannot be denied that Jesus Christ, as the Son of His Love, as the One upon whom the εὐδοξία, the "beneplacitum" of God, rests, is the Elect of God,[5] and that, on the other hand, as the One who Himself calls His own to Himself, He is the One who elects.[6] But, above all, the fundamental idea in this view is that to speak of Election means to speak of Jesus Christ, in entire harmony with the witness of the Scriptures.

And yet we cannot accept this view: that the Subject of the

[1] Eph. 1: 4 and 2: 10.  [2] John 8: 36.
[3] 2 Cor. 3: 17.  [4] See Appendix, pp. 346 ff.
[5] Thus explicitly in 1 Peter 2: 4, 6.  [6] See John 15: 16.

Eternal election is Jesus Christ. Where the New Testament speaks of the eternal election of the faithful in Christ Jesus, the Subject of Election is solely, and without exception, God, just as the Subject of Creation solely, and without exception, is God. Jesus Christ is the Mediator of Election, as He is the Mediator of Creation. *In* Him, *through* Him, but not *by* Him we are elect, as the world has been created in Him, through Him, and unto Him, but not by Him. What is the meaning of this distinction? Not only loyalty to the explicit witness of the Scriptures is here involved, but far more than this: the freedom of God. God has freedom in Jesus Christ to elect, and outside of Jesus to reject. But if Jesus Christ Himself becomes the Subject of the eternal Election, then there is no Divine freedom, *in* Christ to elect, *outside of* Christ to reject. Then neither in God nor in man is an "Either-Or" possible; then in Jesus Christ the decision for every human being has been anticipated; then the elect alone exist and there are no more reprobate than there is a wrath of God; for then the only one who is rejected—and this conclusion is explicitly drawn by those who take this view—is Jesus Christ the Crucified, who is at the same time the One who is the Elect from all eternity. But this means that—not only for those who believe, who are "in Christ", but for all, whether believers or not, the Judgment has been abrogated, the possibility of being "lost" has been taken away from everyone. There is no decision. Thus the result of this view is the most thoroughgoing doctrine of Universalism that has ever been formulated.[1]

Hence in the witness to revelation in the New Testament the Subject of election is God alone. It is His free purpose which places us sinners, through faith, in the reality of the Son of His Love, as it is His purpose to send us His Son, to reveal Himself to us, and to impart Himself to us. All the expressions used in the New Testament which deal with eternal Election point to this purpose.[2] The fact that He places us within the "Kingdom of the Son of His love"—is His *beneplacitum*, this is the "mystery of His will". In Himself the Son signifies Election: where the Son is, there is Election; but where the Son is not, there is no election. But the Son is only present where there is faith, hence in the New Testament the "elect", and they alone, are those who believe. For this cause alone faith is decision in which the stakes are salvation or ruin; it is not a sham decision,

---

[1] On this see Appendix, p. 348.
[2] So above all προορίζειν, and πρόθεσις, strengthened by βουλή and θέλημα.

where everything has already been decided beforehand. The consequences may be serious, if, in order to escape from the doctrine of a double predestination, we take the wrong path, and end up with Universalism. Here a mistaken emphasis upon "Christ alone" has led to a "solution" which is no less dangerous than the opposite view which it desires to rule out. It is the same erroneous Christ-Monism which we have met already in the doctrine of the Trinity; the absolute equation of God and Christ, by means of which the Son, from being the Mediator of Creation becomes the Creator, which leads necessarily to the view that the Son is the Subject of the eternal Election, and in so doing the idea of Judgment is ignored, and the possibility of being finally lost is eliminated.

The two other misunderstandings lead in the opposite direction. Through two ideas, which have crept in through philosophy, the connexion between election and responsibility has been obscured: the idea of Causality, and a wrong idea of Eternity.

### (6)

*Causality.*—It was especially the Reformers' interest in the *"sola gratia"*, the desire to get rid of all traces of synergism, which led the Reformers to understand Man as a mere *object* of Grace, and thus faith simply as the working of divine Grace. The dubious middle term here was *"mere passive"*, that is, in relation to the reception of grace man is wholly passive. The right element in this idea was that man is solely receptive, that faith is neither a merit nor an achievement. But now, this theological idea led to a psychological idea of passivity. Instead of that which is "purely receptive" arose the idea of "purely effected". Thus Man became the object of the working of grace, *"truncus et lapis"*.[1] The personal relation between God and Man became a causal relation: God the cause, faith the effect. At that time men did not know that even in the sphere of physical causality there is no mere passivity but only re-activity. From the theological postulate of the *"sola gratia"* men built up the theory of a purely passive process in the soul, that is, a process in which faith was understood simply and solely as the effect of divine grace as its cause. Of course, such a faith has no connexion with that which the Bible calls "faith", it is a purely artificial theory of theologians, which had no basis in anything men could imagine in the rest of their experience.

[1] Thus Formula of Concord *Sol. Decl.*, II, 19, 24.

The postulate was laid down: That which we know as faith is solely the effect of the divine grace as cause, without asking any further, whether the application of the *causal* idea to the *personal* relation between "Word of God and Faith" is in any way permissible or possible.

This mistaken view of faith, however, also affected the understanding of Election. Election, then, became "determination". Through the eternal election man is determined, his lot has been fixed. The pattern on the tapestry has already been woven before man begins his actual existence: life only means the unrolling of the tapestry which is already finished. If this is what Election means, then certainly there is no more radical determinism than that which is contained in the doctrine of Election or Predestination. It was indeed Luther himself who, in his eagerness to combat the doctrine of freedom taught by Erasmus, the wrong kind of indeterminism, and thus to ward off the menace to the doctrine of the *"sola gratia"*, slipped into this deterministic line, and could not do enough to express the complete passivity of man, by the use of all kinds of causal images and ideas. At a later stage Luther became aware of his error, being enlightened by the true Scriptural doctrine.[1]

Behind this dangerous doctrinal development there lies a fatal confusion of ideas. What these theologians really want to say is that of himself man is incapable of doing the will of God and of believing in Christ, and thus that faith and freedom are wholly the gift of God. That is, in point of fact, the teaching of the Bible and its view of God and His relation with sinful man which springs from revelation. But all this lies within the dimension: "Word—responsibility", "Divine Person—human person". This means that man can never *earn* grace, and further, that he cannot even rightly understand the word of grace and believe it, save as the Holy Spirit opens his heart to do so. But in all this man remains "person", and the transaction between God and man remains a personal one, something which takes place within the sphere of responsibility, and it ought never to be transferred into the dimension of "power—thing", "cause—effect". Even sinful man is a subject, not an object, and even "given" grace is a personal act, and not the cause of an effect. In the truth of Scripture this personal fundamental relation is never affected, but it is explicitly preserved; hence man, even as the recipient of grace, remains a responsible subject, and never becomes *"truncus et lapis"*.

[1] See Appendix, pp. 343 ff.

That is why we do not find in the Bible any traces of the interpretation of Election in the sense of a deterministic doctrine of Predestination.

(7)

*The Concept of Eternity.*—Just as devastating in its effect as the introduction of the idea of causality was the introduction of a wrong idea of Eternity. The eternal Election was understood purely theoretically as the verdict of God which had been pronounced before Time was, and in so doing it was likewise torn out of the sphere of personal relation. It is, of course, true that some of the Biblical terminology seemed to support such a view; eternal election is always connected with the idea of "before": προ-ορίζειν, προ-τίθεσθαι. For a non-reflective faith this was enough; for such a faith can tolerate the paradox: being predetermined and being responsible. But when men began to *think*, this primitive formulation was not sufficient; for once the process of reflection had begun, almost inevitably a "personal" way of thinking tended to drift into an "impersonal" point of view.

The Biblical understanding of Time is very closely connected with the understanding of the personal. It is therefore radically different from the physical and mathematical concept of Time.[1] In the thought of the Biblical writers Time is always human time, historical time, time of decision. In Jesus Christ, as "Messianic Time" it becomes the *"ultimum tempus"*, which means both "high time", and "the last times". Through Jesus Christ, for the believer Time acquires an otherwise unknown quality of decision; decision between Heaven and Hell, between being saved and being lost for ever, between the absolute fulfilment of meaning and the absolute loss of all meaning. This decision took place in Jesus Christ, in the "fulness of the time". But that which has taken place once for all in Jesus Christ as an universal event of History, must be "appropriated" by the believer. He, too, is placed within the sphere of decision, and this decision is faith. In the sphere of faith earthly Time is filled with the tension of eternity. In faith we, as it were, anticipate eternity by sharing in it; we have already been received into the heavenly citizenship of the supratemporal aeon. Hence in faith Time is not simply contrasted with Eternity; it has itself a share in Eternity. It is controlled

[1] Cf. my article, *"Das Einmalige und der Existenzcharakter"* in *Blätter für deutsche Philosophie*, 1929.

and filled with significance from thence. Thus it stands at the furthest end of the scale, at whose opposite end there stands the neutral, atomized Time of mathematical physics, which is composed of purely time atoms. Between these two extremes, of Physical Time and Messianic Time, there lies our ordinary historical Time, where, it is true, decisions are made, but not "the" Decision. But Messianic Time, the time of Jesus Christ and of those who belong to Him, is the opposite of that atomized time of the physicists; it is held together by Eternity, just as the bars in a musical work of art are held together by the sign which denotes a "phrase". In Christ we live at the same time both inside and outside of the sphere of ordinary time.

Thus the eternal Election is something quite different from a decision which was made about us a very, very long while ago. The eternal Election is rather that which in Jesus Christ becomes "Event" in Time. The eternal Election means that God's Word of Love which now reaches me in Jesus Christ, reaches me out of Eternity, that it goes "before" my existence, and my decision, as that which makes it possible. Hence it does not make my existence and my decision, which take place in time, futile, it does not reduce my decision to an illusion; on the contrary, through the truth of the eternal election my decision of faith is seen to be one with the gracious choice of God. The "Yes" of God to me, and my "Yes" to Him are one, indissolubly united. God loves me, before I exist, from all eternity, in such a way that He wills me to be one who in the freedom of decision says "Yes" to His call of love. The human answer is included in the divine will as a free personal decision. Conversely, it is only the free personal decision in which this eternal destiny is realized as a temporal act, in faith in Him in whom God's eternal "Yes" to me reaches me in Time, in Jesus Christ. The eternity grasped in faith does not eliminate the freedom of the decision, indeed it constitutes its basis. In all the world there is nothing so free, nothing which has so much the character of decision, as the decision of faith, which in Jesus Christ lays hold of the eternal "Yes", the eternal love of God to me. And faith knows no other eternity, and should know no other than that which thus establishes our decision of faith as an act of freedom, as the answer to God's original Word.

(8)

There is, however, yet another misunderstanding to be removed, which (with the two others) is the cause of the false idea of Election, the doctrine of a "double predestination". Along with the idea of "Election" there arose, first of all, the view that One who elects picks out certain individuals from a given number, and thus we get the idea of "selection". The Greek word ἐκλέγεσθαι expresses this still more clearly than our German word *Erwählen*. This idea is at first inseparable from the Biblical idea of Election. Israel alone was chosen "out of all nations" as the People of the Covenant and the revelation. The phrase "you alone" is constantly used, and with special emphasis.[1] But this idea of selection should not be understood to mean that God was thus of necessity bound, or that He wills to be so bound, to the recipient of His grace and His choice. The "choosing" is merely the substratum of the divine freedom. All that this means is that the application of grace is wholly based on God's generous love, that it is an act of royal sovereignty. Israel, who has been thus "chosen" can also be "rejected",[2] and this election may be extended to other nations. It has nothing to do with Israel as such, nothing to do with "numbers", it is entirely a matter depending on the freedom of God. In the election or choice or singling out of Israel God demonstrates His absolute freedom, the freedom, the unmotivated character of His loving and His giving. And this choice of selection always remains, it is true, on the part of God, absolute and free, but on the part of man, of the People of Israel, conditioned. There is contained within it a *"conditionalis divinus"*: In so far as Israel obeys . . . Hence Election may also give place to Rejection. It is indeed a *"foedus monopleuron"*,[3] the making of a Covenant, which is wholly based on God's turning towards Israel, but is also a Covenant which includes obedience, the correspondence of Israel, a genuine Covenant.

This preparatory stage of revelation, the election of Israel, becomes, through the complete revelation in Jesus Christ, the election of *all who believe in Him*. Here the idea of a "number", from whom a selection is made, falls away; election no longer has the apparent substratum of selection. The grace of God in its absolute freedom is now wholly "localized" in Jesus Christ; in Him the grace of God is present, therefore everyone who is in Christ is of the "elect". The "elect" are the same as the genuine believers.[4] There is a "selection" only in the sense that that human condition, which was always included with-

---

[1] Amos 3: 2; Deut. 7: 6.   [2] Hosea 5: 12 ff.; Is. 49: 6; 42: 1; 60: 3.
[3] A one-sided Covenant. Cf. Heppe, *Dogmatik der ev. reformierten Kirche*, pp. 279 ff.   [4] 1 Peter 1: 1.

in the idea of Election, the election of Israel—here now quite clearly stands out as the sole principle of selection: "that all who believe in Him should not be lost";[1] that is the continuation in the particular sense of the universal statement: "God so loved the world that He gave His only Son." The absolute free grace of God, purely generous love—that is Jesus Christ. It is applied to the world as a whole, it applies to all; but it applies *to all in so far as they believe*. Whoever excludes himself, is excluded; he who does not allow himself to be included, is not included.[2] But he who allows himself to be included, he who believes, *is* "elect". To believe in Jesus Christ and to be of the elect is one and the same thing, just as not to believe in Jesus Christ and not to be of the elect is the same thing. There is no other selection than this, there is no other number than that which is constituted by the fact of believing or not believing.

As time went on, this identity of "being elect" and "faith", which is obvious in the witness of the New Testament, was no longer understood. When "faith" and "election" were severed from the "personal" sphere; when "faith" had come to mean theoretical doctrinal statement, since faith was no longer understood as an "I-Thou" encounter, but as "truth" in the third person, this correlation of election and faith was broken, the *conditionalis divinus* which it contains was ignored, and instead there was postulated a theoretical *Numerus*. It was at this point that the doctrine arose that "some" are elect from all eternity, and "others" are not. The doctrine of double predestination has been formulated, and in the name of the God of Love, the "*horribile decretum*" was taught, that just as some have been "elect" from eternity, others, and indeed the large majority, the "*massa perditionis*", have been condemned from all eternity to everlasting destruction. And yet it was not some of the lesser known and less important teachers of the Church who held this terrible doctrine, but some of the best and greatest. The fact that they did hold it, although it compelled them to declare their belief in what they called a *horribile decretum*—was because they believed that in so doing they were being faithful to the teaching of the Bible. How they managed to come to this position, and with what right they appeal to the Scriptures for support, must now be examined in closer detail.

[1] John 3: 16; 1: 12.
[2] The question whether the possibility of the decision of faith is limited to *this* earthly life, in view of 1 Peter 3: 19, remains open.

## CHAPTER 23

# THE PROBLEM OF "DOUBLE PREDESTINATION"

IT is particularly important for the Reformed theologian to come to terms with this problem, because for centuries this doctrine has been regarded as the typical doctrine of the Reformed Churches, not only in contrast to the doctrine of the Catholic Church, but also to that of the Lutheran Churches. It is, of course, true, that Luther, in his earlier days, and especially in his controversial pamphlet against Erasmus, did defend this doctrine, but later on, without explicitly revoking this view, he ceased to hold it in practice; possibly because he was not fully aware of the extent to which his outlook had changed.[1] He urged people not to devote too much attention to the theme of Predestination. To a certain extent, therefore, his successors were justified in appealing to his example when they were endeavouring to controvert Calvin's teaching, which, coupled with that of Zwingli, contains the most ruthless statement of the idea of a double predestination. On the other hand, the verdict of history, namely, that in Reformed theology the doctrine of a double predestination is the "central dogma",[2] ought to be modified, at least to this extent; we should recognize that in Calvin's theology the doctrine of Predestination has been wrongly equated with the actual heart of his belief, namely, the doctrine of Election in Christ. How did our Fathers in the Reformed Churches manage to teach this terrible theological theory in the name of the Biblical Gospel?

## (1)

In the case of Zwingli, the answer we must give to this question is very different from that which we must give when we come to consider Calvin, although both Reformers have certain common ideas which point in the same direction. In the main, Zwingli's doctrine of Predestination is presented in his great sermon, *De Providentia*, delivered at Marburg. His very starting-point shows that we are here dealing with speculative philosophy, and not with Christian theology. This starting-point, from which all that follows is developed, is the idea of God as

[1] See Appendix, pp. 343 ff.
[2] This has been the general view, especially since the publication of A. Schweizer's book, *Die protestantischen Zentral dogmen.*

the "*Summum bonum*". This idea does not belong to the Idea of God of the Bible and of revelation but to that of Platonist speculation. The "*Summum bonum*", which Zwingli uses here, is simply the Neo-Platonist idea of Absolute Being with which, with all the consequences which it entails, we are already familiar in the doctrine of the Divine Attributes. Thus there is nothing accidental in the fact that at the very outset Zwingli appeals to the Greek pagan philosophers, who identified the Good with the True, and that he further describes this as the Unchangeable and the Simple. Zwingli is here developing the idea of the "ἕν καὶ πᾶν," under the impression that he is expounding the Christian doctrine of God. "Only the One, single Highest Good is true, that is, simple, pure and sincere." From this beginning he then—in a speculative, rational manner—proceeds to derive the idea of Omniscience and Omnipotence, supporting his argument by appeals to Moses, Paul, *Plato and Seneca*. He is entirely unaware of the immense gulf which separates this speculative idea of the Absolute from the Biblical Idea of God. Hence he does not hesitate to draw obviously pantheistic conclusions from this conception: "Since there is only One who is Unconditioned there can be no Other. . . . From this it follows . . . in view of Being and of existence all must, without doubt, be divinity; for that is the being of all things." But when he expresses this view, even *he* seems to wonder whether this sounds too philosophical, so he comforts himself and his readers with the remark: "Does it matter if we *do* speak of Divine and Religious truth in philosophical terms? For if we leave everything to the philosophers, without reflecting that Truth always proceeds from the Holy Spirit, and that all Truth is the same, whatever be its source, we risk making men hate the Truth." He then further expounds the idea of the "ALL-One": "Since all comes from the One, and is, consists, moves, works, in the ONE, so this One is the only and real Cause of all things. The so-called immediate causes (creaturely causality) are actually not causes at all." In support of this evident Pantheism Zwingli appeals to Pliny to defend him against the reproach of calling Nature "God".

Secondly, with this speculative doctrine of the Absolute Zwingli here combines a Platonic conception of Evil, which derives evil from the lower sphere of sense. "Of itself, the mind would love truth and righteousness like an angel, but it becomes obscured by the lower material of the body which makes it powerless to follow the guidance of the spirit." In the further development of his thought Zwingli uses the Neo-Platonic idea that evil is "necessary", in order that virtue should exhibit its beauty. Only now, in the sixth chapter, do we come to the actual subject itself, introduced by the transitional phrase that he wrote the previous part of the work in order to show that not merely the righteousness—as the theologians have taught —but also the "goodness" of God, is the source of Predestination; here again, the "goodness" of God is not understood in the Biblical sense as a good disposition, but in the Neo-Platonist philosophical sense as the *"Summum Bonum = Summum Ens"*.

After this the doctrine of Predestination develops quite simply, and as it were inevitably, out of the doctrine of God as the sole Cause of all that happens. Not even the idea of Evil frightens Zwingli away from this "single-track" argument. For he says that if a man commits a crime, as we call it, that is an improper expression; for here God is acting, only we cannot call His action a "crime", since it comes under no law. "The adultery of David, so far as God was the cause of it, is no more sinful than the action of the bull who leaps upon the herd." Another analogy he uses is that of a robber who kills his victim: God incites the robber to the fatal act of killing. But if it is God who incites the robber to commit this assault, then "is not the robber forced to do this? I admit that he is, but then he is obliged to be executed". Thus everything is said to be derived from the pan-causality of God; if God is the Cause of sin, and of the condemnation which this incurs, then still more is He the Cause of the Good, and of salvation, to eternal life. Then everything is determined in the will of God; indeed, Zwingli goes further still and declares that everything is God's work alone.

All this has nothing, nothing whatever, to do with Christian theology, but it is a rational metaphysic, partly Stoic in character, and partly Neo-Platonist; it is a "foreign body" in the theology of the Reformer which is otherwise so clearly Biblical, and can only be understood in the light of the whole theological tradition. Bullinger, Zwingli's successor, redressed his friend's error by the wholly Scriptural exposition of the doctrine of Election, which he has given in the *Confessio Helvetica*, X.

(2)

Calvin's doctrine of Predestination is quite different, both in character and origin. But first of all we must clear away various views which have been expressed in the history of dogma. It is

323

not true that the idea of the Divine Omnipotence, in the sense of the *"potestas absoluta"*, is the axis round which Calvin's thinking revolves. Rather, it is quite evident that the centre of his theological thinking, as well as of his preaching, is the historic work of revelation and redemption in Jesus Christ. Secondly, it is not true that Calvin's thought is dominated by the idea of the Divine Glory. It is true that, as in the Bible, it does play a large part; but it is never severed from that of salvation; the Holiness of God, His will to manifest His Glory, and the Mercy through which God gives Himself to the sinful creature to redeem it, are all equally emphasized by Calvin— when we look at his work as a whole. We must never separate his emphasis on the *"soli deo gloria"* from the *"sola gratia"*. If we must speak of a "central point" in the theology of Calvin, then we can only single out this one: the doctrine of Election in Jesus Christ. Then how are we to understand Calvin's doctrine of a double Predestination when we take these presuppositions into account, and add to them the formal principle of absolute loyalty to the Scriptures, the determination never to teach anything that is not taught by the Scriptures?

(1) Like Luther's doctrine of Justification "by faith alone", Calvin's doctrine of "the grace of Jesus Christ alone" leads to the idea of free divine Election. *This* central truth of the Biblical Faith must be secured at all costs, against all attack. Since the opponents of the *"sola fide"* or of the *"sola gratia"*, in order to discredit this doctrine, argued that "Grace" must then be an arbitrary "choice", and thus that the *"sola fide"* implies the doctrine of double predestination; Calvin, if we may thus express it, seems to have taken up this challenge, saying: "Very well, then! So be it! Let us admit this 'double predestination!'"
Two observations seem to prove that this was actually the case: Calvin's first outline of the *Institutio*, of 1536, does not mention the doctrine of double predestination: on the other hand, there is a great deal about Election in Jesus Christ, and about God's operations in the hearts of the "reprobate".[1] The second fact is still more striking. Although the idea of Election in Jesus Christ must be regarded as the central theme of Calvin's preaching, in the hundreds of sermons which Calvin preached he rarely mentions the doctrine of double predestination; even his commentaries—although not to the same degree—show a similar unequal emphasis on the doctrines of Election and Predestina-

[1] *Werke*, I, pp. 7 ff. and 60 ff.

tion.[1] The fact remains, however, that there *is* a danger of misunderstanding the doctrine of Election, which practically equates the latter with the doctrine of a "double predestination". This we have already noted (in the previous chapter) in our discussion of the three erroneous subordinate conceptions: causality, a wrong idea of Eternity, and a mistaken view of the idea of "choice".

(2) The idea of Omnipotence plays a secondary part in this discussion. But even Calvin, whose mind was not very philosophical, had to utilize, to some extent, the conception of Omnipotence of the philosophical-theological tradition, that is, the idea of *"potestas absoluta"*.[2] Since it was already established that at the end of History there would be a Judgment, a separation between those who go into Eternal Life and those who are given over to eternal destruction—which, indeed, is general Christian teaching—it was not difficult to take a further step, and to ascribe this twofold result to the Almighty Will of God, and thus to deduce a double predestination. For how could anything take place at all which had not been willed by God? And if it has already been willed by God, then it has been willed from all eternity. Calvin does not make Luther's distinction— which Luther feels to be so important—between the "revealed" and the "hidden" will of God, or if he does think of it, he takes a quite different view. Hence, from the standpoint of the idea of Omnipotence, Calvin believed that there was an exact parallel between the negative and the positive will of God, between the Omnipotence which achieves salvation, and the Omnipotence which achieves man's ruin. If the accomplishment of man's salvation is based upon an eternal Decree, then the accomplishment of man's destruction is also based upon a divine decree. This kind of argument fitted in exactly with the result of the idea of selection: if there is a *"numerus electorum"*, then there is also a *"numerus reproborum"*.

(3) A third *motif* in the development of Calvin's thought, which ought not to be under-estimated, is the example of his revered ecclesiastical leader, Augustine. Augustine was the only great teacher of the Early Church who gave reliable Biblical teaching on the subject of Sin and Grace, that is, who was occupied with the main problem of Reformation theology. He, too, was the first to combine this doctrine of Grace with that of

[1] See the excellent Zurich Dissertation of P. Jacobs, *Erwählung v. Verantwortlichkeit bei Calvin*, 1927.

[2] The fact that in his *doctrine* of Omnipotence Calvin rejects this idea of the *"potestas absoluta"* is no proof to the contrary (cf. above, p. 306).

a double predestination. It was not difficult to follow his example in this respect.

Last on the list of these influences we may name that of exegesis: for though it is perfectly true that Calvin desired to be first and foremost a Biblical theologian, it is, on the other hand, equally evident that no one has any right to read the doctrine of double predestination into the Bible, and, indeed, that if we pay proper attention to what the Scriptures say, it is impossible to deduce this doctrine from the Bible at all. Thus the Bible can only be regarded as a source for Calvin's doctrine on this point in this sense: that if one has finally embarked on the movement of thought which culminates in the doctrine of a double predestination, it *is* possible to find passages which seem, at least, to teach it, and thus could easily be misunderstood in this sense; but once this had taken place, this apparently "Scriptural" support gave the doctrine of a double Decree a weight which no further arguments could remove. If the Bible teaches double predestination—then what Biblical theologian would dare not to teach it?

(3)

After all that was said in the previous chapter, and all our discussion of the doctrine of the Divine Omnipotence in another passage, our final task is to examine the statements of Scripture which appear to support the doctrine of Predestination. We will now anticipate the results of this examination, and give the reasons for these conclusions in the paragraphs which follow. Here is the result of this study: The Bible does not contain the doctrine of double predestination, although in a few isolated passages it seems to come close to it. The Bible teaches that all salvation is based upon the eternal Election of God in Jesus Christ, and that this eternal Election springs wholly and entirely from God's sovereign freedom. But wherever this happens, there is no mention of a decree of rejection.[1] The Bible teaches that alongside of the elect there are those who are not elect, who are "reprobate", and indeed that the former are the minority and the latter the majority; but in these passages the point at issue is not eternal election but "separation" or "selection" in Judgment.[2] Thus the Bible teaches that there will be a double outcome of world history, salvation and ruin, Heaven and Hell. But while salvation is explicitly taught as derived from the eternal Election, the further conclusion is

[1] Cf. Rom. 8: 28 ff.; 1: 2; Eph. 1: 5 = 4: 28.        [2] Matt. 22: 14.

not drawn that destruction is also based upon a corresponding decree of doom. To the Elect it is said: "Come, ye blessed of My Father, inherit the kingdom prepared for you from the foundation of the world"; but to the rejected: "Depart from Me, ye cursed, into the eternal fire which is prepared for the devil and his angels."[1] The distinctive element in the Biblical statement is not the "congruity" but the "incongruity" of the "right hand and the left hand". The Bible teaches, it is true, that God is also at work in evil and in sin where men harden their hearts and betray the Highest; but this "working" is not ascribed to an eternal decree,[2] and the "hardening of heart"— particularly in the decisive case of Israel—is not conceived as irrevocable. Israel, which at present is hardened and therefore rejected, can—and indeed will—still be saved if it does not remain in a state of disobedience.[3] The Bible teaches that Judas commits his act of treachery in order "that the scripture should be fulfilled",[4] but it does not say that this is the result of an eternal decree. It teaches that men are children of wrath,[5] in so far as they do not believe in Christ, and that "the wrath of God abideth upon them", if they do not turn to Christ;[6] but it does not teach that this wrath is based upon a divine decree. It teaches that in one house there are vessels of honour and vessels of dishonour; but it also teaches that if a man purify himself "he shall be a vessel unto honour".[7] In one passage—and here we come very near to the doctrine of a double predestination— the Bible speaks of those who find the "chief corner stone" to be a "stone of stumbling and a rock of offence", "whereunto also they were appointed".[8] But here, too, there is no suggestion of an eternal decree of rejection, nor even that this unbelief or disobedience was caused by God; what the passage does say is that the "stumbling" against the "rock of offence", which is the result of their disobedience, the ruin which is caused by their unbelief, is "appointed" by God as a necessary result. Even in their unbelief men do not fall out of the sphere of the Divine Will. Even in their ruin God's will is at work.

The Bible teaches "that the Lord hath made everything for His own purpose: yea, even the wicked for the day of evil".[9] Here the actual words seem to come rather close to the idea of a decree of rejection; but the idea itself is simply this: that the

---

[1] Matt. 25: 34 and 41. (R.V.)  [2] Exod. 4: 21; Isa. 6: 10; Rom. 11: 8.
[3] Rom. 11: 23.  [4] Acts 1: 16.  [5] Eph. 2: 3.
[6] John 3: 36.  [7] Rom. 9: 21; 2 Tim. 2: 21.
[8] 1 Peter 2: 8.  [9] Prov. 16: 4. (R.V. margin.)

godless man, by the very fact that in the day of evil it will become evident that he *is* godless, must serve the divine purpose. The writer of the Apocalypse speaks of those "whose names were not written in the Book of Life";[1] but this Book is the Book of the Judge, even though the Judge knows all things beforehand. Here, too, there is no idea of a decree of rejection.

The Ninth chapter of the Epistle to the Romans is usually regarded as the *"locus classicus"* of the doctrine of a double predestination, and for this reason it requires very careful consideration. Hence it is extremely important to show very clearly the connexion of this chapter with the two which follow. They do not deal with the salvation and damnation of the individual, but with the destiny of Israel. Thus the point of view itself is entirely different from that of the doctrine of predestination. The *"probandum"* is not a "double decree", but, on the one hand, the validity of the divine promises to Israel, in spite of the hardening of heart of the empirical contemporary Jewish people; and, on the other hand, the reason for the defective development in Israel, namely, from the human point of view the self-righteousness of Israel, instead of the recognition of the Grace of Christ; and, from the point of view of God, God's all-inclusive plan of redemption, which even the temporary rejection of Israel must serve.

All this looks very different from the doctrine of a "double decree" by means of which a *"numerus electorum"* from all eternity is confronted by a *"numerus reprobatorum"*. The *"nervus probandi"*, the main argument, is not the parable of the potter and the clay, but primarily the freedom of God in his Election and "hardening", and, secondly, the impossibility of making any claim on God. This freedom of God is balanced by the doctrine of righteousness through faith alone. Because Israel is self-righteous, it loses salvation; but if Israel abandons its self-righteousness and becomes converted, then it will receive salvation. When it seems, in the middle of the chapter, as though Paul will finally argue for a decree of rejection, then— quite apart from the detailed exegesis which we shall carry out in a moment—we should reflect that those who are here called "vessels of wrath", are the same as those who, in Chapter 11, will be represented as having finally been saved. Thus the fact that they are *now* "vessels of wrath" does not prevent them

---

[1] Rev. 17: 8. On the other hand, it is said of others that their names are removed from the Book of Life.

from being the "saved" at the end of the ages. So far as the details of this chapter are concerned, which has so often been used in support of the doctrine of predestination, the following needs to be said:

(a) As in the whole context, so also in the example of Jacob and Esau, in the movement of thought of the Apostle Paul, this is not an argument in support of a "double decree", but it is an illustration of the freedom of God in His action in the history of salvation. When we read: "For the children being not yet born, neither having done anything good or bad, that the purpose of God according to election might stand, not of works but of Him that calleth . . ." this does not refer to a double "decretum", but to the freedom of the divine election. Here there is no question of the eternal salvation of Jacob and the eternal doom of Esau; the point is simply the part which each plays in the history of redemption. Paul wishes to show that God chooses the instruments of His redemptive action, the bearers of the history of the Covenant, as He wills. The theme of this passage is not the doctrine of predestination, but the sovereign operation of God in History, who has been pleased to reveal Himself at *one* particular point in History, in Israel.

(b) Likewise in the following verses Pharaoh is simply an historic redemptive instrument in the hand of God, that instrument which, through its "hardening", must serve God's purpose. There is no question here of his salvation or condemnation. All the argument is concentrated on one point: God has mercy on whom He will, and hardens whom He will. The point of the whole is the freedom of grace.

(c) Finally, we come to the critical main passage, verses 19–22, the point in the whole Bible which comes closest to a doctrine of a double decree—and yet is separated from it by a great gulf. The parable of the potter and the clay, taken from Isaiah 28: 16 and Jeremiah 18: 6, expresses the absolute right of God to dispose of His creature as He chooses. The creature has no right to claim anything over against God; He may do with it what He wills. He does not have to account for His actions to anyone. God is the Lord, and His authority knows no limits.

The difficult verse is 22: "What if God, willing to show His wrath, and to make His power known, endured with much long-suffering vessels of wrath fitted unto destruction: and that He might make known the riches of His glory upon vessels of mercy, which He afore prepared unto glory . . ." The sentence breaks off here. The whole phrase is a conditional question: If God does this, what will you say? The "vessels of wrath" which are here mentioned as the means of the divine plan of salvation, are the Jews. The passage does *not* say that they have been *created* as vessels of wrath, still less that from all eternity they have been destined for this, but that, on account of their unbelief, they are "fitted unto destruction".[1] Paul never uses the idea of the "wrath of God" save in the sense of the divine reaction to human sin and man's refusal to obey. There is no more reference here to a negative decree, or to a negative purpose in creation, than there is to a negative ultimate end; for in Chapter 11 it is said of the same Jews that after their temporary rejection has served the purpose of God, they will be restored to the Divine favour, *as soon as they repent, and are converted*. Paul never forgets for a moment the *personal* relation and that *conditionalis divinus*, that is, the Living God.

In any case, the "vessels of wrath" mentioned in this passage are not the *"reprobi"* of the doctrine of Predestination. Here, indeed, there is no mention of individuals as individuals at all, but the whole People of Israel is being discussed, and the point is not that the "People" as a whole will be lost eternally, but that now, for the moment, they play a negative part in the history of salvation, which, in the future, after they have been converted, will become a positive one. The final issue of the judgment of wrath will be their salvation. Here, again, we notice that there is a remarkable "incongruity" between those "on the left hand" and those "on the right", as in Matthew 25. The "vessels of wrath" are designated by an impersonal passive, κατηρτισμένα εἰς ἀπώλειαν, they are "ripe for destruction". Thus it is explicitly stated that it is *not* God who has *made* them what they are. The linguistic phrase is deliberately in the passive, denoting a present condition, and can equally well be translated "ripe for condemnation". Over against them stand the "vessels of mercy" whom God "hath afore prepared unto glory". In the first case *no* active subject, and no indication of an act of predetermination; in the second instance, an active Subject, God, and a clear indication of eternal election. Thus even in this apparently clearly "predestinarian" passage there is no suggestion of a double decree! The examination of the statements of Scripture regarding this doctrine leads, therefore,

---

[1] "Ripe and ready to be destroyed." Moffat's Trans. (TR.)

330

to a completely negative result. There is no doctrine of a double decree in the New Testament, and still less in the Old Testament.

(4)

The doctrine of the double decree is, however, not only *not* supported by the evidence of Scripture, it is also impossible to equate it with the message of the Bible. It leads to an understanding of God and of man which is contrary to the idea of God and of man as given in revelation. It leads to consequences which are in absolute and direct opposition to the central statements of the Bible. Of course, the champions of the doctrine of Predestination have never admitted this, but, on the contrary, they have taken great pains to evade these conclusions, and to smooth out the contradiction; but in this speculative effort which, from their own standpoint, was inevitable, their process of argument becomes sophistical and contradictory. If God is the One who, before He created the world, conceived the plan of creating two kinds of human beings—*non pari conditione creantur omnes*, Calvin says explicitly[1]—namely, those who are destined for eternal life—the minority—and the rest—the majority—for everlasting destruction, then it is impossible truly to worship this God as the God of love, even if this be commanded us a thousand times, and indeed at the cost of the loss of eternal salvation. Essentially, it is impossible to regard the will which conceives this double decree as the same will which is represented as *Agape* in the New Testament. All Calvin's arguments against these objections come to the same point in the end: these two conceptions *must* be kept together in thought, because both are stated in the Word of God. God is Love, that is the clear Biblical message; God has conceived the double decree, that is—according to Calvin's erroneous opinion —equally clearly, the Biblical message; thus one *must* identify the God of the double decree with the God who is Love. But when we reveal the error in the second statement, the whole argument, which demands the impossible, falls to the ground. The Bible does *not* urge us to believe that the God whom it reveals to us as the God of love has created some human beings for eternal life and the rest for eternal doom. Equally inevitably the double decree contains a second consequence for the Idea of God which is in opposition to the Biblical message: God is then unmistakably *"auctor peccati"*. Zwingli drew this conclu-

[1] *Institutio*, III, 21, 5.

sion courageously, without "turning a hair", only making the excuse that the moral standard which is valid for us cannot be applied to God. This at least can be said, and in itself the idea is not contradictory. Calvin, on the contrary, is terrified of this conclusion, and calls it blasphemous. In point of fact, it is impossible to say of the God whom the Biblical revelation shows us, that He is the Author of Evil. But Calvin tries in vain to eliminate this conclusion from his doctrine of predestination. Here, too, his argument simply ends in saying: "You must not draw this conclusion!"—an exhortation which cannot be obeyed by anyone who thinks.

The consequences of the doctrine of predestination are just as disastrous for the understanding of Man as they are for the Idea of God. Predestination in the sense of the "double decree" means unmistakably: All has been fixed from eternity. From all eternity, before he was created, each individual has been written down in the one Book or the other. Predestination in the sense of the double decree is the most ruthless determinism that can be imagined. Before there was any world at all, before there was anything like time, causes, things, and creatures, it was already fixed—not only that there will be these two kinds of human beings, sinners who will be lost and sinners who will be saved, but also to which of both groups each human being, whom God will create, belongs. And here, indeed, we are not concerned with the milder exposition of the Infralapsarian theory—*lapsus est primus homo quia Dominus ita expedire censuerat*[1]—that God does indeed (it is true) *see* all beforehand, but that He only *wills* one thing beforehand, the positive—no, eternal destruction is willed by God in exactly the same way as eternal salvation, and those human beings who are doomed to destruction have been created by God for this end in exactly the same way as the others have been destined for salvation. For every human being who *thinks*, and does not force his mind to accept sophistries, it is clear that the net result is that there can be neither freedom nor responsibility, that decision in the historical sense is only an illusion, since everything has already been decided in eternity. Calvin—and Calvin in particular, who cares so much about moral responsibility—tries to avoid this conclusion, but all his arguments are logically untenable, and all end in the postulate: we must hold both ideas *together* in our minds, since the Bible teaches both.

Finally, the consequences for soteriology are no less sinister.

[1] *Institutio*, III, 23, 8.

If this doctrine be true, what use is it to preach the Gospel and to call men to repentance? He who is going to be saved will be saved in any case, and he who is doomed to destruction will in any case be lost. The summons to decision which all preaching contains is merely a trick, because decision is an illusion. All these absolutely devastating consequences of the doctrine of predestination for the Christian Faith and for the activity of the Church must, we feel, have been dimly felt by Calvin and the other theologians who held these views, but they did not allow them to obtrude. The fact that they must have been aware of them seems evident when we reflect that—with a few exceptions—they did not dare to preach this doctrine, nor to include it in the Catechism. It was *"de facto"* an artificial theological theory, an esoteric doctrine for theologians, which they did not dare to preach to the people as a whole. We can, however, only explain the fact that these theologians themselves believed that they were able to evade these conclusions, and that they did evade them to the extent that they did not let them rob them of either their faith in the God of love or of their belief in human freedom and responsibility, by suggesting that in their own thought the true Biblical doctrine of Election and this false and unscriptural doctrine of predestination were continually being confused with one another. Because, in the genuine understanding of faith, they knew that Election and responsibility, Election and the Love of God, not only do not contradict one another, but that they are one, they were able to hold firmly to the doctrine of the double decree without drawing these conclusions from it. The harm caused by this doctrine was felt less in the sphere of Christian faith and life than in that of theological reflection, and indeed only in the comparatively tolerable form of the impossible sophistical argument. This had to be included out of—so-called—"loyalty" to the Bible. The fact that men were able to hold the doctrine of predestination with a good conscience was due to the unconscious confusion of Election and Predestination. Because they were aware that the doctrine of Election is the heart of the Bible, but did not perceive that this is very different from the doctrine of Predestination, the genuine sentiment regarding the doctrine of Election was transferred to that of Predestination. But the conflicts which this caused were made to some extent innocuous by the fact that the clear Biblical teaching prevented them from drawing the logical conclusions of the doctrine of Predestination. The logical impossibility of this situation was supported by the conviction that in so doing they were standing on the bedrock of Holy Scripture.

### (5)

But the doctrine of double predestination is not the only misunderstanding which menaces the genuine Biblical doctrine of Election; on the other, opposite side, lies the no less dangerous false doctrine which is equally inconsistent with the Faith taught in the Scriptures of the ἀποκατάστασις τῶν πάντων, the doctrine of the final restoration of all men—the statement: All have been elect from eternity, therefore all will participate in eternal life. From the days of Origen onwards this heretical doctrine appeared in the Church, but from the beginning it was recognized and condemned as heresy.[1] It could not gain a footing within the teaching of the Church because it too obviously contradicted the clear Biblical teaching on Judgment and the possibility of being lost. The testimony of the Apostles, as well as the teaching of Jesus Himself, spoke too clearly of the Last Judgment, of the separation between those who are saved and those who are lost, and the idea of the Last Judgment was too firmly anchored in the creed of the Church, and in its practical activity in teaching and pastoral work, to allow the danger from this side to become acute. This only happened at a period when the Biblical foundation of the Church had become precarious as a whole, and an optimistic self-glorifying picture of man occupied a position which could no longer tolerate the idea of a Final Divine Judgment. But, as we know to-day, the doctrine of Universal Salvation may also arise from other causes, namely, from a mistaken "objectivism" in the doctrine of Jesus Christ, which lays stress on the words "God so loved the world", and pays no attention to those which follow, "that whosoever believeth on Him should not perish . . ." If the divine revelation of love in the sense of monergism is emphasized in such a one-sided way that no room is left for human decision, then we cannot avoid the conclusion that the universal will of God for man's salvation—"God our Saviour who willeth that all men should be saved, and come to the knowledge of the truth"[2]—means the doctrine of universal salvation. The absolute character of the divine offer of grace is emphasized—in such a one-sided way—at the expense of the *conditionalis divinus*—to such an extent that in the end the other side disap-

---

[1] See below, pp. 352 ff.     [2] 1 Tim. 2: 3–4.

pears altogether; the result is that the gravity of the element of decision is entirely ignored.

The Church had good reason to reject the doctrine of universal salvation, not only on formal "Biblical" grounds, but also from the point of view of the actual teaching of the Bible. This does not mean that the final salvation of all men must be denied as a divine possibility, but only that it cannot be established as a positive human doctrine. All that we would urge is that we should not allow ourselves to be lulled into a false security by taking the possibility of an incomprehensible, gracious decision of God for granted; we do not deny that this possibility may exist. The error in the doctrine of universal salvation is not that it leaves the door of divine possibility *open*, but that it leaves *this door only* open, and closes the door on the other possibility. That which is an incomprehensible divine *possibility* is here arrogantly taken for granted by man as a *certainty*. This is in absolute opposition both to the Biblical understanding of God and to the Biblical understanding of man and of salvation.

(*a*) Just as it is impossible to combine the idea of the double decree, in the sense in which Calvin uses it, with the love of God, so is it impossible to combine the doctrine of universal salvation with the idea of the Holiness of God. Men will say arrogantly: "God cannot decide against me, against anyone." Then perhaps it is not true that "God is not mocked", that "man must reap what he has sown"? Then it is not true that the man who will not submit to God must be shattered to pieces on the rock of God's immovable righteousness? Then, too, it is not true that the Gospel is a Gospel of deliverance from absolute and imminent danger—for there is no such danger? Then the very use of the term "deliverance" is a vast exaggeration, a sort of bluff, which is only used as a means of frightening men into repentance and conversion, a threat, which is not intended seriously. If there is no possibility of being "lost", there is no rejoicing at being "saved".

Once again: The point at issue is not that we deny the possibility that God *can* save all men, but that this possibility implies the *impossibility* of the opposite. The error in the doctrine of *Apokatastasis* is not the assertion of the positive possibility, but the exclusion of the negative possibility. This doctrine destroys the dialectical unity of Holiness and Love, and this is the Biblical idea of God. The Bible allows for both possibilities; but the negative possibility excludes the decision

335

of faith. Faith knows that "nothing can separate us from the Love of God, which is in Jesus Christ our Lord".[1] But faith at the same time knows that only in Jesus Christ, only in faith, can this decision be made, and is made, and thus that outside of faith the other possibility remains open, and in a case where unbelief is final, must become a reality.

(b) Again, by the doctrine of *Apokatastasis*, human responsibility becomes an illusion, and indeed not only—as in the theory of a double predestination—because it is not possible, but because it is not necessary. For this doctrine excludes, from the outset, any idea that the danger could be serious. There are no longer two ways—one that leads to life and one that leads to death—but only the one way which leads to salvation, which is certain for all. All ways lead to this end; thus neither the decision of faith nor the atoning work of Christ have any final, absolute seriousness. The view which regards the final salvation of all men as an ultimate Divine possibility is compatible with a profoundly serious view of life; it is only when the other possibility is ruled out that seriousness is lost. If there is no possibility of being lost, then the danger is not grave. If the danger is not grave, then salvation is not a real deliverance. The doctrine of universal salvation robs life of its genuine seriousness of decision. If there is no negative possibility, but only a positive final possibility, then all roads lead to the same goal. Thus it is not necessary to make any effort to find the right way. Certainly the champions of this doctrine will not admit this conclusion—but who can prevent those who are careless and superficial from drawing this conclusion? We ought not to say that this line of argument is the same as that followed by Paul in Romans 6, which he rejects: "Shall we then continue in sin, that grace may abound?"[2] For in the Pauline understanding of faith fear is included in this disastrous possibility, and preserves faith from frivolity. As the champion of a double predestination tries in vain to preserve the real possibility of a decision, just as vainly does the protagonist of the doctrine of Universal Salvation try to maintain the real necessity for decision.

(6)

Both errors, the doctrines of the Double Decree and of Universal Salvation, equally eliminate the vital tension, based on the dialectic of God's Holiness and Love, by means of a

[1] Rom. 8: 39.　　　　　　[2] Rom. 6: 1.

monistic *schema*. Both try to evade the truth of the freedom of
God, which is intolerable to logical thought, by establishing a
settled doctrine: on the one side, in a dark, pessimistic manner,
and on the other side cheerfully and optimistically. Both seek
a solution which will satisfy the mind. Logically satisfying,
although terrible for the heart, is the doctrine of the double
decree. Logically satisfying, although devastating for the
conscience, is the doctrine of the certain salvation of all men.
The Biblical doctrine of Election knows neither the one nor the
other of these logical rational solutions. It teaches the doctrine
of the Holy and Merciful God, who in Jesus Christ has chosen
all who believe in Him from all eternity, but who rejects those
who refuse this obedience of faith.

The right understanding of Election is, therefore, only
possible where that dialectical relation of Holiness and Mercy
is rightly understood, which is the fundamental characteristic
in the Biblical Idea of God, and also corresponds—in the
doctrine of the Trinity—to the truth that the Father and the
Son are One, and yet not one. The Holiness of God is identical
with the Love of God—in Jesus Christ, in faith. What God is in
Himself is identical with that which He is for us—in Jesus
Christ, in faith. God's Decree is the decree of Election—in
Jesus Christ, in faith. But outside of Jesus Christ, outside of
faith, God's Holiness is not the same as His Love, but there it is
His wrath; there what God is "in Himself" is not the same as
that which He is "for us", *there* it is the unfathomable, impenetrable mystery of the *"nuda majestas"*; *there* is no election, but
rejection, judgment, condemnation, but not an eternal decree.
For *there* is there indeed no word, no light, no life. The Light,
the Word, and the Life are where the Son is, and in the Son
alone can we perceive a divine decree.

This dialectic is in harmony with the a-symmetry of the
Biblical statements. God's will of wrath is not in the same way
"His" will as His will of Love; His ruling in wrath is His
"strange", not His "own" work. God is never called "Wrath",
it is never said of God that He *is* "wrath", as it is said that He
*is* Love. Hence it is never said of Him that from eternity He
has willed the doom of some, whereas it is constantly asserted
that from all eternity He has chosen His own. This incongruity
of the "left" and of the "right" hand, is, in contrast to that
"congruous", rational, "single-track" way of thinking, the
characteristic of the freedom of God, which includes within

itself the freedom of decision for man, and is the basis of his freedom of decision. Only because it is so, namely, logically so unsatisfying, is there room for the freedom of decision, for the true responsibility of faith. We have to choose between that which is logically satisfying and leaves no room for decision, and that which is logically unsatisfying, but leaves room for decision. Or rather, it is not that we "have the choice", but that in faith "we have decided", and since we have decided in faith, we know that from all eternity the decision has been made for us. But if we have decided in *faith*, then we know, too, that outside of this decision of faith there are only two non-dialectical, "single-track", rational possibilities, the pessimistic and the optimistic, which are excluded by the act of faith itself.

The doctrine of Election is therefore not intelligible in theory, but only in the decision of faith, not as a doctrine— "about", but only as an address to the "Thou", as the Word of God, which in Jesus Christ, through the Holy Spirit, addresses us in such a way that we *ought* to believe, we *are able* to believe, and we *must* believe. As soon as that which is known in faith becomes petrified into an objective impersonal doctrine, it either becomes unintelligible or it remains one of those only too intelligible possibilities: double predestination or universal salvation. This, too, helps us to understand how it is that when the Bible approaches one alternative or the other, at one moment it seems to teach the double decree, the divinely willed particularism of salvation, and at another, the doctrine of *Apokatastasis*, that of sure and certain salvation for everyone, without taking faith into account—yet, in point of fact, it never actually commits itself to either view.

Thus the Christian doctrine of the will of God is in entire harmony with the Christian doctrine of the Divine Nature. The paradox of faith of the Holiness and the Love of God which are identical in Christ, but are contradictory, apart from Him, corresponds to the paradox of faith that God in Christ has elected all who believe in Him, but not those who refuse to give Him the obedience of faith. This paradox of faith, again, is in accord with the character of faith itself, decision which is Faith or Unbelief is a matter of life or death, heaven or hell, of real deliverance, or the real possibility of being lost. The Christian revelation, with its demand for obedience, confronts us with this summons to decision; indeed, it is only in the Christian revelation that we see that this "life or death"

338

decision has to be made; it is only from the standpoint of revelation that human existence acquires this infinite tension. Outside of faith man knows nothing of this, but he lives, taking things very much for granted, whether he is an optimist or a pessimist, either in Utopian self-deception or in despairing resignation. Faith alone knows the abyss from which Christ saves.

## (1) ON THE HISTORY OF THE DOCTRINE OF PREDESTINATION

BEFORE Augustine, there was no doctrine of Predestination. In a world like that of declining antiquity, dominated by the idea of Fate, it was far more important to stress the freedom and responsibility of man than the fact that he is determined. This concern led the Early Church Fathers to the other extreme from that of the doctrine of predestination: to the doctrine of Free Will, which they developed in connexion with the Stoic idea of αὐτεξούσιον as the presupposition of moral responsibility.

Augustine's great achievement was the rediscovery of the Biblical "*sola gratia*"; this was why he meant so much to the Reformers. Augustine was, however, also responsible for connecting the doctrine of Election (against the teaching of Scripture) with the psychological-anthropological problem of Freedom. From the time that Augustine came decidedly under the influence of Pauline thought, the idea of Grace predominated in his theology. As a genuine disciple of the great Apostle, he saw how man was hopelessly entangled in the net of sin, and he understood the Gospel message more and more as the doctrine that God, by His Grace, sets man free from this bondage to sin. In all this he remained true to the genuinely Christian New Testament line of thought. It is true that here there is a trace of a movement in the direction of anthropology, which comes out in the Augustinian concept of Grace: Augustine is not so much concerned about the gracious *action of God* in Jesus Christ, as he is in the *transformation of man*, who was in bondage to sin, into a free *man*, by the working of Grace. The *infusio caritatis*, not the *remissio peccatorum*, accepted in faith, is his main idea; he did not understand that the justification of the sinner does not follow the inpouring of love, but precedes it.

From this transformation which takes place in man he proceeds to argue further, in terms of causality. If this transformation is really due to Grace alone, then this divine factor, which alone counts, must be traced back to its eternal origin. This origin is the divine choice in grace. Then Election is no more the state of "being-elect-in-Christ" than faith is the state of "being-justified-in-Christ". Rather, the psychological separation of grace from Christ (*gratia infusa*) corresponds to the separation of Election from Christ. Election is that pre-temporal act of God to which the *causal* consideration of the divine work of grace in the human soul leads. Election is wholly severed from the revelation in Christ, it is the metaphysical postulate which results from the causal consideration of the experience of Grace.

The great gulf, in Augustine's thought, between faith in Christ and Election, comes out very clearly in the fact that— for Augustine—"faith" does not necessarily imply the certainty of Salvation and Election: *Quis enim ex multitudine fidelium quadiu in hac mortalitate vivitur, in numero praedestinatorum se esse praesumat? (Opp.* X, 999). Thus Election is not that which one accepts in Christ, but it is a metaphysical "X", to which the causal retrospective conclusion—or, to put it more exactly: the causal consideration of Grace in the abstract—leads. This severance of Election from Faith in Christ now means that Election is more narrowly defined as the selection of a "*numerus praedestinatorum*" from the "*massa perditionis*". The misunderstanding of the Scripture passage, Matt. 22: 14, which contrasts the great number of those who are "called" with the small number of those who are "chosen", seemed to provide a Scriptural basis for this view. Actually, this passage does not refer to the subject of eternal *election* at all, but merely to the separation of one group from another at the Judgment.

Otherwise Augustine does not yet develop the idea of predestination to its most ruthless conclusion of a *gemina praedestinatio*. Rather, in his thought we can still detect a trace of the unequal emphasis of the Bible, in that he speaks of a "*praedestinatio*"·to salvation, but not of a "predestination" to destruction; he only speaks of a "foreknowledge" of rejection and of the reprobate. This distinction makes it possible for him to understand predestination in an infralapsarian and not in a supralapsarian sense: out of those who were affected by the Fall of Adam God chooses some to be saved; the rest He leaves to their self-chosen fate. The first man to pronounce the terrible phrase "*praedestinatio gemina*" was a monk named Gottschalk, in whose writings we already find the expression "*pariter*", which Calvin's formula revived. The fight against Gottschalk, and his champion Ratramnus, shows that the Catholic Church was still less inclined to accept this extreme idea of Predestination, since in practice it was moving far more in the direction of Semi-Pelagianism. On the other hand, Aquinas again adopted the doctrine of Augustine on this point; he, too, speaks of a "*certus numerus praedestinatorum*" (I, 23, 7); he, too, distinguishes between the *predestination* of the Elect and the *foreknowledge* of the non-elect. In spite of his emphasis on the "pan-causality" of the Divine Will, Duns Scotus became the forerunner of the Pelagianism of the Catholic rank and file, against which the Thomist Bradwardine, and Wyclif, reacted with a revival of Augustinian conceptions containing a very strong element of determinism: "*omnia quae evenient, evenient de necessitate causae primae . . . omnia illa evenient de voluntate divina, quae . . . necessaria et inevitabilis in causando est*" (*De causa Dei*, III, 27).

If we are to estimate Luther's and Calvin's doctrine of Predestination aright we must start from the fact that for them the problem was regarded entirely from the standpoint of the question of Augustinianism *versus* Pelagianism. Thus from the very outset they adopted the position of the "Either-Or" set up by Augustine, and thus they accepted that fatal perversion in the idea of Election, which we have seen to be present in the thought of Augustine. Once they had embarked on this path, they followed it to the bitter end, to the "*horribile decretum*" of a double predestination. Calvin expressed this view in terms which exactly convey his meaning: "*non pari conditione creantur omnes, sed aliis vita aeterna, aliis damnatio aeterna praeordinatur*" (*Institutio*, III, 21, 5). This formula leaves us in no doubt whether Calvin really taught this doctrine in the Supralapsarian sense or not. Luther, too, in his work, *de servo arbitrio*, argued the strict determinism of Bradwardine through to the bitter end, with extreme, one might even say brutal, logic.

In Luther's teaching, however, this was not his last word. This predestinarian determinism was later contradicted by his new understanding of Election, gained from a fresh insight into the New Testament. Luther, it is true, never revoked what he said in *de servo arbitrio*; but from 1525 onwards his teaching was different. He had freed himself from the Augustinian statement of the problem, and from the causal thinking of Augustine. He saw that this doctrine of predestination was speculative, natural theology, and he understood the Biblical idea of Election in and through Jesus Christ. Since this change in Luther's thought is still too little known—in spite of Th. von Harnack's remarkable evidence (*Luthers Theologie*, I, pp. 148–190)—and since we are here concerned with a most important, not to say fundamental truth, we must now deal with this subject in greater detail.

Whereas before 1525, and especially in *de servo arbitrio*, Luther explicitly denies the universalism of the divine will of salvation, he now emphasizes the truth that God in Christ offers us, as His sole will, the Gospel of Grace—*"nec est praetur hunc Christum alius Deus aut aliqua Dei voluntas quarenda"*—and to this he adds that whoever speculates upon the will of God outside of Christ, loses God (40, 1, 256). In Christ, the Crucified, "thou knowest the certain hope of the Mercy of God towards thee and the whole race of mankind" (*ibid.*, 255). He now makes an explicit distinction between the universalism of the promise and the particularism of the way in which the world will end. "For the Gospel offers to all men, it is true, forgiveness of sins, and eternal life through Christ; but not all men accept the promise of the Gospel . . . but the fact that all men do not accept Christ is their own fault. . . . *"Interim manet sententia Dei et promissio universalis*. . . . For it is the will of God that Christ should be a *communis thesaurus omnium*. . . . But the unbelieving withstand this gracious will of God" (*Erl. ed.*, 26, 300).

Thus henceforth he makes a distinction between the universalism of the divine will of Salvation and the particularism in the Judgment, and all the blame for man's ruin is laid at his own door: *"Non culpa verbi quod sanctum est et vitam offert, sed sua culpa quod hanc salutem quae offertur rejiciunt . . ."* (40, 2, 273).

Here, then, in the fact of man's unbelief, the doctrine of double predestination begins, since here the cause of man's unbelief is said to be derived from the will of God, and thus from God's "decree". Here, however, there follows the decisive turning-point in Luther's thought. From 1525 onwards he warns his hearers against seeking for a hidden divine decree of this kind. In exalted tones he exhorts his students, in his *Lectures on Genesis*: *"Vos igitur qui nunc me auditis, memineritis me hoc docuisse, non esse inquirendum de praedestinatione Dei absconditi. Sed ea aquiescendum esse quae revelatur per vocationem et per ministerium verbi. Ibi enim potes de fide et salute tua certus esse. . . ."* The grace of God in Jesus Christ—this is the true *"beneplacitum Dei patris"* (43, 463).

Luther perceives that the question of predestination lies outside the sphere of Christian revelation and of faith, and that it is a question of speculative natural theology. It is the scholastic speculative theology which makes the distinction between a *"voluntas signi"* (the revealed will) and the *"voluntas beneplaticiti"*, the unsearchable divine election or rejection. "No one ought to dispute about the *"nuda Divinitas"* (that is, about the will of God that has not been revealed), but we ought to flee from such thoughts as from Hell itself, and as from temptations of the devil". In the *Verbum Dei* alone do we have the true knowledge of the will of God: *"aliae cogitationes de voluntate beneplaciti—occidunt et damnant"*. And yet they (the Scholastic theologians) wrongly call them *"dies die voluntas beneplaciti"*. For that which the Gospel shows must be called *"voluntas beneplaciti"*: *"Haec voluntas gratiae recte et proprie vocatur voluntas beneplaciti. . . . Haec voluntas beneplaciti divini ab aeterno disposita est in Christo revelata."* It is the *"Primus gradus erroris"*, says Luther, "when men leave the God Incarnate in order to follow the *Deus nudus"*. For then there is nothing left save the Wrath of God. The sight of this "naked God" would inevitably annihilate us, as we would be burnt up if exposed to the unshaded rays of the sun (42: 297 ff.). "If we approach the *non*-revealed God, there is no faith, no word, *no knowledge*; for it is the Invisible God, whom thou wilt not make visible. Hence God has forbidden most strictly this idea of God (*istam adfectationem divinitatis*) . . . *quia scrutator majestatis opprimetur a gloria . . ."* "I, however," says God, "will make known to thee magnificently my foreknowledge and my predestination, but not by this way of reason and of carnal science, as thou dost imagine. But thus will I do it. Out of the non-revealed God will I become a revealed One, and yet will I remain the same God. . . ." Other ideas, and the ways (*viae!*) of reason, or of the flesh, are futile, because God abominates them: *"Si vis effugere desperationem, odium, blasphemiam Dei, omitte speculationem de Deo abscondito et desine frustra contendere ad videndum faciem Dei. . . ."* "If thou dost believe in the revealed God and dost receive His Word, then soon also the hidden God will reveal Himself unto thee. . . . If thou dost cling with firm faith to the revealed God . . . then art thou certainly predestined and thou knowest the hidden God" (43: 460).

In all this Luther has perceived two truths: first of all, that the traditional doctrine of Predestination, as he himself had taken it over from Augustine, is *speculative* theology, and thus does not create a real knowledge of God, but on the contrary, drives men to despair—and, secondly, that the true doctrine of Predestination is simply the knowledge of Election in Jesus Christ through faith. Thus at this point, as at so many others, Luther has freed the Gospel from the burden of tradition which had almost entirely obscured it, and he once more bases theological truth upon the revelation of God in Jesus Christ.

With Calvin the situation is different. In so far as he was a preacher of the Gospel, for him, too, Election in Jesus Christ through faith was the centre round which all his thinking circled (cf. the fine Zürich Dissertation of G. Jacobs, *Erwählung und Verantwortlichkeit bei Calvin*, 1927). As a dogmatic theologian, however, he was entirely of the same opinion as Augustine, whose doctrine of predestination he intensifies in the sense of the *"gemina praedestinatio"*, and the Supralapsarian equation of fore-knowing and fore-willing. The Biblical inequality of election and rejection is in his *theory* entirely removed, but in *practice* it appears in the fact that apart from a very few exceptions, Calvin never preached about the Double Decree, but only about Election. Calvin fails to perceive the real origin of this doctrine of double predestination—that is, speculative natural theology—from the application of the causal concept to unbelief—owing to the fact that he believes that he has derived his doctrine entirely from the Holy Scriptures, in that he combines certain Bible passages with one another—no one of which really contains this doctrine—in such a way that, together, they appear to provide the Scriptural proof for the *gemina praedestinatio*.

The further development of the doctrine of predestination is of little interest. No new ideas were introduced into it. Beza moves one step ahead of Calvin, to this extent, that he does not place the doctrine of predestination, like his master, in connexion with the doctrine of the Grace of God in Christ, the doctrine of Justification, but he sets it at the beginning of his Dogmatics, and develops it in connexion with the doctrine of Creation, and thus shows unmistakably that it is not derived from the Christian revelation, but from the process of speculative thought: as we have already seen (pp. 321 ff.) this comes out very clearly in Zwingli's teaching.

The controversy between the Lutherans, who, following Luther's later utterances, reject the *gemina praedestinatio* and teach the universalism of the Gospel, and the Calvinists—as well as the controversy between the Supralapsarians and the Infralapsarians among themselves—is of no interest for us here. The doctrine of Calvin to some extent culminates in the Articles of Dordrecht. In the first of these Articles, on the doctrine of Election, the double decree is formulated in an Augustinian, that is to say, an Infralapsarian form: *"non omnes*

*homines esse electos, sed quosdam non electos sive in aeterna dei
electione praeteritos quos scilicet deus ex liberrimo, justissimo . . .
irreprehensibili et immutabili beneplacito decrevit in communi
miseria, in quam se sua culpa praecipitarunt, relinquere"* (*Müller:
Die Bekenntnisschriften der reformierten Kirche*, pp. 845 ff.).
With this statement the doctrine of predestination returns to
its origin, to the doctrine of Augustine, without, however,
actually condemning the more extreme doctrine of Calvin.

In modern times the doctrine of Augustine has found a
champion in Schleiermacher's deterministic speculative theology—certainly with pantheistic modifications—and has found
its historian in one of the most outstanding of his pupils,
Alexander Schweizer (*Die protestantischen Zentraldogmen*).
Otherwise in later theology the less biased view of the doctrine
of the New Testament is emphasized. Even the Reformed
theologian Böhl no longer speaks of a *double* Decree, but of
"the" Decree of God, even when he is contending against the
Lutheran "universalism", which he evidently confuses with the
general theory that "everyone will be saved" (*Dogmatik*,
p. 289). Only within the strictly Calvinistic theology of Holland
(Kuyper and his school), and in America, has the Calvinistic
doctrine of the Double Decree, mostly, however, in the modified
form of the Articles of Dordrecht, been maintained.

## (2) KARL BARTH'S DOCTRINE OF ELECTION

The monumental presentation of the doctrine of Predestination, and of that of Election in particular, which we find in the
*Dogmatics* of Karl Barth (*Kirchl. Dogm.*, II, 2, pp. 1–563),
justifies us in making our own critical estimate of it, partly
because it is the most detailed and comprehensive discussion of
the problem in modern theology, but, above all, because here
some entirely new ideas have been introduced into the whole
question.

From the outset I would observe that in the *main tendency*
there is firm agreement between the doctrine of Barth and that
which is represented in this book: Barth's concern is the same
as ours, namely, the desire to state the doctrine of Election
which is in harmony with revelation and the thought of the
Bible as a whole; hence it is our common concern to reject the
speculative doctrine of Predestination inaugurated by Augustine, the most intense and logical expression of which is Calvin's
doctrine of the Double Decree. Our concern is that Election

should never be mentioned save on the basis of the revelation in Jesus Christ, that we only know the "divine decree" in Jesus Christ, and that we have nothing to teach about a "hidden decree" of God concerning those who do not accept the promise of Jesus Christ.

However, with this subject Karl Barth has combined a number of his own ideas, which, because they are completely new, need to be specially examined.

Barth presents the connexion between Election and Jesus Christ by the twofold thesis: Jesus Christ is the sole God who elects; Jesus Christ is the only Elect Man.

(i) Jesus Christ is the sole God who elects; He is the Subject of eternal Election. This idea is the necessary consequence of the doctrine of the Trinity, as Barth understands it. We have already discussed Barth's doctrine of the Trinity (see above, pp. 235 ff.) as well as its consequences for the doctrine of Election (see above, pp. 313). At this point we must deal more fully with these statements, and the conclusions to which they lead.

(ii) The second main article of his doctrine is thus expressed: Jesus Christ is the only Elect Man. In order to develop this point further he has to make a third statement: "Jesus the eternally Elect Man" (p. 111), "the pre-existing God-Man, who, as such, is the eternal ground of all election" (p. 119).

No special proof is required to show that the Bible contains no such doctrine, nor that no theory of this kind has ever been formulated by any theologian. If the eternal pre-existence of the God-Man were a fact, then the Incarnation would no longer be an *Event* at all; no longer would it be the great miracle of Christmas. In the New Testament the new element is the fact that the eternal Son of God *became* Man, and that henceforth through His Resurrection and Ascension, in Him humanity has *received* a share in the heavenly glory; yet in this view of Barth's, all this is now anticipated, as it were, torn out of the sphere of history, and set within the pre-temporal sphere, in the pre-existence of the Logos. The results of this new truth would be extraordinary; fortunately Barth does not attempt to deduce them. The idea of the pre-existent *Divine Humanity* is an *ad hoc* artificial theory of the theological thinker, who can only carry through his argument that the Man Jesus is the Only Elect Human being by means of this theory.

(iii) Here we cannot go any further into Barth's remarks about the doctrine of Predestination in general; some are very valuable, others are confusing. Anyone who has once understood that Barth's aim is the exact opposite of Calvin's doctrine of the Double Decree, will find it very strange that Barth continually constitutes himself the champion of Calvin's doctrine, as against the Lutheran view, and that he even defends the more extreme Supralapsarian view against the milder doctrine of the Infralapsarians. One cannot escape the impression that Barth is playing with fanciful ideas in theology when he says (of Jesus Christ): "from the very outset, and in Himself, *He* is the double predestination" (p. 170). But it sounds not merely strange, but horrible, when he says that, on the basis of the divine decree, "the only person who is really 'rejected' is His own Son" (p. 350). This view is the inevitable inference from his first statement. But what does this statement, "that Jesus is the only really rejected man" mean for the situation of Man? Evidently this, that there is no such thing as being "lost", that there is no possibility of condemnation, and thus that there is no final Divine Judgment. Karl Barth has been charged with teaching Universalism. When he denies this he is not altogether wrong. He knows too much about the not particularly illustrious theologians who have taught this doctrine of *Apokatastasis* in Christian history to be willing to allow himself to be numbered among them. "The Church ought not to preach Apokatastasis" (p. 529). Thus Barth's doctrine is not that of Origen and his followers.

(iv) Rather, Barth goes much further. For none of them ever dared to maintain that through Jesus Christ, all, believers and unbelievers, are saved from the wrath of God and participate in redemption through Jesus Christ. But that is what Karl Barth teaches; for Jesus Christ is, as the only Elect, so also the only Reprobate man. Thus, since Jesus Christ appeared, and through Him, there are no longer any who are rejected. Not only for those who are "in Him" through faith, but for all men, Hell has been blotted out, condemnation and judgment eliminated. This is not a deduction which *I* have drawn from Barth's statement, but it is his own. Since Jesus Christ has taken the condemnation of sin upon Himself "rejection *cannot* again become the portion of man" (p. 182). "He cannot undo the decision made by God in eternity . . . he cannot create any fact which takes away the Divine choice" (p. 348). The condemnation, therefore, because Jesus Christ has anticipated it for all men, will not affect any godless person. The godless may do what they can—there is one thing they will not reach: "the position and the lot of the rejected, after which—since they reject God—in their foolishness they stretch out their hands, but, *certainly*, they will not reach it" (p. 351). The godless man is also one of the Elect; only he does not know it, and does not yet live in accordance with this truth. But Jesus has "destroyed the terror which menaced him" (p. 353). "They may, it is true, bring shame upon the gracious divine choice; but they *cannot* overthrow it, and they cannot undo it" (p. 385). "If the proper object of His love be none save Him alone (Christ), then apart from Him can none be consumed by the heat of the wrath of God" (p. 391). "Outside of Jesus Christ there are no rejected ones" (p. 389). "Even the rejected stand in this light of Election" (p. 552).

There is no doubt that many people at the present time will be glad to hear such a doctrine, and will rejoice that at last a theologian has dared to throw on the scrap-heap the idea of a final divine Judgment, and the doctrine that a man may be "lost". But there is *one* point which even they cannot gainsay: that in so doing Karl Barth is in absolute opposition, not only to the whole ecclesiastical tradition, but—and this alone is the final objection to it—to the clear teaching of the New Testament. How can we eliminate the proclamation of a divine final Judgment from the Parables of our Lord, from the teaching of the Apostles—of John as well as of Paul, and of the writer to the Hebrews as well as of the Epistles of Peter and the book of Revelation—without entirely destroying their meaning? What the Bible says about deliverance from condemnation and Judgment is this, that "there is no condemnation *to them who are in Christ Jesus*", that Jesus Christ saves *believers* from the coming judgment of wrath, that through His rescuing love in Jesus "all who believe in Him shall not perish", that the foolishness of the Cross "is the power of God unto us who are being saved", but to those who are lost it is "folly", that the newly granted divine righteousness is "for all who believe", and that Jesus Christ makes him righteous who "has faith in Christ"; hence that there are two Ways: the broad way "which leads to destruction"—"and many there be that find it"—and the narrow way which leads to Life, and "few there be that find it". How, then, is it possible for Barth to arrive at such a fundamental perversion of the Christian message of Salvation?

(v) The answer to this question lies in an element peculiar to his teaching, which has always been characteristic, and permeates his teaching as a whole: namely, its "objectivism", that

is, the forcible severance of revelation and faith, or rather—
since Barth also naturally wishes to make a basis for faith—
the view that, in comparison with revelation, with the objective
Word of God, the subjective element, faith, is not on the same
level, but is on a much lower plane.

Whereas in the message of the New Testament, Christ and
faith, participation in salvation in Christ and faith, Justification and faith, absolutely belong together, and are on exactly
the same level, so that we may say: "Where there is no faith,
there Christ is not; where there is no faith, there, too, there is
no salvation in Christ," Barth does not admit that this correlation exists. Thus he says explicitly: "If, however, the nature of
faith consists in the fact . . . that man is wakened by the grace
of God and is born again as a new subject, then, for that very
reason, it is not possible to place him absolutely over against
one who, different from himself, does not make real and visible
the attitude of faith, its form, so that we regard the former, in
contrast to the latter, as 'elect', and the other, conversely, as
'rejected'. If a person, as a member of the Elect, is that new
subject, then as such (and only in Jesus Christ is this possible)
to a certain extent he is raised above himself in his best, and
above the other in his worst, behaviour. Thus, seen from
thence, the contrast between them becomes a *relative contrast*
. . . How could the Grace of God mean His absolute favour for
the one, and His absolute disfavour for the other?" (p. 360).
The believer in particular cannot possibly recognize, in the
unbelief of others, an *ultimate* given fact" (*ibid.*).

Once again we must say: It may be that this "objectivism",
this "relativization" of faith, may seem illuminating to many,
and may evoke their enthusiastic agreement. But there is one
thing that even they cannot gainsay: that in so doing they are
in clear opposition to the teaching of the New Testament,
where countless passages repeat the truth thus expressed in
John 3: 36: "He that believeth on the Son hath eternal life;
but He that believeth not the Son shall not see life, but the
wrath of God abideth upon him."

(vi) Augustine deduced his doctrine of double predestination
from the fact—which he felt sure was proved by the evidence
of Scripture—that there will be two kinds of persons at the
Judgment—those who will be saved and those who will be
condemned; from this he looked back to the divine causality,
and then drew this conclusion. It was a speculation: Natural
Theology on the basis of a statement which had a Biblical core.

Karl Barth takes the opposite line. From the fact that—according to the teaching of Scripture—Jesus Christ is the divine offer of salvation for all, he concludes that in consequence all are saved; this, too, is Natural Theology on the basis of a statement which has a Biblical core. In assigning condemnation to an eternal decree Augustine leaves the ground of the Biblical revelation, in order to draw a logical conclusion which seems to him illuminating. Karl Barth, in his transference of the salvation offered to faith to unbelievers, leaves the ground of the Biblical revelation, in order to draw a logical conclusion which to him seems illuminating. What, however, is the result?

(vii) First of all, the result is that the real decision only takes place in the objective sphere, and not in the subjective sphere. Thus: the decision has been made in Jesus Christ—for all men. Whether they know it or not, believe it or not, is not so important. The main point is that they are saved. They are like people who seem to be perishing in a stormy sea. But in reality they are not in a sea where one can drown, but in shallow water, where it is impossible to drown. Only they do not know it. Hence the transition from unbelief to faith is not the transition from "being-lost" to "being-saved". *This* turning-point does not exist, since it is no longer possible to be lost. But if we look at this view more closely, we see also that the turning-point in the historical Event is no real turning-point at all; for Election means that everything has already taken place in the sphere of pre-existence. In actual fact: the turning-point in the historical event absolutely depends upon whether the unbeliever also experiences a change of mind and heart which leads him to faith. For it was for the sake of this "turning" that Christ became Man and died on the Cross. If the decision of faith is not deadly serious, then salvation through Jesus Christ is not deadly serious either; everything has already been decided beforehand. Thus Karl Barth, far more decidedly than any other champion of the doctrine of *Apokatastasis*, finally reaches the exactly opposite pole from the doctrine of double predestination. But in spite of the contrast, there is also an affinity between the two: in both cases everything has already been decided beforehand, and there remains no room for man to make a real decision. In the older doctrine everything has already been decided in anticipation in the sense of a terrible duality: eternal destiny of salvation for some, eternal destiny of doom for the rest. In this latest doctrine everything is decided in the sense of an encouraging unity: eternal destiny to salvation for unbelievers as well as for believers, the impossibility of anyone ever being lost.

From the standpoint of Barth's doctrine we cannot see what can be brought against this final conclusion. But we cannot see, either, how he could accept it. It is therefore definitely to be expected that in this matter he has not yet said his last word.

### (3) ON THE DOCTRINE OF APOKATASTASIS

The expression which has become the *"terminus technicus"* to describe a doctrine which the Church as a whole has recognized as a heresy, comes from Acts 3: 21. But in this passage the reference is not to the salvation of all men, but to the "restoration of all things, whereof God spake by the mouth of His holy prophets, which have been since the world began". The Bible does not speak of universal salvation, but, on the contrary, of judgment and of a twofold destiny: salvation and doom. Then, too, one of the first protagonists of the doctrine of the "restoration of all" was a theologian who, in spite of his high reputation in the life of the Church, had several of his views condemned later on: Origen. Even the wicked, says Origen, after this earthly life—some sooner some later—"according to their merit, and the endurance of heavy or light punishment, after that they have been restored by this severe method of education, and after they have gone forward from stage to stage and reached a better condition, will finally "enter into that which is eternal and invisible" (*De princ.*, I, 6, 3). Thus in his thought the doctrine of *Apokatastasis* is evidently connected with his educational idea of development, which is itself again based on his Platonist anthropology. The second theologian who supported this view was the equally strongly Platonist pupil of Origen, Gregory of Nyssa (*Orat. catech.*, 8: 35). Later on the same view was held by Duns Scotus and the Syrian Pantheists of the sixth century (cf. Harnack, *Dogmengeschichte*, II, 113). Along with other heretical ideas of Origen this doctrine was condemned under Justinian at the Synod of Constantinople in the year 543. From that time until the period of the Reformation no serious thinker argued in favour of this view; then the Anabaptists, Denk and Hut, took it up, while the *Augustana*, in the 17th Article, spoke sharply against the "Anabaptists who teach that the Devil and men who are damned will not have to suffer eternal pain and torment". During the Enlightenment and later there was much sympathy for this doctrine among "enlightened" thinkers, as well as among Pietists. But the only important theologian with a Biblical outlook who adopted it was F. Ch. Ötinger. Bengel was wiser, who never taught it, but of whom tradition reports that he once said: "He who has some insight into the doctrine of *Apokatastasis*, and talks about it, is 'talking out of school'!" Among the defenders of the doctrine we naturally find (in accordance with his monistic type of thought)—Schleiermacher (*Ueber die Lehre von der Erwählung*); at least he presents it as an hypothesis—it has as much right as the other doctrine—since his eschatological agnosticism prevented him from holding a definite doctrine.

This genealogy gives food for thought. Certainly, it is difficult for us to conceive that alongside of those who are saved in Christ—to whom every believer thinks he belongs—there must be others who are shut out from the Presence of God for all eternity, and in hopeless misery must eternally live a life which is worse than death. But who can say that this is the alternative of the doctrine of *Apokatastasis*? No doctrine taught in the Bible, least of all that of salvation in Christ, is given to us in order that we should think out what is prepared for those who do not accept this salvation. The Word of Christ is for us the word of decision, which, so far as we believe, gives us salvation, and, precisely because it summons us to this decision, forbids us to believe in a deliverance which awaits us, or anyone else, outside the sphere of faith. Just as we ought to know that God alone in Jesus Christ is the God of Grace, and outside of Jesus Christ the God of Wrath, so ought we to know that He is only gracious to him who believes, but that He is not so to him who is outside the sphere of faith. But this cannot be for us an object of theoretical doctrine or even of imaginary ideas. This is said in order that we may believe, and it is for each of us to tell others as we have heard it, in order that they, too, may come to believe. This is our business, but nothing else. We must absolutely resist the inclination to draw "logical conclusions", since they only lead to one of two errors: either to the doctrine of the double decree or to the doctrine of universal salvation, each of which removes the reality of the decision of faith. Only the renunciation of the logically satisfying theory creates room for true decision; but the Gospel is the Word which confronts us with the summons to decision.

# INDEX OF SUBJECTS

355

# INDEX OF NAMES

357

# INDEX OF SCRIPTURE REFERENCES

359